The Bondage and Liberation of the Will

Texts and Studies in Reformation and Post-Reformation Thought

General Editor
Prof. Richard A. Muller, Calvin Theological Seminary

Editorial Board
Prof. A. N. S. Lane, London Bible College
Prof. Susan E. Schreiner, University of Chicago
Prof. David C. Steinmetz, Duke University
Prof. John L. Thompson, Fuller Theological Seminary
Prof. Willem J. van Asselt, University of Utrecht
Prof. Timothy Wengert, Lutheran Theological Seminary
Prof. Henry Zwaanstra, Calvin Theological Seminary

Volume I.   Caspar Olevianus, *A Firm Foundation: An Aid to Interpreting the Heidelberg Catechism,* translated, with an introduction by Lyle D. Bierma.
Volume II.   John Calvin, *The Bondage and Liberation of the Will: A Defence of the Orthodox Doctrine of Human Choice against Pighius,* edited by A. N. S. Lane, translated by G. I. Davies.
Volume III.   *Martin Luther: Prophet, Teacher, Hero: Luther's Function in the Life of the Church, 1520–1620,* by Robert Kolb. (forthcoming)
Volume IV.   Jerome Zanchi, *On the Christian Faith,* translated, with an introduction by John L. Farthing. (forthcoming)
Volume V.   Heinrich Heppe, *Reformed Dogmatics, Set Out and Illustrated from the Sources,* translated by G. T. Thompson, with a new introduction and corrections by Richard A. Muller. (forthcoming)
Volume VI.   Theodore Beza, *Eternal Predestination and Its Execution in Time: Beza's* Tabula Praedestinationis *or* Summa totius Christianismi *(1555),* translated, with an introduction, notes, and appendices by Richard A. Muller. (forthcoming)
Volume VII.   Benedict Pictet, *Christian Theology,* translated by Frederick Reyroux, revised, edited, and with an introduction by Martin I. Klauber. (forthcoming)

The Bondage and Liberation of the Will

A Defence of the Orthodox Doctrine of Human Choice against Pighius

John Calvin

Edited by A. N. S. Lane
Translated by G. I. Davies

a Labyrinth Book

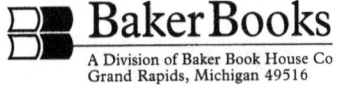

A Division of Baker Book Co
Grand Rapids, Michigan 49516

© 1996 by A. N. S. Lane and G. I. Davies

Published by Baker Books
a division of Baker Book House Company
P.O. Box 6287, Grand Rapids, MI 49516-6287

Second printing, September 2002

Printed in the United States of America

All rights reserved. No part of this publication may be reproduced, stored in a retrieval system, or transmitted in any form or by any means—for example, electronic, photocopy, recording—without the prior written permission of the publisher. The only exception is brief quotations in printed reviews. Labyrinth Books is an imprint of Baker Book House Company.

Library of Congress Cataloging-in-Publication Data

Calvin, Jean, 1509–1564.
  [Defensio sanae et orthodoxae doctrinae de servitute et liberatione humani arbitrii adversus calumnias Alberti Pighii Campensis. English]
  The bondage and liberation of the will : a defence of the orthodox doctrine of human choice against Pighius / John Calvin ; edited by A. N. S. Lane ; translated by G. I. Davies.
      p.   cm. — (Texts and studies in Reformation and post-Reformation thought ; v. 2)
  "A labyrinth book."
  Includes bibliographical references (p.   ) and indexes.
  ISBN 0-8010-2076-X (pbk.)
  1. Free will and determinism. 2. Pighius, Albertus, ca. 1490–1542. De libero hominis arbitrio et divina gratia libri decem. I. Lane, A. N. S. II. Davies, Graham I. III. Title. IV. Series.
BX9420.A32D38   1996
234'.9—dc20   96-25635

For information about academic books, resources for Christian leaders, and all new releases available from Baker Book House, visit our web site:
http://www.bakerbooks.com/

To
Maggie
and Nicola

Contents

Series Preface   *ix*
Preface   *xi*
Introduction   *xiii*
Abbreviations   *xxxv*
List of Works Cited   *xxxvii*

The Bondage and Liberation of the Will

  Preface   *3*
  Book 1   *7*
  Book 2   *35*
  Book 3   *87*
  Book 4   *137*
  Book 5   *171*
  Book 6   *203*

Subject Index   *245*
Scripture Index   *253*
Patristic and Classical Index   *257*

Series Preface

The heritage of the Reformation is of profound importance to the church in the present day. Yet there remain many significant gaps in our knowledge of the intellectual development of Protestantism in the sixteenth century, and there are not a few myths about the theology of the Protestant orthodox writers of the late sixteenth and seventeenth centuries. These gaps and myths, frequently caused by ignorance of the scope of a particular thinker's work, by negative theological judgments passed on the theology of the Reformers or their successors by later generations, or by an intellectual imperialism of the present that singles out some thinkers and ignores others regardless of their relative significance to their own times, stand in the way of a substantive encounter with this important period in our history. Understanding and appropriation of that heritage can occur only through the publication of significant works—monographs and sound, scholarly translations—that present the breadth and detail of the thought of the Reformers and their successors.

Texts and Studies in Reformation and Post-Reformation Thought proposes to make available such works as Caspar Olevianus's *Firm Foundation*, Theodore Beza's *Table of Predestination*, and Jerome Zanchi's *Confession of Faith*, together with significant monographs on traditional Reformed theology, under the guidance of an editorial board of recognized scholars in the field. Major older works, like Heppe's *Reformed Dogmatics*, will be reprinted or reissued with new introductions. These works, moreover, are intended to address two groups: an academic and a confessional or churchly audience. The series recognizes the need for careful, scholarly treatment of the Reformation and of the era of Protestant orthodoxy, given the continuing presence of misunderstandings particularly of the later era in both the scholarly and the popular literature as well as the recent interest in reappraising the relationship of the Reformation to Protestant orthodoxy. In addition, however, the series hopes to provide the church at large with worthy documents from its rich heritage and thereby to support and to stimulate interest in the roots of the Protestant tradition.

Richard A. Muller

Preface

As regards the division of labour, the translation is the work of G. I. Davies, with some input from A. N. S. Lane, especially regarding theological terminology and the correlation with the French translation and the text of Augustine. The editing of the Latin text, the introduction, and the notes are the work of Lane, with some input from Davies, especially regarding the editing of the Latin text.

Two other people deserve especial mention. David Wright has been unstinting both in offering advice and in pursuing enquiries. The tying up of many of the loose ends, especially in the notes, is due to his generous assistance. Those familiar with the magisterial work of Luchesius Smits on Calvin's Augustine citations will be aware of the extent to which he has broken the ground. His work has immeasurably eased the task of tracing Calvin's citations and lightened the load of the editor. His work has, however, been treated only as a starting point. The conclusions reached in the notes vary from his in a number of minor points and in a smaller number of major points. The editor has, of course, had the luxury of confining his attention to only one of Calvin's works, where Smits sought to cover them all.

In addition, others have helped with individual points. Allan Fitzgerald of Villanova University kindly provided from his Augustine Index the material consulted for book 6, note 9. Christoph Burger of the Free University of Amsterdam located a quotation from Luther. Irena Backus and Peter Fraenkel of Geneva offered helpful assistance. Douglas de Lacey enquired on the Internet about an elusive quotation, and G. W. Pigman III provided the source. The editor's colleagues Peter Hicks, Ian Macnair, David Payne, and especially Steve Motyer have offered valuable assistance in classical matters, as has Jean-Marc Heimerdinger with some obscurer points of sixteenth-century French.

Introduction

John Calvin's *Bondage and Liberation of the Will* is undoubtedly the most significant of his works hitherto not translated into English. This is in striking contrast with Martin Luther's study on the same topic, his *Bondage of the Will*, which is one of his best-known publications. While Calvin's work may not be of such crucial significance as Luther's, it is still his fullest treatment of the relation between grace and free will, and contains important material which is not found elsewhere in his writings. It also contains far more discussion of the early church fathers than does any other of Calvin's works, apart from the *Institutes*, and is important for appreciating his use of the Fathers. It is high time that this major work be made available to those whose knowledge of Calvin is confined to English translations.

1. The Debate with Pighius

The first edition of Calvin's *Institutes* was published in 1536.[1] Four of its six chapters covered the same material as did traditional catechisms: the Ten Commandments, the Apostles' Creed, the Lord's Prayer, and the sacraments (baptism and the Lord's Supper). The other two chapters discuss the five remaining Roman Catholic sacraments and the issues of Christian freedom, ecclesiastical power, and political administration.

The second edition of the *Institutes,* which appeared in 1539, was nearly three times as long, the six chapters having become seventeen.[2] Two of these concern us here: chapter 2 on "The Knowledge of Hu-

---

1. F. L. Battles has produced an English translation of the 1536 edition, entitled *Institutes of the Christian Religion, 1536 Edition,* rev. ed. (Grand Rapids: Meeter Center/Eerdmans, 1986).

2. The text (with concordance) of this edition has been edited by R. F. Wevers (Grand Rapids: Meeter Center, 1988). Considerable use has been made of both text and concordance in the preparation of this volume. There is no English translation of the 1539 edition, but almost all of the text survives in the 1559 edition. The English translation by F. L. Battles & J. T. McNeill (LCC 20–21) indicates the edition (1539, 1559, etc.) in which each portion of text first appeared.

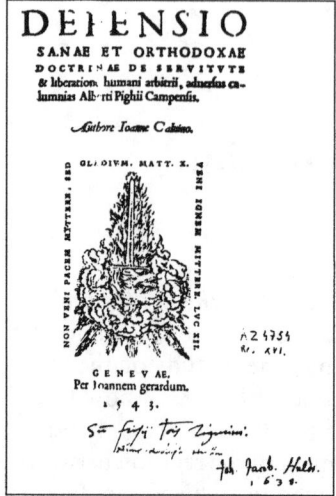
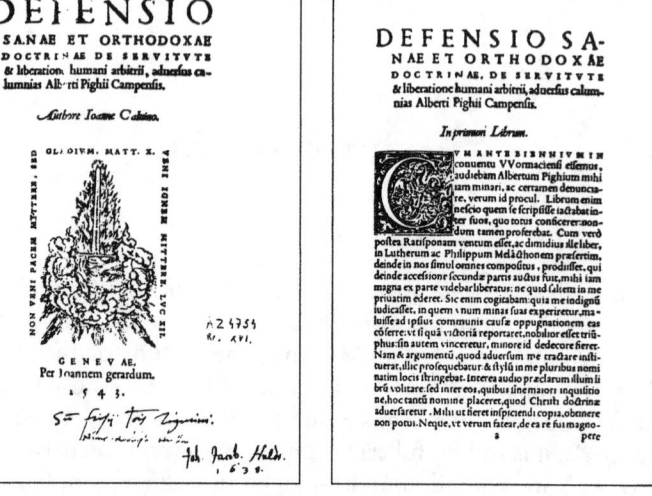

Title and First Page of Calvin's *Bondage of the Will*

manity and Free Choice" and chapter 8 on "The Predestination and Providence of God." When this edition appeared, Bernardus Cincius, the Roman Catholic bishop of Aquila, showed it to Cardinal Marcello Cervini. Agreeing that this work was more dangerous than the other "Lutheran" writings, they showed it to the Dutch Roman Catholic theologian Albert Pighius.[3] He wrote a response which was published in August 1542, his *Ten Books on Human Free Choice and Divine Grace*.[4] Of the ten "books" (like modern chapters), the first six respond to Calvin's second chapter, the remaining four to chapter 8.

Calvin, when he saw Pighius's work, felt a pressing need to respond lest the evangelical cause be lost by default. Because he wanted his reply to be ready for the 1543 Frankfurt book fair, he had time to answer only Pighius's first six books, that is, those on free choice.[5] Sometime in February 1543 Calvin's *Defence of the Sound and Orthodox Doctrine of the Bondage and Liberation of Human Choice against the Misrepresentations of Albert Pighius of Kampen* was published. It was Calvin's intention to write an answer to the remaining four books (on providence and predestination) for the 1544 book fair.[6] In the meantime, however,

---

3. C. Schultingius, *Bibliothecae catholicae et orthodoxae, contra summam totius theologiae calvinianae in Institutionibus Ioannis Calvini, et Locis Communibus Petri Martyris* (Cologne, 1602), 1:39–40; H. Jedin, *Studien über die Schriftstellertätigkeit Albert Pigges* (Münster: Aschendorff, 1931), 163 (Pighius's own account).

4. *De libero hominis arbitrio et divina gratia, Libri decem* (Cologne: Melchior Novesianus, 1542). Never reissued in any language, it is referred to hereafter simply as *Free Choice*.

5. See *BLW*, preface, 229–30; 1.233–34, 236–37 (*Bondage and Liberation of the Will*, preface, cols. 229–30; book 1, cols. 233–34, 236–37). On the debate with Pighius see L. F. Schulze, *Calvin's Reply to Pighius* (Potchefstroom: Pro Rege, 1971).

6. See *BLW* 6.404.

Introduction

Title and First Page of Pighius's *Free Choice*

Pighius had died, so Calvin decided to drop the project in order "not to insult a dead dog."[7] But the controversy over predestination did not cease, and in 1551 it burst into life at Geneva itself, as Calvin's doctrine was attacked by Jerome Bolsec.[8] Calvin responded to Bolsec, while also settling the old score with Pighius, in his *Eternal Predestination of God*, which appeared in 1552. It was not only Calvin who was critical of Pighius. In fact, his *Free Choice* was eventually placed on the Index of Prohibited Books (Lisbon, 1624).[9]

Calvin responded to Pighius in one other manner—in the ongoing revisions of his *Institutes*. Pighius is only once named there, and that in connection with another of his works,[10] but there are other places where it is possible that he is one of the opponents that Calvin has in mind.[11] There are also places where the influence of the present debate can be discerned in the argument. The 1543 edition of the *Institutes* was already largely complete by early 1542 and may even have been with

---

7. John Calvin, *Concerning the Eternal Predestination of God*, trans. J. K. S. Reid (London: James Clarke, 1961), 54. There is also a nineteenth-century translation by H. Cole, *Calvin's Calvinism* (Grand Rapids: Eerdmans, 1956).

8. For a full account of the Bolsec controversy, see P. Holtrop, *The Bolsec Controversy on Predestination from 1551 to 1555* (Lewiston, N.Y.: Edwin Mellen, 1993).

9. F. H. Reusch, *Der Index der verbotenen Bücher*, vol. 1 (Bonn: Cohen, 1883), 565.

10. 1550 *Institutes* 3.2.30 (LCC 20:576 n. 44).

11. In the English translation Pighius's *Free Choice* is four times identified as one of the unnamed works attacked by Calvin (LCC 20:295 n. 11, 302 n. 23; 21:926 n. 15 [where Pighius's *Free Choice* is wrongly said to be part of his *Controversies*; see at n. 17], 982 n. 26). Such identifications should always be treated with extreme caution since the same ideas may also be found in many other works. Of these four passages, the first is from 1539 and the substance of the last is also from 1539, so Calvin could hardly have had Pighius's *Free Choice* in mind!

the printer by the time Calvin was replying to Pighius,[12] so any influence on that edition is unlikely. The 1550 revision was minor, and the new material did not deal with the present topic. It is in the definitive 1559 edition that any influence of the debate with Pighius is to be sought.[13]

2. Albert Pighius

Albert Pighius was born at Kampen, in Holland, around 1490.[14] In 1507 he went to study philosophy and theology at Louvain, where he remained until 1517, after which he spent some time in Paris. At this stage he was very much an Erasmian humanist, and his early writings were all in the area of astronomy. But the direction of Pighius's life changed in 1522 when one of his teachers at Louvain, Adrian Florents of Utrecht, became Pope Adrian VI. He called Pighius to join him at Rome, where he turned his attention from science to theology. There he stayed after his master's early death, and continued to serve the following two popes.

At some stage in the early 1530s Pighius returned to the Netherlands, and in 1535 he became provost and archdeacon of St. John's Church at Utrecht, a post he continued to hold until his death at the end of 1542. During these years he rose to prominence as one of the most influential Roman Catholic polemicists against Protestantism. In 1540 and 1541 he was appointed to the Roman Catholic delegations to the interconfessional colloquies at Worms and Regensburg. But his unremittingly hostile attitude towards Protestantism did not fit him well for such a role, and his Catholic colleagues took care to marginalise him. Indeed it has been suggested that Pighius was appointed in order to act as a dampener upon the proceedings. Calvin was also at Worms and Regensburg, where he presumably met Pighius.

Pighius was the author of a number of works, both scientific and theological.[15] Perhaps the best known is his *Defence of the Ecclesiasti-*

---

12. OS 3:xix–xx.
13. See LCC 20:302 n. 23 & 21:926 n. 15, both with reference to 1559 material. For Pighius's influence upon the 1559 edition see A. N. S. Lane, "Did Calvin Believe in Freewill?" *Vox Evangelica* 12 (1981): 81–83; idem, "The Influence upon Calvin of His Debate with Pighius," in *Auctoritas Patrum II: New Contributions on the Reception of the Church Fathers in the 15th and 16th Century*, ed. L. Grane, A. Schindler, and M. Wriedt (Mainz: Philipp von Zabern, forthcoming).
14. Not much has been written in English on Pighius (whose name in the vernacular was Pigge). For two extremely succinct accounts of his life see H. de Vocht, *Literae virorum eruditorum ad Franciscum Craneveldium 1522–1528* (Louvain: Librairie Universitaire, 1928), 256–60; idem, *History of the Foundation and Rise of the Collegium Trilingue Lovaniense, 1517–1550*, vol. 4 (Louvain: Bibliothèque de l'Université, 1955), 197–200.
15. For a brief account of some of Pighius's works see Schulze, *Calvin's Reply to Pighius*, 14–18. For a full account see Jedin, *Studien*, 7–47.

cal Hierarchy,¹⁶ in which he argued vigorously for papal infallibility. He regarded the pronouncements of the apostolic see as the third principle of faith, alongside Scripture and tradition. In particular, he denied that a pope could become a heretic, despite the condemnation of Pope Honorius I at the Third Council of Constantinople. In the sixth book he anticipated the decisions of Vatican I by arguing for the primacy of the pope over general councils.

Pighius's magnum opus was to have been a three-volume work entitled *First Principles*, a response to the 1537 Danish Church Order drawn up with the help of the Lutheran Reformer Johannes Bugenhagen. The Lutheran Augsburg Confession was also singled out for attention. The first volume, *The Mystery of Our Salvation and Redemption*, was complete by March 1540 and survives in manuscript, but Pighius decided to revise it to include a response to Calvin's 1539 *Institutes*. It was then incorporated into Pighius's modestly entitled *Diligent and Lucid Exposition of the Controversies by Which the Faith and Religion of Christ Are Being Disturbed*,[17] which also took up the issues debated at the Regensburg colloquy. The second volume of the *First Principles* was to have covered free choice, nature, grace, and sin, as well as divine foreknowledge and predestination. This saw the light as Pighius's *Free Choice*, to which Calvin responded.

Two doctrines found in the *Controversies* were especially controversial. In expounding the first controversy Pighius posited a novel theory of original sin according to which the only effects of the fall of Adam were the introduction of death and the imputation of the guilt of Adam's sin to all humanity. There was no talk of the corruption of human nature as a result of the fall. The lust that human beings experience derives from nature as created and was experienced by Adam before the fall. This issue resurfaces in the debate with Calvin over free choice, where Calvin points out that Pighius is heretical by the criteria of Roman Catholic orthodoxy. The same conclusion was reached by the delegates at the Council of Trent,[18] and Pighius's material on the first controversy was placed on the Index of Prohibited Books (Lisbon, 1624).[19]

Pighius's doctrine of justification, expounded in the second controversy, likewise provoked criticism. He put forward a doctrine of "double justification" which was also discussed at Trent. In the last hundred

---

16. *Hierarchiae ecclesiasticae assertio* (Cologne: Melchior Novesianus, 1538).

17. *Controversiarum, quibus nunc exagitatur Christi fides et religio[,] diligens et luculenta explicatio*, first published in 1541 in two parts and often reprinted with slightly different titles (hereafter referred to simply as the *Controversies*). Most of the earlier material was incorporated into the second controversy, which was on justification.

18. H. Jedin, *A History of the Council of Trent*, vol. 2 (London: T. Nelson, 1961), 145, 153, 162.

19. See n. 9.

years or so there has been prolonged debate over the exact nature of Pighius's doctrine, which need not detain us here. Calvin complained that Pighius in his second controversy had plagiarised the *Institutes* to the extent of copying whole passages.[20] Already in 1565 a colleague of Pighius was complaining that in regard to the doctrine of justification Pighius had been bewitched by error and seduced by the reading of Calvin's *Institutes*.[21]

3. Synopsis of Contents

The structure of the first six books of Pighius's work can be seen from his own summary, which we reproduce here.[22] (A summary of Calvin's argument can be found in the margins of the translation.)

Book 1: Pighius begins by showing that knowledge of God and knowledge of ourselves are closely interrelated and interdependent. He then describes an opinion which completely contradicts the goodness of God. Some people, denying free human choice entirely, state that all things happen to us by an inevitable and absolute necessity arising from the will of God. Others concede something to human choice in matters which do not relate to salvation, but in matters which do they concede nothing to human choice but clearly consider it a slave.

Book 2: Pighius refutes these opinions about the inevitable necessity of those things which happen to us and about the bondage of human choice. He shows how much these views contradict the goodness of God and what monstrous blasphemies they imply. Then he clearly demonstrates that the faith, tradition, and definition of the Catholic church of Christ as well as the consensus of all the holy and orthodox fathers from the beginning affirm the freedom of human choice.

Book 3: Augustine in places appears even to the most orthodox to be hostile to the idea of freedom of choice. Indeed, those who see the will as being in bondage cite him as the one ancient father who makes definite assertions on the dispute and agrees with their opinion. But Pighius demonstrates copiously that all the works of Augustine have a certain and clear opinion on this matter, and that throughout he is consistent both with himself and with all the other fathers.

Book 4: Pighius lucidly demonstrates how miserably those who deny freedom of choice and assert the bondage of the will labour to distort those Scriptures which are manifestly opposed to their opinion.

Book 5: Pighius demonstrates the orthodox and catholic truth which walks the regal middle path between the irreverence of the her-

---

20. *BLW* 1.246 (at n. 58).
21. Jedin, *Studien,* 115–17.
22. *Free Choice* **1a–b. The value judgments expressed are, of course, all Pighius's.

Introduction

etics who, on the one side, deny freedom of choice and, on the other side, deny the need for divine grace. This truth affirms the need to combine grace and free choice.

Book 6: Pighius examines very accurately the opinion of the self-designated "evangelical" sect concerning divine grace and the way in which it works in us. He manifestly exposes the falsity of the sect's reasons and arguments.

4. The Theological Issues

The structure of Calvin's *Bondage and Liberation of the Will* is not primarily related to the theological issues. Calvin mainly follows Pighius's order,[23] which was itself related to the structure of Calvin's 1539 *Institutes*. Also, wherever the text spends considerable time debating the views of the Fathers, it often moves from author to author, and from book to book, with the theological issues emerging wherever they happen to be discussed. It might help, therefore, to have an overview of the issues which arise and an indication of at least the major places where they are discussed.

The central issue is, of course, the freedom/bondage of the human will and human choice.[24] Almost all of the other topics are introduced as they bear on this issue. Considerable space is devoted to discussing the views of the early fathers in general[25] and of Augustine in particular.[26] Unfortunately, the issue was obscured by the fact that Calvin, unlike Augustine, chose to reject the term "free choice." Pighius seizes on this, assuming that because Augustine and the Fathers affirmed free choice while Calvin rejects it, Calvin is opposed to the Fathers. Calvin responds by saying that while he accepts free choice as Augustine defined it, he thinks that the term is best dropped because of possible misunderstanding. But he is willing to affirm that the will is free in the sense that we have wills which are not coerced but self-determined, choosing voluntarily, of their own accord.[27]

In an important passage[28] Calvin clearly defines his terms. The will is not free in the sense that Pighius understands it to be free, namely having the power to choose good or evil. Neither is it coerced in the sense of being forcibly driven by an external impulse. Instead it is self-

---

23. See *BLW* 1.237.
24. In this section, the word "will" is used more often than "choice" (see §10 on these two words). This is primarily for stylistic reasons, that is, to avoid repeated references to "the choice and the will." In most instances the word "choice" can be substituted.
25. *BLW* 2.278–92.
26. *BLW* 3.
27. *BLW* 2.279–80; 3.293–94, 302–3, 310–13, 315–19; 4.329, 340; 5.357–58.
28. *BLW* 2.279–80.

determined in that we will voluntarily, of our own accord. Yet because of the corruption of the will it is in bondage and subject to a necessity of sinning. Much of Calvin's work is devoted to explaining and defending these statements.

Underlying the bondage of the will is the doctrine of original sin, which surfaces a number of times in the debate. Calvin repeatedly criticises Pighius's understanding of the effects of Adam's fall, accusing him of Pelagianism.[29] Roman Catholics also had reservations about Pighius on this point.[30] Calvin, by contrast, held that the fall affected every aspect of human nature.[31] Fallen human beings are in bondage to sin. Before the operation of God's grace there is no good at all in the human will.[32]

Because of this view Calvin was accused of Manichaeism, of teaching that God's original creation was evil. He responded with one of the most important distinctions of the whole work, that between human nature as created and as fallen.[33] Human nature was good as originally created, but has become corrupted as a result of Adam's fall. This distinction Calvin also uses as a tool to interpret the Fathers[34] and the early writings of Augustine.[35] He develops it in detail, distinguishing between natural human feelings as given by God's original creation and the way in which sin has turned these feelings into lusts.[36]

Because of the bondage of the will, there is no way in which people can prepare themselves to receive God's grace. This point surfaces repeatedly in the debate.[37] The corollary is that grace is prevenient—that God's grace precedes any human good will.[38] But Calvin wishes to say more than this. Prevenient grace does not simply make it possible for people to respond. Grace is efficacious and effects conversion.[39] This is true not just of the beginning of the Christian life. Grace is needed at every stage and, in particular, for final perseverance. This is a gift of God, not something that is merited by previous obedience.[40]

Other doctrines enter the debate as they relate to free choice and grace. A recurring issue is whether it is possible to obey the law. Calvin

---

29. *BLW* 3.303–5, 310; 4.332; 5.359–61.
30. See §2, esp. the text at nn. 18–19.
31. *BLW* 3.306; 5.350–54; 6.381.
32. *BLW* 3.304, 311, 313, 320–21, 322, 325.
33. *BLW* 2.259, 262–64; 3.308–9; 4.334; 5.350–51; 6.378–79, 381.
34. *BLW* 2.281–86, 290–91; 4.339.
35. *BLW* 3.294–301.
36. *BLW* 5.361–62.
37. *BLW* 1.248; 3.308, 312, 316, 325; 4.329; 5.352, 354, 362–67, 370; 6.383, 387–90, 393–94.
38. *BLW* 2.288–89; 3.304–11, 314, 316, 319, 321; 5.366; 6.382–91.
39. *BLW* 3.310–11, 313–17, 321–26; 5.352–55, 368–69; 6.374–75, 379–80.
40. *BLW* 3.311, 322–25; 5.353, 355–56; 6.397, 400–401.

Introduction xxi

rejects the assumption that "ought" implies "can."[41] This might be true for human nature as created, but Calvin argues that fallen humanity cannot even begin to observe the law.[42] The function of the law is not to show human ability but to point to grace. Grace gives what the law commands.[43]

Related to the law is the question of "good works." Calvin argues that even the best of human works are tainted by sin. Thus it is by his grace and generosity that God rewards them.[44] Furthermore, all good works are the gifts of God's grace and thus, as Augustine put it, when God rewards our merits he crowns his own gifts.[45]

Human responsibility is also a recurring theme of the debate. Pighius objects that human responsibility is incompatible with Calvin's teachings on God's sovereign providence[46] and the human necessity to sin.[47] He also asks why one should bother to preach the gospel if conversion is the work of grace alone.[48] Calvin answers these objections, stressing that God's sovereignty is exercised through human means. Pighius also complains that the character of God is impugned by the doctrines of the bondage of the will[49] and election.[50]

5. The Debate over the Fathers

As can be clearly seen from even a cursory examination, the debate over the teaching of the early fathers is central to Calvin's *Bondage and Liberation of the Will*.[51] A considerable proportion of Pighius's *Free Choice* had been devoted to refuting Calvin's contention in his 1539 *Institutes* that apart from Augustine the early fathers were so confused, vacillating, and contradictory on the subject of free choice that almost nothing can with certainty be ascertained from their writings. Pighius sought to refute the claims both that the early fathers were inconsistent and that Augustine supported Calvin. Calvin joins battle with zest; in fact, about a third of the text of book 3 is composed of patristic quotation.

---

41. *BLW* 1.248; 2.259, 266–67; 3.313; 4.327–30, 339–46; 6.387.
42. *BLW* 2.267; 4.346–47.
43. *BLW* 2.259–60; 3.313; 4.329–30; 6.376–77.
44. *BLW* 1.248–50; 4.328, 336–37.
45. *BLW* 3.312, 316, 318; 4.329, 337–38.
46. *BLW* 2.255–58.
47. *BLW* 4.328, 331–33, 336.
48. *BLW* 1.252–54; 4.344–46; 6.381–82.
49. *BLW* 2.259, 264; 6.381.
50. *BLW* 4.338; 6.385–86.
51. This section is a summary of A. N. S. Lane, "Calvin and the Fathers in His *The Bondage and Liberation of the Will*," in *Calvinus sincerioris religionis vindex*, ed. W. H. Neuser (Kirksville, Mo.: Sixteenth Century Journal, forthcoming).

Which patristic writings does Calvin use? He names or cites twenty-five of Augustine's works, three of Pseudo-Augustine (whose inauthenticity he recognises), and thirty-three from other authors. This impressive array of patristic learning is not quite what it seems. First, on top of his other responsibilities Calvin wrote his reply in a couple of months. Given the time pressure, we must expect to find evidence of haste and of shortcuts. Secondly, Calvin's personal library at this stage is unlikely to have been large, and resources at Geneva were probably meagre. We need to ask, therefore, not just which works Calvin mentions, but which works he shows evidence of having consulted in the preparation of his reply. With some works he is simply repeating his citation from the 1539 *Institutes* or responding to Pighius's quotation. With others it looks as if he is relying on his memory of earlier reading.

Of the twenty-five works of Augustine that he cites, it seems that Calvin consulted the printed texts of fourteen or fifteen of them. This involved making use of at least five of the ten volumes of one of the current editions of Augustine's works. This reading was, as one would expect, confined almost entirely to Augustine's anti-Pelagian writings and to the *Retractations,* where Augustine reviews his earlier writings. In addition, Calvin clearly read for himself two of the three works of Pseudo-Augustine that Pighius had introduced.

Which edition of the works of Augustine did Calvin use? There are two clues which might enable us to trace the specific edition. On one occasion he refers to a passage "five lines earlier,"[52] and another time he talks of "turning the page" to move from one passage to another.[53] An examination of all of the editions available to Calvin suggests that he used one of two editions published in Paris in, respectively, 1531–32 and 1541.[54]

What of the thirty-three non-Augustinian writings? Here the evidence that Calvin consulted them while preparing his reply is equally meagre. For three works of Basil he certainly used the translation by Janus Cornarius, recently published and probably recently purchased by Calvin.[55] Moreover, in a discussion of a passage that Pighius quotes from a work of Ambrose, Calvin's precise indication pointing to other passages "on that very page"[56] would suggest both that Calvin had Ambrose to hand and that he was using one of the editions published by Chevallon at Paris.[57] Calvin also appears to have had Irenaeus's

---

52. *BLW* 3.293 (at n. 16).
53. *BLW* 3.296 (at n. 39).
54. IA 110.201, 258. Both of these are revisions of Erasmus's 1528–29 edition (IA 110.175).
55. (Basel: Froben, 1540 [IA 114.485]).
56. *BLW* 2.287 (at n. 228).
57. In 1529 and 1539 (IA 104.651, 663). It is only in these editions that Pighius's quotation and those of Calvin (*BLW* 2.287 [at nn. 229–30]) are on the same page (i.e., folio).

Against Heresies open before him, and possibly also the *Recognitions* of Pseudo-Clement. Thus of the thirty-three non-Augustinian writings cited, Calvin probably consulted only five or six.

Calvin also quotes from a number of councils: those of Carthage, Milevis, and Orange. He clearly had the source open before him. This must have been volume 1 of Peter Crabbe's *Concilia omnia,* the only printed work at this time to contain the canons of the Second Council of Orange (529).[58] Thus for the wide range of patristic material cited, Calvin need have consulted no more than nine volumes: five of Augustine and one each of Basil, Ambrose, Irenaeus, and Crabbe.

But why did Calvin bother with the Fathers? As a Protestant who held to the final authority of Scripture, why did he need to bicker over the interpretation of Basil or Augustine? At one level, he did not need to. Calvin is perfectly frank in stating that if the Fathers' teaching is contrary to Scripture it is invalid. Even the consensus of the Fathers does not count if it is contrary to Scripture.[59] For Calvin every doctrinal belief must be tested by Scripture, while for Pighius the pronouncements of the pope are the final norm. As they are arguing from different premises, there is little chance of a meeting of minds. But there is also a secondary battle under way. What is historic Christianity? Pighius claims that his view is in accord with the universal consensus of the Catholic church over the centuries. While Calvin theoretically could have conceded this claim, to have done so would have gravely undermined the plausibility of his case.[60]

This is not to say that Calvin's appeal to the Fathers was not sincere. He genuinely believed that Augustine supported him on the issue of the will. Repeatedly he claimed that Augustine was on his side.[61] But how accurate was Calvin's claim? It must be admitted that his quotations of Augustine (and other writers) are often very loose. For example, he omits words, adds words, changes words, changes tenses, changes word order. He also on occasions paraphrases, using similar words, or just summarises the meaning of passages in his own words. Such a method of working was not unusual in the sixteenth century, whose scholarly standards were different from today's. The reasons for Calvin's looseness in citation are simple—lack of resources and pressure of time.[62] For some works he relied upon his memory of earlier

---

58. See n. 94.
59. See, e.g., BLW 2.288.
60. See A. N. S. Lane, "Calvin's Use of the Fathers and the Medievals," *Calvin Theological Journal* 16 (1981): 165–74.
61. BLW 3.301, 312, 317, 326; 5.359. Calvin claims Augustine as "completely ours" (*prorsus nostrum,* 3.301, 320) and "completely with us" (*prorsus nobiscum,* 3.312).
62. Calvin wrote the whole work in a couple of months. The tracing and checking of his quotations have taken a considerably longer period of time.

reading, either because he did not have the volume to hand or because he did not have time to consult it. For the major works of Augustine, it is likely that having studied what Pighius had to say, Calvin read through the work of Augustine in question and then wrote his response from memory of that (recent) reading. At times he would have had the work open before him and have taken longer quotations from it, but again without bothering about total accuracy.

Pighius, by contrast, quoted longer passages than did Calvin and generally much more accurately, though not with total accuracy. Why was this? As Calvin notes in his preface, his Roman Catholic adversaries had considerably more time, leisure, and peace to prepare their attacks.[63] In addition, while Calvin laments his lack of books while writing the 1539 *Institutes*,[64] Pighius had an extensive personal library, an inventory of which was made after his death.[65]

But how accurate was Calvin's interpretation of Augustine? For centuries there has been controversy between Catholics and Protestants over this issue. But in recent times it has become easier for both sides to acknowledge historical development and to interpret the Fathers more objectively.[66] An influential essay by the Benedictine Odilo Rottmanner in the nineteenth century marked a new willingness by Roman Catholics to admit that in the areas of grace and predestination the Reformers were largely justified in their appeal to Augustine.[67] A few notes indicate areas where Calvin's interpretation of Augustine is open to question, but it is very widely conceded today that the main thrust is accurate.[68]

6. Calvin's Use of Aristotle

Luther, in the early years of the Reformation, was unremittingly hostile towards the use of Aristotle in theology. Compared with the medieval Scholastics, Calvin made little use of Aristotle, but was not unwilling to invoke Aristotelian distinctions when these suited his purpose, as with

---

63. *BLW* 229-32. Pighius wrote the prefatory material for the 1542 Cologne edition of his *Controversies* on 5 January 1542, and the prefatory material for his *Free Choice* on 13 August. The intervening seven months were probably mainly devoted to writing the latter work.

64. *BLW* 4.336 (at n. 94).

65. M. E. Kronenberg, "Albertus Pighius, proost van S. Jan Utrecht, zijn geschriften en zijn bibliothek," *Het Boek* 28 (1944-46): 125-58.

66. See O. Chadwick, *From Bossuet to Newman: The Idea of Doctrinal Development*, 2d ed. (Cambridge: Cambridge University Press, 1987).

67. O. Rottmanner, *Der Augustinismus* (Munich: J. J. Lentner, 1892).

68. For a recent Roman Catholic writer who argues that the Reformers (especially Luther) were basically justified in their claim to represent the Augustinian tradition of the church on this issue, see H. J. McSorley, *Luther: Right or Wrong?* (New York: Newman & Minneapolis: Augsburg, 1969).

Introduction

his 1539 discussion of the four causes of salvation.[69] In his *Bondage and Liberation of the Will* he makes a larger than usual use of Aristotle.

The first reference appears to be somewhat slighting, when Calvin says that the teaching attributed to the apostle Peter in the (apocryphal) Clementine *Recognitions* is "no more redolent of the apostolic spirit than is Aristotle's *Metaphysics*," though he goes on to say that the comparison does Aristotle an injustice![70]

Later on Calvin introduces an extended discussion of Aristotle. First he makes a statement about Aristotle's understanding of "necessity."[71] Then, shortly after, he quotes Aristotle's discussion (in his *Nicomachean Ethics*) of circumstances in which the will becomes impotent.[72] Here Calvin takes the battle onto the enemies' ground, showing that even the philosopher beloved of the medieval Scholastics offers support for his doctrine of the bondage of the will.

This use of Aristotle could be described as opportunistic in that it provides further ammunition for Calvin but does not actually affect the case that he is arguing. But elsewhere Calvin makes use of Aristotelian distinctions as a vital part of his argument. Pighius seeks to identify the Protestant doctrine of the bondage of the will with the teaching of the Manichees and other early heretics that evil is a part of human nature as initially constituted.[73] Calvin responds to this charge with two distinctions. First, he differentiates between human nature as created by God in the beginning, which was good, and human nature as it has become through Adam's fall, which is evil.[74] Secondly, in order to make this clearer, Calvin repeatedly invokes the Aristotelian distinction between substance and accidents.[75] The Manichees taught that evil is part of the substance of human nature, that it is inherent to human nature through its origin. The Reformers teach that human nature was created good and that, while it has become evil, this evil is "accidental." In other words, it is contingent, something that has in fact happened but need not have happened. Just as we may be happy or sad without ceasing to be human (happiness and sadness are "accidental" to humanity), so also the human race, after having been created good, became evil without ceasing to be human.

This use of the Aristotelian distinction is fundamental to Calvin's argument. It is, one might say, not merely accidental to it but part of its

---

69. *Inst.* 3.14.17 (LCC 20:783–84).
70. *BLW* 2.261 (at n. 42).
71. *BLW* 4.335 (at nn. 78–79).
72. *BLW* 4.335–36 (at nn. 81–84).
73. *BLW* 2.262–63.
74. *BLW* 2.259, 263–64.
75. *BLW* 2.263 (at n. 58), 264 (at nn. 63, 65), 284 (at n. 213), 290 (at n. 259); 4.331 (at n. 45); 5.361 (at n. 100); 6.381 (at n. 59).

substance. "Without this distinction it is not surprising if [Pighius] gets everything confused."[76] Calvin also develops similar and related contrasts. Calvin's use of Ezekiel 36:26 led Pighius to accuse him of teaching that conversion involves the destruction of the faculty of the will and its replacement by a new will. He cites, against Calvin, Ambrose's statement that the substance of the heart is not removed. Calvin mocks Pighius's accusation, insisting that he had never taught the destruction or removal of the substance of the heart or will. What is changed in conversion is not the faculty or substance of willing, nor merely the actions of the will. It is, rather, something in between, the quality or "habit" (Latin, *habitus*) of the will.[77] These contrasts are related to the distinction between substance and accidents, as becomes clear when Calvin shortly after refers to the "accidental qualities" of the soul.[78]

Calvin's use of the word "habit" is significant. This was a Scholastic technical term that was used to describe "a kind of predicamental quality in that it is a modification of the substance not easily changed."[79] Calvin repeatedly contrasts it with substance.[80] Elsewhere he uses it in a less technical way, as we talk of having good or bad habits.[81] Ironically, although Calvin maintains that the distinction between substance and habit was the plain teaching of his 1539 *Institutes,* he did not introduce it into any edition of that work.[82]

Finally, Calvin also uses the Aristotelian distinction between form and matter. The human will is described as matter which receives form — a bad form from the corruption of original sin, a good form from the operation of grace.[83] The explicit distinction occurs just two times, but should be kept in mind on the numerous occasions where Calvin talks of the will being "formed" by grace.[84]

This extensive use of Aristotle and of Aristotelian distinctions shows that while Calvin did not share the medieval Scholastic enthusiasm for Aristotle, he also did not share the early Luther's programmatic rejection of Aristotle.

---

76. *BLW* 5.361 (at n. 100). The distinction referred to is that between human nature as created whole and its *accidental* corruption, a combining of the two distinctions mentioned in the previous paragraph.

77. *BLW* 6.377–79, 392.

78. *BLW* 6.381 (at n. 59).

79. R. J. Deferrari, *A Latin-English Dictionary of St. Thomas Aquinas* (Boston: St. Paul, 1960), 453–56.

80. *BLW* 6.378–79; cf. 4.336 (at n. 85).

81. *BLW* 3.304–5; 6.380.

82. The Latin word *habitus* occurs once, in *Institutes* 4.4.9 (from 1543), where it probably simply means "habit" in the colloquial sense and is translated "exemplary life" (LCC 21:1077).

83. *BLW* 3.312 (at n. 178); 6.391–92 (at n. 131).

84. *BLW* 3.314, 316; 4.329, 342–43, 345; 5.353; 6.374–75, 380, 389.

7. Erasmus and Luther

Calvin and Pighius were not the first in Reformation times to debate the issue of the human will. That distinction goes to Luther and Erasmus.[85] On 15 June 1520 a papal bull was proclaimed condemning as heretical forty-one errors drawn from Luther's writings.[86] The thirty-sixth of these was that "free choice after sin is a reality only in name, and while it does what it can, it sins mortally." This was the thirteenth of the theological theses defended by Luther at the Heidelberg disputation in May 1518.[87] Luther responded to the papal bull with various works, including his *Defence of All the Articles of Martin Luther Condemned by the Latest Bull of Leo X*.[88] Article 36 receives a lengthy and vigorous treatment.[89]

In the early years of the Reformation, Erasmus, the leading scholar of the day, lent tacit support to Luther. But eventually he was persuaded to oppose him, and in 1524 he published his *Diatribe concerning Free Choice* in which he attacked Luther's treatment of the thirty-sixth article.[90] Luther responded the following year with his *Bondage of the Will*.[91] Erasmus had the last word, replying at great length in his *Hyperaspistes*, which appeared in two parts in 1526 and 1527.[92]

How do the two debates compare? In many ways it is remarkable how little they have in common. Erasmus's *Diatribe* is brief and eloquent while Pighius's work is longer and more thorough. In particular, Pighius devotes considerable attention to the writings of the early fathers, while Erasmus mentions them only briefly and in passing.[93] What Pighius and Erasmus do have in common is that both of them were later thought to have strayed beyond the bounds of Catholic orthodoxy in their exaltation of free choice. This was in main part due to the fact that the condemnation of semi-Pelagianism at the Second Council of Orange (529) was overlooked from the tenth century to 1538.[94]

---

85. On Luther and Erasmus see McSorley, *Luther: Right or Wrong?*
86. J. Atkinson, *The Trial of Luther* (London: B. T. Batsford, 1971), 83–89; McSorley, *Luther: Right or Wrong?* 251–53; L. Grane, *Martinus Noster* (Mainz: Philipp von Zabern, 1994), 231–37.
87. LW 31:40, 48–49.
88. WA 7:94–151; see also Atkinson, *Trial*, 102–12. Luther also produced a briefer German version, which has been translated into English (LW 32:7–99).
89. WA 7:142–49; see also McSorley, *Luther: Right or Wrong?* 253–73.
90. LCC 17:35–97.
91. LCC 17:101–334.
92. LB 10:1254–1536.
93. LCC 17:42–43.
94. The medievals relied on compilations for their knowledge of the councils; these compilations, including the most influential, the ninth-century Pseudo-Isidorian *Decretals*, did not include Orange. Thus the canons of this council were unknown and unquoted from the tenth century until 1538, when Peter Crabbe published his two-volume *Concilia omnia* (Cologne: P. Quentel, 1538); see H. Bouillard, *Conversion et grace chez S. Thomas d'Aquin* (Paris: Aubier, 1944), 98–102, 114–21.

Calvin in his response met Pighius on his own ground by arguing at length from the writings of the church fathers. This was not uncongenial for him as he was much more interested than Luther in defending his teaching in this way. Calvin also adopted a more moderate position than did Luther. Luther, in his defence of the thirty-sixth article quoted above, ironically retracted what he had said earlier: He should not have said just that "free choice after sin is a reality only in name"; he should have said frankly that "free choice is something imaginary, a name without substance." Indeed, it is true that "all things happen by absolute necessity."[95] This last claim caused Calvin some embarrassment. His concern for Protestant solidarity prevented him from openly criticising Luther's assertion, but he was annoyed by the attention that Pighius devoted to it at the beginning of his work, especially as the subject belonged in the last four books, where providence was treated.[96] Calvin glosses over the differences between Luther and Melanchthon concerning human free choice in external and secular matters.[97] When he does eventually deal with the issue, in his 1552 *Eternal Predestination of God* and his 1559 *Institutes,* he puts clear water between Luther and himself. Calvin, contrary to his more usual practice, explicitly approves two Scholastic distinctions which Luther had rejected: between relative and absolute necessity and between necessity of consequence and consequent necessity.[98] The purpose of this atypical foray into "Scholastic subtlety" is to enable Calvin to dissociate himself from Luther's doctrine of absolute necessity.[99]

Finally, to what extent do Pighius and Calvin draw upon the earlier debate? The answer appears to be none at all. Pighius attacks Luther's *Defence,* but to the best of my knowledge makes no mention of either Erasmus's *Diatribe* or Luther's *Bondage of the Will*.[100] Calvin makes no allusion to the earlier debate. In the notes to this work a number of parallels are noted,[101] but none of these amounts to clear proof that either Pighius or Calvin had the earlier works in mind. What is remarkable is not the occasional parallel, nor the inevitable fact that certain

---

95. WA 7:146; cf. *BLW* 1.248 (at n. 70).
96. *BLW* 1.248 (at n. 70), 250 (at n. 78); 2.255 (at n. 2).
97. *BLW* 1.250–51.
98. Luther rejects these distinctions in, among other places, *The Bondage of the Will* (LCC 17:120–21, 247–49); Calvin approves them in *The Eternal Predestination of God*, 170, 177–78 (unfortunately the English translation is unreliable, on p. 170 conflating the two distinctions into one), and the 1559 *Institutes* 1.16.9 (LCC 20:210).
99. For a fuller discussion see A. N. S. Lane, "Did Calvin Believe in Freewill?" *Vox Evangelica* 12 (1981): 74–75.
100. Pighius's library at his death included neither work (Kronenberg, "Pighius, proost," 132–58). But it did not include Calvin's *Institutes* or Luther's *Defence* either.
101. *BLW* 1.238 n. 30, 244 n. 47; 2.256 n. 8; 3.294 n. 17; 4.350 n. 216; 5.362 n. 102; 6.398 n. 192.

Introduction

commonplace arguments are reiterated, but the lack of similarity between the two debates.

8. The History of the Editions

Calvin's *Bondage and Liberation of the Will* was published three times in his lifetime.[102] The first edition was published at Geneva in 1543 by Jean Girard.[103] In 1552 Nicolas Des Gallars published at Geneva an edition of all of Calvin's treatises, including the *Bondage and Liberation of the Will*. This all-encompassing edition also was printed by Jean Girard.[104] A smaller collection of treatises published in 1563 by Nicolas Barbier and Thomas Courteau does not contain the *Bondage and Liberation of the Will*.[105]

A translation of the work into French was published at Geneva in 1560 by François Jaquy, Antoine Davodeau, and Jacques Bourgeois.[106] No indication is given of the identity of the translator. There is no evidence that Calvin made the translation; given the interval of nearly twenty years and Calvin's work load in 1560, it is very unlikely that he did it. This translation reappears in a collection of Calvin's treatises in French; this collection was published at Geneva in 1566 by Baptiste Pinereul, and a second edition appeared in 1611.[107] There is no other translation, in any language, until the present one.

The Latin text reappears in various collections of Calvin's works, beginning with an edition by Calvin's successor Theodore Beza in 1576 and again in 1597.[108] It was republished in 1611 and 1612 at Geneva by Jacob Stoer, and again in 1617 as part of a multivolume set of Calvin's works.[109] It also appeared in the multivolume set published at Amsterdam in 1667–71 by Jacob Schipper.[110]

After an interval of nearly two hundred years, a fifty-nine-volume set of Calvin's works was published in the nineteenth century as part of the *Corpus Reformatorum* series, which also includes the works of Melanchthon and Zwingli. The best Latin edition so far of Calvin's *Bondage and Liberation of the Will* is in that series.[111] Before too long,

---

102. The editor has personally checked all of the editions mentioned in this section.
103. For bibliographical details see R. Peter and J.-F. Gilmont, *Bibliotheca Calviniana*, 2 vols. (Geneva: Droz, 1991, 1994), 1:122–25; OC 6:xxiii–xxv.
104. For bibliographical details see *Bibliotheca Calviniana* 1:456–62; OC 5:ix–xiii.
105. For bibliographical details see *Bibliotheca Calviniana* 2:1017–19; OC 5:xiii–xiv.
106. For bibliographical details see *Bibliotheca Calviniana* 2:767–69; OC 6:xxiv.
107. IA 130.101; OC 5:xiv–xix, xxv–xxviii.
108. IA 130.142, 267; OC 5:xix–xxiv.
109. OC 5:xxiv–xxv.
110. OC 1:xii.
111. OC 6:229–404.

however, it will be superseded by a critical edition prepared by the editor of this translation and published in the new *Editio Recognita* of Calvin's works.[112]

9. The Text

The translation has been made from the original 1543 edition. Textual variants in later editions were examined, but are noted only where they appear to present the correct reading. Simple cases of correcting a printer's error in the first edition have not been noted. Anyone interested in details of the textual variants should consult the forthcoming critical edition. At times Calvin's text includes words in Greek. Those he left untranslated have translated into English, with a footnote indicating that the original was in Greek.[113] Those he translated have been left in Greek.[114]

The French translation has been treated not as an authoritative interpretation, but as an example of a previous translation, an indication of how a contemporary of Calvin's interpreted the text. In general it is a looser translation than the present one, and there are places where it appears to be inaccurate. It has been consulted where there have been difficulties in translation; also, the whole has been compared with the present translation.

The text of the present translation contains only Calvin's original text and his marginal notes (which are given in parentheses).[115] The reader may be confident, therefore, that all of the references found in the text are Calvin's. This is not at all true of the *Corpus Reformatorum* edition, which drops or changes some of Calvin's references and adds many biblical references of its own, a high proportion of which are inaccurate.

There are, however, three types of situations in which we have altered Calvin's references. First, his seven marginal references to Pighius have been relegated to footnotes,[116] as have five erroneous references.[117] Secondly, Calvin's references to Augustine's *Benefit of Perseverance* have been changed to *The Gift of Perseverance* (the usual title today). Thirdly, Calvin numbers Augustine's letters according to the numeration of his time. The late-seventeenth-century Maurist edition

---

112. To date, two volumes in this series, which is being published by Droz at Geneva, have appeared.
113. See, e.g., *BLW* 2.268 (at n. 102).
114. See, e.g., *BLW* 2.270.
115. Calvin's marginal notes, which may span a number of lines, have been placed at the end of the passage to which they refer. This has, of course, necessarily involved an element of judgment on our part.
116. *BLW* 1.247 n. 59, 248 n. 69; 2.263 n. 60, 265 n. 83, 292 n. 269; 6.401 nn. 226–27.
117. *BLW* 2.265 n. 80; 4.344 n. 172; 5.352 n. 13, 368 n. 140; 6.399 n. 209. Where there is a merely numerical error, the marginal reference has been retained in the text.

introduced a new numeration that has since become standard. Calvin's numbers have been converted to the Maurist system as part of the process of translation into modern English.

Calvin's paragraph breaks have been followed and, in the interests of clarity, others have been added. The subheads in the text and the summary in the margins are ours, not Calvin's. The text also contains column numbers from the *OC* edition. The latter are given to enable the reader to move from the translation to the *OC* edition and to the new critical edition, which will also give these column numbers. They are also used as a means of cross-referencing within the present text.

10. The Translation

The translation sets out to be as close to the original as is compatible with readable contemporary English. The latter requires some compromise of the former, but this has been kept to a minimum. Material added for the purposes of clarity is normally placed within square brackets. The translation has been revised a number of times, especially as a result of comparison with the French translation and the text of Augustine.

The translation was well under way before the issue of gender-free language became prominent. We then had to decide whether or not to revise it in the direction of political correctness. After careful consideration we opted for a partial revision reflecting two basic guidelines: (1) In translating the Latin word *homo* (human being) we have sought to represent its meaning accurately without either producing stilted English or departing excessively from the phraseology of the original. In many places it has been possible to use terms like "human being(s)," "people," "someone," "those (who)," and the adjective "human." But there are also many places, especially in the doctrinal passages, where any translation other than "man" or (rarely) "men" would be extremely stilted. It should be clear in these passages that the word is being used in its traditional inclusive sense. (2) Calvin was a writer of the sixteenth century; it is not our aim to pretend otherwise. Just as we have left unaltered those sections which some modern sensibilities might consider too polemical or (rarely) vulgar, so also we have not sought to make his language politically correct in an anachronistic fashion.[118] Not all will agree with our policy. But we trust that the modest use, where appropriate, of the alternatives mentioned above will help to prevent misunderstanding or misinterpretation.

---

118. M. Potter's translation of Calvin's "Warning against Judiciary Astrology and Other Prevalent Curiosities," *Calvin Theological Journal* 18 (1983): 157–89, keeps to the traditional usage of "man." For her justification see p. 161 n. 3.

With an issue like grace and free choice the language can be quite technical. In order to convey the meaning as accurately as possible we have sought to translate the more technical terms consistently. First, the word *arbitrium*. This is always translated "choice"; *voluntas,* on the other hand, is almost always translated "will." There is a long tradition of translating *liberum arbitrium* as "free will," but this can only cause confusion in a work where *arbitrium* and *voluntas* are often used in relation to each other.[119]

Other terms are also translated consistently, at least in the context of the debate about the freedom of the will. *Coactio* and *cogo* are translated "coercion" and "coerce." *Electio* is translated "decision" or "choosing" or "to choose." *Invitus* is translated "unwillingly." *Spontanea* and *sponte* are respectively translated "self-determined" and "of its own accord." *Ultro* is translated "of itself." *Voluntarius* is translated "voluntary" or "wilful." Finally, *voluntate* as an adverb is translated "wilfully."

Where theological precision does not call for uniformity of translation greater scope has been left for stylistic variations. In particular, *servus, servitus,* and their cognates are translated both as "bound/bondage" and as "enslaved/slavery." To have restricted the translation to one or the other of these possibilities would have entailed stylistic impoverishment with no compensating gain in clarity. The reader should be aware that there is no theological significance in the variation between the two sets of words, both going back to the same Latin originals.

For the most part, quotation marks have not been used for biblical quotations, nor for quotations from Pighius.[120] Where Calvin cites other authors, such as the Fathers, the classics, or even his own *Institutes,* quotation marks have been used for quotations, some of which may be very loose. Where the citation takes the form of paraphrase or summary, quotation marks have not been used. The limits of the citation should be clear, usually from the position of the introductory words at the beginning and the footnote at the end. The boundary between loose quotation and paraphrase is blurred, but it is hoped that the criteria used have at least been consistent throughout.

Most of the patristic works cited by Calvin have titles like *[Three Books] on Free Choice* (Augustine). The word "on" is the link between the number of books and the subject matter. In translation such a title is more often than not rendered *On Free Choice*. But this is not how

---

119. While in LCC 17 the title of Luther's *De servo arbitrio* is rendered *The Bondage of the Will,* in the text itself *arbitrium* is translated "choice"; see LCC 17:29.

120. Since these quotations often overlap patristic quotations, to use quotation marks for both would at times result in chaos.

Introduction

titles are normally given in English, which prefers simply *Free Choice*. That is the style adopted here.

11. The Notes

It is always difficult listening to one half of a telephone conversation. One has to guess at the other half, and the result is often lack of understanding or misunderstanding. The problem is exacerbated with Calvin's *Bondage and Liberation of the Will*. Calvin is responding to Pighius's work, often page by page or even line by line. He has the work in front of him and at times assumes that his reader knows what is there. Furthermore, Pighius in turn has been responding to Calvin's 1539 *Institutes*. There are places where the significance of Calvin's comments becomes clear only when one looks back at these earlier works.

The situation is yet more complicated. For much of the time Calvin and Pighius are debating the interpretation of Augustine. Augustine in turn discussed Pelagius, Paul, and several of the church fathers. Thus "he" in Calvin's text may turn out to be Pighius, Augustine, Pelagius, Paul, or _____. Often it is impossible to tell who is in view without going back to the original texts. That is the responsibility not of the reader but of the editor. The fruits of his labours are to be found at times in the text, where "he" may become, for example, [Pighius]; but they are more often to be found in the footnotes. These aim not just to give the source of quotations but to help the reader to understand the text. The complexity of the structure has necessitated full notes. To make Calvin's meaning as clear as possible, there has on occasion been a willingness to state the obvious.

All of Calvin's explicit biblical references have been identified.[121] Biblical allusions by Calvin have also been identified where noticed. But where he is quoting from another writer, such as Augustine, only the explicit biblical references are identified.

Notes are supplied wherever Calvin specifically identifies his citations of the church fathers. These notes give page references for the Ante-Nicene and Post-Nicene Fathers series. This is not because these series offer the best translations (they do not), but because they are the most comprehensive set of translations available. Other English translations are cited for works not found in these series. Where there is no English translation, reference is made to Migne's *Patrologiae*, again not

---

121. With quotations from the Synoptic Gospels, the aim has been to identify the specific Gospel used. Where more than one Gospel equally fit the evidence, the references are linked by (/); see, e.g., *BLW* 1.249 n. 75. In the case of other parallel passages, e.g., Ezek. 11:19–20 and 36:26–27, care has been taken to ascertain which passage Calvin has in mind.

because they constitute the best editions, but because they are the most comprehensive and are widely accessible. Similarly with all other works, reference is made to an English translation where possible and, failing that, to an edition in the original. With Augustine's *Retractations* there are references to English translations both of that work itself and of passages of the *Retractations* that occur in editions of the work which Augustine is discussing.

Classical allusions and proverbs have been sought primarily in Erasmus's *Adages*, a work with which Calvin would certainly have been familiar. This is not to deny that Calvin may have made direct use of some of the classical originals that are referred to in the *Adages*.

Except where explicitly indicated, all references to the *Institutes* are to passages which appear in the 1539 edition, the most recent one at the time Calvin wrote *The Bondage and Liberation of the Will,* and the one which Pighius and he had in mind. But as there is no English translation of the 1539 edition, the references point to the definitive 1559 edition. (The English translation of the 1559 edition indicates which material originated in each edition.) Sometimes the 1539 text has been rewritten in the 1559 edition, in which case the reference is to the equivalent passage in the 1559 edition, and the phrase "as rewritten in 1559" is added.

The one work which is not always noted is Pighius's *Free Choice,* both because it is cited so frequently and because it is available only in the original Latin edition. Wherever it is mentioned in the notes, folio numbers are given in parentheses; (5a–b), for example, means the first and second side of folio 5. Where the source is not given in the notes, readers have two possibilities for tracing the passage in Pighius to which Calvin is responding. They may wait for the forthcoming critical edition, which will contain both full references to Pighius and a facsimile of his text. Alternatively, since Calvin normally worked through Pighius's text in order, they can make a calculated guess by looking at the references to Pighius that occur in the footnotes in the immediate context.

Abbreviations

ACW   *Ancient Christian Writers* series (London: Longmans, Green; Westminster, Md.: Newman; New York: Paulist)
ANF   *Ante-Nicene Fathers* series (Grand Rapids: Eerdmans)
BLW   *Bondage and Liberation of the Will*
CCL   *Corpus Christianorum: Series Latina* (Turnhout: Brepols)
CFS   *Cistercian Fathers* series (Kalamazoo: Cistercian)
CWE   *Collected Works of Erasmus* (Toronto: University of Toronto Press)
FoC   *Fathers of the Church* series (Washington: Catholic University of America Press)
IA   *Index Aureliensis* (Baden-Baden: V. Koerner, 1965ff.)
Inst.   *Institutes* (used only of material in the 1539 edition)
LB   Desiderius Erasmus, *Opera Omnia* (Leiden, 1703–6)
LCC   *Library of Christian Classics* series (London: SCM & Philadelphia: Westminster)
Leith   *Creeds of the Churches*, ed. J. H. Leith, 3d ed. (Atlanta: John Knox, 1982)
Loeb   *Loeb Classical Library* series (Cambridge: Harvard University Press)
LW   *Luther's Works* (Philadelphia: Fortress)
Müller   *The "De Haeresibus" of Saint Augustine,* ed. L. G. Müller (Washington: Catholic University of America Press, 1956)
NPNF   *Nicene and Post-Nicene Fathers: First Series* (Grand Rapids: Eerdmans)
NPNF2   *Nicene and Post-Nicene Fathers: Second Series* (Grand Rapids: Eerdmans)
OC   *Ioannis Calvini opera quae supersunt omnia,* ed. J. W. Baum et al. (Brunswick, 1863–1900)
OS   *Joannis Calvini Opera Selecta,* ed. P. Barth et al. (Munich: Chr. Kaiser, 1926–68)
PG   *Patrologia Graeca,* ed. J. P. Migne (Paris: Migne, 1857–66)

PL	*Patrologia Latina*, ed. J. P. Migne (Paris: Migne, 1844–64)
Smits	L. Smits, *Saint Augustin dans l'oeuvre de Jean Calvin*, 2 vols. (Assen: van Gorcum, 1956, 1958)
SW	*Selected Works of John Calvin*, ed. H. Beveridge & J. Bonnet (Grand Rapids: Baker, 1983)
Tappert	*The Book of Concord*, ed. T. G. Tappert (Philadelphia: Fortress, 1959)
WA	*D Martin Luthers Werke* (Weimar: Hermann Böhlaus, 1883ff.)
Walther	*Proverbia Sententiaeque Latinitatis Medii Aevi*, ed. H. Walther (Göttingen: Vandenhoeck & Ruprecht, 1963–69); and *Proverbia Sententiaeque Latinitatis Medii ac Recentioris Aevi: Nova Series*, ed. P. G. Schmidt (Göttingen: Vandenhoeck & Ruprecht, 1982–86). Items given by number.
Works	*Works of Saint Augustine* (New Rochelle, N.Y.: New City)

List of Works Cited

This is a list not of suspected patristic and classical allusions, but of (1) works named by Calvin; (2) works not named but clearly cited by Calvin (*); (3) works named by Pighius and referred to by Calvin (#); (4) works clearly quoted by Pighius, without naming them, and referred to by Calvin (§); (5) works named by Calvin in the 1539 *Institutes* and here referred to by him (¶); and (6) unnamed but clear intermediate sources of Calvin's quotations (◊).

Patristic Works

Ambrose	*Commentary on Luke*
	Flight from the World
	/#Jacob and the Happy Life
Augustine	*Against Faustus the Manichee*
	Against Felix the Manichee
	Against Julian
	Against Two Letters of the Pelagians
	City of God
	**Confessions*
	Enchiridion
	Expositions on the Psalms
	Free Choice
	The Gift of Perseverance
	Grace and Free Choice
	The Grace of Christ and Original Sin
	The Greatness of the Soul
	Heresies
	Letters
	The Merits and Forgiveness of Sins
	Nature and Grace

	The Perfection of Righteousness
	The Predestination of the Saints
	Rebuke and Grace
	Retractations
	Sermons on John
	The Spirit and the Letter
	True Religion
	Two Souls
Pseudo-Augustine	The Dogmas of the Church
	Hypognosticon
	§Sermon 236
Basil	#Ascetic Constitutions
	*/#Homilies
	*Homilies on Psalms
Pseudo-Basil	*Sermon on Free Choice
Bernard	*Grace and Free Choice
Cassiodore	◊Tripartite History
Chrysostom	#Homilies on Genesis
	*Homilies on Matthew
	*Homily on Reproaches to Be Borne
Pseudo-Chrysostom	¶Homily for the First Sunday in Advent
Clement	Letters
Pseudo-Clement	Recognitions
Cyprian	*The Lord's Prayer
	*Testimonies
Cyril	§Commentary on John
Eusebius	The History of the Church
Hilary	#Treatise on Psalms
Irenaeus	*Against Heresies
Jerome	§Against Jovinian
	¶Dialogue against the Pelagians
	Letters
	#Questions on the Hebrew of Genesis
Origen	#First Principles
Pamphilus	#Apology for Origen
Peter Lombard	¶Sentences
Prosper	#The Call of All Nations
Rufinus	The Adulteration of the Works of Origen

List of Works Cited xxxix

Tertullian	*Against Marcion*
	The Prescription against Heretics
Theodoret	**The History of the Church*

Councils

Council of Carthage (416)
Council of Milevis (416)
Council of Carthage (418)
African councils in the time of Boniface I and Celestine I
Council of Orange (529)

Classical Works

Aristotle	**Categories*
	Metaphysics
	Nicomachean Ethics
	*Topics
Cicero	*#Nature of the Gods*
	◊Tusculan Disputations
Erasmus	*◊Adages*
Aulus Gellius	**Attic Nights*
Horace	**Art of Poetry*
Gnaeus Naevius	**Hector's Departure*
Terence	**Eunuchus*
Virgil	**Aeneid*

*Defensio sanae et orthodoxae doctrinae
de servitute et liberatione humani arbitrii
adversus calumnias Alberti Pighii Campensis*

*Defence of the Sound and Orthodox Doctrine
of the Bondage and Liberation of the Human Will,
against the Misrepresentations of Albert Pighius of Kampen*

Preface

§ *John Calvin, to a most famous man, Philipp Melanchthon*[1]

Although I am well aware of that special sharpness of your judgment, which all rightly admire, and respect its criticism, as is proper, yet if I were sending this book privately for you to read I should not employ long excuses, relying rather on the genuineness of my love towards you. But now that I have been so bold as to address it publicly to you, I know that there are sure to be some who will accuse me of rashness in that action. Therefore, because of them, I will briefly explain, as would not be necessary in your presence, from what I have derived this confidence. To begin with, I am dedicating to you a book which I know for certain will be doubly pleasing to you, both because of your love for me the author and because it contains a defence of the godly and sound teaching of which you are not only a most zealous supporter, but a distinguished and very brave champion.[2] There is also a third recommendation and that an unusual one—the fact that the kind of defence which I employ is straightforward and honest. For as much as you shrink from crafty, sidelong devices in argument which serve to draw darkness over things which are otherwise clear and open, in short from all pretence and sophistry, so you are pleased by an unembellished and frank clarity which, without any concealment, sets a subject before the eyes and explains it. This quality of yours has often stirred in me great admiration, just because it is so rarely found, for, although you are outstanding for

229–30

Four recommendations of the book

---

1. Calvin's relations with Melanchthon have been remarkably neglected. For a rare exception see J. T. Hickman, "The Friendship of Melanchthon and Calvin," *Westminster Theological Journal* 38 (1975–76): 152–65, which draws on the earlier work of P. Schaff, "Calvin and Melanchthon," in *History of the Christian Church* (Grand Rapids: Eerdmans, 1953), 8:385–98. Calvin mentions his dedication of this work to Melanchthon in a letter to him of 16 February 1543 (SW 4:374–75).

2. Melanchthon had begun by supporting Luther's *Bondage of the Will*, but by this stage had come to allow more scope to human free will than did either Luther or Calvin. See, e.g., B. Hägglund, *History of Theology*, 3d ed. (St. Louis & London: Concordia, 1968), 249–51. He himself remarked on this difference in his letter to Calvin of 11 May 1543 thanking him for the dedication (OC 11:539–42, cited in Schaff, *History of the Christian Church*, 8:391–92) and in a letter of 12 July the same year (OC 11:594–95). Calvin refers to the difference in his preface to the 1546 French translation of Melanchthon's *Loci communes* (OC 9:848–49).

your amazing insight, you still rank nothing above straightforwardness. Therefore this reason too will, I know, be of no little effect in winning your favour for this modest volume. Besides I remember that you once assigned me the task of writing something to restrain Pighius's insolence if he should continue to challenge us.

Reply to Pighius is necessary

It is not, however, just your authority that has led me now at last to begin this task. I have also been forced into it by his wickedness. For by his recent publication of ten books on free choice and predestination[3] he undertook, not after judgment and selection but out of a mere passion for fighting, to refute everything that I had put out on these matters. There he throws himself with such insolence and such unbridled ferocity against the pure teaching of godliness which we guard, that I considered it essential to counteract in some way the gross impudence of the man, unless I wanted to betray the glory of Christ by silence. A treatment of this critique demanded somewhat more of both leisure and time. But since I could see that our foe would endeavour, if

and must be prompt

I put it off longer, to use this delay of mine to instil some prejudice in people's minds, I preferred to offer something quickly, even if it was not sufficiently worked out, rather than by remaining silent to lose a good cause and to allow him to enjoy empty boasting of that kind. However, I think my haste has been such that I have not stumbled at all through undue speed. For I hope you will judge that I have to a large extent achieved my main object, which was to say enough to rebut our foe's misrepresentations.

Even so, it would not be right to omit this excuse; and if, in your kindness, you will accept it yourself, you will show others the way and prevent them from being unduly unfair to me or less than generous. It has certainly occurred to me quite often to complain about our situation,

Reformers write under pressure;

that being overwhelmed by such a multitude of tasks which constantly press in on us, weighed down by their frequent recurrence, and perplexed by their variety, we cannot concentrate our minds and attention on the handling of any one of them. We are continually compelled to rush this way and that, like those who are appointed to diverse burdensome offices which they are by no means able to fulfil together, and who, being under pressure from all sides at the same moment, do not

their opponents at leisure

know because of fatigue which way they should turn. Meanwhile, whichever of our enemies decide to attack us are released from all other responsibilities and are at leisure in deep peace for as long as they please,

231–32

and so can concentrate on preparing their § instruments of war and collecting forces to launch against us later when an opportunity arises. If they feel any tiredness as a result of one engagement, then too they se-

---

3. I.e., Pighius's *Free Choice*, to the first six books of which this work is a response.

Preface

cure themselves the refreshment of a truce as they choose, until with mind and strength renewed they are again equipped and prepared to attack us. In addition there is also the fact that because of our separation by large distances we are deprived of that facility from which no little relief could be expected, namely of communicating with one another and discussing plans as the situation and time require.

These things, as I said, I think over and consider, not without a sigh of distress at our lot. But to prevent my being broken by such reflection there comes to mind on the other side a comfort which is not inconsiderable. First, because I resolve that we are not beset and hard pressed by such difficulties as to be in want of human assistance which could help us apart from the sure counsel of God; as a result, we are the better awakened and learn to look to him alone. And secondly, because I recall, as I think, that there is this ancient precedent. For the sacred history reports that the Israelites laboured under an equal difficulty when, after their restoration from captivity, they were building their city (Neh. 4). For when the very greatness and bulk of the task, when the difficulties of the time were putting more than enough pressure on them, they were enduring from their enemies some further trouble and discomfort. And yet we see that this did not prevent them from continuing steadfastly and with unbroken resolve in the work, until the time when their enemies' wicked rage would finally be broken by their own steadfast persistence. For it was no ordinary example of bravery to collect the bricks and mortar with their swords girded on, to hold a sword in one hand and to work wielding a trowel with the other, and thus to pay attention to the building and at the same time be ready for battle.[4]

It is fitting that we too should be awakened by the memory of that history, so that among so many difficulties which tempt us to despair, we may nonetheless recover our resolve. Now that the Lord has by his wonderful power as well as goodness set us free from that frightful tyranny of the Antichrist of Rome,[5] he today assigns to us the responsibility for rebuilding his holy city of Jerusalem, that is, the church. It would be, to be sure, a hard and toilsome task, even if no additional hindrance came in from elsewhere. But the ministers and accomplices of Satan, whose purpose it is not to allow (as far as lies in them) the building of the church to arise, cause additional discomfort by troubling us with continual battles. And so, although the regular labour of repairing the church, to which we were appointed when this seemed good to the Lord, requires time that is free from distraction by other concerns, as soon as we begin to lift a single stone, they are summoning us to battle

Pressure makes us rely upon God

Precedent of Nehemiah

Reformers, like Nehemiah, are

1. rebuilding Jerusalem

2. under constant threat

---

4. Neh. 4:17.
5. For Calvin's view of the pope as Antichrist see *Inst.* 4.2.12 (LCC 21:1052).

with the bugle call. Since we are a tiny body of people and they form a huge army, how could we at the same time both resist them and have our hands busy in the work? Only if it entered our minds that God is now doing as he has long been wont to do, so as to make the power of his hand the more illustrious. So it should be sufficient for us that even if we now seem to have little success from our labour, we are nevertheless as sure of the outcome as if it were already present, since we fight under his banner and command. But if our business, because it smacks of haste somewhere, does not escape the criticism of some, as many today are too fastidious and peevish, then let us be upheld and strengthened by the assurance that we know that it has the approval of God our Judge, Christ our Lord and Guide, and his holy angels. As far as concerns me privately, since I know well enough whose servant I am, I am entirely at rest in the confidence that I have no doubt that any service of mine, of whatever kind, is pleasing to him. But if a human opinion is required, then yours alone will for me always be equal to that of all others, as it ought deservedly to be.⁶

<small>3. helped by God</small>

<small>4. doing God's work</small>

---

6. The 1552 and subsequent editions add "In the month of February 1543." It was on the 16th of that month that Calvin wrote to Melanchthon about this dedication (see n. 1).

On Book One [of Pighius]

Background

§ When we were at the meeting in Worms two years ago,¹ I heard that Albertus Pighius was now threatening me and announcing a fight, but that it was still far away. For he was boasting among his friends that he had written some book by which I should be completely finished; he was, however, not intending to publish it yet.² But when later on, after the Colloquy of Regensburg,³ that half a book—which was written chiefly against Luther and Philipp Melanchthon but secondarily against all of us together—had come out (it was later supplemented by a second part),⁴ I already felt to a large extent liberated from the fear that he might put out something directed particularly against me. For I reasoned as follows: because he had judged me an unworthy victim by myself for him to prove his strength, he had preferred to turn [his book] into an attack on the common cause itself, so that if he were victorious his triumph would be the more renowned, whereas if he were defeated the disgrace would be less. For he there proceeded with the theme which he had resolved to treat in opposition to me, and in many places he turned his pen specifically against me.

Meanwhile I hear that that magnificent book has taken wings⁵— though only among those who, without further investigation, would

233

Pighius (P) threatens to publish his *Controversies*,

and the book appears

---

1. I.e., the Colloquy at Worms between Roman Catholic and Protestant theologians, which took place during the winter of 1540–41 following the Colloquy of Hagenau (summer 1540). Pighius was present at Worms.

2. In a letter of 5 March 1540, Pighius announced his intention to publish his *Mystery of Our Salvation and Redemption* (H. Jedin, *Studien über die Schriftstellertätigkeit Albert Pigges* [Münster: Aschendorff, 1931], 33; see also Introduction §2). It was subsequently incorporated into Pighius's *Controversies* (see n. 4).

3. The Colloquy of Regensburg, April to June 1541, was the third and last of the series of colloquies seeking to restore religious unity in Germany. Pighius was present.

4. Pighius's *Controversies* (see Introduction §2). The first volume ("half a book") was printed at Ingolstadt in 1541, the second ("a second part") at Venice, by the heirs of L. Junta, later that year. A number of one-volume editions followed soon after, with a slightly longer title. The following year Pighius wrote a brief work, *Ratio componendorum dissidiorum et sarciendae in religione concordiae* (Cologne: M. Novesianus, 1542), as a sequel to the *Controversies*.

5. There had been at least five editions of the *Controversies* by this time.

take pleasure in the simple fact that it attacks the doctrine of Christ. I was not myself able to get hold of it so as to have a chance to examine it,[6] but to tell the truth I was not much put out about that, for I thought nothing more certain than that it would be published the next day. Then a whole year passed by before it saw the light of day, either in whole or in part.[7] So I was not in the least doubt that he had changed his plan. Unconcerned now about Pighius I had taken in hand another task,[8] when unexpectedly I am presented with his large volume entitled *Free Choice*.[9] Even though he does not name me right § at the beginning, he shows clearly enough when he gets down to a treatment of the subject itself that his purpose is none other than to overturn my discussion of it in my *Institutes*.[10]

He does indeed frankly declare that he is doing this with the specific intention of (as it were) driving his spear through my side into Luther and the rest of our party. But he issues the challenge to me alone in particular and joins in battle with me because he thinks that I have dealt with the full extent of this subject more carefully and arranged everything in a more orderly and methodical way than others have done. For myself I should not have dared to take up the defence of the common cause if he had attacked all of us together, for fear that I would appear to have wanted to put myself before others who are agreed to be far more competent, and so would seem to be motivated more by my own rashness and foolish self-confidence than by right judgment. Were it not for this fear, I should perhaps have made a response to that earlier book which I mentioned.[11] But now I am glad that, for whatever reason, I held myself back, when I see that Bucer, who was able to give it the better and more brilliant treatment that it deserved, has taken this task upon himself.[12] But in the present case I think that nobody will find fault with me for responding, when no others can be expected to do so and when Pighius would scoff at God so publicly if I were not to intervene in the defence of wholesome doctrine. Therefore no matter how many there may be today in the army of the Lord who are more learned and more practised than I, and who can curb the in-

---

234
P's *Free Choice* attacks Calvin (C) especially,

so he must respond

---

6. I.e., Calvin was unable to see it at the Worms colloquy.
7. The first volume was printed around March 1541, but was withheld until later that year.
8. On 11 September 1542, the Genevan council charged Calvin with working on a new constitution for the city (OC 21:302). This was completed by January 1543.
9. Pighius's *Free Choice* was originally intended to be the second part of his *First Principles*; see Introduction §2.
10. I.e., the second edition of Calvin's *Institutes* (1539); see Introduction §1.
11. I.e., Pighius's *Controversies*; see n. 4.
12. Bucer's *De vera ecclesiarum in doctrina, ceremoniis, et disciplina reconciliatione et compositione. . . : Responsio ad calumnias Alberti Pighii Campensis* (Strassburg, 1542) responded to both of Pighius's works mentioned in n. 4. Pighius replied in his *Apologia adversus Martini Buceri calumnias*, which was published incomplete after his death (Paris, 1543).

solence of this proud Goliath and have been ready to do so if the need arose—since he has passed them by and challenged me by name to a contest, I will advance to meet him, relying on the heavenly strength of my King and Commander and those spiritual weapons which he is wont to supply to his servants, so that my adversary may not be able to pride himself in a victory over even one of the servants of Christ. §

But why Pighius chose to start a dispute with me alone out of so many only he can see—if someone so blinded by madness can see anything at all! For he is mistaken if he supposes that I am in the slightest degree affected by that incidental remark that he devoted to me.[13] Perhaps when he gives me some priority over others, he is making this up for his own advantage, in case he appear to have joined battle with a mere man of the ranks. But whatever he thinks, it is of no importance to me, or very little. For the glory of the faithful is not in their learning or fine speech, but in a pure conscience,[14] and that not according to human judgment but in the sight of God. Moreover, I do not value his judgment so highly that I am on that account pleased with myself. "I am happy that I am praised," said that famous man in the old tragedy, "but only because it comes from someone praiseworthy."[15] Therefore even if I were vain, I should still have no reason to seek praise from these lips which are so foul and fetid and constantly utter nothing but abominable insults against Christ. In addition, during his flights of folly he is completely lacking in judgment and insight, whether because by being given over to a reprobate mind[16] as his impiety deserves he is an evident example of divine punishment, or because the unbearable pride which puffs him up is the most detrimental kind of blindness. Accordingly, just as on the stage "Pentheus sees ranks of Furies, two suns, and Thebes also appearing twice over,"[17] so he has such keen eyes that he thinks he sees what is not there. But at the same time he labours under the affliction that in broad daylight he is just as blind as he would be if struck by the most severe dizziness.

I admit that in other respects the man is clever and learned. I allow that he is an incisive debater and a skilful orator. I recognise that he is, in the popular sense, eloquent—that is, he is strong in that kind of eloquence which is able to captivate and allure those who have not much

---

13. I.e., the compliment mentioned at the beginning of the previous paragraph.
14. 2 Cor. 1:12.
15. From *Hector's Departure* by Gnaeus Naevius (c. 270–c. 201 B.C.), quoted in Cicero (106–43 B.C.) *Tusculan Disputations* 4.31.67 (Loeb 404–5).
16. Rom. 1:28.
17. Virgil (70–19 B.C.) *Aeneid* 4.469–70 (Loeb 426–27). Pentheus, king of Thebes, was driven mad for opposing the worship of Bacchus. The story is the theme of Euripides' tragedy *The Bacchae*. The Furies are mythological spirits of punishment sent to avenge wrongs done to others.

Margin notes:
235 Why did P pick on C?
P's folly
P is gifted,

education, of whom there are many today. But to what end are all those talents when a person's whole mind is disturbed and ruined by madness? Wherefore if he wants to have any place among the educated and enjoy the reputation for which he shows himself so excessively eager, he should first return to a sound mind. But for the curing of this insanity which afflicts him at present the remedies are two, namely these: let him cease to wage war with considered malice against the clear and certain truth of God; and let him strip off and cast away his stupid opinion of himself and the arrogant pride displayed in his threats which makes him entirely devoid of sense. But lest I should appear unduly impelled against him personally by the heat of controversy, I prefer now to bring my readers to his book, as it were to the very spot, so that there they may confirm whatever I say, or even more. §

Method to Be Followed

But before I come to this I must begin with a few words about the order of discussion which I have decided to follow. First, there is no reason for the reader to expect that I should follow in my reply the thread of Pighius's discourse. For if I wanted to examine individual items minutely, leaving nothing untouched, my book would grow to an immense size. For in addition to having an innate fluency of speech, he also constantly puts in a great deal of effort and study, so as both to conceal the matter in hand by his pompous speaking and to overwhelm his opponent by a long and dashing brandishing of words. Perhaps he even covets praise for this, since the best way to make an impression on the ignorant is to run wild with loud cries and a long accumulation of words. For myself I would happily yield the prize to him in this matter, even without a struggle, since I consider looseness with words no less of a defect than looseness of the bowels.[18] But for all his efforts to win his case by this kind of device, by as it were pouring out words, while he may be able to blind his readers by covering their eyes with fog, it will be too weak a defence with those of a sound mind. He will without doubt deceive the simpleminded and those who lack judgment, but anyone who has a spark of right understanding will have no time for those bombastic speeches in which one will find nothing substantial. And so I shall be content to make all devout and perceptive readers see that Pighius "turns brightness [into smoke],"[19] while I bring light out of the smoke"[20]—that is, he has distorted by misrepresentations and ma-

---

18. Calvin had a lifelong concern for and commitment to brevity; see LCC 20:lxx–lxxi.
19. "Into smoke" is required by the context and is part of the passage to which Calvin is alluding (see n. 20). It is supplied by all later editions.
20. Horace (65–8 b.c.) *Art of Poetry* 143 (Loeb 462–63).

licious criticism what had been well written by me, but I seek only to disperse Satan's smoke so that the pure and simple truth of God may shine forth. For I think that better than to weary myself in vain with a long and unnecessary piece of writing and at the same time be irksome to my readers.

To be honest, there is also another reason which compels me to be brief. I am limited by the pressure of time, since I have barely two months before the Frankfurt market,[21] at which I have decided, if possible, to publish this reply. And if only I had half of that time absolutely empty and free for writing! For this reason readers will forgive my haste if anywhere I should too lightly hurry over things which deserve longer reflection and more careful attention. But if anyone objects with that ancient and widely used saying that it is absurd to plead to be spared from blame which I could have avoided if I had wanted to,[22] I have my reply ready. First, I am compelled by force of duty to uphold and defend the truth of God when it is attacked on my own property;[23] secondly, I will write quickly in such a way that my labour will nevertheless be widely useful and not inappropriate § to the seriousness of the matter, even if it fails to match its worth at all points.

C hurrying to make Frankfurt book fair

237

But to help readers, when comparing what he and I have written, more easily and more surely to form their judgment and as it were mark the main points with their fingers, I will follow the order and arrangement which he himself kept to in his work. There will be only this much difference, that whereas he wanted to commend himself with a splendid array of words, I will as far as possible aim at conciseness and simplicity; and secondly, while he took up many pages with virulent insults against us which were born of an arrogance worthy of Thraso,[24] in this kind of thing too I will happily yield to him. For I reckon that if Pighius both is and is called an eloquent name-caller, this causes neither any loss to the glory of Christ nor any harm to the reputation of good people—provided that at the same time all understand that, moved partly by a raving passion for abuse and partly by a bad temper, or rather by madness, he is pulled this way and that indiscriminately.

C will follow P's order

---

21. I.e., the Frankfurt book fair, which in 1543 took place from the 1st to the 20th of March (A.-L. Herminjard, *Correspondance des réformateurs dans les pays de langue française* [Geneva: H. Georg & Paris: M. Levy, 1866–97], 8:341 n. 1). In a letter to Guillaume Farel of 15 December 1542, written at about the same time as this passage, Calvin states that he wants this work to appear at the next book fair (OC 11:474; Herminjard, *Correspondance*, 8:221). In his letter of 11 May 1543, Melanchthon states that he had received from the fair Calvin's letter of 16 February (see preface n. 2), but not the promised copies of the book (Herminjard, *Correspondance*, 8:341). This suggests that the book failed to make the fair, though other explanations are possible.

22. Aulus Gellius (c. 123–c. 165) *Attic Nights* 11.8 (Loeb 318–19).

23. I.e., it is *his* statement of the truth that has been attacked.

24. Thraso is a braggart soldier in the *Eunuchus* of Terence (c. 195–159 B.C.).

Pighius's Letter of Dedication

First let us consider in passing the points which [Pighius] treats in his letter to Sadoleto.[25] Although they are not germane to this discussion, they are nevertheless intended to put pressure on our position. Pighius is surprised and grieved at the torpor of his Germany, which is such that it could be won over to our teaching. After all, we [he says] are undertaking a task far more difficult than that once accomplished by the apostles: our teaching is utterly absurd, and we resurrect all the false teachings of the heretics of the past, which are inconsistent with the true rule of piety—indeed we go beyond the ravings of all of them. And yet we have nothing, even in appearance, which could deceive people by its (of course false) lustre. We excel neither in learning, nor in eloquence, nor in sanctity of life, which would necessarily arouse attention. And so as to enlarge on this the better, he shows how senseless and perverse our way of proceeding is.

I will reply briefly: Pighius is too stupid to recognise that [our success] is an evident and clear miracle of God's power at which he is compelled to marvel, whether he wishes to or not. For the less well prepared and well taught we are for so great and difficult a task, the more clearly God's power, which shakes the whole world through our weakness, shines forth. But if those complaints of Pighius were compared with the time of the apostles, you would say that a Porphyry,[26] or someone else from that century, was speaking. Therefore, lest I spend too long on this, I will reply by quoting Paul: we willingly admit that we have only very little of the many and great defences which would be needed to withstand such great might, so that the truth of our doctrine and faith must be based not on our own fine speaking or education, but on the spiritual power of God.[27] A cause must surely be strong and mighty if it is to continue not on the basis of human protection or of any outside support, but from its own goodness alone. § So let Pighius cease to be amazed about the origin of this new and unheard-of efficacy of our teaching, when the fact itself proclaims that at the beginning it was not Luther who spoke, but God thundered through his mouth, and that now it is not we who speak, but God is displaying his power from heaven.

On the other hand, however, he declares how different we are from

---

25. From here to col. 245 is Calvin's response to Pighius's letter of dedication to Cardinal Jacopo Sadoleto (1477–1547). Sadoleto had in 1539 written a *Letter to the Senate and People of Geneva*, urging them to return to the fold of the Roman Catholic Church; Calvin responded in his *Reply to Sadoleto* of the same year.
26. Porphyry (c. 233–c. 305) was a Neoplatonist philosopher who wrote a treatise *Against the Christians* in fifteen books.
27. 1 Cor. 2:3–5.

the apostles. Certainly if it is a matter of personalities, no words are enough to express the extent by which they surpass us. But in those matters of doctrine in which Pighius makes us differ, I say that we have the greatest likeness. They, he says, described what they had seen with their eyes and drunk with their ears,[28] which had been foretold or sketched in figures. But what of us? Have we hammered out a new gospel, to demand that it should be believed, having said good-bye to that which the apostles proclaimed? We have many disputes on a variety of matters with the realm of the Roman Antichrist, but almost all of them derive from the fact that we want a hearing to be given to Christ, the prophets, and the apostles, while our adversaries, not daring openly to impose silence upon them, require them to take second place to their own imaginings. There was, he says, a wonderful unanimity among the apostles over doctrine. As if the Lord has not given this same unanimity also to those who today seek to restore the teaching of the gospel to its original place. There was present then, he says, the immediate power of divine activity, there was that Spirit of fire who showed himself in their behaviour, their faces, and their eyes. But in fact these things, and whatever else Pighius relates to commend or confirm the teaching of the apostles, are our weapons. For all that we teach comes back to this main point, that the gospel, which he declares to have been confirmed by so many eminent evidences, should be heard by the world. For our complaint that it has been buried and as it were wiped out from human memory is quite justified.

    We have sought nothing else these twenty-five years[29] but that the whole conflict should be ended in such a way that the victory should not fall to men, but should remain, as is fitting, with that teaching which was proclaimed by Christ and the apostles. Now too we are ready, if we are found guilty of teaching something contrary to [their teaching], not only to withdraw it but to attack it with total commitment. Therefore when miracles other than those by which the dignity of the gospel was ratified of old are demanded of us, no others need be produced but those which were performed through the apostles. For they happened once, but served to confirm the gospel for ever. And what a wide field would be open for me here to speak both of the ingratitude and ill will and also of the shamelessness of those who not only demand that the gospel of Christ be established afresh by new miraculous signs, just as if it were new and of recent origin, but turn those very miracles which ought to contribute to its glory into a cause for insults and mockery! But since I have devoted another work

Marginal notes: 1. personalities; 2. doctrine; 3. unanimity; 4. power of the Spirit; Reformers happy to be tested by apostles' teaching; New miracles not needed

---

28. Cf. Virgil *Aeneid* 4.359 (Loeb 420–21).
29. I.e., roughly the time since Luther's *Ninety-five Theses* (31 Oct./1 Nov. 1517).

239

P accuses Reformers of trickery

but their behaviour is superior to that of Romanists

Reformers' task harder than apostles':

1. Reformers face papacy,

to this matter,[30] for the moment I will desist.

But Pighius continues § his efforts to remove this defence of ours by saying that since all our teaching is contrived to subvert every whit of piety and to remove all thought of religion from people's minds, we practise acts of pure trickery, guile and deceit, a wicked abuse of Scripture, exceptional audacity and shamelessness, lies, insults, the plotting of villains, insurrections, and a looseness of living that is worse than the heathen. What will he forbear to say? The former charge will be dealt with later in its proper place.[31] As far as our practice is concerned, I appeal to the facts themselves to refute Pighius's lies. On the subject of our acrimony I will say only this: it has been poured out only upon those to whom the word of God itself is a deadly odour of death,[32] and further it cannot be regarded as excessive if one bears in mind the shameful state of affairs which forced it out of us. Besides, it is exceedingly unfair for a teaching to be evaluated on the basis of the behaviour of those who misuse it. However, if it should be agreed that the decision about us and our opponents be based on our behaviour, we by no means reject this ruling. For whatever we may be, we have nevertheless better cause than we could have wished for to glory in the fact that our behaviour is different from that of all the Romanists who today uphold the rule of Antichrist. Accordingly, I have no fear, if anyone looks carefully at our behaviour and theirs and compares them with equal care, that one will fail to see clearly that we for our part fear God, while they actually despise both him and his law.

What [Pighius] says about our struggling with a more difficult task than did the apostles of old would, if taken in a different sense, not be at all far from the truth. For anyone who considers with insight the conditions of the time when Luther came to prominence will see that he shared almost all other difficulties in common with the apostles, but that in one respect his situation was worse and harder than theirs. In their time there was no kingdom or dominion in the world for them to declare war upon, whereas [Luther] could in no way arise from the depths except by the overthrow and destruction of that empire[33] which not only was the most powerful of all empires, but also held all the others as it were in subjection to itself. This is a difficulty which we also now face. It is well known how powerful the pope is in the power of

---

30. Calvin answers the Roman Catholic demand for miracles in the *Prefatory Address to King Francis* at the beginning of his *Institutes* (LCC 20:16–18). Erasmus made a similar demand for miracles in his *Diatribe concerning Free Choice* (LCC 17:45–46), to which Luther responded in his *Bondage of the Will* (LCC 17:144–47).

31. E.g., in *BLW* 2.257–58 (*Bondage and Liberation of the Will*, book 2, cols. 257–58), where the charge that Reformed teaching subverts piety is answered.

32. 2 Cor. 2:16.

33. I.e., the papacy.

arms and in aid from treaties and in wealth and in the very reverence paid to his title, and then how much security and strength he has in this vast flotsam of his which is scattered all over the world—I mean the cardinals, bishops, and priests. But since they see that their only hope of safety lies in bringing down our teaching, they all turn the whole of their wealth and strength to attacking it, just as if they were fighting for their dearest possessions, indeed for their own lives.

I would say that our troubles exceeded those of the apostles also because of the toil of having to struggle with a deceptive ghost of a church and a concealed hostility to religion which hides itself under the name of God itself, were it not for the fact that several of the prophets § and the apostles had a similar ordeal on the same battleground. But to reply to Pighius's charge once and for all—it is indeed a difficult and tiresome task quickly to overthrow and do utterly away with so many monsters of irreligion, so great a labyrinth[34] of godless teaching, so many varieties of superstition. They have through several centuries gained hold of everyone's mind, they have pushed down such deep roots, and they exhibit such an attractive complexion. It is especially difficult when all the power in the world opposes us and rises up with sword, fire, and every kind of cruelty to defend them. [Our struggle] is a bold enterprise, Pighius says, and I do not deny it—I should even admit that it was rash if it were the work of men and not of God himself. But when we hear Paul discoursing about that invincible power which is given to the ministers of the gospel to destroy all inventions, to undo plans, and finally to bring down every eminence which raises itself against the knowledge of Christ (2 Cor. 10),[35] we gather our spirits to stand unflinchingly against this whole arsenal of Satan by which popery is kept in being.

Furthermore, we always have ready a sponge to remove that paint with which Pighius daubs his harlot, in the fact that we by no means undermine the whole of history together with all the opinions of the saints (as he falsely says), but rather seek only the restoration to their former condition of those things which have been spoiled and lost by the injurious effects of history. He protests; we argue that this is how things are. He offers no proof for the slander which he utters against us; our books are packed with solid clear evidence about this matter. The false charges which he heaps upon us appear convincing—according to him we say that the church has been abandoned by Christ her

2. false church,

240

3. and ferocious persecution

Reformers seek to restore primitive purity

---

34. The image of the labyrinth (the first one being the maze that was built for King Minos of Crete to contain the Minotaur, which was killed by Theseus) is a favourite of Calvin's. For an imaginative account of its significance as a key to Calvin's personality, see W. J. Bouwsma, *John Calvin: A Sixteenth-Century Portrait* (New York & Oxford: Oxford University Press, 1988), esp. pp. 45–48, chs. 4–6. Cf. Erasmus *Adages* 2.10.51 (CWE 34:147–48).

35. 2 Cor. 10:4–5.

husband for fourteen hundred years, and so we make Christ a liar.³⁶ But they are clouds which vanish with a single puff of a true reply. For we say that Christ has faithfully been with his church and always will be, as he promised.³⁷ We say that the church has been preserved by his power, lest she perish, and governed by his Spirit, lest she depart from the truth. But at the same time we say that that event had to happen which is foretold in a clear prophecy of Paul about a frightful rebellion, which he declares will happen not in some distant corner of the earth, but throughout the whole world. He is assuredly speaking about the future condition of the church, that is, the one which followed later. He says that already then Antichrist was setting in motion the mystery of sin, but what he adds immediately afterwards is much more serious, namely that the time will come when he goes about openly and acts tyrannically against the church, and that not as an enemy from outside but after seizing the sanctuary of God (2 Thess. 2).³⁸ When [Paul] speaks of these things, he is saying that a rebellion will come. As we see that they have happened as predicted, we recognise that the Spirit of Christ is true.

At the same time, however, we confess that Christ's own faithfulness to his promise is established, since in so great a disaster he has wonderfully preserved his own, so that they should get away safely from the depths of death, because he did not allow the church to perish in so great a shipwreck, § and when it seemed to have lost all hope he delivered it, as it were, from death itself.³⁹ For it is from that seed that this harvest which we see today has been thrust forth. Now let Pighius, taking our part but speaking from the thoughts of his own mind, go and accuse Christ of lying or faithlessness. For the fact is that when he punished his church for its contempt for his gospel by an almost total blinding of the world, he nevertheless never robbed it of the light of his truth and his life. But indeed I recognise that his faithfulness has thereby been rendered the more glorious, in that through so many obstacles and contrary to the expectation of all it made a way for itself, so as to remain unshaken.

But lest in maintaining the right, or rather the wrong [of his cause], [Pighius] might seem excessively inflexible, he finally admits that abuses have crept into the church, which all the devout would wish to see put right. But [he says] the way to put them right is very different

---

36. Cardinal Sadoleto used this argument in his *Letter to the Senate and People of Geneva*, and Calvin responded to it in his *Reply to Sadoleto* (SW 1:14–21, 37–39).
37. Matt. 28:20.
38. 2 Thess. 2:3–12; cf. preface n. 5.
39. For Calvin's view of the survival of the church in the darkest times see the *Prefatory Address* to the *Institutes* (LCC 20:24–27).

from that which we have tried. For this is the responsibility of the pastors, from whom, he complains, we have taken away the means to do it. Then he says that the vices are not of such a kind as to justify our departure from the church. For as our pretext for having thrown the whole world into confusion and for having deserted the unity of the church we cite the abuses which were dominant in it and the corrupt behaviour of the priests.

To begin with this last point: I should like to know from whose lips he heard this excuse. It is possible that in books written by our company he read that initially Luther criticised only certain very great abuses and the infamous behaviour of the priests, always going further than before because of the wickedness of his opponents. But what resemblance is there between this and Pighius's calumny? Somewhere else Luther himself also writes thus about himself: "Whether I will or not, my opponents compel me to become wiser from day to day."[40] What he says is very true, for they were like a whetstone to sharpen his intellect. While still submerged in that deep darkness which swallowed up almost the whole world, he saw a single ray of light shining as it were from a narrow crack, and he tried to approach it. Just here the enemies of the light, wanting to hinder and violently resist the devout study of this man, opened up by their uproar first a wider window and finally all the doors. We do not say this in order to gain an excuse for our defection from the pope, but to make it clear what forbearance our opponents would have shown if Luther had at a single stroke cut back all the corruption of popery to the quick, when they were unable to bear gentle, modest criticism and that of vices which were blatant. Nor indeed was it then Luther's intention to defect from the tyranny of the Antichrist, but solely to heal those diseases whose cure seemed as easy as it was necessary. But he proved to be mistaken in this view. For popery was swarming with such a purulent mass of every kind of foul practice that once a hand began to be laid on it, since it could not bear any cure, it split down the middle.

Pighius should therefore know that we are not § so scrupulous as to have thought that the unity of the faith should be split for the sake of moral deficiencies, even the most serious.[41] We know that in correcting or rebuking vices moderation is needed to prevent the bond of peace from being broken. But on the other hand we know that there must be limits to patience, lest it encourage sin. For this reason we were bound at the beginning not to approve or conceal by silence or pretence this most infamous way of life of the popish clergy, which was, as all every-

Reform from within was impossible

Papacy was beyond reform

242

Silence was unjustifiable

---

40. Martin Luther *The Babylonian Captivity of the Church* (LW 36:11).
41. See *Inst.* 4.1.13–14, 16–17 (LCC 21:1026–29, 1031–32).

where could see, stained by every kind of dishonourable behaviour. Nor can we even now in duty do so, especially when [this issue] is of importance for the instruction of the people. For since the cause derives from the priests themselves like a common pollution, we could not remove the vices in the body of the population in general without also censuring the priests.

<small>Split was over doctrine, not abuses</small>

But to say that this was the cause of the split is a very wicked lie, when we have always clearly stated that we should be satisfied with agreement on pure, sound doctrine as a bond to hold us together. When it is a question of reviving the church, we do indeed add discipline to doctrine. But it is one thing to be zealous to get the church into good order, it is another to separate from the church. Pighius's reproach against us would be justified if we had because of disapproval of corrupt behaviour abandoned the fellowship of the church and transferred our allegiance to another party. But when it is obvious that the source of the split was the inability of the Antichrist of Rome to tolerate just and holy criticisms of his ungodly teaching, why is the charge of secession still hurled at us, with the addition (please God!) of the facile accusation that mere scrupulosity was the reason why the somewhat disorderly behaviour of the clergy displeased us?

<small>Charge of schism is slander</small>

Pighius does just the same as the boys in their schools, who invent their topics for public speaking. For he takes the following two ideas as his starting points: that we were the instigators of our departure from the church, and that it was due solely to our being offended by some corruptness of life among the priests. We in fact deny that the separation was begun by us and, lest we seem to be holding something back, we will cite the facts themselves as they happened. By themselves they provide us with a clear proof that the responsibility for the division of the church lies with the Antichrist of Rome. By violent and tyrannical means, without any legal trial and contrary not only to ecclesiastical custom but to any humane principles, he drove out all those who either dared to speak for the truth or cherished it. And will the Romanists still hold us guilty of secession when they themselves by their savage and bloodthirsty decrees first excluded us from any fellowship whatever with them? But [he says] it had been better for us to procure peace by forbearance and silence, and so to remain in the unity of faith, than by overviolent cures to kindle a ruinous fire throughout the body.

<small>Reformers were violently expelled</small>

243

<small>Truth too high a price for peace</small>

What is this peace, and what is this unity of faith § which you preach to me, where the truth of God, which ought to be the sole bond of peace, has no place? The Holy Spirit declares that the unity of the church is maintained by agreement in sound and true doctrine,[42] and

---

42. Eph. 4:3–6.

On Book One

Pighius does not dare to contest this in what he says, even if in his mind he thinks otherwise.

Let us then see with what chains or knots popery is fastened together.[43] First, every kind of idolatry predominates there, and not without the open denial of God. Whatever little residue of the worship of God survives stinks of pure superstition, being in part polluted with fabricated rituals and in part corrupted by depraved thinking. True doctrine is either utterly subverted or contaminated. Christ is half-buried, so that he retains only his name, without the glory of his power, and he is in fact more like a ghost than his true self. For his power is hidden in deep darkness, his office is consigned to oblivion, grace is almost brought to nothing. The administration of the sacraments is first maimed and torn to pieces; on top of this it is disfigured by many alien inventions, and finally it is enveloped in the products of ungodly imaginations.

Evils of papacy

What then does Pighius tell us to do? Not to disturb the peace. But on what terms and conditions? Our connivance at all these [evils] of course. But it is an illicit peace which is bought at such a price. He, however, maintains that he and the Antichrist's other dogs, who hunt after priestly offices with barking and fawning, are making no innovations in the faith and are indeed seeking with all their hearts to put right the abuses, but mindful of their station and office they do not arrogate to themselves what is another's responsibility to decide. What? As if it were not the duty of every one of us to shrink from open violations of doctrine and practices of worship which bring the most grievous insults on the most holy name of God. You should have kept silence, says Pighius. It would have been a treacherous and abominable silence by which God's glory, Christ, and the gospel were betrayed. Is it possible? So God shall be held up as a laughingstock before our eyes, all good religion shall be torn apart, wretched souls redeemed by the blood of Christ shall perish,[44] and it shall be forbidden to speak? A faithful dog barks at the first sound of a thief and risks his own life to protect his master's life and his family—shall the church be plundered by the thieving of the ungodly, shall God's majesty be stamped under foot, shall Christ be robbed of his own kingdom, while we watch and say nothing?

Silence would betray Christ

A final point. On behalf of the Antichrist, Pighius sets off enormous tumults when he sees danger threatening his kingdom—shall we do nothing amid the ruin of the kingdom of Christ? Yet we had no right to secure peace even in this way, since we should have had, just by par-

Christ's kingdom more important than pope's

---

43. For Calvin's assessment of the Roman Catholic Church, see *Institutes* 4.2 (LCC 21:1041–53), part of which is from 1539.

44. See 1 Cor. 8:11. Unlike some later Calvinists, Calvin does not appear to limit Christ's redemption to those who will eventually be saved.

ticipating and so by a kind of silent vote, to give approval to the majority of those crimes. Shall the shaking off of this yoke of ungodliness be a breach of the bond of faith, secession from the church, a disturbing of the common peace and concord? Such words were indeed once heard by a holy prophet from an evil king. But how did he defend himself? It is not I, he said, who disturbs Israel; it is you and the house of your father who have abandoned God's § commandments and followed the Baals (1 Kings 18).[45] Our defence is just the same: we are not to blame for the breaking out of whatever disturbances and commotions there are today, nor do we now foster them; the whole responsibility lies with those who have persisted in confounding heaven and earth and sea rather than give ground to the kingdom of Christ. But what is written must be fulfilled, that that wicked one shall remain until the Lord slays him by the breath of his mouth and destroys him by the brightness of his coming.[46]

But Pighius says that by our overhasty action we took away the one and only means which there was for remedies to be applied. For the authority of pastors, to whom this task belongs, has been weakened by us. Who cannot see that this disciple of Lucian[47] is openly having a pleasant game while the church is now suffering such a lamentable disaster? Nothing else, he suggests, is holding back the Roman pontiff and his whole company from correcting faults but the fact that they have been deprived by us of the ability to do so. But what, I demand, were they going to do if we had kept quiet, when now, with so much pressure laid upon them, they show no more concern and activity than they would if they were quite untouched by any responsibility for the church at all? The whole world cries out that the final ruin of the church is imminent if a remedy is not soon applied. The situation itself, which is a very piercing weapon, makes them uneasy and so presses in on them that there is no place left to take refuge. We attack vigorously, as we should, their sluggishness or rather their enormous cruelty, because they do not help the church when it is in danger. When they are not aroused by all these incitements, it is a fine thing to expect, as Pighius recommends, that they would have hastened at the first opportunity to correct the abuses if we had done nothing.

But, he says, they would do something now if they were not prevented by us. Why then, after being asked so many times, have they not given some slight proof of this intent? These tumultuous times, we shall be told, are the least suitable in which to make a change. The truth is

---

45. 1 Kings 18:17–18.
46. 2 Thess. 2:8.
47. Lucian of Samosata was a satirist of the second century A.D. Luther made the same charge against Erasmus in his *Bondage of the Will* (LCC 17:109, 113, 274).

that they are with good reason afraid that, once someone touches this building, which, having already a weak foundation, suffers as well and is almost collapsing from the weight of its decayed and rotten materials, and is now finally tottering and shaken, it will fall headlong and in its collapse overwhelm the architects themselves. It is assuredly this, it is this alone which all those wolves care about: how they may protect their tyranny for the future, by what stratagems they may prop it up, so that no further threat to their desires can arise. What becomes of the church hereafter is of no concern to them; they think it of no importance if it should die a hundred deaths. If Pighius should claim that I am inventing some of this, I shall not name just a few witnesses to support my charge, but I will make the consciences of all the devout my evidence.[48]

Rome fears reform

It is worthwhile too to hear Pighius's complaint that we have severely disrupted the public discipline of the church. As if indeed there had been any discipline in the past, and not § rather chaos horrible to behold and everything in foul, distorted confusion! For what is the relevance of his boasting to us of the ancient canons by which the church had been ordered and shaped, when they were put to no greater use than if they had never been written?[49] So it is just as if, after the suppression of their tyranny, some courtier of Dionysius[50] or Phalaris[51] had come forward and bemoaned the disruption of the state, the overthrow of the laws, the degradation of the courts. Who would endure this defender of liberty and law? But if Pighius does not accept this comparison, I should like him to show me how much better and more orderly the situation has been under the Roman Antichrist than it was under the tyrants of old.

Reformers don't undermine discipline
245

It seemed right to make this short response to Pighius's preface quickly, lest readers should be prejudiced with regard to the matter itself through being preoccupied with his charges, and in this I am sure that I have been successful. For it is not part of my present purpose to refute the insults with which he censures Luther's character and way of life, since they are not of much importance for the matter in hand, nor is Luther in need of defence by me, nor finally is Pighius behaving in any way differently from a ravenous starving dog that takes revenge by barking when he finds nothing to bite! For the most severe of his accu-

Luther's character

---

48. Where the first edition has "evidence," later editions have "judges," involving a change of one letter in the Latin.

49. See *Institutes* 4.5 (LCC 21:1084–1102), mostly from 1543.

50. Dionysius I (c. 430–367 B.C.), founder of the dynasty which ruled Syracuse in Sicily in the late fifth and the fourth century B.C. See Erasmus *Adages* 1.1.83; 1.6.70; 1.7.33 (CWE 31:125–26; 32:49, 87).

51. Phalaris, tyrant of Acragas in Sicily (c. 570–554 B.C.), who had his victims roasted alive in a hollow brazen bull. See Erasmus *Adages* 1.10.86 (CWE 32:273–74).

sations against Luther amounts to no more than his being a hellish monster because he has often been troubled by grave struggles of the conscience equal to the pains and torments of hell.⁵²

But really, if this idiot could imagine even in a dream what this means, what it implies, he would either be struck dumb or he would rather be changed into an admirer and a praiser of Luther. For it is the common lot of the devout to endure from time to time awful tortures to the conscience, so that taught by these they may become more accustomed to true humility and fear of God. Therefore as each is endowed with particular excellence of character in excess of others, so he is sometimes afflicted in strange and unfamiliar ways, so that he can say that he has been not only surrounded and besieged by the pains of death but devoured by hell itself. So it is necessary for the most excellent of the saints to be as it were choice workshops of God for him marvellously to carry out his judgments beyond all fleshly feeling. Lest I be delayed by citing numerous examples, such was the wrestling of Jacob, in which that celebrated wrestler had no human opponent, but encountered God himself.⁵³ Now if you want to understand how much he toiled in that arena, consider first the strength of God, and then draw your conclusion also from the fact that though victorious he nevertheless was lame to the end of his life. Let these words be for the devout. For what can you do with Pighius and those irreligious people who have no conscience or feeling of devotion, and who, if anything is said about the judgments of God, receive it as if they were hearing Homer's stories about the banquets of the gods?⁵⁴ §

Pighius's Book One

P's plagiarism

Since the knowledge of God and the knowledge of man are bound together and connected by a reciprocal relationship, it is with good reason that Pighius begins his argument about free choice at that point. Someone will say that I praise this arrangement because it is my own.⁵⁵ But I will reply that I used it because it seemed the best and the most suited to instruction, and for that reason it is a pleasure that my oppo-

---

52. For Luther's spiritual struggles see A. E. McGrath, *Luther's Theology of the Cross* (Oxford: Basil Blackwell, 1985), 169–75.

53. Gen. 32:24–32. For Calvin's interpretation of this passage see D. C. Steinmetz, "Calvin as an Interpreter of Genesis," in *Calvinus sincerioris religionis vindex*, ed. W. H. Neuser (Kirksville, Mo.: Sixteenth Century Journal, forthcoming).

54. Homer (ninth or eighth century B.C.) was the author of the *Iliad* and the *Odyssey*, the two greatest epic poems of ancient Greece.

55. Book 1, chapter 1, of Pighius's *Free Choice* is on the mutual correlation of the knowledge of God and of ourselves, and has some remarkable parallels with the opening of chapter 1 of Calvin's 1539 *Institutes*. Ambrosius Catharinus, a Catholic contemporary, also accused Pighius of plagiarising his works (Jedin, *Studien*, 2).

nent follows the plan which I judged to be the best. However, I am amazed at the boldness with which, without making any mention of me, he has dared, with such presumption, to lift from my book matter to insert into his own. For I do not see by what right he does it, unless perchance he pleads in excuse that this has long been his regular custom. For in that big book which he put out against our confession[56] he often stuffs in whole pages from my *Institutes* where he thinks fit, and turns them to his own advantage just as if he had not lifted them from elsewhere. I should like to know now by what right or pretext he appropriates what is mine as his own. If there were some close bond between us, I would not find it difficult to overlook this boldness in friendship. But as things are, there is no place for such a pardon. Or is it because I am his enemy that he thinks that he has the right of plunder over all my goods? But this kind of looting is indefensible according to both justice and custom. So only one defence is left, which is to say that what I had said could just as easily come into the mind of any educated person as it had earlier come into mine. But I beg my readers, if they have sufficient time, to compare the first chapter of Pighius's book with the first chapter of my *Institutes*.[57] I will say only that they will not be able to observe the man's utterly depraved and shameless behaviour without jeering and protesting. But if they have the appetite to proceed further, let them run through his treatment of justification in that other work and align it with the sixth chapter of my *Institutes*.[58] It will be remarkable if they can contain their anger. For he does not steal with a little secrecy or selectively, nor does he take pains to conceal his thefts by craftiness, so that what he has gathered from my writings should seem to have originated with him. He rehearses my material word for word so openly that he appears through laziness to have stitched in the very pages to save himself the labour of copying them out. If he named the true author, I would say that he was borrowing them; but as things are, what can he plead to save himself from being publicly called a plagiarist? Anyone who reads his work will wonder how the man could be so senseless as not to fear immediate detection.

Nevertheless, as I think over the whole affair carefully, I have something to say in the man's defence: that he did it out of confidence rather than out of carelessness. For he thought it sufficient if only he could

---

56. I.e., Pighius's *Controversies* (see n. 4), which specifically attacked the Augsburg Confession.
57. I.e., compare book 1, chapter 1, of Pighius's *Free Choice* with the first chapter of the 1539 *Institutes* (see n. 55).
58. I.e., compare the second controversy in Pighius's *Controversies* (see n. 4) with the sixth chapter of the 1539 *Institutes*, the contents of which are to be found in book 3, chapters 11–18, of the definitive edition (LCC 20:725–833). Specific instances of appropriation are given by Jedin, *Studien*, 116.

P is writing only for the prejudiced **247**

please those who avoid reading our writings with no less devotion than the readiness § with which they praise and admire everything which attacks us in any way at all. Let him then indeed enjoy his well-known bragging in the dark. But in the light and in the sight of good people, I hope, my *Institutes* will appear as a witness and an avenger of his unlimited shamelessness. I was not intending to mention this matter, had not his unworthiness forced me to do so. But since he so often pours scorn on us from the high eminence of his boasting, as though we are unlearned, of no intelligence and no judgment, it has been worth the trouble to make it plain that a man who so cruelly savaged those whose guidance had in fact given him some help is neither honourable nor grateful.

Summary of P's book 1

It is not the task of this work to examine what he subsequently inserts of his own, thus distorting or misrepresenting what was well said. What [his argument] adds up to is that, in treating the knowledge of God and of ourselves and comparing them with each other, it is only when we know that our wills are endowed with free choice, and that it is put within our power whether or not to obey the commandments, to refrain from evil and to do good, that we can understand that the judgment of God is just.[59] When [Pighius] has decided this, he quickly moves on to an exposition of our opinion: first in fact from the words of Luther[60] (which he deems insufficiently accommodated to the popular mind), and then from mine,[61] which he also keeps in view throughout the work, so that my head bears the brunt of the attacks on our whole "sect," as he calls us. That brings to an end the first book.

Luther's attitude toward reason

Now since the principal device which he uses to try to overturn our teaching is the charge that it is in the highest degree contrary to common sense, he begins by saying that it is not without reason that Luther schools his disciples, as a first principle, with a requirement that they learn to disown fleshly reason and wisdom.[62] For most of [Luther's] doctrines are so absurd (and especially that one with which we are dealing, concerning the bondage of human choice) that if you want to persuade anyone of them, you have first to pluck out the "eyes" of his mind and take away all his rational sense. With what mean reproaches [Pighius] rails at that proposition [to disown fleshly reason], which among those who bear the name of Christian ought no more to have

---

59. The margin contains a reference to Pighius: "Folio 5, page 1."
60. In book 1, chapter 2 (5b–8b), Pighius quotes from and expounds "Article 36" in Luther's *Defence of All the Articles of Martin Luther Condemned by the Latest Bull of Leo X* (WA 7:142–49). Luther also produced a briefer German version, which has been translated into English (LW 32:92–94). See Introduction §7.
61. In book 1, chapter 3 (9a–15a), Pighius quotes from and expounds the second chapter of Calvin's 1539 *Institutes*.
62. For Luther's attitude toward reason see B. A. Gerrish, *Grace and Reason: A Study in the Theology of Luther* (Oxford: Oxford University Press, 1962).

admitted of debate than that God is one! What laughable criticisms he levels at it! It is in conflict, he says, with the apostle who bears witness that faith comes from hearing the preaching.[63] Again, if it is true, it will follow that infants and idiots are more suited to learn faith than are all others. As if indeed Paul did not immediately afterwards cut this knot of Pighius's by adding that faith depends on the secret revelation of God![64] Or as though he who deprives man of fleshly reason, that is, the vain belief in his own wisdom, makes him a woodenhead! But so that [Pighius] may understand that his struggle is not with us but with Paul himself, let him hear his words, if he has ears: The natural man, he says, does not receive those things which belong to the Spirit of God. They are foolishness to him and he cannot know them because they are discerned spiritually.[65] Let [Paul] also rehearse to us himself the reason why this is so. Surely because God has made foolish the wisdom of this world, § so that through the foolishness of preaching he may save those who believe.[66] To what end? Let him once more reply himself: To confound the glorying of the wise.[67] What, finally, does he deduce from this? Let no one deceive himself. If anyone thinks that he is wise, let him become foolish in this world so that he may be made wise, seeing that the wisdom of this world is foolishness with God.[68]

See how Paul declares that the first foundation of spiritual wisdom is to know that worldly wisdom is reduced to nothing. Now let Pighius spew out against [Paul] his bilious charge that he wants to pluck out the eyes of people's minds, to make them like brute beasts, to treat them worse than idiots! But that none of those who are wise in their own eyes are persuaded of [Paul's declaration] is not surprising, since the only way by which they could reach this position is closed to them as long as they do not condemn the whole of that foolishness in which they take pleasure, namely the appearance of wisdom. For there is no kind of spell more dangerous in its ability to bewitch than confidence in one's own wisdom. To put it briefly, whatever wisdom a person has of himself is pure folly with regard to God; and when self-confidence is added it becomes madness. If nothing else were, Pighius is ample proof of that fact when he says that he will believe no apostles, no Scriptures, nor all the angels, if they teach that very thing in which he supposes Luther to be in error.[69]

---

63. Pighius (5b) cites Rom. 10:17. Calvin is thinking also of 1 Cor. 2:1–5, as is shown by the following sentences.
64. 1 Cor. 2:6–16.
65. 1 Cor. 2:14.
66. 1 Cor. 1:20–21.
67. 1 Cor. 1:19, 27–29.
68. 1 Cor. 3:18–19.
69. The margin contains a reference to Pighius: "Folio 6, page 1."

Luther's teaching, according to P:

1. No free choice

2. All happens by absolute necessity

Good works rewarded by God's generosity

249

When the discussion has reached Luther's actual opinion, [Pighius] reduces everything in it which he desires to condemn to two main charges: namely that he taught that since the fall of the first man free choice has been a reality in name only, and that we can of ourselves do nothing but sin; and that, not content with that, he added afterwards that [free choice] is something imaginary, a name without substance, and then that nothing happens by chance, but everything befalls us by absolute necessity.[70] Under the first heading, many things annoy him. First that it would follow from this that man cannot prepare himself by his natural powers to receive the grace of God. Next that our nature is held to be corrupt, indeed it is as it were regarded as valueless. In addition, the keeping of the law is impossible for us, yet we nonetheless do wrong by not keeping that which exceeds our ability. Fourth, that with this is associated our (that is, the Catholic church's)[71] doctrine of original sin, which he calls monstrous. Fifth, [that according to Luther] the righteous sin even in their good works, and while such good works are pardonable in the mercy of God, of themselves they are mortal sins.

I should like to remind my readers that Pighius is constantly singing the same old song. And so because all the other matters will reappear in their proper place, I will speak here only about the last point. When Luther spoke in this way about good works, he was not seeking to deprive them of their praise and their reward before God. Nor did he ever say that God does not accept them or that he will not reward them; but he wanted to show only what they are worth if they are considered by themselves apart from God's fatherly generosity.[72] It is certain that whatever good works can be cited do not please God § by virtue of their own worth but by his gracious favour, because he wills to value them so much, even though they do not deserve it.[73] But, you will say, Luther exaggerates. I can grant this, but only when I say that he had a good reason which drove him to such exaggeration; that is, he saw that the world was so deprived of sense by a false and perilous confidence in works, a kind of deadly drowsiness, that it needed not a voice and words to awaken it but a trumpet call, a peal of thunder and thunderbolts. Yet

---

70. Pighius (6a–b, 8a) makes these charges against Luther. The first charge is a virtual repetition of the thirty-sixth of the Lutheran articles condemned in the papal bull *Exsurge Domine* (thus the heading of "Article 36" in Luther's *Defence* [WA 7:142]). What he "added afterwards" is Luther's provocative heightening of his claims in the course of the article (WA 7:146). See Introduction §7.

71. Calvin is claiming that *his* teaching is that of the Catholic church. He does not often use the term "catholic," but where he does (e.g., *Inst.* 4.1.2 [LCC 21:1014]) it is with approval; see also *BLW* 2.274 (at n. 146). Calvin chose his ground carefully. Pighius's doctrine of original sin was later deemed by the Council of Trent not to be Catholic; see Introduction §2.

72. P. Althaus, *The Theology of Martin Luther* (Philadelphia: Fortress, 1966), 234–42.

73. This is Calvin's doctrine of "double justification," expounded in *Inst.* 3.17.1–10 (LCC 20:802–14).

there is nothing in those words of his which is not straightforwardly and unambiguously true.[74] For since the worth of good works depends not on the act itself but on perfect love for God, a work will not be righteous and pure unless it proceeds from a perfect love for God. Now I would like you to find for me that much-talked-of human perfection to make me concede that there are some works which are good in themselves.

But, you object, that amounts to disparagement of the Holy Spirit, through whom good works are done. Not at all, if you distinguish clearly and intelligently between what is of human origin in a good work and what is of the Spirit. For however much the saints dedicate themselves sincerely and unfeignedly to obedience to God, it is yet far from being the case that there is present that readiness to render obedience which is demanded by the well-known summary of the law, which requires that we should love God with all our heart, all our soul, and all our strength, and that after God we love our neighbour.[75] Indeed whoever does not know that this is the rule by which the testing of works is to be carried out is incapable of any judgment. Now let Pighius listen. I mean that the saints are held back by a permanent weakness of the flesh from doing perfectly the good works which they do; I mean that they walk when they should be running, often they even limp. It is as a result of this, I say, that there has never been a good work which was entirely pure and perfect, which lacked any blemish at all. But if something base is, as a result of the imperfection of the flesh, always included in the works of the saints, then when they are reviewed by God and weighed in that balance which fills even the very angels with dread, they will there be exposed as corrupt, whatever may be the value set on them by human judgment.[76]

Good works not untainted by sin

But, it is said, it is contrary to reason for complete purity to be spoiled by a tiny blemish. But, first, it is enough to prove my case if there is sin included in every good work. Secondly, I do not at all accept that it would be irrational if complete purity were spoiled by a tiny piece of dirt. For the taste of a wine which is sweet and pleasant in other respects is entirely spoiled by slight sourness, so that it loses the pleasantness which it has; and if so, who will seek to bring charges against God because he declares that a spoiled work displeases him? So it was determined in the law of Moses that if someone in a state of uncleanness touched something holy, it was deemed unclean.[77] By this it was

Any sin spoils purity

---

74. Calvin seems here to withdraw his earlier concession that Luther was exaggerating. For the argument of the next two sentences see *Inst.* 3.12.1–2; 3.14.1–10 (LCC 20:754–57, 768–77).
  75. Matt. 22:37–39/Mark 12:29–31/Luke 10:27.
  76. See *Inst.* 3.12.1–2, 4–8; 3.14.1–10 (LCC 20:754–62, 768–77).
  77. Num. 19:22; cf. Hag. 2:13.

signified that human uncleanness is so powerful and contagious a poison that it defiles by mere contact whatever is otherwise holy. Now how are we all freed from our common defilement except by faith? So then let that conclusion remain, that good works, if they are evaluated in themselves, § are without exception sinful; and that they are good and please God and receive praise and reward through God's fatherly acceptance of them, not by their own inherent merit.

The other point, about the absolute necessity of [all] events, we will postpone to the place where it can be dealt with in its proper order,[78] since of course the question is one about God's providence and predestination. He says afterwards that since we were ashamed of that doctrine we abandoned half of it, because we allow mankind free choice in external matters and in public affairs. But he says that three arguments prevent him from regarding this recantation as genuine: in our published works we claim that it is permitted to advance the gospel by deceitful tricks; we do not heap curses on Luther, the originator of so horrific a blasphemy; and we do not condemn our earlier books and thus openly admit that we were in error.

His accusation that we wrote about advancing the gospel by deceit and trickery is incredible, unless he has been dreaming to himself. For I cannot believe that any such statement has slipped out from any of our party. Concerning Luther there is no reason for him to be in any doubt when now also, as we have done previously, we openly bear witness that we consider him a distinguished apostle of Christ whose labour and ministry have done most in these times to bring back the purity of the gospel.[79] Concerning ourselves we gladly admit what tradition says that Solon used to boast about himself: that we learn every day as we grow old, or at any rate hasten towards old age.[80] But why does Pighius demand of us that we declare that we have taught error, when even now we persevere steadily in our adherence to that totality of doctrine which we have always avowed? It is indeed possible that we use different ways of speaking, that almost every one of us has his own manner of speaking which is different from that of others.[81] But why could we not be allowed something that has been the common

---

78. In the reply to Pighius's last four books; see John Calvin, *Concerning the Eternal Predestination of God*, trans. J. K. S. Reid (London: James Clarke, 1961), 170, 177–79.
79. For Calvin's assessment of Luther see B. A. Gerrish, "The Pathfinder: Calvin's Image of Martin Luther," in *The Old Protestantism and the New* (Edinburgh: T. & T. Clark and Chicago: University of Chicago Press, 1982), 27–48.
80. Cf. Erasmus *Adages* 1.8.60 (CWE 32:159).
81. Calvin is reluctant to admit that there is any variation among the Reformers. With regard to improving his own manner of speaking, Calvin was himself influenced by this controversy with Pighius when he was revising the *Institutes*. See the Introduction §1 for further comments.

practice of everyone in every generation? This too I recognise without reluctance, that when our works are reprinted we improve what was rather coarse, we soften what was too harshly expressed, we clarify obscure points, we explain more fully and at greater length what was too compressed, we also strengthen our argument with new reasons, and finally, where we fear the danger of causing offence, we also tone down and soften our language. For what would be the point of living if neither age nor practice nor constant exercise nor reading nor meditation were of any benefit to us? And what would be the point of making progress if it did not result in some profit reaching others also? On the contrary, if Pighius does not know it, I should like it to be absolutely clear to him that we strive night and day to shape our faithfully transmitted teachings into a form which we also judge will be the best.

It is also true that Philipp Melanchthon, by careful and very adept softening of the outward form of some things which Luther had written in scholastic language, in a style alien to popular taste, accommodated them to the general mass of humanity and to common usage.[82] Likewise when the wording of the Augsburg Confession needed to be produced, § [Melanchthon] desired to linger only on that teaching which alone is peculiar to the church and necessary to know for salvation, namely that natural powers by themselves have no ability to conceive faith, to obey the divine law, and [to attain] entire spiritual righteousness. What they can do in public affairs and outward behaviour he did not want to discuss in too much detail, because it is not of great importance for faith.[83] But that teaching which is the chief issue in this controversy and the cause of everything else that is said we defend today just as it was put forward by Luther and others at the beginning. Even in those matters which I have declared to be not so necessary for faith there is no difference, apart from the softening of the form of expression so as to remove anything displeasing.

When [Pighius] has finished this part of the play, he proceeds to his discredit to another scene: to bring out "the mysteries of our doctrine," as he calls them, into the clear light of day from the darkness in which they have been concealed and submerged in our writings. And here he complains not only about our obscureness but about our diversity; for [he says] since a lie is of itself full of darkness, we seek a hiding place for it to aid our deceit, and besides we are so unlike and different from one another that it would be an endless task to conclude anything definite from all our writings. It is said that there is one kind of poor-

Melanchthon softened Luther's language

251

P accuses Reformers of obscurity and disharmony,

---

82. Calvin in 1546 wrote a preface to the French translation of Melanchthon's *Loci communes*. He there makes a similar observation about that work, specifically applying it to the point being discussed here (OC 9:848–49).

83. Augsburg Confession 18 (Tappert 39–40).

sighted person who can see better at dusk than at midday. And in general we see that those whose eyesight is delicate and weak suffer a greater impediment and disability if they come out into full daylight. Who would deny that Pighius is one such? Yielding praise for fine speech to others, we nevertheless have a tongue that is not so very given to difficult and confusing speaking. And all notice that we strive earnestly to make ourselves understood. It is in fact for precisely this reason that our opponents are so enraged with us: we have made the teaching of Christ too well known to the common people. Only Pighius charges us with excessive obscurity. But it is the same as I have said elsewhere: in the manner of boys who make practice speeches in their schools, he puts all the rules of rhetoric to use without discrimination! He read somewhere that charging your opponent with being obscure will help to damage his cause. [Pighius] seized this weapon, because he liked it, and now he brandishes it mindlessly at us. But there was no place in the present case for this cypress tree,[84] since our books, without need for defence, can protect themselves more than adequately from this empty accusation. Even Pighius himself later, as though forgetting himself, credits me at least with orderliness and clarity. Whether we disagree with one another as he declares, it was up to him to prove. What else is there now for me to say except that he blabs out anything and everything against us indiscriminately, so as to make our teaching detested only by those who do not read it? For he has no regard for those who have had even the slightest contact with our writings.

Next he begins to unfold, using my words,[85] what our party holds in common, though (lest he should seem to be contradicting himself unduly) he treats as an exception any instance where [those in our party] share a single point of view. You can see, reader, that the man is pulled both this way and that. He wants to appear to be opening a battle against the whole party of the Lutherans,[86] § not against any individual member of it. But he cannot attack us all at the same time except as a united body. Grudgingly he is brought to acknowledge that there is agreement between us. Therefore he says both things at the same time, and neither; and in this way he tears apart the knot which he cannot untie. To this he adds a summary of my arguments on this topic in the second chapter of my *Institutes*.[87] I am not so mean and peevish that I would without good cause accuse Pighius of bad faith in reproducing

---

84. A clear allusion to Horace *Art of Poetry* 19–21 (Loeb 450–53). There is a fuller allusion to the same passage in *BLW* 3.296 (at n. 42). Cf. Erasmus *Adages* 1.5.19 (CWE 31:400).
85. See n. 61.
86. Note that Calvin, in the interests of maintaining a united Protestant front against Pighius's charges, is willing to be called a Lutheran.
87. See n. 61.

On Book One

my arguments. But, lest he flatter himself unduly, I perceive that he has somehow described the sum of my argument in such a way that I would be most reluctant to have such summaries made of the whole work, and I accept this one only on the condition that readers remember that it was produced by an adversary. For in what he claims to be throughout a more orderly and coherent discussion than my own, he behaves characteristically in two respects, namely in empty self-importance and in a liberality of untruth.

I will also pass by the remarks with which, like drops of a bitter liquid, he sprinkles my statements here and there to make them less palatable to the reader, saying that I mutilate a statement of Chrysostom which I cite verbatim, just as it appears in his own work;[88] that I falsely attribute an idea to Peter Lombard, when it is clear for all to see that my interpretation is accurate;[89] that in quoting proofs from the prophets I either am dishonest[90] or do not follow faithful translators, because in some places I disagree with the Vulgate. These things are not worth relating, except to show Pighius's remarkable ignorance and malice, which, however, sober readers will notice well enough without need of anyone to point them out. One thing would be worth relating, if he did not repeat it in another place, where it will be dealt with, namely that he deems it pure imagination when I teach that the soul of a believer is by regeneration divided into two parts. For even in this single statement one can observe a clear mark of Pighius's theology. For who could not see that one who regards as imagination an experience so familiar to devout souls treats the soul like salt?[91] But because this is part of the main body of the argument, and Pighius also repeats it there, it will be more useful to defer treatment of it until then.[92]

P's charges against C

For this same reason I will only lightly touch on his last objection, where he mocks our folly in spending so much trouble on instructing people, when we assert meanwhile that faith is not obtained through human efforts at persuasion, but is the special work of the Holy Spirit. For this will arise again in the actual course of the discussion.[93] Even so, because this has been placed by Pighius at the very threshold of his work for the very purpose of blocking the way to our writings, I cannot en-

Why preach when God gives faith?

---

88. In *Inst.* 2.2.9 (LCC 20:267) Calvin quotes from (Pseudo-)Chrysostom's homily for the first Sunday in Advent. This homily appears in Erasmus's edition of Chrysostom's works.
89. In *Inst.* 2.2.6 (LCC 20:263–64) Calvin quotes from Lombard's *Sentences* 2.25.8 (PL 192:708).
90. Latin "infidelem."
91. An allusion to the statement of Chrysippus the Stoic that the "soul" of the pig serves as salt to preserve it from corruption until we are ready to eat it (reported by Cicero *Nature of the Gods* 2.64.160 [Loeb 276–77]). Cf. Erasmus *Adages* 1.1.40 (CWE 31:89).
92. See *BLW* 5.356–57.
93. See *BLW* 4.341–46.

253

Why do farmers labour when God gives fertility?

tirely pass it by. He says that we labour in vain in urging and exhorting people to believe, if it is really the case that they do not conceive [faith] themselves by their own power, but God § inspires it by his grace. For he makes this logical argument:[94] Whatever is done prior to grace by the enslaved choice is necessarily evil and leads away from faith rather than towards it, and faith itself depends entirely on God. Therefore in teaching and exhorting, all effort is vainly cast to the winds. I reply that we are no more labouring in vain than do farmers while they plough the earth and sow seed. For it is written, You shall sow and not gather.[95] By which it is indicated that all labour is in vain without the blessing of God. But where labour brings a good result, so that fruit is gathered from it, it is written: I will answer the heaven, and the heaven shall answer the earth, and the earth shall answer the corn.[96] Now you hear[97] that without the blessing of God all labour is worth nothing. Where however some fruit follows, it results from the fact that God has answered the heaven, so as to make the earth fruitful. God speaks still more clearly elsewhere, when he says that he disciplined his people in the wilderness lest, when they had come to the land promised to them, they should say in their heart, My strength and the might of my hand furnished me with all this.[98] You see there that God causes everything and of necessity, that is, in accordance with his providence. Why is it that the earth waits for the hand of the farmer when its fertility depends entirely on nothing but the blessing of God? Evidently because God has ordained it so.

God works through instruments

I will bring forward another similar example too, but one that is still clearer. The Lord bears witness that, when he rained the manna from heaven, he provided a lasting proof that man does not live by bread alone but by the power of [God's] word.[99] If we are fed and sustained not by bread but by the word of God, why do we still labour for food and drink? Pighius will retort that we do not live by bread alone, but yet we do in some measure. But it is precisely this that I want to maintain, that bread does not have any power of itself, and only the blessing of God is sufficient to nourish us.[100] For where that inner power of God is absent, only that can happen which is written: You shall eat and not be satisfied.[101] Also: I will break the staff of bread.[102] But where

---

94. The next two sentences are Pighius's representation of the logic of the Reformers' view.
95. Mic. 6:15; cf. Deut. 28:38.
96. Hos. 2:21–22.
97. "You hear" and "you see" (which appears in the text after n. 98) are favourite expressions of Pighius and are used some thirty times by Calvin in this work.
98. Deut. 8:17.
99. Deut. 8:3.
100. Cf. *Inst.* 1.16.7 (LCC 20:206, as rewritten in 1559).
101. Lev. 26:26; Mic. 6:14.
102. Lev. 26:26.

[God's power] is present, it supports us and sustains us no less effectively without bread than with bread. Where is the logic of Pighius's argument? God effectively, by his own secret power, feeds man, and he does so in accordance with his providence, so that man's life depends entirely on that and not on food and drink. Therefore we eat and drink in vain. But lest I become too long-winded, I will show what sort of an argument that one is in three sentences. God alone feeds man. Therefore he does not work through intermediaries. That is, he uses no instruments. What boy would escape a beating from his teacher if he argued like that?

Now it remains to apply those comparisons to the present case. Paul, when he speaks about the task of the apostles, compares them to gardeners who plant or water. And immediately he adds that they are nothing; God alone, who gives the increase, § is everything.[103] If one of us simply said that he who teaches is nothing, that he who exhorts is nothing, with what firebrands would Pighius arm the Furies[104] that he would send against us! Now let him bare his teeth for a moment at Paul. Let him mockingly ask what he achieves by writing and speaking so, why he undergoes so many trials, exposes himself to so many troubles and cares, makes no end of travelling around, if all these are nothing. To all these questions Paul replies that he has a ministry of the Spirit by which he is to write the preaching of the gospel on human hearts, not by his own activity and effort or (as they say)[105] by his own exertions, but by the Spirit of the living God.[106] Now you hear where the effectiveness of his ministry comes from, namely from the secret action of the Holy Spirit, not by human labour or desire. You hear also that the instrument which the hand of God uses to complete his work is thereby of no importance. So then let the holy apostle adapt this defence of his to us too in our common cause. Pighius asks, What is the point of our labour in writing and public speaking if man, before he believes, is held captive in Satan's bonds so that he cannot by himself receive and embrace sound teaching, but when he is enlightened by the Spirit of God he effectually and necessarily receives it? Let Paul reply here: it is because God appointed the gospel to be the means to display the power of his Spirit.[107] What more do you want? It is God alone who acts; but because he willed that the power of his Spirit should in some way be enclosed in the preaching of the gospel, our work which serves his providence is not empty or useless.

Paul's answer

254

---

103. 1 Cor. 3:6–7.
104. On the Furies see n. 17.
105. See Erasmus *Adages* 1.6.19 (CWE 32:15–16).
106. 2 Cor. 3:3, 6.
107. Rom. 1:16; 1 Cor. 1:18; 2:4.

God works through preaching

There is therefore no reason for this fellow to seek praise for being funny when he jeeringly ascribes to us the reply that whether for good or ill we [preach] of necessity, without purpose or reason. Now it is true, in case he does not know, that we were not roused to this ministry by our own wisdom or by chance, but by the sure and steady purpose of God and the effective movement of the Holy Spirit. For our reason for [preaching] is no different from that of Paul, who declares both that from the womb he was appointed by divine choice to the task of an apostle,[108] and that he did not begin until the day had come which God had determined. But what justification does this give for Pighius's insipid remark? For at the same time we are sure that, in accordance with this divine election, we are performing a service which is acceptable to [God] and effective for the salvation of believers and wholesome for the church; and, to use also Augustine's words, "we exhort and preach so that those who have ears to hear may hear" *(The Gift of Perseverance).*[109] We do it because we know that it is granted only to a few to understand without human aid, while it is granted to many to believe in God through human agency. But in whatever way we proclaim the word of God to men, it is indubitable that where someone hears so as to obey, it is a gift of God.

---

108. Gal. 1:15.
109. *The Gift of Perseverance* 14.37 (NPNF 5:540).

On Book Two [of Pighius]

§ At the beginning of the second book [Pighius] unfolds all the resources of his oratorical skill. For he is engaged in a public dispute in which he can display himself before the mass of mankind and so win applause. And indeed at the start he is so beside himself with amazement that you might say that he was acting the part of Niobe in a play.[1] But the cause of his amazement [he says] is that we have been smitten with such dizziness, blindness, and madness as to have embraced this doctrine with which he is dealing, when it is more than obvious that it is false, condemned by common sense and by consent of all mortals since the creation of the world, and blasphemous against God like none other. Then, lest he should seem to be raving without good reason, he lists many absurdities which he thinks are included in it.

I could wish that I had an opponent who would attack me from every side but not rush at me in a blind and confused combat as this man does, for, having resolved to discuss two different issues separately, he now mixes them up together. He says: If even to think anything good or evil is in nobody's power, but everything happens by "absolute necessity".... But he has undertaken to deal with the providence of God, on which this necessity depends, elsewhere, and this is just what he does in the last four books of his work. Why then does he now mix up this issue with the other one? Let him say whatever he has to say, even if it is weak, even if it is worthless; if only he will stay in one place, I will let him say it. But now that he has brought forward two issues for debate, and undertaken that he will speak about each one separately, why does he not fulfil in his actual discourse the promise which he made before? When he everywhere boasts that he is a good practitioner of orderly discourse, I dare not ascribe [his mixing issues together] to his inexperience; I know that it is done out of cunning and

255
P says Protestant doctrine absurd

P drags in issue of "absolute necessity"

---

1. The legendary story of Niobe is told by a number of classical writers, starting with Homer. She was the mother of a large number of children who were killed. Calvin is probably comparing Pighius's amazement with that of Niobe at discovering her loss.

malice. For since he could see that the statement of Luther about absolute necessity which he quotes[2] was less in agreement with the common understanding of mankind, he thought that this very point would be the most promising place for him to begin, so as to have the mind of the flesh agreeing with him but shuddering at the teaching of Luther. Therefore he steers clear of the whole subject of the corruption of [human] nature, like some rock. When he is drawn, or rather dragged, towards it by the implications of what he himself is saying, more often than not he shies away from it. For he knows that on this subject his case will find less favour with ordinary people than when he is pushing forward that other argument.[3]

Seven Arguments

1. If God is in control, why bother?

But all right, since our opponent wants it so, let us make our response about both issues at the same time. So the first argument is: If we cannot think of anything good or evil or plan our ways, whether good or evil, but everything is in God's control and happens necessarily in accordance with it,[4] why do we not snore and sleep for ever? Why does the farmer sweat so in ploughing, sowing, and gathering crops? Why does the merchant take upon himself long journeys and dangerous voyages? Why does a worthy head of a household see that his children are well trained to practise virtue and behave honourably? § Why do we call a doctor when we are sick? For nothing is gained by care, hard work, or diligence. If Pighius is waiting for me to fashion some new reply, he is mistaken. Rather, I shall borrow from my *Institutes* just so much as will be enough for an answer. It is as follows: "Human hard work, thoughts, plans, and purposes are easily reconciled with divine providence by Solomon. For just as he mocks the stupidity of those who undertake anything boldly without reference to the Lord, as if they were not governed by his hand,[5] so elsewhere he speaks thus: The heart of a man ought to plan his way, and the Lord will direct his steps (Prov. 16).[6] He thereby indicates that we are not in the least prevented by the eternal decrees of God from, subject to his will, having regard for our interests and managing all that is ours. Nor is that without a clear explanation. For he who set boundaries to our life with his own limits has put the care of it in our hands. He has equipped us with ways

God's providence works through us

---

2. Pighius (15b) cites "Article 36" of Luther's *Defence of All the Articles of Martin Luther Condemned by the Latest Bull of Leo X* (WA 7:146).
3. I.e., the argument about absolute necessity.
4. See *Inst.* 1.16.6, 8 (LCC 20:204–5, 207) and 1.17.2 (LCC 20:212–14, as rewritten in 1559).
5. A reference to the earlier citation of Prov. 16:1 in *Inst.* 1.16.6 (LCC 20:204–5).
6. Prov. 16:9.

and means of preserving it; he has made us aware of dangers, lest they should fall upon us when we are unprepared; and finally he has supplied both ways to prevent them and cures. So those madmen do not consider what is obvious, that the skills of taking counsel and being careful are inspired by God, so that with their help we may be subject to his providence in the preservation of our life. Just as, on the other hand, by carelessness and laziness we invite the evils which he has imposed on us. For how does it happen that a prudent man, when he is consulting his own interest, frees himself even when evils are threatening him, while the fool perishes through thoughtless indiscretion, unless it is because both folly and prudence are instruments of divine governance on either side?"[7] Pighius has what he was seeking, or rather what he was not seeking. For a concern for seeking the truth does not control someone who is so unable to be satisfied with such a clear and simple answer that, having heard it, he pretends that no reply has been given to him, and continues to jeer as if he has heard nothing.

The second argument: Why are crimes punished by the law if they are committed of necessity? Why does the judge pass sentence on the person through whom God has acted? For if a murder has been committed, no punishment will be inflicted upon the sword. But the wicked when they commit their crimes are, according to Luther,[8] in exactly the same position in God's sight as is a sword in someone's hand. I reply[9] that there is an answer to this objection if with due humility rather than ungodly arrogance one reflects on the way in which divine providence governs human affairs. For we do not say that the wicked sin of necessity in such a way as to imply that they sin without wilful and deliberate evil intent. The necessity comes from the fact that God accomplishes his work, which is sure and steadfast, through them. At the same time, however, the will and purpose to do evil which dwells within them makes them liable to censure. But, it is said, they are driven and forced to this by God. Indeed, but in such a way that in a single deed the action of § God is one thing and their own action is another. For they gratify their evil and wicked desires, but God turns this wickedness so as to bring his judgments to execution. This subject is one that I am touching on lightly with, as it were, only a brief mention, since elsewhere it will have to be treated at greater length and with

2. Why punish crimes if they are necessary?

Necessity does not exclude evil will

257

---

7. *Inst.* 1.17.4 (LCC 20:215–16).
8. This is the charge that Pighius brings against Luther (16a), which he justifies with a brief quotation from "Article 36" of Luther's *Defence* (WA 7:144). Pighius is looking back to his earlier (7b–8b) lengthy quotation from this work (WA 7:144–47). Luther himself does not there use the analogy of the sword, but Erasmus uses it in a similar accusation against Luther in his *Diatribe concerning Free Choice* (LCC 17:63–64).
9. See *Inst.* 1.17.3, 5, 9 (LCC 20:215–17, 222).

more attention.[10] But his attempt to heap odium on Luther for comparing the wicked to a sword deceives no one and only shows up his brazen impudence.[11] For they are the Holy Spirit's words, not Luther's: O Assyria, rod of my anger! Again: Why does the axe boast, which is guided by the hand of him that cuts? (Isa. 10).[12]

<u>3. Necessity undermines law and order</u>

The third argument: This doctrine banishes all political authority and order, all instruction in good living, from human life. For the promise of rewards for good deeds would be to no purpose, and the threat of punishment for crimes equally so, if it is necessary that what will happen should happen. As though in fact, when we say that God determines everything by his choice and directs it towards his end, we do not also add that he himself employs certain methods, as it were

<u>God works through secondary causes</u>

means, or secondary causes.[13] So the world is held together by political authority and the instruction given by laws, but, insofar as God uses them, he does so to bring about that preservation of the world which he in his own counsel determined. We are not Stoics who dream up a fate based on a continuous connection of events.[14] All we say is that God is in charge of the world which he established and not only holds in his power the events of the natural world, but also governs the hearts of men, bends their wills this way and that in accordance with his choice, and is the director of their actions, so that they in the end do nothing which he has not decreed, whatever they may try to do. Accordingly we say that those things which appear to be in the greatest degree due to chance happen of necessity—not by their own innate properties but because the purpose of God, which is eternal and steadfast, is sovereign in governing them.[15] But we do not for that reason discount the means which God has appointed to be subject to his will, nor do we say that those things are without effect or superfluous which serve the fulfilment of the divine purpose.

<u>4. Necessity undermines religion</u>

The fourth argument: That all religion is done away [by our doctrine] and human beings are turned into brute beasts, or rather monsters, before which [argument] Pighius goes rigid with wonder like a stone. You would suppose that someone is speaking here who is ardently concerned about religion, as if he were not everywhere breathing forth mouthfuls of Romish theology whose first axiom is: You should

---

10. I.e., in the reply to Pighius's last four books, in *Concerning the Eternal Predestination of God*, trans. J. K. S. Reid (London: James Clarke, 1961), 168–85; cf. *BLW* 1.250 (at n. 78); 5.351 (at n. 5).
11. Cf. Isa. 48:4.
12. Isa. 10:5, 15.
13. See *Inst.* 1.17.6, 9 (LCC 20:218, 221–22).
14. See *Inst.* 1.16.8 (LCC 20:207). For the Stoic doctrine see Cicero *The Nature of the Gods* 1.20.55 (Loeb 54–55); see also at n. 88.
15. See *Inst.* 1.16.1, 6, 8 (LCC 20:197–98, 204–5, 207).

believe as much about God as you like, or find useful. But leaving the man on one side, let us see how true what he alleges is. We say that man not only cannot do anything good but cannot even think it, so that he may learn to depend totally on God and, despairing of himself, to cast himself entirely upon him; and so that [man] may give the credit, if he has done anything good, to God and not to himself, and not render the praise to God for his good works in half measure only, but fully and wholly, leaving nothing for himself but the fact that he has received whatever he has from God.[16] We say that man has inborn in him a perversity derived from inherited corruption, so that he should blame himself § whenever he sins and not fix the blame elsewhere when he finds the root of evil in his own self.[17] We say that human affairs are not, by some blind or random chance, turned this way and that, but are controlled by the fixed purpose of God, so that nothing can happen other than what he decreed at the beginning. All things are subject to his power, and so there is no created thing which does not, either of its own accord or under coercion, obey his will. Accordingly everything that happens happens of necessity, as he has ordained.[18] Satan too and all the wicked are submissive to his authority, so that they cannot move beyond what he has commanded, for they are constrained by his hand as though by a bridle or a halter, so that now he restrains them, since it pleases him to do so, and now he drives them on and guides them to execute his judgments.[19] All this [teaching] has no other purpose[20] but to make the believer rest, free from anxiety, in the omnipotence of God. He then will fear neither fortune nor chance and will not be afraid for himself because of wild animals or human beings or devils, as though the reins had been let go or broken and they came on under their own impulse without any control from above. Instead he will entrust his soul and body to God and so, with a calm and tranquil mind, sink back into the protection of him whose will he knows determines everything and whose hand brings everything to pass. Moreover, since this entire teaching trains a person only to be humble, to fear God, to place his trust in God, and to ascribe glory to God, which are the chief components of true religion, there is no reason why Pighius should direct so awful an accusation against us.

The fifth argument: By speaking in this way we make God the author of all evil deeds, we make him who is the most just into one who

But Reformers teach entire trust in God

258

Rest in God and fear nothing

5. God the author of sin?

---

16. See *Inst.* 2.2.12–16, 18–20, 22–25 (LCC 20:271–75, 277–79, 281–85).
17. See *Inst.* 2.1.8, 10–11 (LCC 20:250–54).
18. See n. 15.
19. See *Inst.* 2.4.5 (LCC 20:313).
20. Calvin was always concerned that doctrine be useful; on the usefulness of the doctrine of providence see *Inst.* 1.17.6–11 (LCC 20:218–25).

is cruel and savage, and we turn his infinite wisdom into folly. I myself do not deny that such an opinion is commonly expressed by people speaking on the basis of their carnal understanding, so that they form this kind of conception of God when they hear his own statements about his secret judgments. But what sort of justice is it if foolish human reason is allowed to assess the incomprehensible judgments of God, before which Paul trembles in adoration and wonder because he dare not scrutinise them?[21] When Paul himself quotes the blasphemous opinions of the ungodly, he adds that he is speaking "humanly."[22] By this word he shows plainly that human beings are bound to judge perversely on such matters, even to the extent of holding ungodly and sacrilegious opinions. Therefore let us turn away from that headlong effrontery of the carnal mind to a pure modesty and reverence for the divine justice. Then we shall understand[23] that God is not made the author of evil deeds when he is said to lead the ungodly where he wills and to accomplish and execute his work through them, but rather we shall acknowledge that he is a wonderfully expert craftsman who can use even bad tools well. We shall be compelled to admire his justice, which not only finds a way through iniquity but also employs that very iniquity to a good end. §

259

The sixth argument: We damn the whole of nature, because we say that everything that man has from his nature is corrupt. Augustine bears witness that it is nothing new for the enemies of grace to hide behind the praise of nature (*To Boniface* 2).[24] However, lest I should seem thereby to be evading the issue, I reply[25] that both Luther and all of us define nature in two ways: first as it was established by God, which we declare to have been pure and perfect, and second as, corrupted through man's fall, it lost its perfection. We assign the blame for this corruption to man; we do not ascribe it to God. If Pighius rejects this teaching, let him find fault with the apostle who expounds it in nearly identical words.[26] Or if he prefers, we will reply with words from Augustine's lips, which are contained in his first book to Boniface: "Human beings are the work of God insofar as they are human, but they

---

21. Rom. 11:33–34.
22. Rom. 3:5.
23. See n. 9.
24. *Against Two Letters of the Pelagians* 2.1.1 (NPNF 5:391), where Augustine is attacking those who use the defense of the goodness of creation (against the Manichees) as an excuse for undermining the reality of grace (Pelagianism). This text is also cited in *BLW* 4.339 (at n. 127).
25. See *Inst.* 1.15.1; 2.1.1, 10–11 (LCC 20:183–84, 241–42, 253–54). For Luther see, e.g., *The Bondage of the Will* (LCC 17:187–88, 231); *Lectures on Romans* on 6:6 (LCC 15:182).
26. Calvin is probably thinking not of any particular passage but of the teaching of Paul as a whole, to which he often turns in this work; see, e.g., at nn. 77–78, 80. The Beza edition adds a reference to Rom. 3:20, which OC changes to 8:20.

are under the control of the devil insofar as they are sinners, unless they are rescued from there through Christ."²⁷ So from God they are good, but from themselves they are evil.

Here I would again like to ask readers to remember that I am not yet dealing with these questions in an orderly way, but only briefly countering Pighius's subtleties. He desired by his false accusations to make our teaching hateful to people before they learned about it and, by as it were standing in the doorway, to prevent them from entering upon any direct knowledge of it. So I have refrained from saying everything about those topics which would be required for a full, well-constructed explanation of them, so as not to be compelled, when the appropriate time for them comes, either to refer the reader to the present treatment or to burden him unnecessarily with excessive repetition. *Fuller discussion to follow*

As for his final objection—to which he is prompted by some quite superficial similarities—namely that if our teaching were accepted the whole doctrine of God would be exposed to ridicule, I will say only that a short and quick answer to all of it can be given in a few words. I mean, of course, if we consider separately what is man's obligation to God and what God does in man. For we ought not to measure by our own ability the duty to which we are bound nor to investigate man's capabilities with this unaided power of reasoning. Rather we should maintain the following doctrine. First, even if we cannot fulfil or even begin to fulfil the righteousness of the law, yet it is rightly required of us, and we are not excused by our weakness or the failure of our strength. For as the fault for this is ours, so the blame must be imputed to us.²⁸ Secondly, the function of the law is different from what people commonly suppose it to be.²⁹ For it cannot make [sinners] good but can only convict them of guilt, first by removing the excuse of ignorance and then by disproving their mistaken opinion that they are righteous and their empty claims about their own strength. Thus it comes about that no excuse is left for the ungodly to prevent them from being convicted by their own conscience and, whether they like it or not, becoming aware of their guilt. They may not always § acknowledge it and admit it but, with the law pronouncing its judgment within, they are aware of it. It also comes about, conversely, that the godly, being thoroughly emptied of all misplaced confidence in themselves, [an attitude] which is true humility indeed, make room for the grace of God, from which they may draw strength. Therefore in issuing commands and exhortations God does

7. Protestant doctrine exposes God to ridicule

"Ought" does not imply "can"

Law teaches duty, not ability

Law's role is to expose guilt

260

---

27. *Against Two Letters of the Pelagians* 1.18.36 (NPNF 5:388). The first edition has "rise," which all subsequent editions rightly change to "are rescued." This quotation, slightly shortened, reappears in *BLW* 5.354 (at n. 35).
28. See *Inst.* 2.7.3–5; 3.12.1–2, 4–8 (LCC 20:351–54, 754–62).
29. For this "first use of the law," see *Inst.* 2.7.6–9 (LCC 20:354–58).

not take account of our strength, since he gives that very thing which he demands[30] and gives it for the reason that by ourselves we are helpless.

Pighius Compares Reformers to Ancient Heretics

Moreover, lest he pass by anything which is able in the slightest degree to stir up hatred against Luther's view and our own, [Pighius] mentions that it is derived from the ancient heretics, Priscillian, Mani, Marcion, Cerdo, and even Simon Magus himself, all of whom however, he says, Luther surpassed in impiety.[31] I would call this a clever device, if it had any substance. But since it is easy to make it obvious that it is a stupid and wicked lie, I do not know what gain he hoped for from it—unless perhaps it is, as I have already said, that he was satisfied as long as he could please people of his own kind, who do not come into contact with our teaching nor ask whether what is said is true or false, but admire everything by Pighius or Eck[32] solely for the reason that it is written against us. The charge is an ancient and well-worn one, not discovered first by Pighius. For so once the Pelagians harassed Augustine, as though he held the same opinions as the Manichees.[33] But truth always has a defence ready against empty, unfounded abuse.

1. Simon Magus

To begin with Simon,[34] what reason does Pighius have to make us his disciples? Indeed why does he mention him at all? Nearly all the ancients refer to Simon and list his errors, but none to my knowledge brings forward anything of the kind that Pighius is throwing about here. A large number of his insanities are reported by Irenaeus in his first book,[35] some by Tertullian (*The Prescription against Heretics* 20),[36] and Augustine in fact collects together whatever he had read or heard (and *Heresies, to Quodvultdeus*).[37] On freedom or bondage of

---

30. An echo of Augustine *Confessions* 10.29.40; 10.31.45 (NPNF 1:153, 155), quoted in *Inst.* 2.5.7 (LCC 20:325). Cf. *BLW* 4.348 (at n. 206). This passage is also quoted by Augustine in *The Gift of Perseverance* 20.53 (NPNF 5:547).

31. The 1543 and 1552 editions erroneously read "piety" for "impiety."

32. Johann Eck (1486–1543) was a German Roman Catholic theologian who opposed Protestantism. He debated with Luther at Leipzig in 1519, and Calvin would have met him at the colloquies of Worms and Regensburg (*BLW* 1.233 nn. 1, 3). Eck also accused the Lutherans of Manichaeism (*Enchiridion of Commonplaces* 28, 31 [Grand Rapids: Baker, 1979], 186, 210, 219).

33. See Augustine *Against Two Letters of the Pelagians* 2.1.1 (NPNF 5:391–92); *Against Julian* 1.3.5 (FoC 35:6–7). Manichaeism was a dualistic religion founded by the Syro-Persian Mani (216–76).

34. Simon Magus appears in Acts 8:9–13, 18–24, and subsequently became a notorious heretic about whom it is hard to disentangle fact and legend.

35. *Against Heresies* 1.23.1–4 (ANF 1:347–48).

36. Tertullian attacks Simon in *The Prescription against Heretics* 33 (ANF 3:259).

37. See n. 39. In the margin of both the first and second editions, "and *Heresies*" goes with the preceding note. Simon is also attacked in Pseudo-Tertullian *Against All Heresies* 1 (ANF 3:649), but "and *Heresies*" probably belongs here, referring to Augustine's *Heresies*, which was addressed to Quodvultdeus.

choice, on necessity or chance, there is absolutely nothing. He taught, [Augustine] says, unrestricted sexual intercourse, and that God did not make the world; he denied the resurrection of the flesh, he claimed that he was Christ and also wanted it believed that he was Jupiter and that a certain prostitute called Selene[38] was Minerva, and he provided images of himself and her to be worshipped. He said that in the person of the Father he had given the law to the Jews, that he thought that under Tiberius he had appeared in the person of the Son, and that afterwards he had come upon the apostles in tongues of fire. These are the teachings which Augustine was able to collect from all other sources and put into a single catalogue.[39] What reason will Pighius find here to make us disciples of Simon?

Yet he is not inventing the evidence; § he gets it from the *Recognitions* of Clement.[40] A fine author indeed to settle a dispute about such weighty matters! For it is common knowledge that [the *Recognitions*] are the imaginings of some stupid monk, which were maliciously put out under Clement's name.[41] Nor is there any need for grand and long arguments—if in fact there is any book in circulation which without need for an informer more fully betrays its own absurdity! The things that are attributed to Peter there are no more redolent of the apostolic spirit than is Aristotle's *Metaphysics*.[42] Indeed I think I do Aristotle an injustice when I compare him to this caricature of a philosopher. I will therefore say no more than I have already said, that it was some stupid monk who wanted to ease the boredom of his leisure by writing nonsense. But he acquired confidence for the use of Clement's name from the fact that it was commonly accepted that Clement had written an account of a dispute between Peter and Simon. Even Rufinus quotes this (*Apology for Origen*),[43] not without the unfavourable comment that it contains many falsehoods[44] and blasphemies, but adding in Clement's defence that the opinions in it could be not genuine but deceitfully interpolated by heretics.

261

Clementine *Recognitions* —a forgery

Its own content betrays it

Testimony of Rufinus

---

38. The prostitute was called Helen, according to the French translation. Augustine's original text also had "Helen," but here as elsewhere the sixteenth-century editions available to Calvin have a divergent text (PL 42:25 n. 1).

39. *Heresies* 1 (Müller 62–65; PL 42:25–26). The final sentence ("He said . . . fire") is found in the sixteenth-century editions of Augustine (including the Erasmian edition used by Calvin), but not in the original (PL 42:26 n. 1).

40. Pseudo-Clement of Rome *Recognitions* 2.19–3.50 describes Peter's confrontation with Simon. For the present topic see especially 3.21–26 (ANF 8:119–21).

41. It is today universally recognised that Clement was not the author.

42. Aristotle (384–322 B.C.). *Metaphysics* is in Greek script.

43. *The Adulteration of the Works of Origen* (NPNF2 3:422–23). This is Rufinus's epilogue to his Latin translation of Pamphilus's *Apology for Origen* and is found in some sixteenth-century editions of the works of Origen.

44. The first edition reads "no falsehoods," which is rightly corrected by all later editions.

However, I am led by the almost universal authority of the ancients, rather than by the opinion of Rufinus alone, to think that the whole book is a forgery and that it bears Clement's name falsely. For if some such book which was considered to be by Clement had existed in the time of Irenaeus and Tertullian, they would surely not have ignored so fine and so useful a support. That very issue which is handled there was the subject of disputes, for the one with Valentinus[45] and for the other with Marcion.[46] They strove for nothing more than to prove that their teaching corresponded exactly to the preaching of the apostles. What was more powerful or more sure than simply to quote this witness, which could by itself put an end to the whole dispute? There was surely no easier or better argument to convince both factions, the Marcionites as well as the Valentinians. For a record which had derived from a disciple of Peter would have been one of undoubted reliability. They would thereby have brought forward the faith of Peter, certified by sure testimony. Surely this would block every subtle way of escape for their enemies? Yet they use a more roundabout argument. They list all the bishops of Rome who had succeeded the apostles up to their own time—indeed among the others they even list Clement—and they bear witness that they teach what had been directly handed down to them by those bishops.[47] Why were inferences necessary in a matter that was so clear? Why do they remain silent about a book on which the whole point at issue turned? Furthermore, why do they not stir up enmity against their foes by naming names, since then everyone detested the name of Simon? So with this one word they could have armed themselves for battle and avoided a longer struggle: "Why, O Valentinus and Marcion, do you bring up Simon to us from the world § of the dead? We must not engage with you in dispute, we must deal with you by anathema. For it is not lawful to call in question a matter on which the apostle has once delivered the verdict."

There is in addition the fact that when Eusebius is speaking about Clement, he says that he left behind one epistle, but he does not venture to assert anything about a second, because he has not seen it (*Church History* 3).[48] Then he immediately adds: "But other works of

---

45. Valentinus founded the Gnostic sect bearing his name. He taught at Rome in the middle of the second century. Irenaeus wrote against him.

46. Marcion of Sinope, who taught at Rome in the middle of the second century, founded the sect that bears his name. He sought to purge the Christian faith of all Judaism, including the Old Testament. Tertullian wrote against him.

47. Irenaeus *Against Heresies* 3.3.1–3 (ANF 1:415–16) lists the bishops; Tertullian *The Prescription against Heretics* 32 (ANF 3:258) mentions Clement only.

48. Eusebius *History of the Church* 3.16 refers simply to the one epistle of Clement. In 3.38 he mentions a second epistle claimed to be by Clement (NPNF2 1:147, 169).

his are also said to be recognised by some, such as the dispute between Peter and Apion, which we find to have been put to very little use by early writers, because the teaching of the apostolic faith is discovered not to have remained pure and without corruption in them."[49] And—to put beyond any doubt how the matter stands—everyone well trained in the histories of those times who ponders it closely either recognises that the controversy between Peter and Simon Magus was fictional and legendary or leaves it undecided, as something doubtful and unknown. For Augustine too writes that in his time rumours were widespread about it which were considered by the Romans themselves to be false (*Letter* 36).[50] I wanted to recall these facts at some length and treat them rather fully, so that readers could decide how much weight is to be given to the proofs which, like fiery darts, Pighius a little later brandishes at us from that forged book of Clement. But suppose we grant that some book bearing this title was composed by Clement—what connection can there be between that and these feeble, or rather foolish, fictions which without ability or judgment were stitched together by an ignorant monk? What a token of Pighius's candour!

and Augustine

I come to the other heretics whose disciples he makes us out to be. Even though they differ somewhat from each other, yet there is a single error which is common to them all. I will therefore take hold of them together, as they say, in a single bundle,[51] and briefly recount what their teachings were and what ours are, so that from a comparison readers may judge what we have in common with them. And I will leave out that indescribable chaos of Valentinus's account of the genealogy of the aeons[52] because it contributes too little to our purpose—except for the fact that he imagines that from the thirtieth aeon was born the devil, who afterwards fathered others by whom the world was made. From that it follows that he ascribes evil not to [human] choice, but to the nature of the world, that is, to its devilish origin.[53] The madness of the Cerdonians, the Marcionites, and the Manichees is simpler, for they establish two opposite principles, as it were two gods, one good and the other evil. Evil things have their source and origin in the

2. Other heretics

---

49. Ibid., 3.38 (NPNF2 1:169–70), which Calvin quotes from the Latin version of Rufinus. Eusebius refers to works of Clement *containing* dialogues of Peter and Apion. For the question of which works these might be see NPNF2 1:170 n. 5.

50. *Letter* 36.9.21 (FoC 12:156).

51. Cf. Erasmus *Adages* 1.6.9 (CWE 32:9–10).

52. "Aeons" (here, not below) is in Greek script. Gnostics believed that under the supreme God there was a hierarchy of aeons and that the creator God of the Old Testament was an inferior aeon.

53. This account of Valentinus is found in Augustine *Heresies* 11. Most of it is not found in the early manuscripts, but only in the sixteenth-century editions of Augustine (including the Erasmian edition used by Calvin) (Müller 68–71; PL 42:28 n. 3).

latter, good things in the former.⁵⁴ The Manichees then go on to contrive further, still more ridiculous doctrines concerning the mixture of good and evil things, which I will refrain from mentioning.⁵⁵ The philosophy of the Priscillianists about the origin of human wickedness is a little different. For they do not suppose that souls are born from an evil [substance] by transmission but that, having been formed from the divine substance, they come down § from heaven and, meeting a prince of evil intent, the maker of the world, acquire pollution from this prince and are implanted in diverse bodies.⁵⁶ They all, however, agree, along with Montanus⁵⁷ and the others like them, in that they teach that man is evil not through the fall and his own fault, but through creation itself. They say that the corruption did not become accidentally attached to our nature but is part of its substance, and so the substance itself is evil and corrupt.⁵⁸ Therefore, lest they be compelled to make the good God the author of evil, they attribute the creation of man to the devil, the prince of darkness.⁵⁹

C's teaching as described by P:

Our own teaching I will relate in the words of none other than my opponent himself. For although there is nothing which he does not twist by false accusations, he could not prevent himself, in such an open debate, from giving evidence in our support.⁶⁰ [For he admits] that we do indeed say that man is to be considered from two points of view, first in that condition of innocence in which he was created, and second in that wretchedness into which he has fallen through his own fault. We hold that Adam was certainly created according to the image of God and adorned with remarkable gifts of righteousness, truth, and wis-

Man was created good

---

54. This account of the three heresies is composed of phrases found in Augustine *Heresies* 21–22, 46 (Müller 72–73, 84–87). The Cerdonians were the followers of the Syrian Gnostic Cerdo, who taught at Rome in the middle of the second century.

55. These doctrines are described in Augustine *Heresies* 46 (Müller 84–97).

56. This account of the Priscillianists is found in Augustine *Heresies* 70 (Müller 110–13). Priscillian, from whom they took their name, was a Spanish bishop who was accused of using magic arts and executed in 385, the first in Christian history to be put to death for heresy. Priscillian was accused of both Gnosticism and Manichaeism, but there is still uncertainty about how guilty he was.

57. Montanus was the founder of a movement ("the new prophecy") that began in Phrygia (in modern Turkey) in the second half of the second century, claiming a fresh outpouring of the Holy Spirit. He took asceticism to extremes that won him Calvin's disapproval (*Prefatory Address to King Francis* in the *Institutes* [LCC 20:21]; 1543 *Institutes* 4.12.23 [LCC 21:1250]; *Commentary* on 1 Tim. 4:3 [*Calvin's Commentaries: The Second Epistle of Paul the Apostle to the Corinthians and the Epistles to Timothy, Titus and Philemon* (Edinburgh & London: Oliver & Boyd, 1964), 238–39]). But he was not guilty of the charges here made against him, which are not found in Augustine's account of the Montanists (*Heresies* 26 [Müller 74–75]).

58. Note here, and in the paragraph after the next, the philosophical (Aristotelian) distinction between substance and accidents; see Introduction §6.

59. The doctrines described in the last three sentences are found in Augustine's account of the Manichees (*Heresies* 46 [Müller 96–97]).

60. The margin contains a reference to Pighius: "Book 1, last chapter." See BLW 1.247 n. 61.

dom, with the added assurance that not only he but all his descendants would live in this state if he continued in the innocence which he had received. But he did not long remain in it, and so, because of his ingratitude, he was stripped of those gifts and thus was deprived of that likeness to God and put on a new image. Being made subject to ignorance, weakness, unrighteousness, and vanity, and having sunk into such wretchedness he also involved his offspring in it.[61] Already I have it on Pighius's own admission that we ascribe the fact that man is evil not to nature nor to the origin of the first man, but only to his wrongdoing, by which he brought this wretchedness on himself. For we do not deny that man was created with free choice, endowed as he was with sound intelligence of mind and uprightness of will. We do declare that our choice is now held captive under bondage to sin, but how did this come about except by Adam's misuse of free choice when he had it? But why do I waste words on this, when Pighius's account of our teaching is more than sufficient to make our defence? For these are my words as he cites them there: "Therefore we recall that our fallenness is to be attributed to the corruption of our nature, lest an accusation be levelled against God, the creator of our nature. It is indeed true that that deadly wound persists in our nature, but it is of great importance whether it befell it due to some external cause or was innate from its beginning. It is agreed, however, that it was caused by sin, and so there is no reason for us to complain, except about our own selves. . . ."[62] *[but fell into bondage to sin]*

Will Pighius still make us out to be like Cerdo, Valentinus, and the Manichees? They imagined that man § was evil in substance and by creation. We, as it is appropriate to speak of God's most excellent work, say that he had been created upright, with a good and pure nature, but he became corrupt through his own fault when of his own accord he rebelled against God. What similarity, I ask, is there between substance and accident?[63] Between God's creation and corruption brought on himself by man? Augustine, when he is dealing with the Priscillianists, says that they err in that they declare that man is evil not through choice but through God's act of creation.[64] In condemning them he not only acquits us, but by that very verdict of his bestows approval on our teaching. Yet more, when against the Pelagians [Augustine] engages in a similar cause to that in which we are now occupied, that is, when he *[C's teaching far removed from heretics'* **264***]*

[Augustine faced the same charges]

---

61. Calvin quotes loosely from Pighius's quotation (9a–b) of a passage in *Inst.* 1.15.4; 2.1.5 (LCC 20:189–90, 246, as rewritten in 1559).

62. Almost exact quotation from *Inst.* 2.1.10 (LCC 20:254), quoted loosely by Pighius (9b–10a).

63. See n. 58.

64. This does not fit Augustine's (or Calvin's) account of the Priscillianists (see text at n. 56). The description used here is taken from Calvin's account of the Valentinians (see text at n. 53) and his more general comments (see text at n. 59).

is defending himself against the same false accusations, he speaks on his own behalf in such a way that his pleading also provides us with all the defence that we need. He does this in many places, both briefly and at greater length. So far as our own dispute is concerned, his main point amounts to this: Those who say that [human] nature must be healed differ greatly from the Manichees, because it could not be healed if the evil were eternal and unchangeable, as in Mani's dreams. Those who say that evil is accidental to our nature are greatly opposed to the Manichees, who assign it to its substance.[65] Those who teach that [human] choice is free only to do evil, but at the same time acknowledge that it originated from that which is not evil, are not at all close to the Manichees, but powerfully refute their error.[66] But which of those doctrines have we not always taught? If Augustine were alive today, and openly took up the case for our defence, he could not express more clearly what is needed to rebut the false accusation made by this heckler!

P says Luther worse than the heretics

But see how scrupulous[67] the man is! He thinks it not enough to make us the disciples of those [heretics], for he adds that we teach doctrines that are still more senseless and more blasphemous. The Manichees, he says, invented two ultimate causes, so that they would not have to attribute the doing of evil to God.[68] But Luther, by stating that in doing such [evil] things we are like saws pulled by [God's] power this way and that, wherever he wills, ascribes crimes and outrages to the one God, who is the most good and the most great.[69] Mani, following those earlier heretics, makes man have two natures, one good, the other evil. Of these the former cannot sin and the latter cannot do good.[70] But Luther claims that human free choice, indeed the whole of human nature, of necessity and without ceasing, even in the case of the saints, opposes the Spirit of God and like an untamable wild animal constantly fights against God's grace.[71] That the wicked are like saws in the hand of God which moves, turns, and directs them where he wills is not derived from Luther but from the Holy Spirit—if Pighius acknowledges that it was he who spoke through the prophets. For Isaiah says concerning Sennacherib: Shall the saw boast against him by whom it is pulled? (Isa. 10).[72] However, Luther always added this explanation: all

---

65. See n. 58.
66. The last three sentences are drawn from Augustine *Against Two Letters of the Pelagians* 3.9.25 (NPNF 5:415).
67. The Latin can mean either "scrupulous" (which would be ironical) or "disgraceful."
68. Pighius 17a; see Augustine *Heresies* 46 (Müller 84–85).
69. Pighius 17a; see n. 8.
70. Pighius 17a; see Augustine *Heresies* 46 (Müller 86–87, 96–97).
71. As at n. 8, Pighius (17a) uses his own words in accusing Luther, looking back to his lengthy quotation (7b–8b) from "Article 36" of Luther's *Defence* (WA 7:144–47).
72. Isa. 10:15.

the wicked are instruments of God in such a way that the doing of evil originates from them, remains in them, and is also to be imputed to them.[73]

Again, it is not on his own § authority that Luther condemns the whole of human nature as it is marred and corrupted after the fall, but he assents to the verdict of God, the most excellent and supreme Judge, against which no appeal is permitted.[74] For who was it who made these declarations? Every imagination of the heart of man is only evil from childhood.[75] The heart of man is wicked above all things and deceitful.[76] All have turned aside, together they have become unprofitable, there is none who does good, not even one.[77] The desire of the flesh is enmity against God. It is not subject to the law, nor even can be[78]—and countless others. Now let Pighius go and, with a single taunt, repeal so many and so great divine verdicts! As far as the saints are concerned, there is no doubt that what remains in them of their own nature resists the grace of the Holy Spirit. For Paul was not speaking falsely on account of humility when[79] he acknowledged that in him, that is, in his flesh, there dwelt no good thing, but it was with unfeigned groaning that he bemoaned his wretchedness.[80] There he declares his whole fleshly nature guilty of wickedness, and indeed he defines his flesh as whatever he has from himself. When, therefore, he complains that the remnants of his flesh resist the righteousness of God, how does he differ from Luther, except that he does not use so many words to say the same thing? Pighius says that he shudders at Luther's saying that in the saints too the fleshly nature, like an untamed beast, struggles against the Holy Spirit.[81] I leave Paul on one side now; what, I ask, do these words of Augustine mean? "Let no one flatter himself; of himself he is Satan. Let man take sin, which is his own, and leave righteousness with God" (*Homily on John* 49).[82] If this had been said by Luther, what an uproar Pighius would now be raising! Augustine is speaking about the saints:

265
Luther's teaching is scriptural

and Augustinian

---

73. Luther did not "always" thus explain himself; in particular, there is no such qualification in the relevant portion ("Article 36") of his *Defence* (WA 7:142–49). Nor does Luther normally thus qualify his use of Isa. 10:5–6, 15. In *The Bondage of the Will* he does safeguard this point (LCC 17:232–34, 246, 248).
74. Luther in "Article 36" of his *Defence* (WA 7:142–49) argues throughout from Scripture, using some of the same verses as does Calvin.
75. Gen. 6:5.
76. Jer. 17:9.
77. Ps. 14:3; 53:3; Rom. 3:12.
78. Rom. 8:7.
79. The first edition reads "but," which is in later editions rightly corrected to "when."
80. Rom. 7:18. The first edition wrongly includes a marginal reference to "Ps. 70," which the French translation rightly corrects to "Rom. 7."
81. See col. 264 (at n. 71).
82. *Sermons on John* 49.8 (on 11:8–10) (NPNF 7:273), which had been quoted with greater accuracy in *Inst.* 2.2.11 (LCC 20:269). It is quoted again in *BLW* 6.380 (at n. 56).

whatever they are or have naturally he declares to be sin, and not content with that he says that every one of them is of himself Satan.

Appeal to Scripture or Tradition?

P refuses even to hear Scripture

I know of course that I shall get nowhere with this crazy individual, who says that he will not believe any Scriptures which teach anything other than what he is already persuaded is true. Indeed he even boasts, in the height of arrogance, that if any such were brought forward he would say without hesitation that they originated from the devil, the source of all blasphemy.[83] What can you do with such madness? He has so intoxicated himself, or rather bewitched himself, with his own imaginings that he will not endure hearing anyone, either human beings or angels or God, contradicting him. For he spews out explicitly the following profanity: If any Scriptures affirmed the teaching of Luther, I would not hesitate to say that they had been dictated by Lucifer, the source of all blasphemy and contempt for religion. Again elsewhere: They are doctrines of such a kind that I do not hesitate to say that I will believe no gospel, no Scriptures, no apostles, nor even all the angels § from heaven, if they uttered them. Someone will say [to me]: Why then do you waste your efforts on someone so beyond hope of cure? Indeed I would not utter even a word for his sake. But I expend this effort for the sake of others who either are ready of their own accord to embrace the truth, or, though held in error, are yet curable, or at any rate do not have their minds so dulled that they cannot perceive what is being said.

This insults the Holy Spirit

But, it may be said, he does not think that he is in any way disparaging the sacred oracles of God, because it is not possible that they should be favourable either to Luther or to us. I, however, maintain that no explanation can be offered to cover the fact that those utterances provide a clear testimony, certified for posterity, that Pighius has displayed no more reverence towards the Holy Spirit speaking in the Scriptures and declaring the eternal decrees of God than he would to Plato[84] philosophising out of his own head. For who with even one spark, however small, of the fear of God left in his heart has dared to speak like this? It is true that Paul commands that an angel from heaven should be held accursed if it has brought another gospel.[85] Certainly, since angels too ought to be submissive and obedient to the word of God, they are rightly subject to a regimen according to which, if they do otherwise, they will be designated as demons. Although that cannot happen, the majesty of the gospel is of such worth that in its defence it is permissible

---

83. The margin contains a reference to Pighius: "Folio 18, page 2."
84. Plato (c. 427–347 B.C.).
85. Gal. 1:8.

in a way to abuse the name of the angels. But what precedent is there for imposing an anathema on God himself? That God speaks in the Holy Scriptures is doubted by no one among the devout.[86] What else, then, did Pighius mean by his statement but that if what are very certainly oracles of God took away free choice from man, he would say that they had been put forth by the devil? Would not anyone devout who heard this say that it is the bark of some Cerberus[87] rather than human speech?

Then, so as to rob us of the Scriptures themselves, [Pighius] uses the following argument: All the Fathers read them, and they were orthodox and saintly, but none of them [he says] deduced from them that everything happens to us by inevitable necessity. None of them said that impossible demands are made of us by God, or that people are condemned for those things which they do not with a free will but driven by the "necessity of fate."[88] None of them considered God to be the source and spring of all crimes and outrages.

P appeals to the Fathers

To this I reply, first, that the Fathers do not, any more than we do, place human life and affairs under the control of chance, but recognise divine providence and define it as the supreme and sole helmsman who presides over people's plans, inclines their wills, and governs events. They do not conceive of a providence whose movements are sudden and random, or one which is dependent upon secondary causes, or wavers uncertainly this way and that in response to events caused by chance, but one which moves unchanged on a course which is firm, steady, and constant.[89]

but they acknowledge God's providence

On the possibility or impossibility of keeping the law there is no reason for him to put us in contention with the Fathers. For when we affirm that it is impossible for man to keep the law, we have two things in mind: first, that the perfection which is there demanded of us far exceeds § our natural strength; and, secondly, that no one has ever existed who has rendered in full the righteousness demanded by the law. No such person will or indeed could exist. We are not saying by this that God could not bestow on someone such perfection of grace as would match the righteousness of the law. But since he has said that he will not do this, we say that it becomes in a straightforward sense impossi-

Impossibility of keeping the law:
1. Reformers

267

---

86. See n. 114.
87. Cerberus was the mythical dog of Hades, guarding the entrance to the lower world.
88. This is a phrase of Cicero *Nature of the Gods* 1.15.40; 1.20.55 (Loeb 42–43, 54–55); cf. at n. 14.
89. In *Retractations* 1.1.2 (FoC 60:6–7), Augustine qualifies his earlier references to fortune. (References to this work are given as in PL. In the English translation the two books are combined into one series of chapters.) In this work Augustine is not "retracting" his earlier works, but re-treating them—listing them, reviewing them, explaining how they should be understood, and, occasionally, revising his opinion.

ble.⁹⁰ Lest we seem to speak without authority, here we are following Paul, who, by the very argument that all are cursed who have not continued in all the commandments which are written in Scripture, proves that all who are under the law are subject to the curse.⁹¹ But that argument would not hold unless he took it for granted that no one could fulfil [the commandments]. For let us grant that someone could—what would become of the logic then? God curses all who do not fulfil his law; therefore all must be cursed, who ever have been, who are, and who will be. But Paul has a principle, albeit one unknown to Pighius, that what is declared by the Scriptures must be deemed inevitable. Therefore when Scripture makes all the saints guilty of transgression, he does not hesitate to deduce from that that there is no one who can exempt himself from guilt.

> 2. Paul

When the Fathers said that the observance of the law was possible, they did not in fact attribute this to the ability of free choice, but to the power of grace. For Jerome himself, whom Pighius quotes, explains it in this way *(Letter to Ctesiphon)*.⁹² Augustine does so even more clearly: "It is not in question whether man has been commanded to be without sin—for that is clearly so—but whether he can fulfil the command in this body, where the flesh lusts against the Spirit" *(The Perfection of Righteousness)*.⁹³ A little later he adds: "No one will attain to abundance of righteousness in the hereafter, who has not run his course by hungering and thirsting."⁹⁴ Here he speaks of the saints, who are now led by the Spirit of God into obedience to the law. But where he is dealing with [unregenerate] nature he agrees that it cannot even begin the law,⁹⁵ as we shall see elsewhere.⁹⁶ For we are not yet entering upon our real discussion of these matters, which is why I am only touching on them lightly, so as to reach the proper place for them more quickly.

> 3. Jerome
> 4. Augustine

However, the principle to which Pighius always and especially here calls us back, that we should seek our rule of faith not from the word of God, but from the tradition of the church, ought by no means to be accepted. Far be it [from us] indeed that the Christian faith should be supported by so weak and shaky a foundation! For what more is left in the power of the living God than to dead idols if his everlasting truth is

> Rule of faith is God's Word, not tradition

---

90. The argument of the paragraph to this point is drawn from *Inst.* 2.7.3–5 (LCC 20:351–54).
91. Gal. 3:10–12, quoted in *Inst.* 2.7.5 (LCC 20:353).
92. *Letter* 133.8 (NPNF2 6:277). The thrust of the letter is the rejection of the Pelagian idea that sinlessness is possible (NPNF2 6:272–80).
93. *The Perfection of Righteousness* 8.17 (NPNF 5:164).
94. Ibid.
95. *Against Two Letters of the Pelagians* 2.9.21; 2.10.23 (NPNF 5:400–401).
96. Especially *BLW* 4.346–47.

said to stand or fall by man-made decrees? And what will be the stability of faith, which ought to stand firm and unconquered against all the armaments of hell, if it should depend on the approval and decision of human beings?

But let us hear the fine arguments of the man by which he tries to cajole us.[97] § It was foretold, he says, that there would be sects and heresies; there would be those who would confess Christ with their lips and be teachers of error, ravening wolves concealed in sheep's clothing, who would seduce the unwary from the sheepfold of Christ, and teach Christ contrary to Christ, in the desert, in corners, and in coverts. He also names the weapons with which heretics attack the church, indeed with which Satan their leader and master attacked Christ, that is, texts of Scripture twisted against their true meaning. In the third place he gets down to the cure: the faithful must not let themselves be separated from the unity of the church.

P warns against false interpretations of Scripture **268**

I acknowledge that the church always has been, and to the end of the world always will be, subject to the evil of being severely troubled by enemies within. This was more than adequately proved by the experience of all previous times and is now experienced by us to our great trouble and most bitter anguish. Pighius gives good advice when he says that the more horrible and harmful a plague is, the more thought must be taken about a remedy. But the question is: what should it be? I am surprised that the man is so borne headlong by his own passion that he does not notice himself falling upon the true remedy at his first step. There is no doubt, he says, that heretics now attack the devout in just the same way that Satan once attacked Christ, namely by the false interpretation of Scripture. Who would not instantly draw the conclusion that we should resist them according to Christ's example? Why not? Or will the wicked be lined up under Satan's leadership to attack the faith and Christ not arm his followers to defend it? Now it is well known what shield, what sword, and what armour he used then to drive Satan back. "It is written," he said.[98] Since he emerges as the victor by relying on Scripture alone, the enemy overcome and subdued, surely, as though by raising a standard, [Christ] calls us to that same way and promises certain victory! But what does Pighius say against this? The heretics imitate the craftiness of their head, Satan, in that they administer their poison under a false pretence based on Scripture. The faithful must beware of an ambush; they must put on their shield and armour. Indeed, by taking refuge together with Christ in Scripture. Not at all, he says; there is no safety

Christ's remedy was Scripture

---

97. Pighius (20a–21b) argues from Scripture. Many of the passages are considered in cols. 268–74.
98. Matt. 4:4, 7, 10/Luke 4:4, 8, 12.

P says Scripture is unclear

there. They must go back to the tradition of the church as being their only refuge. Would he sink into such inept stupidity if he had even an ounce of sound understanding?

But the Scriptures, he says, are pulled this way and that according to the whim of the ungodly, so that without definition by the church there can be no sure meaning to which we can give our assent.[99] Of course that is the well-worn, commonplace taunt of the Lucianists[100] about the most holy word of God, that it is a waxen nose[101] which can be bent into any shape, as each person is inclined to invent one interpretation or another. Is that really so? So that there is no school of philosophy, however despised or worthless, which does not with certainty derive its founder's thoughts from his writings, while Christians alone, when the teaching of their master is sought, look elsewhere? So that in the school of Pythagoras that "he said" prevails,[102] while Christ does not have sufficient § honour among his disciples for them to listen in silence to his sacred oracles? So that Epicurus's[103] short, fragmentary, and obscure little pronouncements are understood by his followers, while God has not succeeded in making us know what he means by books which are so numerous, so extensive, so reliable, so clear? What moreover is the point of such a great heap of [biblical] books if we may not derive anything certain from there?

The Old Testament teaches otherwise

It is a very different testimony which God himself gives to his own word. Do not say in your heart, he says, Who shall ascend into heaven [to bring us the word]? or, Who shall go down to the abyss? or, Who shall cross over the sea? The word is near, in your mouth (Deut. 30).[104] Why does he call us back to a word over which we can only waver and vacillate? But he anticipates that objection when he bears witness that he has put it in our mouth and our heart, so that we may both perceive it with a sure faith and confess it with confidence. And at what point in time was this said? When the sun of righteousness[105] had not yet risen in its full brightness, but only the law had appeared, like a kind of dawn of faith. Moses also says in that same solemn speech: This is the way, walk in it.[106]

---

99. It is ironical that while Calvin argues for the impossibility of *obeying* God's Word, Pighius argues for the impossibility of *understanding* it.

100. See *BLW* 1.244 n. 47.

101. Pighius repeatedly made this claim (see P. Polman, *L'Elément historique dans la controverse religieuse du XVIe siècle* [Gembloux: J. Duculot, 1932], 286–87).

102. "He said" is in Greek; cf. Erasmus *Adages* 2.5.87 (CWE 33:279–80). Pythagoras (6th century B.C.) was a philosopher and mathematician.

103. Epicurus (c. 342–270 B.C.) was a famous philosopher.

104. Deut. 30:12–14.

105. Mal. 4:2.

106. Calvin is quoting Isa. 30:21. The passage in Deut. 30 of which he is thinking is probably v. 16 or vv. 19–20.

If when the quantity of light was so little, veiled by the darkness of the words and the shadows of figurative speech, God yet declared that there was no longer any excuse for ignorance or hesitation because he had handed down teaching that was sure, teaching that should both be received with sure confidence of heart and be proclaimed in a free and bold confession, if he testified through Moses that the way was clear and open—what depravity it is, at high noon, with the sun of righteousness clearly visible before [Pighius's] eyes, to brand the word of God with this dishonour, that it leaves the minds of the faithful no more than uncertain, confused, and anxious! Let us also hear another testimony of God. I did not speak in secret, he says, not in a corner of a land of darkness. I did not say in vain to the seed of Jacob, You shall seek me.[107] Or does God not speak to us today through the Scriptures? Or does he not do so more clearly than formerly to Israel? He says that he does not teach in vain. Therefore in his word we shall certainly find what he commands us to seek. If this were not so, what would this mean: "Hear me, and your soul shall live"?[108] This then is the peaceful and safe harbour, to fall back on the holy oracles of God—from which Pighius teaches us to flee as though they were a dangerous rock!

How much more now that we have the New Testament

But perhaps he will retort that God is not to be heard in Scripture alone but through the tradition of the church. Nonsense! For the Holy Spirit long ago removed any occasion for this mockery. For Isaiah, when he warned the people not to follow anyone besides the one God, at the same time also indicated the way. To the law, § he said, and to the testimony! (Isa. 8).[109] By what spirit then[110] does Pighius shout back that the law is equivocal and the testimony dark and uncertain? Malachi too, when he wants to strengthen the people in waiting for Christ until his coming and to arm them against all hindrances, sends them only to the law itself (Mal. 3).[111]

P says God is heard in tradition as well

270

It is according to the same principle that Peter says that we have a more secure prophetic message to which, until the morning star rises in our hearts, we ought to give heed as to a lamp burning in a dark place (2 Pet. 1).[112] But what immediately follows seems to be somewhat favourable to Pighius's opinion. For [Peter] warns that prophetic Scripture is not of private interpretation.[113] I myself take it in the same way that he explains it, that is, that it was not at the impulse of their own intentions but through the stirrings of the Holy Spirit that the prophets

2 Pet. 1:19–20

---

107. Isa. 45:19.
108. Isa. 55:3.
109. Isa. 8:20.
110. I.e., the spirit animating Pighius is not the Holy Spirit who inspired Isa. 8:20.
111. Mal. 4:4.
112. 2 Pet. 1:19.
113. 2 Pet. 1:20.

spoke. But where the noun "interpretation" stands it would be appropriate to say "movement," a meaning which is sometimes given to the Greek word which is used here, ἐπίλυσις. But let us grant that he himself is speaking about interpretation. What other meaning can you derive except that the Scriptures should in no way be stretched to suit each person's own interpretation? For the only proper interpreter of them is the Holy Spirit who dictated them.[114] What will Pighius say to this? Will he still continue to call the Scriptures a complicated labyrinth,[115] when Peter ascribes to them such clarity as can guide us surely, so that we do not go astray even in the deepest darkness of this world?[116]

Psalms

And so that you may see that the Holy Spirit declares concerning the law only what the faithful experience in themselves, hear what a description David applies to it[117] on the basis of a true experience of faith: Your word, he says, is a lamp to my feet, and a light to my paths.[118] Also: The testimony of the Lord is sure, giving wisdom to the young.[119] Of course he is saying only what ought to be a matter of intimate knowledge to all the devout. Readers should infer from this how well Pighius is practised in earnest understanding of Scripture, and indeed what taste he has for it at all. For when he says that it is a waxen nose[120] that can be bent in any direction, he denies that we can rest secure in it and therefore orders us to flee to the authority of the church, as if it were a holy place of security.

P's rule of faith is church's definition

But to settle the whole matter once and for all: because Pighius sees that it is of no advantage to him at all for this controversy to be ended on the basis of the word of God, he contends that Scripture, being vulnerable to the ungodly, wicked lies of the heretics and capable of being twisted to bear various meanings, is uncertain and obscure. Therefore he calls us straightaway back to the church's definition, which, not being subject to any accusations, is to be regarded as a true and certain rule of faith.

But this is contrary to Paul

271

I should like him now to answer me: what new form has the word of God put on since Paul affirmed that faith comes from the hearing of it?[121] § For by speaking in this way he makes it not only the true and certain rule of faith but the only rule. But when there is a struggle with

---

114. Here, as elsewhere, Calvin speaks of the Scriptures as being dictated by the Holy Spirit. While this indicates that he believed firmly that they are the Word of God, it does not stop him from holding strongly to the human authorship of Scripture.
115. See *BLW* 1.240 n. 34.
116. 2 Pet. 1:19.
117. The first edition mistakenly has "of faith," which all later editions correct to "to it."
118. Ps. 119:105.
119. Ps. 19:7.
120. See text at n. 101.
121. Rom. 10:17.

heretics, [Pighius] says, you cannot accomplish much with Scripture, which is easy for them to evade entirely. Again, let him answer me: what change has occurred since Paul called the word of God a spiritual sword by which Satan could be wholly overthrown?[122] If the sword is victorious and triumphant over the head of all heretics, how does it happen that against the members [of Satan's body] it is blunted and as it were [becomes] a weapon made of reed? And where will be that power of penetration which is elsewhere attributed to it, so that it reaches the division between soul and spirit, distinguishes between the thoughts of the heart and so on?[123] Let him further answer me, Is the following statement of permanent validity or only for a single age? All Scripture inspired by God is useful for teaching, for refutation, for correction, for instruction, so that the man of God may be complete.[124] Here also he will shake his head, as though the Holy Spirit did not foresee what subtlety heretics would exhibit in twisting and distorting the Scriptures. But whom will he persuade that he is wiser than God? If he even now continues to say that Scripture is inadequate to confute heretics, what remains but to dismiss him with an anathema as an avowed and obstinate enemy of the truth? Paul, in that passage, brings forward exactly what he had learned by his own experience. For when he disputed against the Jews, however unrelenting and obstinate they might be, he drew his weapons from no other source, if Luke reports truly (Acts 17).[125] Finally, where there has been much lengthy controversy, this is the touchstone[126] by whose standard all doctrines are to be tested. For the Holy Spirit praises the Thessalonians who, having received the word with all readiness, inquired from the Scriptures whether these things were so.[127] Surely either the use of Scripture as a standard to test doctrines is illegitimate, or a sure and clear definition of belief can be had from there.

Augustine puts it excellently: "When there is dispute over an obscure matter, and there is no help from sure and clear proofs in the divine Scriptures, human audacity must restrain itself, since it accomplishes nothing by turning in one direction or the other."[128] What room will there be for this opinion if God's truth does not have a solid and constant reliability in the Scriptures, which is invulnerable to any artillery? So afterwards he concludes by saying that he believes that nothing

and to Augustine

---

122. Eph. 6:17.
123. Heb. 4:12.
124. 2 Tim. 3:16–17.
125. Acts 17:2–3.
126. Literally "Lydian stone"; cf. Erasmus *Adages* 1.5.87 (CWE 31:459–60).
127. Acts 17:11.
128. *The Merits and Forgiveness of Sins* 2.36.59 (NPNF 5:68). In the *Prefatory Address* in the *Institutes* (LCC 20:21) Calvin alludes to this passage without naming Augustine.

which it is necessary to believe for salvation is without clear confirmation in the Scriptures.[129] Now let Pighius make fun of the lack of experience of that holy man, because not being accustomed to disputes he wrongly thought this to be so! Yet he wrote this when he was already an old man,[130] when, almost worn out by continuous struggles against various heresies throughout the course of his life, he knew well enough by experience how powerful the Scriptures are both for teaching and for contending. §

272
P appeals to Matt. 24:5

And what is certainly utterly laughable is that when [Pighius] wants—because the meanings of Scripture are uncertain and obscure—to drag us to the church's definition, he takes his axiom from the Scriptures. But axioms ought to be self-evident,[131] which demands the utmost clarity in them. It is written, he says, False prophets shall arise and shall lead astray many in my name.[132] What does "[to lead astray] in the name of Christ" mean? By false interpretation of Scripture [he says]. What if I said that it does not? For there is more than one way of deceiving in the name of Christ. But suppose it has this meaning. The next question is: what is "to lead astray"? To lead apart from the unity of the body [according to Pighius]. On the contrary, it is what Pighius says that is a going apart. For Christ uses the word πλανήσουσιν,[133]

but mishandles it

which means "deceive" and "beguile." But [Pighius] childishly plays the philosopher over the etymology of a word[134] which Christ never used! It is not surprising if Pighius finds the Scriptures so uncertain, when he plays and sports on them with such irreverent boldness. But it is a mark of his utter depravity that he is not at all ashamed so boldly to present, and even as an axiom, such empty and worthless fabrications of his own instead of the authentic meaning of Scripture.

Matt. 24:26

But let us continue with this fine exposition! He understands the wilderness, the corners, and the inner chambers[135] in the allegorical sense of new and extraordinary opinions foreign to the common mind of the body. But what if Christ himself speaks differently in Luke? The kingdom of God, he says, will not come with observation, nor shall they

---

129. *The Merits and Forgiveness of Sins* 2.36.59 (NPNF 5:68).
130. In A.D. 412, when he was fifty-eight.
131. "Self-evident" is in Greek. Calvin uses the Greek word because he is quoting a Greek philosophical principle. See Hero Alexandrini *Definitiones* 136.6, in *Opera quae supersunt omnia*, ed. J. L. Heiberg (Leipzig: Teubner, 1912), 4:112–13.
132. Matt. 24:5.
133. Ibid.
134. Pighius interprets "they shall lead astray" (*seducent* in the Vulgate of Matt. 24:5) as "they shall lead in separation from *(seorsum ducent)*, they lead away from that body of ecclesiastical unity . . ." (20b).
135. Matt. 24:26 has the wilderness and inner chambers. Pighius refers to two places: "in the desert" and "in the corners and inner chambers of the houses" (20b–21a). Calvin makes of these three separate places.

say, "Behold here!" or "Behold there!" For behold, the kingdom of God is within you.[136] It is the same incident which the two Evangelists are recounting, although in different words. Pighius fabricates an allegorical meaning in the words of Matthew. I say that there is no more faithful interpreter than Christ himself, who in Luke, without any symbols, shows that he means only that the kingdom of God is spiritual, and so is not to be tied down by fabricated observations. Meanwhile, he says, until I come for judgment, God will reign in you spiritually; he will reign in your consciences by means of righteousness, truth, peace, and courage of the Spirit, not according to the external splendour of the world. But when I come, I will appear suddenly like the lightning, contrary to the expectation of all. And just as the lightning comes forth from the east and is seen as far as the west, so in a single moment, in the twinkling of an eye, I will reveal myself, I will ascend the judgment seat, and I will summon the whole world to me.[137] There is therefore no reason why Pighius should search desperately for "inner chambers" and "coverts" in such clear and simple words as these.

But let us hear his subtle conclusion. Therefore, he says, Christ warns us not to go out. From where? From the body. And lest any pretend that they do not know where that body is, [Christ] quickly puts forward a clear and infallible sign: Where the body shall be, there will the eagles gather together.[138] What eagles are they? Surely those people who, as mentioned by the prophet, though they are burdened by the flesh, are carried high up by the wings of assisting grace.[139] Wherever those eagles gather together, have no doubt that there is the body to which you ought to adhere and conform. § Certainly if it is permitted to wield the Scriptures up and down like this, I do now concede to Pighius what he insists upon, that one must seek elsewhere a sure rule of faith. And he seems to me to have wanted deliberately to provide an example of what he was saying, that there is almost nothing in Scripture which the heretics in their wickedness will not corrupt.

Matt. 24:28

273

But I will prove, on the contrary, that the truth of God is not so open and vulnerable to their scoffing that it cannot be bravely defended against them. The clouds can overshadow the sun for a time, but they cannot extinguish or put out its blaze and prevent it from finally triumphing. [Pighius] takes the body in this passage[140] to refer to the church. But the Evangelist has πτῶμα, which to the Greeks signifies a

C's reply

---

136. Luke 17:20–21.
137. Matt. 24:27–31, with an echo of 1 Cor. 15:52.
138. Matt. 24:28.
139. Isa. 40:31.
140. Matt. 24:28 has πτῶμα (corpse); Luke 17:37, however, has σῶμα (body). The Latin Vulgate translates both verses identically, using the word *corpus* (body), the word which Pighius uses (21a–b).

corpse. The meaning of the parable is easy and obvious to anyone: just as a number of eagles are wont to fly to a single corpse, so all the elect, from every direction, go back to the one Christ. So Christ makes himself, rather than the agreement of men or their large numbers, the bond of unity. Now let my readers consider what a faithful interpreter Pighius is. Christ speaks about a corpse, to whom he compares himself, because he is responsible for the fact that his elect come together and assemble together with him. [Pighius] thinks of the body of the church. Christ names eagles, just as we in our common way of speaking would say crows. [Pighius] fabricates a piece of subtle reasoning to make ["eagles"] refer to the doctors of the church. The application of the parable is this: Where Christ will be, there all his elect from throughout the world will come together. [Pighius] interprets it in a quite different way: Where the eagles shall be, there we ought to gather together. If he thinks that by such empty fabrications the whole reliability of Scripture is not only overthrown but far removed from human minds and hearts, there is good reason why even the children should make fun of his foolishness.

P appeals to Gal. 1:8

He then shows how truly great the authority of church tradition is by citing the testimony of Paul when he pronounces an anathema against any, whether human beings or angels, who have dared to preach anything contrary to the gospel which he had once delivered to the Galatians.[141] [Pighius] argues that this was a tradition because [Paul] speaks not of writing but of word of mouth. I will speak briefly about this, without any hint of controversy, [an approach] which will be enough for all good people but will shut the mouths of the wicked. At the beginning the Lord gave the law, so that the people of Israel should have in it an expression of his will. Then there was added the teaching from the prophets, which was not different or new, but fuller and richer. Consequently before the prophets the law alone had unquestioned authority, so as to be received as the word of God. Afterwards, until the Christ should be revealed to the world, Scripture was contained in the law and the prophets. So we see that Moses and the prophets are quoted by Christ and the apostles, as it were as classical witnesses whose writings, just like public records, were recognised without dispute among the people of God. The apostles at first bore their witness by word of mouth, as they had been commanded. Then it seemed good to the Lord that the main points of their preaching § should be put into written form, so as to reach later generations uncorrupted. For what other reason was there why he wanted the law and the prophets to be committed to writing except to ensure that the sure

C replies: origin of Scripture

274

---

141. Gal. 1:8.

teaching which all ages should follow should survive for perpetual remembrance? For such is the tendency of human beings on the one hand to fickleness and inconstancy, and on the other to boldness and wilfulness in making innovations, that they would forthwith seek for a new form of religion if they were not held back, as if by some fences, by fixed boundaries of teaching. The Lord cries out: I am always the same, and I do not change.[142] But that would be of little benefit if people could not see his constancy in verbal form, as in a mirror,[143] so that as long as they remain constant by it they cleave to their God without any change.

Therefore the same process took place with the teaching of the apostles as earlier with the prophets. Of course not all their sermons were written out word for word, but the whole of their gospel was faithfully reduced to a summary which could be fully sufficient for us. Thus God formerly spoke in many places and in many ways through the prophets, and finally in his beloved Son in the last days.[144] Why are the "last days" said to begin with the revelation of Christ? Surely because God has spoken for the last time. Through whom? Through his Son. What did he speak? To learn that, Pighius sends us away to the tradition of the Fathers. I say that it is contained in the writings of the apostles, as John testifies that he writes so that those who read may have eternal life.[145] So we do not now have the gospel of Paul or anyone else as an individual, but we call it the gospel of the catholic church,[146] which after it had been reduced to written form God sealed as his word. As for the fact that Paul sometimes commends his own preaching or specifically that gospel which he himself had handed on,[147] he does this to distinguish the pure, genuine teaching of Christ from the counterfeit gospel of the false apostles. For they too claimed that they preached Christ, although in doing so they misused his name so as to corrupt the truth. Therefore it was necessary for the pure, uncorrupted gospel to be marked by some special sign, so that the faithful should not receive the lies of the false apostles as the word of Christ.

Apostolic gospel found in the New Testament

Did the Fathers Appeal to Scripture or Tradition?

But [Pighius says] Irenaeus, Tertullian, and Origen, when they were engaged in doctrinal controversy with the heretics, did not appeal to

P says Fathers appealed to tradition, not Scripture,

---

142. Mal. 3:6.
143. The mirror was a favourite analogy of Calvin's; see W. F. Keesecker, "John Calvin's Mirror," *Theology Today* 17 (1960): 288–89.
144. Heb. 1:1–2.
145. John 20:31.
146. See *BLW* 1.248 n. 71.
147. 1 Cor. 15:1, 3; Eph. 3:2–6. Paul can refer to "my gospel" (Rom. 2:16; 16:25; 2 Tim. 2:8) and to "our gospel" (2 Cor. 4:3; 1 Thess. 1:5; 2 Thess. 2:14).

the Scriptures but to the tradition of the church. Pighius behaves just as if he had their books buried at his house, so that he could not by [someone's] mere reading of them be found guilty of such a blatant lie.[148] I acknowledge of course both that [tradition] is brought forward openly by them, to establish their case by its authority, and that they make respectful references to it. But we must look first at the reason, then at the contemporary circumstances, and then also at the manner and the moderation which they employ.

275

Irenaeus had § to deal with the most outrageous heretics, who could be influenced no more by the authority of Scripture than by the agreement of the universal church. So he complains that nothing can be brought forward which they cannot evade. For they were not at all concerned to escape by crafty stratagems, but they would shamelessly repel whatever was thrown at them. If they were shown by the Scriptures to be wrong, they would say that they had a deeper and more complete wisdom than did the apostles. If they were called back to the consensus of the church, they would say that the church did not keep its doctrine pure, for [the church] had received it in a corrupted and "leavened" form not only from the disciples but from the Lord too.[149] What does Irenaeus say to this? "It is through the apostles alone," he says, "that we receive the account of our salvation; what they had declared by word of mouth they later handed on to us in writing to be the foundation and the pillar of our faith" (book 3).[150] Later he also presses this second point, that all the churches, taught and instructed by the apostles, nurture the unity of faith which is founded on the Scriptures.[151] But nevertheless he always holds on to the fact that Scripture is a school where wisdom complete and entire is taught.

Tertullian writes about the "prescription"[152] of the truth in opposition to the heretics for two reasons. He saw that there was no [other] way to prevent them from, in their impudence, continuing the dispute, though they might be defeated a hundred times. Also he considered that the greatest aid to the establishment of the truth would be agreement that it originated from the apostles themselves, while on the other hand it would be a strong and powerful stratagem for undermining the heretics' lies if they could be shown to be changing something in the teaching of the apostles.[153] But although in a just cause that

---

148. I.e., he behaves as if no one else were able to check the volumes.
149. *Against Heresies* 3.2.2 (ANF 1:415).
150. Ibid., 3.1.1 (ANF 1:414).
151. Ibid., 3.5.1 (ANF 1:417–18).
152. Tertullian *The Prescription against Heretics*. For the meaning of "prescription" see LCC 5:29–30.
153. For the first point, *The Prescription against Heretics* 15–19 (ANF 3:250–52); for the second point, 29–35 (ANF 3:256–60).

could be supported by other arguments the heat of controversy makes him proceed somewhat beyond the proper limits, his sole intention is to establish in the minds of the simple and weak the teaching which was assuredly propounded in the Scriptures; [he does so] by the additional token of the fact that the apostles had handed it on directly by word of mouth.[154]

[Tertullian] says that "no appeal should be made to the Scriptures, since on that ground victory is uncertain, or not certain enough."[155] But what does he himself do in so many writings? What weapons does he use against Marcion, Praxeas, Hermogenes, and the others, but the unadorned word of God? What then? Is he not fully consistent? But he had already quoted the passage of the apostle where he forbids further debate with a heretic after one or two warnings.[156] It is therefore not in doubt that he has this in mind when he says that arguments about the faith are not to be conducted on the basis of the Scriptures.[157] "There is no need for us to be curious after [knowing] Christ Jesus, or inquisitive after [believing] the gospel."[158] In sum, he wants only to place a limit on disputations which sharpen the heretics' dexterity, so that they are better prepared for battle, and increase their obstinacy, while weak consciences are disturbed § without any benefit.[159] But where circumstances demand it he shows, not by words alone but also by example, that it is only from the word of God itself that arguments and definitions about the faith are to be made.

but uses Scripture

276

The same method was followed by all the orthodox teachers when they defended the true, pure faith against heretics. Theodoret reports that when Constantine had gathered together the Council of Nicaea he addressed the bishops in these words: "We have the books of the apostles and the decrees of the prophets which teach us what we ought to think about sacred things. Therefore, putting aside unfriendly rivalry, let us seek the answer to the questions from the divinely inspired Scriptures."[160] Why did the Fathers not object, if this was not a legitimate course for the debate? Indeed why did they willingly accede to this de-

Constantine at Nicaea

---

154. Ibid., 20–21 (ANF 3:252–53).

155. Ibid., 19 (ANF 3:251–52).

156. Titus 3:10, cited in *The Prescription against Heretics* 16 (ANF 3:251; LCC 5:42). Tertullian, unlike Paul and Calvin, allows only *one* warning. The ANF translation, unlike LCC, brings Tertullian into line with Paul.

157. Ibid., 15–19, 37 (ANF 3:250–52, 261).

158. Ibid., 7 (ANF 3:246).

159. Ibid., 17–18 (ANF 3:251).

160. *The History of the Church* 1.6 (NPNF2 3:44). Calvin's Latin is closer to the text of Cassiodore's *Tripartite History* 2.5 (PL 69:925). Calvin made heavy use of this Latin mosaic of the three Greek church histories of Socrates, Sozomen, and Theodoret (R. J. Mooi, *Het kerk- en dogmahistorisch element in de werken van Johannes Calvijn* [Wageningen: H. Veenman, 1965], 292).

mand, as the records of the council bear witness?[161] In fact, it is natural to think that they would of their own accord have done what they were being told to do, in view of the fact that they had come already prepared and instructed by the Scriptures for this very thing. Why does Pighius not make mockery of their foolishness in that, leaving behind that sure rule of faith on which they could in safety have taken their stand, they allowed themselves to be abducted to that rambling labyrinth[162] of Scripture?

Augustine

Indeed why does he not lay a capital charge against Augustine, who refused to agree when the condition was laid down that he should use the writings of the earlier fathers to determine the very issue that is in dispute between us? For although he uses their statements and shows that they are not opposed to him, he does not allow the dispute to be settled on that basis, but appeals to Scripture. "The books of God are open; let us not look away from them. Scripture cries out; let us pay attention and listen."[163] In addition, speaking of his own book, [he says]: "So that it may be of the greatest benefit to you, do not be reluctant to read it again often. It will show you the identity and nature of the disputes for whose resolution and healing an authority then prevailed which is not human but divine. From that authority we may not depart if we wish to reach our goal."[164] Now Pighius has someone to contend with! When he has overcome him, he may come on to us!

Tradition has a role

but is to be tested by Scripture

However, I do not want what I am saying to be understood as though I leave no place for the agreement of the churches in determining questions about the faith. But it is proper that Scripture be accorded the honour of having everything tested by reference to it. Whatever is proved by its authority should not be questioned further; on the other hand, nothing should be accepted except what is in conformity with it. Whatever is divergent from it should be condemned, so that the whole body of definition of the faith may depend on it alone and be founded on it alone. When the agreement of the churches is added to this, it has no little importance for confirmation.[165] But great care must be taken lest it be separated from it. So a singular proof to seal the certainty of our faith is that we know that it is this very faith which all the saints throughout the world embraced in time past, and persevered in till death, for which so many of

---

161. *The History of the Church* 1.6 (NPNF2 3:44), where Theodoret goes on to note that most members of the council were won over by Constantine's arguments. Calvin makes the same point in the 1543 *Institutes* (4.8.16), where he appeals to Theodoret's account of the council fathers' consent (LCC 21:1165–66).
162. See *BLW* 1.240 n. 34.
163. *The Gift of Perseverance* 9.21 (NPNF 5:532–33).
164. *Rebuke and Grace* 1.1 (NPNF 5:472), referring to his *Grace and Free Choice*.
165. Calvin believed in church statements of faith such as the *Zurich Consensus* on the Lord's Supper, which he negotiated with Heinrich Bullinger.

them endured chains, exiles, banishments, stonings, and dishonour, and finally shed their blood. § But all this would be of little importance if the knowledge had not first been engraved in our hearts that [this faith] was founded on the word of God and not on human opinion.[166]

Accordingly Pighius is seriously in error when, in calling us away from Scripture on the pretext of ecclesiastical tradition, he makes a divorce of that perpetual union without which the teaching office of the church is not sufficiently well founded. He will say that he does not do this, because he gives Scripture second place. What this means, of course, is to give to the sacrosanct word of God its due glory in such a way that, since human judgments are assigned a secure place of honour, it must afterwards be twisted in any way possible so as to agree with them, so that it becomes subject to them. For is not this what he is explicitly saying? It is an essential first principle, he says, that the rule of orthodox belief be derived from the tradition of the church, because only that truth is to be believed which in no respect departs from it. Therefore it is from this in the first place and before all else that we shall begin, since it is not vulnerable to the stratagems, opposed interpretations, and accusations of the heretics in the way that the Scriptures are. Nonetheless, in the second place we will also show the judgment of the Scriptures. Behold the fellow's splendid theology: whatever human beings have determined must be certain and genuine, but as for the word of God we shall have to see afterwards! What if in the process a clear contradiction should reveal itself between human decrees and the oracles of God? For that very thing has been clearly shown by our people. How will the disagreement be resolved according to Pighius, who wants the word of God to remain in a subsidiary place, if not by his imposing silence upon it?

But to save us from wasting time battling over something unnecessary I should like readers to be warned that it would not be difficult for Pighius and me to reach agreement on this topic. Let him only demonstrate the church's tradition on the basis of the certain and lasting agreement of the saintly and orthodox, and not by quotations badly selected from here and there. Then let him use [the Fathers] straightforwardly and frankly to prove the true and authentic teaching of the church and not misuse them to decorate unholy teachings of this present time.[167] The church is the pillar and support of the truth, says

---

277

P makes Scripture subordinate to tradition

P's "tradition" is partial and selective

---

166. For the importance of the inner witness of the Holy Spirit to Scripture see *Institutes* 1.7 (LCC 20:74–81), some of which is from 1539. This is the ultimate basis for Christian confidence, but does not rule out other, secondary aids such as rational argument or, as here, the witness of the church (*Inst.* 1.8.1, 12–13 [LCC 20:81–82, 91–92]).

167. Calvin is here raising a hermeneutical issue: which passages should be used from which Fathers and how should they be interpreted? Calvin's accusations against Pighius are typical of the charges made by the Reformers against Roman Catholic appeals to the Fathers and vice versa; see the *Prefatory Address* to the *Institutes* (LCC 20:18).

Paul,[168] surely because God has entrusted his word to her so that it might be handed on by her ministry. That body is therefore to be considered a church which is a faithful guardian of the word of God, which by means of its ministry keeps it pure and uncontaminated by any leaven and passes it on to the next generation.[169] The individual churches claim for themselves a certain portion of this honour and responsibility, but they would not lay claim to have always possessed it throughout all their parts. In view of this, if Pighius wants to make up the common agreement of the church out of the private opinions of a few writers and affirm that this was derived from apostolic tradition, I will not accept it.

<small>Origen and Tertullian are unreliable</small>

He will say that Origen, Tertullian, and others like them refute my objection when they begin by saying that they will say nothing which is not the shared belief of the churches, which were instructed by the apostles themselves.[170] But what if what they do does not correspond to this opening statement? § Indeed, since it is agreed that in vital topics of the faith they do err greatly after such an introduction, how safe is it to take up without any distinction or selection whatever they hand down as the tradition of the church? And that is what I said, that individual statements are to be tested by reference to the word of God, from which it will become clear what is the genuine tradition of the church and what on the other hand is either inconsistent with it or does not belong to it. Otherwise those crazy ideas of Tertullian and Origen which we all equally reject will have to be accepted as [divine] oracles.

<small>278</small>

<small>Tradition more reliable in the time of Irenaeus and Tertullian</small>

But his other stratagem is much more improper still. For statements which had no bad sense as spoken by the holy fathers, provided only that they find a rational and honest interpreter, become, through Pighius's artful mixing, a cosmetic to make attractive and colourful wicked ideas which those very fathers would, if they were alive today, repudiate no less than we do. Irenaeus had seen the followers of the apostles.[171] He and Tertullian mention the small number of bishops who had been in succession to the apostles up to their time.[172] Many

---

168. 1 Tim. 3:15.
169. On the marks of a true church see *Inst.* 4.1.9 (LCC 21:1023–24).
170. Tertullian *The Prescription against Heretics* 20–21 (ANF 3:252–53); Origen *First Principles,* preface (ANF 4:239–41). But while Tertullian claimed to believe nothing *beyond* the apostolic tradition, Origen claimed only to teach nothing *contrary* to it.
171. Irenaeus as a boy had heard the teaching of Polycarp, who had himself known the apostle John and others who had seen Jesus (Irenaeus *Against Heresies* 3.3.4 [ANF 1:416]; idem, *Letter to Florinus,* preserved in Eusebius *The History of the Church* 5.20 [NPNF2 1:238–39]).
172. Irenaeus *Against Heresies* 3.3.3 (ANF 1:416) lists the bishops, without himself commenting on the smallness of the number; Tertullian *The Prescription against Heretics* 32 (ANF 3:258) mentions succession lists recorded by the apostolic churches, but does not himself give any lists or comment on their length.

old people were still alive then during whose lifetime the very words uttered by the apostles had been well known from the reports of their fathers. So it is not surprising if they put forward as apostolic tradition what at that time not only had been accepted in common by the first churches, but was considered fixed and unchangeable as the sure doctrine of the faith which Paul, Peter, and their other colleagues had only lately delivered to them. But even Origen, whose time was not much different from theirs, counts among the essentials of the faith certain opinions which, if Pighius does not anathematise them, will get him stoned by his own side too.[173]

So now, after so many and so great upheavals, after such undoing or rather collapse of the churches, to try with haughty disdain to sell as church tradition whatever has found its way in, by whatever chance, with no certainty about the occasion or the author—how much of a guarantee is there in that, I ask? But it may be said that Pighius quotes only those leaders of the church under whose guidance pure religion still flourished. But to what end, except to put whatever colour or mask he can on grossly wicked doctrines to which it never entered the minds of those holy men to give the slightest opening, so far from it being the case that[174] they would now want their writings to support such views? I urge readers merely to compare those ancient times with our own; then they will be able to judge how much sincerity or alternatively disgrace there is in his building his case on [the Fathers'] support.

P's appeal to tradition insincere

The Fathers and Free Choice

Let us hear, however, what evidence [Pighius] brings forward from those authors. His intention is to show that all of them, with a single voice, affirm free choice, and from this he afterwards draws two conclusions. [He deduces] that we are obvious heretics, since we dissent from the continuous consensus of the church, that is, the apostolic tradition. Secondly, [he claims] that I have lied shamelessly, since I have said, "All ecclesiastical writers § except Augustine have spoken so ambiguously or diversely on this matter that nothing certain can be derived from their writings."[175] But first he defines the force and meaning of the expression. He wants "choice" to be understood as "choosing" or more fittingly as "will," and, according to his definition, that is called "free" which is autonomous or its own master, without doubt in

P claims Fathers all affirm free choice

279

---

173. See col. 291.
174. The first two editions wrongly have "and" in place of "that."
175. Quotation from *Inst.* 2.2.9 (LCC 20:266), where Calvin is referring back to an earlier statement (2.2.4 [LCC 20:259]). Cols. 279–80 are of crucial importance for Calvin's view of free choice.

the sense of doing whatever it does in such a way that it does not do it of necessity, but is able not to do it.

<small>Different meanings of free choice</small>

Now as far as the term is concerned I still maintain what I declared in my *Institutes,* that I am not so excessively concerned about words as to want to start an argument for that cause, provided that a sound understanding of the reality is retained.[176] If freedom is opposed to coercion, I both acknowledge and consistently maintain that choice is free, and I hold anyone who thinks otherwise to be a heretic. If, I say, it were called free in the sense of not being coerced nor forcibly moved by an external impulse, but moving of its own accord, I have no objection. The reason I find this epithet[177] unsatisfactory is that people commonly think of something quite different when they hear or read it being applied to the human will. Since in fact they take it to imply ability and power, one cannot prevent from entering the minds of most people, as soon as the will is called free, the illusion that it therefore has both good and evil within its power, so that it can by its own strength choose either one of them. I am therefore not making an issue out of nothing or for the sake of a single phrase, but think that I have just cause to wish this phrase, against which almost the greater portion of humanity dashes itself at so great a risk, to be removed from common use.

<small>Scripture proclaims bondage of the will</small>

In any case, it does not even seem to agree very well with the usage of Scripture. For freedom and bondage are mutually contradictory, so that he who affirms the one denies the other. Accordingly, if the human will is in bondage, it cannot be said at the same time to be free, except improperly. Now let us hear what the Holy Spirit declares. I will be content with a single passage, since the argument is not about the thing itself, but only about what it is called. When Paul describes the state of the saints, he affirms that they are bound as prisoners with the chains of sin insofar as they have not yet been set free by the Spirit of God.[178] And when he speaks of man's nature, he says that he is sold under sin.[179] If the saints are in bondage to the extent that they are still left to themselves and their own nature, what is to be said of those in whom their nature alone flourishes and reigns? If after regeneration man has only half freedom, what has he in the time of his original carnal generation but total bondage? Paul had also said this very thing earlier. For in the sixth chapter he gives thanks to God that the Romans have been set free from sin, to which they were previously in bondage.[180] We see how before regeneration it is not the remnants of the flesh but the

---

176. *Inst.* 2.2.7–8 (LCC 20:264–66).
177. I.e., "free."
178. Rom. 7:23.
179. Rom. 7:14.
180. Rom. 6:17.

whole person which he yields up to bondage. Therefore anyone who claims that choice is free uses a different expression from that of the Holy Spirit.

And yet if there is agreement among the learned about its meaning, I will allow them to make § use of that word.[181] And I will not even impede its use before the general public, if that which is designated by it is clearly explained. Where this cannot be achieved, I now warn readers to pay attention to the thing itself rather than to its name. But since Pighius is always craftily confusing coercion with necessity, when it is of the greatest importance for the issue under discussion that the distinction between them be maintained and carefully remembered, it is appropriate to note how the following four [claims] differ from one another: namely that the will is free, bound, self-determined, or coerced. People generally understand a free will to be one which has it in its power to choose good or evil, and Pighius also defines it in this way. There can be no such thing as a coerced will, since the two ideas are contradictory. But our responsibility as teachers requires that we say what it means, so that it may be understood what coercion is. Therefore we describe [as coerced] the will which does not incline this way or that of its own accord or by an internal movement of decision, but is forcibly driven by an external impulse. We say that it is self-determined when of itself it directs itself in the direction in which it is led, when it is not taken by force or dragged unwillingly. A bound will, finally, is one which because of its corruptness is held captive under the authority of evil desires, so that it can choose nothing but evil, even if it does so of its own accord and gladly, without being driven by any external impulse.

According to these definitions we allow that man has choice and that it is self-determined, so that if he does anything evil, it should be imputed to him and to his own voluntary choosing. We do away with coercion and force, because this contradicts the nature of will and cannot coexist with it. We deny that choice is free, because through man's innate wickedness it is of necessity driven to what is evil and cannot seek anything but evil. And from this it is possible to deduce what a great difference there is between necessity and coercion. For we do not say that man is dragged unwillingly into sinning, but that because his will is corrupt he is held captive under the yoke of sin and therefore of necessity wills in an evil way. For where there is bondage, there is necessity. But it makes a great difference whether the bondage is voluntary or coerced. We locate the necessity to sin precisely in corruption of

"Free choice" all right if correctly understood
280

Coercion versus necessity

Will as free,

coerced,

self-determined,

or bound

C's position

---

181. Where the first edition and the French translation have "that," later editions clarify the meaning by adding "word."

the will, from which it follows that it is self-determined. Now you see how self-determination and necessity can be combined together, a fact which Pighius craftily tries to conceal when he thinks that man's freedom consists of acting (whether well or badly) without necessity.

Origen

But what does Origen say? He declares those to be heretics who take away free choice from man.[182] If he is talking about the original, natural state, he is telling us nothing that we ourselves do not also acknowledge. If he makes no distinction between a nature that is corrupted and one that is unspoiled, then everyone who is devout will declare that he is bringing basic principles[183] of the faith into confusion. "We are not," he says, "subject to necessity in such a way that in every respect we are coerced, even if we do not wish it, to act either § well or badly."[184] We for our part affirm nothing that is opposed to this opinion. On the contrary, this conclusion of Origen[185] is an indication that he seeks only to establish by the exclusion of coercion that there is a self-determined will in man. We do the same in a similar way. But I do not deny that elsewhere[186] he extols free choice more generously, though in such a way that he nowhere explains definitively how extensive it is. For all the passages which are quoted by Pighius[187] deal with the nature of the man who was formed by God; they are completely silent about what kind of man he began to be after his fall and rebellion. What then will you derive from this so as to get a full and clear resolution of the question that is now at issue? For we are considering man, not as God created him, but on the basis of that corruption which he obtained for himself by his own fault.[188] As I said, Origen does not touch on this aspect, although it is the more important one.

Pseudo-Clement

As for Clement I have already said enough about him above.[189] But in calling up such a one to be a leading advocate of his cause what is Pighius doing but wanting to frighten us off with the noise? Even if I were to pretend otherwise, I say the book itself cries out that it was stuffed full by some incompetent would-be philosopher. It is opinions

---

182. Origen's comments on Titus, as quoted by Pighius (23b–24a) from Pamphilus *Apology for Origen* 1 (PG 17:555).

183. A play on the title *First Principles*?

184. *First Principles*, preface 5 (ANF 4:240), as quoted by Pighius (22b), who has taken it from Pamphilus *Apology for Origen* 1 (PG 17:551).

185. I.e., the passage just quoted (at n. 184).

186. Calvin may be thinking of *First Principles* 3.1.5–6 (ANF 4:305–6), cited by Pighius (31a), this time from the original.

187. Pighius quotes (19a–b, 21b–24a, 31) from the passages given in nn. 182, 184, 186, and from *First Principles*, preface 2 (ANF 4:239), taken from Pamphilus *Apology for Origen* 1 (PG 17:549); *Commentary on Matthew* 10.11 (on 13:47–48) (ANF 10:419); *Commentary on Romans*, preface (PG 14:833).

188. The word "fault" is missing from the first edition.

189. See cols. 261–62.

plundered from there that [Pighius] pushes in front of us as though they came from the mouth of Peter himself. For my part my conscience, in the presence of God, will not allow me to take trouble over a reply, lest I provide him with an opportunity for error and cause him to put even the slightest value on that book.

When he wants to bring Tertullian forward, he begins by saying that his opinion about freedom of choice is so clear that anyone who cannot see it must certainly have closed his ears and eyes to the truth. But what in total do the texts which he brings forward[190] contain except that man as created by God was free and in control of himself? For he is there arguing against Marcion, whose idea about the nature of man was, because it was insulting to God, both wicked and irreligious. For he said openly that man was not evil through his own fault, but he traced back the cause of his being evil to God, who was the author of his being. I will leave it for sound and impartial readers to judge from this whether all Tertullian's responses in opposition to him do not likewise have reference to man's original condition. But I would not want anyone to take merely my word for it. Whoever reads the book itself or even the passage which Pighius quotes will find there what I am saying.

My response to all the testimonies from Irenaeus which he goes on to throw at me[191] is no different. Irenaeus is concerned there with the refutation of the ravings of Cerdo, Valentinus, Marcion, and others like them. When they invented a plurality of gods, they built up their error from the doctrine that man was evil. An evil being could not have been created by a good God. Therefore there is § also an evil god. You see the nature of the argument. Now that holy man, as the situation demanded, replies that man is not by nature evil, that is, by God's creation, but was made with free choice and received a soul that was capable of both good and evil. Since it is not in dispute that he is dealing with man's original condition at a time when he was still pure and possessed the image of God, why is this opposed to us, who locate the bondage of [human] choice only in a corruption and depravity of [our] nature? In one place Irenaeus says, among other things, "Wheat and chaff are produced naturally, but man is rational and as a result like God, since he was made free in his choice and in control of himself, and was responsible for his becoming now wheat and now chaff. Therefore he will justly be condemned, because having been made rational he lost true reason and by living irrationally he opposed the righteousness of God, delivering himself to an earthbound spirit and

Tertullian

was referring to man as created

Irenaeus

282

was dealing with unfallen human nature

---

190. Pighius quotes (26a–28a) much of Tertullian *Against Marcion* 2.5–10 (ANF 3:300–306).

191. Pighius quotes (29a–30b) from Irenaeus *Against Heresies* 4.4.3; 4.37.1–7 (ANF 1:466, 518–21).

being in bondage to all kinds of pleasure. As the prophet said: Man, when he was honoured, did not understand. He was made the equal of cattle and became like them."[192] This we say happened to all of us through the fall of our first father, and in this we have the whole church in agreement with us. In addition [Irenaeus] says that the freedom with which he is dealing is the image of God, in accordance with which Adam was created.[193] But Paul teaches that this needs to be restored from day to day in the faithful, and that not by their own power but by the power of the Holy Spirit.[194] It follows therefore that it has been erased and corrupted.

<small>Irenaeus was either ignorant of original sin</small>

<small>or referring to unfallen nature</small>

Now let Pighius choose whichever alternative he will. Either the inherited corruption which Adam passed on to his descendants was unknown to Irenaeus, or it was omitted by him because it was irrelevant to the refutation of the ravings of Cerdo and Valentinus, and his statements were made only about the pure state of creation. He must make one or the other of these two replies. But either way I am set free.[195] For not even Pighius will recommend that Irenaeus should be listened to if with the unanimous agreement of the church against him he makes no distinction between a corrupted and an unspoiled nature. But if he is describing only what man was like before the fall, that is of no concern to us, who derive the bondage of [human] choice not from God but from man's fault.

<small>Cyprian</small>

<small>affirms freedom of choice</small>

When he comes to Cyprian, [Pighius,] anticipating the objection that he nowhere deals with this question explicitly, cites a passage from Augustine[196] avowing that [Cyprian] does not deny freedom of choice. The meaning of the expression "freedom of choice" for Augustine will be the subject of clearer exposition by us elsewhere,[197] but it is also evident from this passage. For he says that Cyprian does not abolish freedom of choice when he ascribes entirely to God the fact that we live uprightly. He cites[198] that saying of Cyprian: "We should boast of nothing, because nothing at all is of ourselves."[199] How magnificently, do you see, he thinks of our own capacity, when he attributes everything good entirely to God, § while to us he leaves absolutely nothing!

283

---

192. *Against Heresies* 4.4.3 (ANF 1:466), quoting Ps. 49:12 according to the LXX (48:13).
193. Ibid., 4.4.3; 4.37.4 (ANF 1:466, 519).
194. 2 Cor. 3:18.
195. This is a standard argument which Calvin employs with patristic passages which might have a Pelagian interpretation.
196. Augustine *Against Two Letters of the Pelagians* 4.9.26 (NPNF 5:428).
197. Especially in *BLW* 3, e.g., cols. 302–3.
198. "He cites" is not found in the first edition, but is rightly supplied by all later editions.
199. Cyprian *Testimonies* 3.4 (ANF 5:533), which is quoted often by Augustine. The source in mind here is *Against Two Letters of the Pelagians* 4.9.25–26 (NPNF 5:428). This passage had already been quoted in *Inst.* 2.2.9 (LCC 20:266).

Where then is that freedom of man's choice which is ascribed to him by Cyprian? Surely in that he understood that man sinned or acted well of his own accord whenever by sinning he became the slave of Satan, under whose tyranny he was held captive, or was guided to live a good life by the Spirit of God, without any impulse from his own flesh. The issue here is not the words used, but the actual power of free choice. Besides Cyprian's opinion of it is shown not only by that noble sentiment so often praised by Augustine which we reported just now,[200] in which he declares that every kind of human merit is absolutely excluded, but also by another passage: "When we pray that we may not fall into temptation, we are (so long as we pray in such a way that no one exalts himself haughtily, that no one proudly and arrogantly claims something for himself, that no one draws glory for himself either from his confession or from his suffering) reminded of our helplessness and weakness. For the Lord said, Watch and pray etc., so that, so long as there is first a humble, meek confession and all the credit is given to the Lord, whatever is sought humbly with fear and respect towards God may be furnished by his kindness."[201] What does Cyprian here call arrogance? Not only claiming all the credit for oneself, but taking any at all.

and human bondage

I come to Hilary, whose first passage describes the nature of man without any mention of corruptness.[202] But I always have this defence open to me: either he did not mean to deny the depravity which is innate in man as a result of original sin, or if he did mean to deny it, he is in disagreement with the church's agreed teaching. Since his intention there was only to deprive men of any excuse, lest they cast the blame for their wrongdoing on God, it is not at all surprising if he calls them back to their first origins to make them learn thereby to level the accusation against themselves and their free choice, to which they ought to ascribe the fact that they are evil. But why not a single word about the downfall of human nature, or about its restoration through the grace of God? Let Hilary himself, I say, consider how he might justify his strategy. For me it is sufficient if I make it clear that he is not opposed to us in the way that Pighius pretends. There is no difficulty in the fact that he sets against the will not coercion or outside force but necessity, since by the word "necessity" he undoubtedly means not the wretched state to which man is delivered through his sin, but an external cause which compels what happens to happen.

Four passages of Hilary: the first

---

200. See text at n. 199.
201. Cyprian *The Lord's Prayer* 26 (on Matt. 6:13) (ANF 5:454), cited by Augustine *Against Two Letters of the Pelagians* 4.9.25 and *The Gift of Perseverance* 6.12 (NPNF 5:428, 530). Cyprian is quoting Matt. 26:41/Mark 14:38.
202. *Treatise on Psalms* 2.13–17 (on Ps. 2:5) (PL 9:269–70).

> the second

In the second passage[203] [Hilary] does not dispute what human choice can achieve if the grace of God is excluded, but he calls to mind that through the whole course of this present life man is given time and space to give thanks to God, an opportunity which is brought to an end by death. In his own words he expresses this somewhat differently, but it will be easy for anyone who wishes to determine that this is their meaning.

> the third

In the third passage[204] [Hilary] does not ascribe as much importance as is fitting to the grace of God, and he assigns to man what God claims as his own, namely to turn the heart to obedience to the law. He himself

> 284
> the fourth

states the reason which drove him both here and in § the next passage[205] to share the praise for good works between God and man. He was concerned to refute the wicked teaching of those who sought in the frailty of the flesh the resources and opportunity to excuse themselves. Since he could not extricate himself in any other way, he took refuge in the reply that God's grace works in us in such a way that at the same time it leaves some contribution for us to make; and if one fails in this, then [Hilary] says that it is purely by one's own idleness and neglect that he sins.

> C's claim in *Institutes*

And that is exactly what I put in print in my *Institutes:* "The ancient [fathers] seem to me to have deliberately exalted human powers more than was right [for two reasons]. First, to avoid arousing by an explicit acknowledgment of [human] impotence the laughter of the very philosophers with whom they were in controversy. Secondly, so as not to give a fresh opportunity for laziness to the flesh, which was of itself excessively reluctant to do good."[206] Then immediately afterwards I add: "Therefore, so as not to teach something absurd in the general opinion of mankind, they were anxious to half-reconcile the teaching of Scripture with the doctrines of philosophy. But that they particularly aimed not to provide room for laziness is clear from their words."[207] If I had not then acknowledged this explicitly and with straightforward integrity of mind, Pighius would now rightly be attacking me. But as it is, what justification is there for his lashing me so brutally with a succession of pages as though I lied about the ancients, when nevertheless he brings against me nothing which is not in agreement with what I have said?

> Hilary

He puts forward the fact that Hilary ascribes to the power of free choice a contribution of its own [in partnership] with the grace of

---

203. Ibid., 51.23 (on Ps. 52:8–9 [51:10–11 in the Vulgate]) (PL 9:323).
204. Ibid., 118.14.20 (on Ps. 119:111–12 [118:111–12 in the Vulgate]) (PL 9:598–99).
205. Ibid., 118.5.11–12 (on Ps. 119:36 [118:36 in the Vulgate]) (PL 9:538–39).
206. *Inst.* 2.2.4 (LCC 20:259).
207. Ibid.

God.[208] I reply that I admitted this already in my *Institutes*.[209] The words which he quotes show that Hilary's intention was the same as I there expounded it. And yet he continually cries out shamelessly that I am lying. I said that the ancient [fathers] spoke too obscurely or with too much disagreement for their opinion to be deducible with certainty,[210] to which [he responds that] these passages are quite lacking in either obscurity or disagreement. I reply, in accordance with the facts, that Hilary did indeed ascribe some power to free choice, since he would have been prevented from removing objections if he had acknowledged that it is absolutely without power. But he did so without any clear definition which would make it possible to know how much is in man's control. I have certainly never denied that the ancients frequently extol free choice and ascribe to it more than is proper. But I gave a warning[211] which I repeat now, that their teachings are either so divergent or so inconsistent or so obscurely expressed that almost nothing certain may be stated on their authority.

and C's claim

From Basil he quotes two passages, of which the former[212] contains nothing but a description of human nature as it was created by God, a description designed to prevent people from passing on to God the blame for the evils they commit. At the beginning therefore he says that sin was not inherent in man's substance, but befell him through his own fault,[213] something which we not only acknowledge but carefully safeguard. Later he says: "Virtue is voluntary and not of necessity, and free choice is present in us."[214] Here Pighius § is exultant, as though he has secured a victory. But I say that these words are not to be understood of our present condition, but show only the nature of man at the time of his creation and first origin. [Basil] explicitly explains what man was like at creation; he does not mention the corruption which followed his fall. When he does want to state the cause of his being evil, he speaks only as follows: "Why is man evil? As a result of his own will. Why is the devil evil? For the same reason. For he too has in himself a free existence and free choice placed in his

Basil's first passage refers to human nature as created

285

---

208. *Treatise on Psalms* 118.14.20 (on Ps. 119:111) (PL 9:598–99); cf. n. 204.
209. See nn. 206–7.
210. See at n. 175.
211. See at n. 175; for further clarification see cols. 291–92.
212. *Homily* 9.6–7 (PG 31:343–46). Pighius (33a) was using the Latin translation by Raphael Maffei Volaterranus, which appeared in five editions of Basil's *Opera* between 1515 and 1531 (IA 114.428, 440, 448–49, 486; I. Backus, *Lectures humanistes de Basile de Césarée* [Paris, 1990], 15–27).
213. Basil says this in the passage quoted by Pighius (n. 212) and also, in words similar to Calvin's, shortly beforehand (*Homily* 9.5 [PG 31:341–42]). Note the Aristotelian contrast between substance and accidents ("befell" = *accidisse*); see n. 58.
214. *Homily* 9.7 (PG 31:345–46). This is part of the passage which Pighius cites (33a) (n. 212).

power, either to remain with God or to become estranged from him."²¹⁵

Basil elsewhere on bondage

How should we judge [Basil] in the light of this? Did he not notice what a great wound was inflicted on our nature by sin? But it must be said that he elsewhere absolves himself from such suspicion when he touches on the wretchedness of the human race in these words, which may be brief but are not at all ambiguous: "It is salvation that is needed by the weak and deliverance by those who are held in captivity. He therefore who is placed under the power of death, and knows that there is one who delivers and one who saves, says, In you have I hoped. Save me from weakness, deliver me from captivity."²¹⁶ When someone makes man weak and a captive and indeed declares him to be held in a kind of bondage from which he can be delivered only by God and not by himself, how greatly he diminishes that first [unfallen] condition!

and limitations of free choice

But [replies Pighius] in this state of captivity too [Basil] leaves much to free choice. Let us hear how much that is. "Those who are not schooled in the word of God believe in vain presumption that they can remove the assaults of sin through free choice, when sin can be removed only by the mystery of the cross. For the free choice which is placed in man's power lies in choosing or not choosing to resist the devil, not in the ability to remain strong against the passions."²¹⁷ And a little later: "For unless we have been delivered by a more powerful helper from the fiery darts of the adversary and received into adoption, all our efforts are in vain, as being far from the power of the cross."²¹⁸ If you carefully evaluate all this, he leaves in man's power only the judgment in choosing, which is both utterly ineffective and powerless by itself to overcome the passions. Even though he does not say here all that he should have said, it is nevertheless possible to see how far he withdraws from that splendid description of freedom.

Basil's second passage

In the second passage²¹⁹ I notice nothing which is even slightly opposed to our position. He teaches that the rational part of the soul is

---

215. *Homily* 9.8 (PG 31:345–46), shortly after the passage quoted by Pighius (33a) (n. 212). Calvin's quotation follows the translation by Janus Cornarius, found on p. 181 of the edition of the *Opera omnia* published in 1540 by Froben at Basel (IA 114.485). On this edition see Backus, *Lectures humanistes*, 43–48, 232–38.

216. *Homilies on Psalms* 2.2 (on Ps. 7:1–2 [7:2–3 in the Vulgate]) (PG 29:231–32), found on p. 68 of the Froben edition.

217. Pseudo-Basil *Sermon on Free Choice*, found on p. 383 of the Froben edition. This is today known as Pseudo-Macarius *Spiritual Homilies* 25.1 (*Fifty Spiritual Homilies of St. Macarius the Egyptian*, ed. A. J. Mason [London: S.P.C.K. & New York: Macmillan, 1921], 178).

218. Pseudo-Basil *Sermon on Free Choice* = Pseudo-Macarius *Spiritual Homilies* 25.2 (Mason, 179).

219. Pighius's quotation comes in a section which is a paraphrase of Basil's *Ascetic Constitutions* 4 (PG 31:1345–60), translated by Raphael Maffei Volaterranus and found in each of the editions mentioned in n. 212. On the inadequacies of the translation at this point see Backus, *Lectures humanistes*, 21, 23–24.

within our control. But to say no more myself, it is evident enough that there it is the nature of the soul in its pure state that is under consideration, as is usual when definitions are being given. We also, when we debate about the soul, first define clearly its parts, the mind and the will, and we teach that it is the function of the mind to go before the will and to guide it—hence its name ἡγεμονικόν. Then we go on to say that the will is in a good condition when it does not expose itself to be dragged this way and that by the passions, but attends to the rule of the mind. Finally § [we teach] that the whole person is properly constituted when right reason rules in him, which both guides the will in the appropriate direction and restrains the sensual passions by its reins as a charioteer does to a team of wild horses.[220] But at the same time we show that our reason is blind, because through sin it has been deprived of the light of God and cannot rule well until it has handed itself over to the Spirit of God to obey him, or rather has actually been subjected, like a handmaid, to his service.[221] Similarly we say that the desires of the flesh have seized dominion in man and cannot be prevented or repressed by any power in the soul from exercising their tyrannical rule. For the will is so overwhelmed by wickedness and so pervaded by vice and corruption that it cannot in any way escape to honourable exertion or devote itself to righteousness.[222]

As for the statements of Jerome which [Pighius] adduces,[223] I do not deny that free choice is affirmed in all of them. However, I would like to know what certain conclusion he wants to derive from them. We have been endowed with free choice, he says, and each one of us lives not according to divine command or authority, but by our own consent.[224] But what if, on the other hand, I qualify this by saying (which is true) that that freedom was wounded, nay done for and extinguished, when man by the binding act of sin yielded himself to bondage to Satan? Or can I reach a certain conclusion about [his] opinion on the matter as a whole, since he does not touch on its principal aspect? I say that no clear and solid teaching about free choice is transmitted by all those who do not at the same time add [the following]: what loss this liberty suffered through the fall of Adam; what the faithful recover through

compared with C's teaching

286

Jerome

---

220. See *Institutes* 1.15.7–8 (LCC 20:194–96), part of which is from 1539.
221. See *Inst.* 2.2.12–16, 18–20, 22–25 (LCC 20:271–75, 277–79, 281–85).
222. See *Inst.* 2.2.26–2.3.5 (LCC 20:286–96).
223. Pighius here (33b–34b) quotes Jerome *Letters* 21.5–6 (ACW 33:113–14), 120.10 (PL 22:999), and *Questions on the Hebrew of Genesis* 4.6–7 (PL 23:993). He also claims to quote from *Commentary on Matthew* 1.5, but the quotation, which is cited by Calvin in *BLW* 3.299 (at n. 71), actually comes from *Against Jovinian* 2.3 (NPNF2 6:389). Pighius probably derived the quotation from Augustine *Nature and Grace* 65.78 (NPNF 5:149) and incorrectly copied down the source of another quotation that appears there.
224. In this sentence Calvin is quoting not Jerome, but Pighius's summary of or "conclusion" (34a) from *Letter* 21.5–6 (ACW 33:113–14), which comes in his comments after the quotation.

the grace of regeneration; how great, moreover, is the perversity of the nature that has been corrupted and its rebellion against the righteousness of God; on the other hand, what is the operation of the Holy Spirit in the elect, both to enlighten the mind and to guide the heart. On all these matters there is a deep silence in Jerome's works.[225]

Ambrose: voluntary slaves

Regarding Ambrose, [Pighius] either should not have brought him in at all, or should have introduced him speaking in different terms. For what does he bring forward? "The devil buys a voluntary slave; he holds no one bound by the yoke of slavery, unless one has first sold himself to him for the price of his sins. Why do you accuse the flesh as being weak? Desire is the source of the fault; the flesh is the handmaid of the will. Therefore let not our will sell us off, for it is through it alone that we are delivered into slavery."[226] Of course he is answering the empty subterfuge of those who blame whatever sins they commit on the weakness of the flesh. But he immediately explains what he means by the word "flesh," when he calls it the "handmaid of the will."[227] It is therefore the inferior and, as they call it, the sensual part of man, which, with the bodily organs, is signified by "flesh." Now, one who diverts the blame for his evildoing to [the flesh] is deservedly brought back to the will, so that once he has been convinced that the root of evil is fixed there, he may learn that it is to himself alone that he ought to ascribe the blame. If Pighius can deduce from this what the capability of free choice is and the extent of its power in itself, he will be an exceedingly clever arguer! §

287

But [he says] everyone understands that [we use the word] "voluntary" whenever whether something should happen or not happen is in our control and is not subject to necessity. But of the different understanding which Ambrose himself has I will seek proof no further away than on that very page[228] from which Pighius took what he quotes. For when he is dealing with the use of the law, he uses these words, among others: "There came a chain, not release; there was added the recognition of sins, not their forgiveness. But it was for my good. I began to acknowledge what I used to deny" etc.[229] Again: "That too is of benefit to me, namely that we are not justified on the basis of the works of the law. For I have nothing of which I can glory in my works, I have nothing of which to boast, and therefore I will glory in Christ."[230] Would

---

225. For a revision of this unfair generalisation see col. 291 (at n. 265).
226. Pighius quotes (34b–35a) from Ambrose *Jacob and the Happy Life* 1.3.9–11 (FoC 65:124–27); Calvin reproduces part of this (1.3.10–11 [FoC 65:125–26]). In the second half of the last sentence Calvin is quoting Pighius's summary of Ambrose (35a). There is a briefer mention of the passage in *BLW* 6.395–96 (at n. 167).
227. The last sentence but one of Calvin's previous quotation (n. 226).
228. Regarding the edition used by Calvin see Introduction §5.
229. *Jacob and the Happy Life* 1.6.20–21 (FoC 65:132–33).
230. Ibid., 1.6.21 (FoC 65:133).

these words be valid if man when left to himself were not in subjection to the necessity to sin?

Here too Augustine comes to my aid in that by bringing forward three quotations he proves that nothing was further from Ambrose's mind than what Pighius falsely ascribes to him. First, when in his book *Flight from the World* he urges us to seek the help of God, he openly confirms that our heart and our thoughts are not under our control.[231] Secondly, he comments like this on Luke: "What is good is not discerned by human will alone, but as it is granted by Christ, who brings it about that what is good also seems to us to be good. For him on whom he has mercy he also calls. Therefore when someone says that he wanted to have faith, he does not deny that God wanted [him to have] it. For the will is prepared by God.[232] For [faith] is God's gracious gift, so that he may be honoured by the saints."[233] Thirdly, "Him whom God deems worthy he calls, and whom he wills he makes godly."[234] From these words Augustine does not hesitate to deduce that Ambrose ascribes to God alone both the beginning and the continuance not only of faith but of good works, not only of thoughts but of good desires, and takes them away from human beings.[235] If anyone does not take my word for this, let him read his book *The Gift of Perseverance*.

Augustine on Ambrose

When quoting Chrysostom, to save himself much sweat, [Pighius] simply copies out a passage which I brought forward, where (to shut off from sinners all pretence at an excuse) he lays down that good and evil lie within human control; therefore nothing prevents them [from doing good], except that they are unwilling, for they can do it if they so will.[236] That the cause of evil is to be sought nowhere else but in man's own will,

Chrysostom

---

231. Ambrose *Flight from the World* 1.1 (FoC 65:281), which is quoted five times by Augustine (FoC 65:281 nn. 1, 3). In *The Gift of Perseverance* 19.48–49 (NPNF 5:545–46) Augustine quotes not only this passage, but also the two quotations from Ambrose that follow (at nn. 233–34). Augustine does not there give the source of this quotation, but it is found earlier in the same work where there is a longer quotation (ibid., 8.20 [NPNF 5:532]).

232. Prov. 8:35 according to the LXX. This was a favourite verse of Augustine's, which he cited fifty-three times in all and which he came to know through this passage of Ambrose (A. Sage, "Praeparatur voluntas a Domino," *Revue des études augustiniennes* 10 [1964]: 1–20). The many comments in the Augustine quotations below about the will's being prepared by the Lord are all allusions to this verse.

233. Ambrose *Commentary on Luke* 1.10 (PL 15:1538), quoted in Augustine *The Gift of Perseverance* 19.49 (NPNF 5:546).

234. Ambrose *Commentary on Luke* 7.27 (PL 15:1706), quoted in Augustine *The Gift of Perseverance* 19.49 (NPNF 5:546).

235. Augustine *The Gift of Perseverance* 19.48–50 (NPNF 5:545–46).

236. This is a summary of Pighius's quotation (35a) of Chrysostom *Homily on Genesis* 19.1 (on Gen. 4:8) (FoC 74:21). Calvin had quoted from this passage, much more briefly, in *Inst.* 2.2.4 (LCC 20:259). Thus Calvin can justly charge Pighius with looking no further than a source that he himself had brought forward in 1539, but not with "simply copying it out" from the *Institutes*.

lest by removing the blame elsewhere he should want to discharge himself from it, is an opinion with which I have more than once indicated myself to be in agreement.[237] Indeed this is one of the main principles on which I insist in my *Institutes*. But I made no secret there of what I thought of the fact that Chrysostom so exalts the power of free choice.[238]

Conclusion

P claims consensus of Fathers

288

After heaping up all these quotations, as though the matter were now finished, Pighius at length deduces what he had put forward from the beginning. That is, that the view which we advocate about the bondage of human choice is condemned by the unified agreement of all the devout who have ever lived, and that the falsity of my claim has been clearly shown up, when I said that the ancients spoke about this matter either so obscurely or so differently that almost nothing certain may be gathered § from their writings.[239] I would like readers to forgive me if in replying to him I do not put on those exotic stage clothes in which our adversary assaults us. For I have decided to contend with him not in grandeur of speech but in truth, which, being simple, is content with a simple style of speaking.

True consensus is in agreement with God's Word

First of all, therefore, when he flings at us the consensus of the church, let him have this single sentence as his reply: the only consensus of the church is that which is throughout suitably and fittingly in agreement with the word of God.[240] Moreover, one should not, to fit human judgments, twist what the Holy Spirit, who is certainly the best practitioner of speaking, has without doubt dictated[241] to the prophets and the apostles. He did this for the very purpose that on this basis all teachings, both of human beings and of angels, should be evaluated. Whenever, therefore, [Pighius] sings that old song at me about the consensus of the universal church, I will at once object that it is wrong that things which God has joined by a perpetual bond should be separated. And I will cast back at him, with an improved interpretation and in a more suitable place, that proverb of Christ's: Where the corpse is, there are the eagles.[242] For if the opinions of the faithful are to be considered as the unchanging consensus of the church, it is necessary for them first, like eagles by a corpse, to congregate around the truth of Christ and as it were be united with it.

---

237. E.g., *Inst.* 2.1.10–11; 2.3.5; 2.5.1–2 (LCC 20:253–55, 294–96, 316–18).
238. *Inst.* 2.2.4 (LCC 20:259–60).
239. See text at n. 175.
240. Calvin's respect for the Fathers was great, but subject to the final authority of Scripture. See Introduction §5.
241. See n. 114.
242. See cols. 272–73 (at nn. 138, 140).

Nor in addition will I yield to him what he takes to be generally acknowledged, that what they have put out in six or eight writings is to be immediately accepted as the sure and fixed consensus of the church. Nor indeed do those statements themselves encourage me to yield it. But, it might be objected, would they dare to lie about a matter that was well known and commonplace among all their contemporaries? And if no trust is placed in them, what will be left of the testimony of antiquity? I of course am not implying that they were lying, nor do I so entirely discount what they testify about the common teaching of the church that I think it valueless, as though it had not been spoken. I say only that it is not sufficient for complete and sure certainty. For it ought not to seem absurd if I say that what was then commonly accepted in the churches they relate in such a way that they add something fashioned by their own minds, either because they were prevented from doing otherwise by having already formed their opinion or because sometimes they were deprived of their natural clear manner of speaking. For where did Irenaeus, Tertullian, and Hilary get that harsh, rough manner of speech, unless from an impediment which prevented them from saying what they wanted to say? Everyone knows that it makes a great deal of difference what words are used to express each particular thought.

Pighius's quotations are no consensus

Moreover, let Pighius answer me this question: should greater trust be placed in a private individual, as evidence of the consensus of the church, than in many people gathered together in a council who declare in the name of the church and as though from its mouth what they have considered together? But now I turn to the question at issue. Pighius cites the following words from Hilary: "Our will has of itself a natural capacity to will, but once it begins to do so God gives an increase, and the merit of what is added derives from the will's § initiative."[243] Now I will bring forward on the other side a decree of the Council of Orange: "If anyone argues that God waits for our desire that we should be cleansed from sin, and does not acknowledge that it is by the work of the Holy Spirit in us that we are even caused to want cleansing, he resists the Holy Spirit as he speaks through Solomon: The will is prepared by the Lord" (ch. 4).[244] Hilary divides the credit between the human will and the grace of God, in that he ascribes the initiative to the former and says that it is helped afterwards by the grace of God;[245] the council declares to be enemies of the Holy Spirit those who think or speak

Hilary versus Council of Orange

1. Third passage

289

---

243. *Treatise on Psalms* 118.14.20 (on Ps. 119:111 [118:111 in the Vulgate]) (PL 9:598–99); cf. nn. 204, 208.

244. Council of Orange (529), canon 4 (Leith 38), citing Prov. 8:35; see n. 232. This is also quoted in *BLW* 3.305 (at n. 116); 3.319 (at n. 252); and 5.363 (at n. 104).

245. See text at n. 243.

so.²⁴⁶ Where is that very certain [ecclesiastical] definition now, which Pighius flaunts with every other word?

2. Fourth passage

In a second passage of Hilary there is the following statement: "When we pray, therefore, the beginning is made by us, so that a gift may come to us from God."²⁴⁷ Here again I set against him another declaration of the same synod: "If anyone says that mercy is bestowed on us because apart from the grace of God we will, toil, desire, try, ask, seek, or knock, and does not acknowledge that it is from God through the Spirit that we are enabled to believe, will, ask, and do all these things as we should, he resists the apostle when he says: What do you have that you have not received?" (ch. 6).²⁴⁸ With particular reference to faith Hilary affirms that its beginning is located in us.²⁴⁹ But the words of the council have a very different sound: "If anyone says that both the beginning and the increase of faith and the very desire to believe come not as a gift of grace (i.e., through the working of the Holy Spirit reforming our will from unbelief to belief, from irreligion to religion), but are innate in us by nature, he is opposed to the apostle when he says: He who began a good work in you will complete it at the day of the Lord Jesus."²⁵⁰ Whatever Pighius quotes from Hilary he wants considered as the official tradition of the church. Where then shall we put that council, which even though later in time ought not to take second place in authority? Especially since it approved nothing that was different from the earlier councils at Carthage and Milevis.²⁵¹

3. Third passage again

Councils have greater authority

246. See text at n. 244.
247. *Treatise on Psalms* 118.5.12 (on Ps. 119:36) (PL 9:539); cf. n. 205.
248. Council of Orange (529), canon 6 (Leith 39), citing 1 Cor. 4:7. This is also quoted in *BLW* 5.363 (at n. 105).
249. *Treatise on Psalms* 118.14.20 (on Ps. 119:111) (PL 9:598–99), ending with the passage quoted above (at n. 243). In this discussion Calvin refers to none of Hilary's writings outside the passages quoted by Pighius (31a–32b; see nn. 202–5).
250. Council of Orange (529), canon 5 (Leith 39), citing Phil. 1:6. This is also quoted in *BLW* 5.363 (at n. 103).
251. Relevant councils are the Council of Carthage (c. 416) (Augustine *Letter* 175 [FoC 30:85–90]); the Council of Milevis (c. 416) (Augustine *Letter* 176 [FoC 30:91–94]; for both councils see Augustine *Letter* 177 [FoC 30:94–108]); and the Council of Carthage (418), which produced nine anti-Pelagian canons (C. J. Hefele, *A History of the Councils of the Church*, vol. 2 [Edinburgh: T. & T. Clark, 1876], 458–60) that came to be falsely ascribed to the earlier Council of Milevis (CCL 149:xxxi). Calvin was himself misled by this false ascription (*BLW* 3.305 n. 119). Contrary to Calvin, there is a difference between these councils and Orange in that while the former insist on the need for grace, the latter insists on the need for *prevenient* grace (canons 3–8, 14, 18–20, 23 [Leith 38–43]). For further reference to these councils see *BLW* 3.300 n. 79; 3.305 (at n. 119). For a mistaken reference to Milevis see 3.319 (at n. 252). An earlier synod at Carthage (411) had condemned Celestius for his teaching on original sin rather than on grace, the topic here (Augustine *The Grace of Christ and Original Sin* 2.2.2–2.4.4 [NPNF 5:237–38]). There were also a council at Carthage in 417 and a second council there in 418 (CCL 149:xxx–xxxi, xxxiii), but nothing survives from these to which Calvin could be referring. Calvin's source is Peter Crabbe's two-volume edition of the proceedings of the councils (Cologne: P. Quentel, 1538), the only edition which at that time included the canons of the Council of Orange (529). In this work Calvin would have found the canons of the Council of Milevis (= Carthage [418]) (1:284a–87a) and the letter of the Council of Carthage (c. 416) to Pope Innocent I (Augustine *Letter* 175 [FoC 30:85–90]) (1:277a–78a). This is what Calvin means by Carthage and Milevis here.

I will continue to say nothing of Augustine yet, who when he does come forward later separately in his due place[252] will disrupt utterly the whole harmony [alleged by] Pighius. [But] if enough time and leisure were available to do justice to this matter, I would display, by comparing with one another opinions of the ancients collected from all sides, how feeble a proof can be had from them of any lasting consensus of the church. But seeing that shortage of time compels me to hasten on to other things, I must now forgo this task. It was, however, my wish to bring forward this example in passing, so that readers could[253] guess what would be the level of certainty of our faith if we yielded to Pighius, when he allows to be certain in religion only that which has emerged from the church's § tradition and continued in a perpetual succession from the very beginnings of the church down to our own time.[254]

But if I should wish to borrow from Augustine the counter-argument which he uses in the same debate, only a very unreasonable person, I think, will object, since it is so very reasonable. For when certain opponents of his were claiming that they would be ready to agree with him if he proved his teaching by the authority of the Fathers, he replied in these words: "What then is the use of our examining the works of those who, prior to the rise of the heresy at issue, had no need to engage in this question which is so difficult to solve, although they undoubtedly would have done so if they had been compelled to reply to such teachings? This is why in certain passages of their writings they touched only briefly and incidentally on their opinions about the grace of God, whereas they spent much time on their arguments against the heretics [of their own era]."[255] If I now confront Pighius with these words, to make him desist from what he so mightily insists upon, that a resolution of this issue is to be sought only from the writings of the ancients, when Augustine is witness that they touched on it only briefly and in passing, he will belch out a mouthful of that abuse with which he is stuffed full. So, since nothing reasonable can be got out of that Fury,[256] I address my appeal instead to my readers, with whom I hope that an argument based on such fair reasoning will carry some weight.

No consensus among the Fathers on this issue

290

Writings before Pelagian controversy of limited value

---

252. I.e., *BLW* 3 especially.
253. The first edition puts this verb in the indicative. Later editions, followed here, put it in the subjunctive.
254. This requirement is similar to the so-called Vincentian canon of Vincent of Lérins that the catholic faith is that which "has been believed everywhere, always, by all" (*Commonitory* 2.6 [NPNF2 11:132]). Vincent's aim was, in part, to exclude Augustine's doctrines of grace on the grounds of novelty. Modern historical scholarship has shown that very few beliefs fully satisfy the criterion of the Vincentian canon.
255. *The Predestination of the Saints* 14.27 (NPNF 5:511).
256. See *BLW* 1.235 n. 17.

But the most important issue on which our defence turns, as I say, is that Pighius in part uses counterfeit names to make up the number of his witnesses and in part incorrectly and falsely twists the evidence which he quotes against us, when it in no way contradicts us. For in naming Peter and Clement,[257] what is he practising if not plain deceit? In calling me shameless so often he wanted, I suppose, to take the precaution of getting in first, lest he should hear from me the charge which *he* deserves. But by what name shall we call that depraved and deplorable villainy which lets him so confidently thrust Peter and Clement upon us in the garb of a counterfeit, forged book?

As for Irenaeus and Tertullian,[258] they ascribe freedom to man only at the time of his first beginnings and in that wholeness of his nature with which he was created, but make no mention of the corruption which he brought upon himself by his own fault. Therefore what they say does us no harm at all, since we locate the cause of [human] bondage not in the natural state but in the fall of the first man. So they teach that man was created free; we do not deny this, but say that he fell into bondage because he declined from his original condition. They argue that sin is not attached to his substance; we too affirm the very same thing, but we add that the first man, after he fell from his wholeness, underwent[259] the corruption of his good nature and passed this on to all of his descendants. So Pighius must § also delete these two from the list of his witnesses.

Of the six[260] who still remain, two, Ambrose and Basil,[261] give only the slightest help to his cause, or rather none at all. For what does that description of human nature which they lay down have to do with this corrupt, degenerate nature which, being robbed both of the other gifts of God and also of its freedom, ought to lament its present poverty rather than boast of the powers which it has lost? For the freedom of the will is its soundness. So then whoever wants to make the will free must restore its soundness.

There follows Origen, the authority of whose opinion in determining the church's doctrines may be left to Jerome to decide.[262] But, it may be said, it is beyond belief that he could have lied about a matter so well

---

257. See cols. 261–62.
258. See cols. 274–78, 281–82, 288.
259. Latin *accidisse*; note the contrast with substance at the beginning of the sentence; see n. 58.
260. The first edition has "but," which all later editions correct to "six." The six are Ambrose, Basil, Origen, Hilary, Jerome, and Chrysostom. At the end of book 2 (36b) Pighius lists these six and adds Peter, Clement, Irenaeus, Tertullian, and Augustine. Thus he omits Cyprian, whom he had earlier (31a) cited (see cols. 282–83).
261. For Ambrose and Basil see cols. 284–87.
262. For Origen see cols. 274, 277–78, 280–81. Jerome was one of the most zealous fourth-century opponents of Origen.

known in his time, that is, about a prominent principle of our faith. What do I hear? Or are the following declarations not among the principal doctrines of our faith: that the Son is begotten from the Father and of one nature with the Father, that the Holy Spirit shares a single divine nature with the Father and the Son, that this very flesh, which we now bear, will rise again, and such things? But Origen teaches that the Son was made, not begotten; he says that [the Son] is not good by nature and of himself; his view of the Holy Spirit makes him no more than a mere activity; and he thinks that the flesh is to be annihilated when Christ appears.[263] Now if Pighius should chant that party piece of his, that Origen could not have lied about things so well known, surely he deserves to have everyone spit in his face!

But he still has Hilary—one, however, whose opinion we have shown was condemned by an orthodox council.[264] He has Jerome, who being aroused in the depths of old age by Pelagius eventually began to speak somewhat more moderately.[265] He has Chrysostom, who I have always acknowledged was excessive in his praise of human powers.[266] And indeed elsewhere he does not hesitate to bring forward Bernard,[267] but if the dispute were to be decided on his vote, I would, even if I did not get his absolutely full support, still come out on top by a long way.

Hilary
Jerome

Chrysostom

Bernard

Where is that so well attested agreement of all the ages which should because of its certainty be considered as the sure and unambiguous tradition of the church, and therefore be preferred to the word of God? Where is that lie of such capital magnitude of which he so loudly boasts that I have clearly been found guilty? I said that the ancients unjustifiably exalted free choice, the Greeks especially and among them particularly Chrysostom. But I added that they themselves spoke in such confusion or obscurity or with such variety that it is not easy to deduce anything certain from their writings.[268] I took "spoke with variety" to mean that one ascribes more, another less, to free choice; one locates freedom in one faculty, another in another, so that when the opinions of all of them are considered together they can only keep one in uncertainty. § Pighius interprets me as if I said that each one of them is inconsistent with himself. But who can endure this filthy slanderer? Moreover, why should I not say that they speak obscurely and in confusion when they talk about man as if he still existed in his wholeness,

Where is P's "consensus"?

Fathers inconsistent with each other

292

Fathers were confused

---

263. These accusations seem to be drawn from Jerome *Letter* 124.2, 4–5, 10–11 (NPNF2 6:238–40, 242–43).
264. See cols. 283–84, 288–89.
265. See cols. 267, 286; Calvin's unfair comments about Jerome there (at n. 225) are here qualified.
266. See col. 287.
267. For Bernard see *BLW* 4.333–35; 6.378.
268. See text at n. 175.

though he has [in fact] fallen into a desperate and ruined condition from which he is unable to arise by his own power, and when they assign to man a power of free choice as if it had not been lost by the fall? But since it would take too long to argue this out, I will say nothing further—except that I should like to hear from him what he means when he declares elsewhere[269] that before the Pelagian heresy broke out all the ancients indiscriminately exalted free choice. If, when the distinction between divine grace and human power is absent, clarity is easily and quickly acquired, then I admit that I was wrong. If on the other hand the reader cannot avoid being left, doubtful and anxious, in confusion about what should be ascribed to God and what should be left to man—why, when I have done nothing wrong, am I so atrociously abused?

---

269. The margin contains a reference to Pighius: "around the beginning of book 3."

On Book Three [of Pighius]

Introduction

There follows the third book, which [Pighius] has devoted entirely to Augustine. For since I appropriated him alone out of all the rest, [Pighius] tries not only to snatch him away from me, but even to bring him over to his own side. This, I say, is what he declares at the beginning, but when he has entered a little upon the matter itself, he frequently lingers and hesitates, now hunting for a hidden escape, now openly repudiating the very Augustine whom he had proposed to make his ally. Now what good is it with puffed-out cheeks to promise absolutely everything and then, after you have awakened the readers' desire and attention, to send them away unsatisfied? I for my part mean first to ensure that all readers who have sound judgment and are not ill disposed towards the truth can see the following: that Pighius has approached this dispute not out of a love of sound teaching but through an unseemly and frenzied hatred of us; that in pursuing it he has been impelled and driven on not by a desire to discover the truth but by vanity and by a propensity for brawling; and finally that he does nothing sincerely or genuinely, but is satisfied if in any way at all he can blind the eyes of those who read him, or rather win praise from his cunning and ability to deceive. Secondly I want them to recognise my honesty and frankness when I claimed[1] that at least one of the ancients, Augustine, supported our position.

P claims Augustine,

but not sincerely,

unlike C

First, [Pighius] complains that I quote passages from Augustine out of context and without understanding them. But which are these?[2] [One is] where he writes that the human will is not free without the help of the Spirit, since it is held back by conquering and binding de-

P claims that C quotes six passages out of context
First passage

---

1. I.e., in the statement which Pighius disputes throughout most of book 2 (see *BLW* 2.279 at n. 175). In his reply to book 3 Calvin defends his earlier appeal to Augustine in the 1539 *Institutes* (cols. 292–94), attacks Pighius's appeal to Augustine in book 3 of his work (cols. 294–320), and finally expounds the teaching of Augustine in support of his own position (cols. 320–25).

2. In cols. 292–94 (at nn. 3, 8–10, 12, 15–16) Calvin reviews six of his seven Augustine citations from *Inst.* 2.2.8 (LCC 20:265–66). The seventh is reviewed in col. 315 (at n. 219).

sires. I noted the place: it occurs in the *Letter* (145) *to Anastasius*.³ What is torn from its context or obscure here? Likewise his statement in the book § *The Perfection of Righteousness*. For there he sets out the dilemma posed by Pelagius: "We must enquire how it is that man becomes a sinner. Is it by natural necessity, or through freedom of choice? For if it is by natural necessity, he is free from blame; if it is through freedom of choice, we must ask from whom he received this. From God, of course. Therefore it is a good gift from him who is good. Why then is it said to have a greater propensity toward evil?" Then he himself replies: "It was through freedom of choice that man came to be a sinner, but now the corruption which followed as a punishment has turned freedom into necessity. As a result faith cries to God: Deliver me from my necessities.⁴ Being subject to such necessity, we are either unable to understand what we will, or we will what we understand but we are not able to accomplish it. For even freedom itself is promised by our deliverer: If the Son shall set you free, etc.⁵ For since the will has been conquered by the corruption into which it has fallen, [human] nature lacks freedom. For another [passage of] Scripture says: If someone has been subdued by another, he is assigned to him as his slave.⁶ Just, then, as the healthy have no need of a doctor, but only those who are ill, so those who are free have no need of a deliverer, but only those who are slaves, so that we say to him: You have saved my soul from its necessities.⁷ For its very health is genuine freedom, which would not have been lost if the will had remained good. But because the will sinned, the sinner is pursued by a harsh necessity to possess sin, until his sickness is fully healed."⁸ Now let Pighius say that I quote isolated, incomplete extracts!

Again, where [Augustine] writes to Laurentius that "Man misused his free choice and so lost both himself and it,"⁹ and the passage with a similar meaning which I quoted from the third book addressed to Boniface.¹⁰ If this seems to be torn from its context or obscure to Pighius, let him hear its interpretation from the same book: "The righteousness of the law is not fulfilled when the law commands and man

---

3. *Letter* 145.2 (NPNF 1:495–96), cited in *Inst.* 2.2.8 (LCC 20:265).
4. Ps. 25:17 in the Vulgate translation, where it is numbered 24:17.
5. John 8:36, which shows that freedom is a gift of grace, not an attribute of (fallen) nature.
6. 2 Pet. 2:19; cf. Rom. 6:16.
7. See n. 4.
8. *The Perfection of Righteousness* 4.9 (NPNF 5:161–62), cited in *Inst.* 2.2.8 (LCC 20:265). It is cited again shortly after (2.3.5 [LCC 20:295]). Part of this passage is also quoted below in *BLW* 3.299 (at n. 69) and in 4.328 (at n. 21); see also 4.332 (at n. 55).
9. *Enchiridion* 30.9 (NPNF 3:247), cited in *Inst.* 2.2.8 (LCC 20:265). This passage is quoted again in *BLW* 3.295 (at n. 32) and more briefly in 4.336 (at n. 98).
10. *Against Two Letters of the Pelagians* 3.8.24 (NPNF 5:414), cited in *Inst.* 2.2.8 (LCC 20:265); see text at n. 12.

performs it as though by his own strength, but when the Spirit helps him, and man's will, being not free but liberated by the grace of God, performs it."[11] Again a little later on: "And free choice, since it is a prisoner, is capable only of sinning; but for righteousness, without divine liberation and assistance, it is inadequate."[12] And in the first book he had said: "The power for someone to become a son of God can in no way derive from free choice, since it is not free to do good, because the liberator has not liberated it."[13] In the fourth book he affirms this again as follows: "Why do you parade free choice before me, when it will not be free unless you become a sheep? Therefore it is the one who makes men into sheep who sets their wills free for obedience to the truth."[14] Pighius is certainly an unduly captious fellow, if he should dare to raise any further objections here.

The final passage was taken from the book *Rebuke and Grace*, where I say that Augustine is making fun of the use of the expression when he says in words of jest: "Free choice is free from righteousness and in bondage to sin." For he acknowledges no other human freedom except liberation from righteousness, which is a most miserable bondage to sin. Five lines earlier he had said that choice § is free only when it is set free by grace.[15]

Fifth passage

294

The first passage, from the second book against Julian, where [Augustine] describes [choice] as bound, reads as follows: "You want man to be made perfect here—and O that he were, by the gift of God, and not through the free, or rather the bound, choice of his will!"[16] Will Pighius here too continue to bark back that I do not understand what I quote, or that I pluck out words deprived of their context, which will in no way convey Augustine's meaning? And in any case I did not [in the *Institutes*] introduce these proofs with the intention, as this trifler falsely suggests, of having the whole issue decided on the basis of them, but only to show the reader in passing what the force of the epithet "free" is when it is applied to human choice in Augustine.[17] So while I

Sixth passage

---

11. *Against Two Letters of the Pelagians* 3.7.20 (NPNF 5:412), which is added in the 1543 *Institutes* 2.2.8 (LCC 20:265).

12. *Against Two Letters of the Pelagians* 3.8.24 (NPNF 5:414), which is cited more briefly in *Inst.* 2.2.8 (LCC 20:265). A shorter quotation is found in *BLW* 5.354 (at n. 42).

13. *Against Two Letters of the Pelagians* 1.3.6 (NPNF 5:379), the second half of which is added in the 1543 *Institutes* 2.2.8 (LCC 20:265).

14. *Against Two Letters of the Pelagians* 4.6.15 (NPNF 5:423).

15. *Rebuke and Grace* 13.42 (NPNF 5:489); the direct quotation is a shorter version of a citation in *Inst.* 2.2.8 (LCC 20:266). On the edition used by Calvin see Introduction §5.

16. *Against Julian* 2.8.23 (FoC 35:83, where it is mistranslated). The 1539 *Institutes* contain a brief reference to book 2 of this work (2.2.8 [LCC 20:265]). This passage is "the first" in that it is the first of the series of Augustine citations in 2.2.8. Luther had quoted it briefly in his *Bondage of the Will* (LCC 17:174).

17. *Inst.* 2.2.8 (LCC 20:265–66).

am dealing [only] with the word itself, he pretends that I base the whole resolution of the matter on [these] very few words.

But before beginning to bring Augustine forward into contention with us, he advises that it is not irrelevant that we should consider at what periods [Augustine] wrote each of his works. And so [Pighius] makes three groups of his works, insofar as [they relate] to the question under discussion. The first he allots to those which he wrote before the Pelagian heresy arose, the second to those which he published against Pelagius himself when the battle itself was raging, and the third to those which he composed after its heat had diminished and been calmed.[18] I too willingly accept this apportionment, except that I will not concede the truth of that criticism which he repeatedly adds. For because he knows that in the whole of that second class of books Augustine will give him little support, he seeks to deprive them of their reliability or at least to reduce their authority. He says that they smack of the heat of controversy, and that therefore a plain explanation of the truth can better be obtained from other, later works, in which [Augustine], with a mind composed and at peace, gives his teaching about the matter itself more clearly. But while I am not at all against deciding the issue from these later books,[19] if it should be necessary, I deny that Augustine was so on fire with a desire to fight in the others that he was unable always to maintain a clear, lucid account of the truth. For he was not a young man, as he was when he wrote against the Manichees.[20] Also, while he carefully in many places withdrew his excessive praise for free choice, he never recalled that he had diminished it too much.[21] By this he showed that after the end of the controversy he did not hold a different opinion from what he had held at the time of writing.

Three groups of Augustine's writings

1. Before Pelagian controversy
2. In the heat of controversy
3. After the heat

Division acceptable, but second group not unreliable

First Group

1. Free Choice

First passage

After this introduction let us listen to the way [Pighius] begins with the first group of writings. He says that in the second book on free choice, which [Augustine] wrote against the Manichees, he declares that a free will was of necessity given to man and that to the end that he might live

---

18. According to Pighius (38a, 53a), the third group consists of works that were written after the beginning of the Pelagian controversy and that are more positive in tone, as opposed to those written in the heat of controversy. He never, contrary to Calvin's report, stipulates that all of them were written *after* the more polemical writings. He includes in this group two earlier writings, *The Merits and Forgiveness of Sins* (cols. 312–13) and *The Spirit and the Letter* (col. 314).
19. As he does in cols. 320–26.
20. Augustine was born in 354; his main anti-Manichean works were written between 387 and 400; his anti-Pelagian works were written between 412 and his death in 430.
21. In his *Retractations* (FoC 60), completed in 427, Augustine qualified his earlier anti-Manichean enthusiasm for free choice, as Calvin frequently points out in *BLW* 3. But he never, as Calvin notes, qualified his reservations about the freedom of the will.

uprightly. If this be denied, the fairness of divine judgment is removed.²² And to prevent us from quibbling that this should be understood to refer to the freedom which is given us by grace, he resorts to an anticipation of the objection—as if indeed there were a danger that we might as though caught in a trap search around for ways out, when Augustine himself by his own words not only refutes Pighius's objection, but shows that it is silly and flimsy, in the first book of the *Retractations*, chapter § nine. "On the grace of God," he says, "by which he prepares the wills of his people, there was no controversy in these books. For it is one thing to ask about the origin of evil, and another to ask how there may be a return to the original state or an advance to a greater good."²³ You see that his aim was to show that the origin of sin derived from man's voluntary fall, not from God's act of creation. Now our view of man after the fall is far different, and it is a far different question how or by what power the sons of Adam may recover what they lost in their father. Therefore as often as Pighius chants at me that human free will is being eulogised, let him in turn hear that refrain which comes not from my mouth but from Augustine's: the will was free when it was whole, but now that it is so gravely and mortally wounded it needs humble confession, not proud defence.²⁴

₂₉₅

_{Issue was Adam's fall}

He adds a second proof from book three, where [Augustine] argues that the change by which man through sinning turns away from what is unchangeably good to lower things is voluntary and free, since otherwise he could not properly be praised or blamed, or even admonished.²⁵ He goes on to say that the foreknowledge of God is not the cause of sin,²⁶ for man's will can be a will only if it is under his own control.²⁷ In case something that I might bring forward of my own should be open to suspicion, let Augustine himself make his own response. He does this in a single sentence when he says that he is not discussing what the human will is like now, but what it was like when it was made by God.²⁸ Moreover, the nub of the controversy between

_{Second passage}

_{Issue was unfallen human nature}

---

22. *Free Choice* 2.1.3 (LCC 6:135).
23. *Retractations* 1.9.2 (LCC 6:102–3; FoC 60:33), quoted more briefly in *BLW* 4.328 (at n. 18). Pighius quotes from *Free Choice*, without ever mentioning *Retractations*; Calvin's response is based on Augustine's treatment of that work in his *Retractations*. For evidence of this beyond the fact that all of Calvin's quotations are found in the latter work see nn. 39, 44. At no point in *BLW* does Calvin reveal a direct knowledge of *Free Choice*.
24. The second part ("but now . . . defence") is a loose quotation from *Nature and Grace* 53.62 (NPNF 5:142); the first part ("the will . . . whole") summarises much of the argument of the work. Calvin had already quoted (slightly differently) from the same passage in *Inst.* 2.2.11 (LCC 20:269).
25. *Free Choice* 3.1.2–3 (LCC 6:170–72).
26. Summary of *Free Choice* 3.3 (LCC 6:173–76).
27. *Free Choice* 3.3.8 (LCC 6:175); cf. *BLW* 4.344 n. 73; 336 n. 96.
28. *Retractations* 1.9.5 (LCC 6:104; FoC 60:38), quoting *Free Choice* 3.18.52 (LCC 6:201–2); cf. n. 36.

us is what now remains in man since he was robbed of those spiritual riches with which he was by nature endowed. "The will," he says, "is the means of sinning and of right living, the point I was then wanting to make. So unless the will itself is liberated by the grace of God from the bondage that made it the slave of sin and is helped to overcome its faults, it is impossible to live an upright and godly life. And if this God-given benefit, by which [the will] is liberated, did not come first, it would be given according to its merits and there would be no grace, which is of course given freely."[29] And in case he should seem to be repudiating what he had said before, he quotes the passage from there, so that it may be evident that those remarks which glorify our nature so much referred not to its corrupt state but to when it was [still] innocent. "Let us hold with a sure faith that because man is not also able to raise himself of his own accord in the way that he fell of his own accord, God's right hand, that is, the Lord Jesus, was stretched down to us from above."[30] You see how he is searching only for the original source of evil. The Manichees imagined that it was God; he himself affirms that it originated from man's free choice.[31] So he was created free—who denies it? But now that he has sold himself into bondage, now that "by misusing free choice he has lost both it and himself,"[32] where does it get us to remind ourselves of what he was like then?

296

Dispute with P not about original creation

but about fallen nature

To speak even more clearly, there is full agreement between us[33] § about the original creation of man. For Pighius lays down that man was made with free choice. We accept this, and did not wait for him to demand this of us; we have always[34] owned this belief. Now Augustine everywhere proclaims the entirely different and unlike natures of man when he was still innocent and now that he has been corrupted through the fall.[35] The present dispute is about the latter. But Pighius, in a long rambling discourse, relates what Augustine thinks and says about the former. Augustine strongly objects: "When we speak about a will that is free to do right, we are of course talking about the will with which [man] was created."[36] For these are his words in that same book from which Pighius boasts that he quoted evidence with such accuracy and

---

29. *Retractations* 1.9.4 (LCC 6:103; FoC 60:35–36).
30. *Retractations* 1.9.4 (LCC 6:104; FoC 60:37), quoting *Free Choice* 2.20.54 (LCC 6:169). It is quoted again, more loosely, in *BLW* 4.328 (at n. 19); see also 3.296 n. 40.
31. *Retractations* 1.9.2 (LCC 6:102–3; FoC 60:32–33).
32. *Enchiridion* 30.9 (NPNF 3:247). For the other uses of this passage see n. 9.
33. I.e., between Calvin and Pighius.
34. See *Inst.* 2.3.13 (LCC 20:307). For a later more explicit statement (from 1559) see *Institutes* 1.15.8 (LCC 20:195–96).
35. See cols. 294–96 (especially at nn. 23–24, 28, 32, 36).
36. *Retractations* 1.9.5 (LCC 6:104; FoC 60:38), quoting *Free Choice* 3.18.52 (LCC 6:202). The same passage is quoted more loosely in col. 295 (at n. 28).

exactness. Surely this is a case of what the proverb means: "I asked for scythes, but he says that there are no hoes."[37]

Now let Pighius raise his eyebrows and cry out, as he does, that there is nothing uncertain in these words when Augustine teaches that nothing is more in man's power than his will![38] I reply: why does he not turn the page, where he will find something to curb this foolish uproar of his? "If that is not man's punishment but his nature, then those things are in no way sins. For if man does not depart from that state in which he was naturally made (without the possibility of improvement), he is doing what he ought when he does these things. If man were good, he would be other than he is. But now, because he is as he is, he is not good and does not have it in his power to be good. Who can doubt that to be a punishment?"[39] Then he adds: "From this wretchedness the grace of God frees him, because of his own accord, that is, by free choice, man was able to fall, but not also to rise."[40]

Third passage

These are Pighius's invincible weapons, on which he relies as he snatches away Augustine's patronage from me. Now, he says, Calvin is forsaken by Augustine, who he pretended was on his side. Is it so? You will certainly be a marvellous deceiver if you can persuade anyone of this. But, just as if he had given Augustine his weapons to fight against me, he is soon girding himself to bring him aid, in case he gets into difficulties while attacking me. He is a ridiculous fellow indeed who so wearies himself in a pointless struggle which he rashly and without reason brings upon himself, since Augustine needs no defence against me. For I welcome without a struggle all those statements of [Augustine's] which Pighius brings forward; and if he needed it, all this equipment designed to break the connection between the will and necessity is of no avail at all. Whether necessity is compatible with will or not we shall see elsewhere.[41] But this is not the place for that question, no more than a picture of a shipwreck is the place for a cypress tree.[42]

P's boasts

---

37. Erasmus *Adages* 2.2.49 (CWE 33:99–100).
38. *Free Choice* 3.3.7 (LCC 6:174), quoted in *Retractations* 1.9.3 (FoC 60:34).
39. *Retractations* 1.9.5 (FoC 60:37–38), quoting *Free Choice* 3.18.51 (LCC 6:201); see also n. 44. There is clear evidence that Calvin (unlike Pighius) is quoting from *Retractations* rather than *Free Choice*: (a) the text in the former is slightly closer to his quotation; (b) "turn the page" makes perfect sense if the two quotations are taken from *Retractations*, but not if they are taken from *Free Choice*; and (c) the following quotation from the same source ("he adds") is found in the former, but not the latter. On the edition used by Calvin see Introduction §5.
40. *Retractations* 1.9.6 (LCC 6:104; FoC 60:39), where Augustine summarises *Free Choice* 2.20.54 (LCC 6:169), which he had quoted earlier (*Retractations* 1.9.4 [LCC 6:104; FoC 60:37]); cf. n. 30.
41. See cols. 299–300, 301–2.
42. A clear allusion to Horace *Art of Poetry* 19–21 (Loeb 450–53). There is a briefer allusion to the same passage in *BLW* 1.251 (at n. 84). Cf. Erasmus *Adages* 1.5.19 (CWE 31:400).

Fourth passage

Issue was Adam's fall

§ 297

Augustine's (in)consistency

Then he proceeds to add that Augustine denies that someone can sin by doing what can in no way be avoided.[43] Anyone who wishes may look at the passage [to see] whether he is not speaking about the beginning of sin, so that he may prove, of course, that this necessity with which we are burdened today originated precisely from the voluntary fall of the first man.[44] This detail Pighius, who claims to be such a faithful reporter, concealed by omission.[45] In case anyone should initiate a dispute about this, [Augustine] himself removed all doubt in his *Retractations*, as I said a little while ago.[46] And at the same time he gave the reason why he did not in that place expound original sin and the corruption of our flawed nature more openly. His reason was that his argument was with the Manichees, who rejected the Holy Scriptures and especially the Old Testament, from which it would have been necessary to prove [original sin].[47] Add the fact that many of the passages which Pighius cites were said by way of concession. Augustine wrote them not because this was how he saw the matter, but because he did not want to disregard means which he could use to overcome his opponents, either by accepting the view which they professed or by conceding what they demanded of him.[48] Nor do I want readers to believe me or my guesses on this matter, unless they see the real thing with their own eyes.

Finally with his usual modesty [Pighius] boasts that he will have enough for victory if he can show Augustine opposing me only once, because I said that he always speaks consistently and uniformly about this matter. But what devil revealed to him that I had said this? For I am not so simpleminded as not to perceive how much Augustine changes if one compares his first writings with his latest.[49] He was still a young man and not very experienced when he refuted the Manichees. Therefore

---

43. *Free Choice* 3.18.50 (LCC 6:201), quoted in *Retractations* 1.9.3, 5 (LCC 6:103–4; FoC 60:35, 37). Cf. *BLW* 4.328 (at n. 14) and 4.332 n. 59.

44. *Retractations* 1.9.5 (FoC 60:37–38), quoting *Free Choice* 3.18.51 (LCC 6:201). Part of this is quoted above (at n. 39). Calvin is able to give the impression of having used *Free Choice* itself because *Retractations* 1.9.5, after quoting the passage from *Free Choice* cited at n. 43, reads, "Immediately I proceeded to add: . . ." (FoC 60:37).

45. Pighius (42a–b) in his long quotation from *Free Choice* 3.18.50–51 (LCC 6:200–201) leaves out the middle third of 3.18.51, where Augustine clearly makes the point that Calvin has stated in the previous sentence.

46. *Retractations* 1.9.2 (LCC 6:102–3; FoC 60:33), cited above at n. 23, which is the only earlier passage where Calvin has named the *Retractations*, suffices to make the point claimed here.

47. *Retractations* 1.9.6 (LCC 6:104–5; FoC 60:39).

48. I.e., Augustine was using ad hoc arguments.

49. Calvin and Pighius both recognise that there is development in Augustine's views. Neither of them acknowledges that the fundamental shift took place not with the beginning of the Pelagian controversy but nearly twenty years earlier, in the mid-390s. See E. TeSelle, *Augustine the Theologian* (London: Burns & Oates, 1970), 156–65, 176–82. Augustine himself describes this shift in *The Predestination of the Saints* 4.8 (NPNF 5:501–2).

you would find more natural ability, keenness of mind, and profane philosophy there than you would sacred, spiritual teaching. As far as free choice is concerned, provided he could extract an admission that it was given to the first man and that the source of his ruin derived from it, he did not labour over a deeper investigation. But when Pelagius and Celestius emerged with their followers, as if aroused out of sleep he began to think and investigate more thoroughly. It is from this that there arose that clear, sure, and precise explanation of the true, wholesome teaching which before [all] others I credit to Augustine alone; it is from this also that the agreement derives which I pride myself exists between him and us. He might, perhaps, have like others allowed the grace of God to lie hidden in obscurity, if he had not opened his eyes more widely under the impact of Pelagius's insolence. Thank God, therefore, that he wonderfully used the wickedness of the godless, both to embellish the praise of his grace and to abase the pride of the flesh!

In Pighius's book there follows another passage, from the book *Two Souls, Against the Manichees*, where Augustine defines [the will as] "an uncoerced movement of the mind, directed either towards not losing or towards obtaining something."[50] [Pighius] supposes that this definition puts us under enormous pressure, which I for my part do not see and do not acknowledge. But to avoid an unduly long dispute between us about this, let Augustine himself come between us to settle the argument. "The purpose of the definition was," he says, "to distinguish someone who wills from someone who does not and thus to ascribe intention to those who, as the first humans in paradise, were the source of sin for the human race by sinning without coercion" (*Retractations* 1.15).[51] A little later: § "The will is free insofar as it has been liberated, and to this extent it is called 'will.' Otherwise it is rather wholly passion. The latter is not, as the Manichees foolishly say, something of a foreign nature which is added to us, but a corruption of our own nature, from which we cannot be healed except by the Saviour's grace. But if anyone says that passion itself is nothing other than will, except that it is corrupted and in the service of sin, we should not object, or make a dispute about words, when there is agreement about the reality."[52] Here you hear concerning which will he wants this saying to be understood; you hear with what thunderbolts he lays low the strength of a corrupted will, to the extent that he does not even count it worthy of its own name.

2. *Two Souls*

First passage: Augustine's definition of will—

298

not applicable to fallen will

---

50. *Two Souls* 10.14 (NPNF 4:102–3). As with *Free Choice* (see n. 23), Pighius is working with the original alone, Calvin with *Retractations* alone.
51. *Retractations* 1.15.3 (FoC 60:66).
52. *Retractations* 1.15.4 (FoC 60:67). Calvin refers back to this quotation in *BLW* 5.362 (at n. 101).

Second passage: Augustine's definition of sin—

Then Pighius goes on to mention the definition of sin which is laid down there, namely that "it is the will to hold on to or to pursue that which righteousness forbids, and from which it is free to refrain. But if it is not free, then it is not will."[53] Now let Augustine explain his thoughts to us in the following words: "It is a true definition because what is defined there is sin alone, not also the punishment for sin. For when sin is such that it is also the punishment for sin, how much strength does the will then have when it is dominated by passion, unless it happens to be devout? For it is free only to the extent that it has been liberated."[54] Do you see by the testimony of the author himself, who certainly ought to have the right to interpret what he has said, that this definition suits only the initial sin of Adam? For by his fall we fell from our original lordship[55] into wretched bondage. You should gather from this, then, the effrontery with which Pighius insults me at this point with his dramatic declamations. Augustine [Pighius says] states as a fact familiar to all: "Nobody deserves criticism or punishment who does not do what he cannot do. This is declared and repeated over and over again by shepherds on the mountains, by poets in the theatres, by the uneducated in their gatherings, by the learned in their libraries, by teachers in schools, and by theologians in their precincts."[56] But he bears witness at the same time that it is a wrong interpreter of his words who makes this apply to all sins. For he meant only that man could not be deservedly condemned if he had not sinned with a free will. But that bondage in which we are held captive in mind and in will is now part of our condemnation until we are liberated by the unmerited benefits given by Christ.[57] What now remains but for [Pighius] to call Augustine a beast because he does not support his own madness? For he does brandish this very reproach: "What if [Augustine] said the opposite elsewhere? If he had done so, or did so, I would reckon him with Luther's people, and say that he had degenerated into a brute beast."[58] [Augustine] not only says the opposite to Pighius's opinion, but in those words also bears witness that their opinions are contrary to one another.

not applicable to fallen humanity

3. *True Religion*

The passage which [Pighius] mentions from the book *True Reli-*

---

53. *Two Souls* 11.15 (NPNF 4:103), the first part of which is quoted in *Retractations* 1.15.4 (FoC 60:66).
54. *Retractations* 1.15.4 (FoC 60:66–67). The last sentence is the first sentence of the passage quoted above (at n. 52).
55. The French translation explains this as "the lordship which we once had over ourselves and our affections."
56. *Two Souls* 11.15 (NPNF 4:103).
57. A summary of the argument of *Retractations* 1.15.2, 4 (FoC 60:64–67), which is not addressed specifically to the passage cited by Pighius.
58. A loose quotation of Pighius 45a; cf. col. 326 (at n. 320).

*gion*⁵⁹ § does seem, I acknowledge, apparently to contradict us. But if we accept Augustine as his own interpreter, then the whole problem will be very easy to solve. He says that sin will not be sin without its being voluntary, and further that free choice resides in the will. "For God judged that his servants would be better if they served him freely. But this would happen only if they served him with a will, not by necessity."⁶⁰ Now let us make space for the interpretation. "That sin which is sin alone, and not also the punishment for sin, should be understood to be meant" (*Retractations* 1.14).⁶¹ Later, when he asks in what sense those deeds too which are done by us are voluntary, he teaches that they can be called this for the reason that they are done with an evil will. But for the will to be good, it must be healed and prepared by the Lord.⁶² Could he more clearly find fault⁶³ with Pighius for inflicting a serious wrong on him by twisting his writings to a different meaning?

[Augustine, he claims,] begins by making an inference from what is voluntary to what is free and goes on to make necessity opposed to the will.⁶⁴ I myself would not disapprove of this inference, if the will were whole and in control of itself. Just as if someone should say, "Man is a two-footed animal; therefore he can walk and go along," it would be no bad or improper argument. But if someone wanted to transfer this to a paralytic, the reply is to hand that from another source there is a fault which impedes his nature. Concerning the will exactly the same kind of reply should be given: it is indeed free by nature, but by corruption it has been made a slave, and it is held back by this bondage until it is set free by the hand of God. But since a response from Augustine's own lips will be less open to question, let Pighius hear him speak: "If we want to defend free choice, let us not attack the source of its freedom. For he who attacks grace, by which [the choice] is set free to shun evil and do good, wants it to remain in captivity" (*Letter* [217] *to Vitalis*).⁶⁵ Or, if he prefers a briefer statement: In this inquiry it is not nature, but the corruption of nature which must be reflected upon (*The Grace of God, against Celestius*, 2.33).⁶⁶ But there⁶⁷ it is certain that the discourse is about the natural state.

299

Freedom of will inalienable?

---

59. *True Religion* 14.27 (LCC 6:238). As with *Free Choice* and *Two Souls* (see nn. 23, 50), Pighius is working with the original alone, Calvin with *Retractations* alone.
60. *True Religion* 14.27 (LCC 6:238), which Calvin has taken from Pighius (45a).
61. *Retractations* 1.13.5 (LCC 6:219; FoC 60:53).
62. Summary of the rest of *Retractations* 1.13.5 (LCC 6:219–20; FoC 60:53–54).
63. For "could he . . . find fault," the first edition has "could fault be found" (passive instead of active). This is corrected in later editions.
64. Pighius's comment (45a-b) on the passage of Augustine cited in n. 59.
65. *Letter* 217.3.8 (FoC 32:80).
66. A paraphrase of *The Grace of Christ and Original Sin* (against Pelagius and Celestius) 2.33.38 (NPNF 5:251). Celestius was a more extreme associate of Pelagius.
67. I.e., in the passage cited in n. 59.

As regards the second part[68] the solution is the same: "For it was through freedom of choice that man came to be a sinner, but now the corruption which followed as a punishment has turned freedom into necessity."[69] Therefore when Pelagius asked whether sin was [an act] of the will or due to necessity, [Augustine] replied: "So that we may be healed, we call upon him to whom it is said in the Psalm, Deliver me from my necessities" *(The Perfection of Righteousness)*.[70] These statements could, I think, suffice, [even] if I added nothing else. But what is contained in the book *Nature and Grace* is fuller still. The followers of Pelagius were quoting at [Augustine] that saying of Jerome which Pighius too has not failed to quote against us: "We were created with free choice and are not drawn either to virtue or to vices by necessity."[71] "Who would deny," [Augustine] responds, "that our nature was created in a state § different [from the present one]? But in right action there is no chain of necessity, because freedom comes from love. Now go back to the saying of the apostle: The love of God has been poured out in our hearts by the Holy Spirit, who has been given to us.[72] But by whom, unless it is by him who ascended on high and led captivity captive? So let man hear that the necessity of sinning derives from the corruption of nature, not from its creation; and so that he may cease to continue in it, let him learn to say to God: 'Deliver me from my necessities'" (chs. 65–66).[73]

Necessity compatible with will?

300

4. The Greatness of the Soul

The passage from *The Greatness of the Soul*[74] does not even require a reply. For if we can believe Augustine, wherever he praises the capacity for free choice he is thinking of the original creation of our nature, not of its present wretchedness into which it has fallen headlong through a fault of choice.[75] If we do not believe him, at any rate he [later] withdraws what he had said.[76] When [Pighius] rushes at us with such mighty armaments, are you surprised, O reader, if he is paralysed with amazement when he sees that we are not at all disturbed by them? Indeed I myself am surprised that such a windbag does not immediately break wind in public.

---

68. I.e., the second part of the inference at n. 64.

69. *The Perfection of Righteousness* 4.9 (NPNF 5:161). For the other uses of this passage see n. 8.

70. *The Perfection of Righteousness* 2.2 (NPNF 5:160), quoting Ps. 25:17 in the Vulgate translation, where it is numbered 24:17. This passage is mentioned in *BLW* 4.331 (at n. 43).

71. Jerome *Against Jovinian* 2.3 (NPNF2 6:389), also quoted in *BLW* 4.333 (at n. 68); see also 2.286 n. 223 and 4.336 n. 90.

72. Rom. 5:5.

73. *Nature and Grace* 65.78–66.79 (NPNF 5:149), quoting Ps. 25:17 in the Vulgate (24:17).

74. *The Greatness of the Soul* 36.80 (ACW 9:110). Calvin passes over this work because *Retractations* 1.8 (FoC 60:28–30) has no material useful to his cause.

75. I.e., in *Retractations*; see nn. 28, 36.

76. Calvin acknowledges the possibility that Augustine in his *Retractations* as well as explaining his earlier writings also sometimes explains them away.

But we must proceed. In book 22 of *Against Faustus the Manichee* [Augustine] says that man was created such that there was within him the possibility or the capacity to control his desires.[77] This contains nothing that is at issue between us. For he is dealing with the original creation. But afterwards he adds something which can be understood only of our present condition: "Man is renewed through that possibility through which, if he had wished, he was able not to have fallen."[78] The possibility, Pighius says, is the capacity for free choice. Augustine bears witness that man revives through it. But far from that holy man let this wicked delusion be, which he so often repudiates and which all the African bishops at his instigation deemed worthy of an anathema![79] What then does he mean by these[80] words? Surely only that we are restored by the kindness of God from the bondage of sin into that freedom by which we may overcome the world, the flesh, and all our lusts. For this is that possibility for us, which he everywhere praises, that we should be strong in the power of the Lord. But why did he not declare this explicitly in that passage? He himself replies: "I call it nature rather than grace [when writing] against the Manichees, because the issue with them was over nature. And in any case what grace does is to make the restored nature capable of what the corrupted nature cannot do" (*Retractations* 1.16).[81] He acknowledges that he ascribed to nature what belongs only to grace, because of course the only purpose of grace is to restore the nature that has fallen and has been overturned and make it stand upright.

The words which Pighius then quotes from the second book *Against Felix* are much less impressive. For all that is being dealt with there is the pristine state of our nature.[82] But Augustine himself in the *Retractations* also excuses himself for not saying anything there about the liberation of our captive nature and the renewal of what was ruined, because the argument § did not require it (book 2).[83] What difficulty would there be here, I ask, if Pighius's disturbed brain had not unnecessarily, by its own madness, created trouble both for himself and for others?

5. Against Faustus

6. Against Felix

301

---

77. *Against Faustus the Manichee* 22.28 (NPNF 4:284).
78. Ibid.
79. Calvin is probably thinking of the councils of Carthage and Milevis, as set out in *BLW* 2.289 n. 251. But these councils rejected the idea that humans can keep the law by free choice without grace, not the idea that free choice can seek grace.
80. See quote at n. 78.
81. *Retractations* 1.15.8 (FoC 60:70), where Augustine is commenting on *Two Souls* 13.20 (NPNF 4:106).
82. *Against Felix the Manichee* 2.3–4, 8, 12 (PL 42:537–38, 541, 544).
83. *Retractations* 2.8 (FoC 60:136).

Second Group

<small>Augustine's consistency</small>

When he wants to move over to the second category of Augustine's books,[84] fearing that I may in my reply claim that Augustine later withdrew things which he had written rather inadvisedly as a young man, he anticipates this insult, as he himself calls it, and refutes it. First he says that by that means he has won [the argument], because I will be held convicted of a most shameless lie in that I have said that Augustine everywhere speaks clearly, everywhere speaks surely and consistently on this matter.[85] Let him show where I said this, if he wants to be believed. [In the *Institutes*] I affirmed that Augustine is certainly on our side;[86] but that he constantly in all his books speaks consistently, it never entered my mind to affirm. No, rather am I accustomed to say that all other heresies were of the greatest disadvantage to the church, but that the Pelagian heresy was much more of a help than a hindrance. For it aroused the spirit of this holy man to purify the church from that pagan philosophy about free choice which was by then generally prevalent, so that he might restore to the grace of God its proper honour. This was hidden and, as it were, half-buried by the false view of human ability which had then seized the minds of the masses.[87] But suppose things are as Pighius imagines. Let me have said that Augustine is everywhere consistent. What more has he brought out into the open which would show me guilty of lying? He makes a lot of noise, of course, but I think I have sufficiently exposed his Thrason-like[88] vainglory when I set against the empty sound of his words the facts themselves, which are so clear and solid, even though I did so without [making] a loud noise about it. Likewise I will pass by that second claim which he makes, that [Augustine] could in no way have retracted the things which he had previously declared. This, I say, I do not oppose if only he can bear to take them in the sense in which Augustine himself instructs us that they are to be taken,[89] seeing that on these terms they are not at all opposed to us.

<small>Benefit of Pelagian controversy</small>

<small>P boasts of Augustine's support</small>

After this introduction, he repeats that splendid promise in his characteristic way, saying that he will ensure that it is soundly accepted that Augustine is always and uniformly not only opposed to us, but our most bitter enemy. But when he endeavours to come closer to the point

---

84. I.e., writings from the second period mentioned in col. 294.
85. Cf. text at n. 1 and at n. 49.
86. *Inst.* 2.2.4, 9; 2.3.13–14 (LCC 20:259, 266, 307–9).
87. Cf. *True Religion* 8.15 (LCC 6:233) and *Letter* 194.10.47 (FoC 30:332), where Augustine himself makes a similar comment, but about heresy in general.
88. See *BLW* 1.237 n. 24.
89. I.e., if Augustine's earlier writings are interpreted as Augustine himself interprets them in his *Retractations*.

(that is, ten lines later), he forgets that confidence of his and as much as he can disparages Augustine's reliability in this second category of books. For [Pighius says] he quibbles over individual words used by his opponents and is always looking for something to criticise. So in some cases, if the accepted mode of argument did not excuse it, you would feel a lack of candour in him. He pours out so much in disputing, so as to entrap his enemy with tricks of sophistry, that it would otherwise be unworthy of him, if he had said it seriously. If Augustine [really] so tenaciously supports [Pighius's] point of view, to what end was it useful to diminish his reliability? And because he dare not open up the wound too deeply, he cites as proof only two passages, which he thinks cause him little difficulty.

<small>but belittles his polemical works</small>

To the well-known objection (he says) of Pelagius that whatever is constrained by natural necessity is deprived of choice of will, Augustine replies § that it is of necessity that we desire to be happy, but we none the less [do so] with our will.[90] [Pighius] judges this a sly piece of sophistry. But on what grounds? Because elsewhere Augustine has said much about free choice.[91] But does it therefore follow that nothing is at the same time both voluntary and necessary? [Pighius claims that] this is how Augustine had put it. Of course, since he was [there][92] confusing necessity with coercion. Here,[93] however, it is clear that [Augustine] distinguishes the one from the other.

<small>1. *Nature and Grace*
First passage
302</small>

The other passage is where [Augustine] tries to refute Pelagius's objection: "Because not to sin is within our power, we are able both to sin and not to sin." [Augustine] sets up a similar inference against him, in which there is an obvious flaw: "Because not to want unhappiness is within our power, we can both want it and not want it."[94] But in this passage [Pighius] finds nothing to criticise, except to say that this argument has no validity if twisted to attack the papists. We will look at this point later on. But ought Augustine, who had deserved nothing of the kind, to have been treated so spitefully and churlishly on this basis?

<small>Second passage</small>

Finally [Pighius] infers that [Augustine's] real, considered view should be sought from those books which he has quoted and from others.[95] Why is that? Because in the heat of an argument [Augustine] is sometimes carried away off course. What then? Will not all the books

<small>Status of Augustine's polemical works</small>

---

90. *Nature and Grace* 46.54 (NPNF 5:139).
91. In the anti-Manichean writings and in his other writings, as Calvin himself concedes in *Inst.* 2.2.8 (LCC 20:265).
92. See the previous note.
93. I.e., in the passage just quoted (at n. 90), where Augustine does not explicitly distinguish between necessity and coercion, but rather shows the compatibility of necessity and will.
94. *Nature and Grace* 49.57 (NPNF 5:140).
95. I.e., not just from his early polemical works against the Pelagians, but from his later writings; see col. 294.

which Pighius has quoted so far be suspect for a similar reason? For what do they contain but [Augustine's] disputes with the Manichees? See the subtlety of Pighius, which I offer to children to laugh at! Augustine, while still a young man, amid the passion of youth, full of confidence in his eloquence, fresh from the orator's school, better practised in disputes than in dignity, deeply influenced by profane learning and [only] moderately suffused with knowledge of Holy Scripture, attacked the Manichean heresy in many books in which he stretched all the sinews of his mind for combat. Whatever is read there, Pighius orders to be treated as an oracle. The same Augustine also wrote when already an old man, when already far more learned and controlled, and he wrote so as to attend more to accuracy than to subtlety. It is not safe, says Pighius, to judge his view from here, because, driven on by passion, he does not control himself well.

2. Against Two Letters of the Pelagians

Now let us hear what he brings forward, as he said he would, from Augustine to storm our stronghold. In the first book of *Against Two Letters of the Pelagians* it reads as follows: "Which of us would say that free choice was lost to the human race by the sin of the first man? A kind of freedom was lost by that sin, but it was the freedom which existed in paradise of enjoying complete righteousness with immortality."[96] In case these words should cause anyone difficulty, we must immediately observe the sense in which he is wont to call choice free. I made no secret in the *Institutes* of the fact that this term occurs repeatedly in his writings. But I warned that it was necessary to bear in mind what its sense was, and that could be seen clearly from many passages, of which I have recently cited a few.[97] As in other matters, so in one's manner of speaking, common usage has great power. As someone has said, "This governs the choice, meaning, and rule of speech."[98] That expression[99] had already § gained a hold in common speech, so that Augustine saw that he would have more trouble eliminating it than explaining the whole matter properly. So he yields to custom, but at the same time he takes careful precautions to prevent the name from giving birth to a mistaken understanding. In the thirtieth chapter of the book *The Spirit and the Letter*, for example, he says that free choice is made secure through grace, because only when it is redeemed from captivity through grace does it begin to be free. But as long as it is left to itself, it is in bondage.[100]

Meaning of "free"

---

96. *Against Two Letters of the Pelagians* 1.2.5 (NPNF 5:378). See n. 102.
97. *Inst.* 2.2.8 (LCC 20:265). For passages found there and also "recently cited," see cols. 292–94 (at nn. 3, 8–10, 12, 15–16).
98. Horace *Art of Poetry* 72 (Loeb 456–57).
99. I.e., "free choice."
100. Summary of *The Spirit and the Letter* 30.52 (NPNF 5:106). This passage is discussed in col. 307 (at nn. 140–42) and again summarised in *BLW* 4.338 (at n. 114).

But, so as not to depart too far from the present discussion, this passage[101] which Pighius wrongly uses against us is sufficient for us. [Augustine] says that free choice was not lost to the human race. Why does he say that? "Because it is by means of [free choice] that those who sin with enjoyment sin. So they are not free from righteousness except by a choice of the will, nor do they become free from sin except by the Saviour's grace."[102] Therefore it is free not because it can turn itself in either direction by its own power, but because by a voluntary movement it proceeds to evil. But I have always borne witness that I do not want to fight over words if it is once and for all established that freedom should be applied not to a power or ability to choose good and evil alike, but to a movement and an agreement which is self-determined.[103] And what other meaning do Augustine's words bear? Man, he says, has a will that is free, but to do evil. Why? Because he is moved by enjoyment and his own appetite.[104] He adds later: "But this will which is free in the wicked, because they enjoy evil, is not free to do good, because it has not been liberated."[105] These words are so in agreement with our teaching that you would think that they had been written to support it.

Augustine's meaning of "free choice"

But Pighius, so as to avoid these snares, lays down a far different distinction. He says that a free will exists naturally in man, through which [the will] has its own movements and all its actions under its control, so that [man] wills and does each action in such a way that he has at the same time the power not to will it and not to do it. And he understands this to be the freedom which Augustine everywhere affirms. But because the will not only gives its assent to its own actions but holds control over the whole person, it also has authority by nature over all the members of the body. So all the members which are endowed with voluntary movement are obedient to it when it uses its power in earnest and effectively. He then acknowledges that everyone does indeed experience difficulty as a result of a certain weakness in the flesh. While the members are sluggish in performing their duty of righteousness, being more devoted to the indulgence and pleasures of the flesh, so also the will too readily inclines towards the desires of its kindred flesh and does not readily make use of the power of its authority to restrain them. But when it wants to demonstrate the greatness of its power, [he continues,] all the members must necessarily follow its direction into obedience to righteousness.

versus P's

---

101. I.e., the passage quoted at n. 96.
102. *Against Two Letters of the Pelagians* 1.2.5 (NPNF 5:378). "Free choice . . . human race" is a paraphrase of what precedes the quotation, including the passage quoted at n. 96. A shorter version of this quotation is added in the 1543 *Institutes* 2.2.8 (LCC 20:266).
103. E.g., *Inst.* 2.2.7–8 (LCC 20:264–66).
104. *Against Two Letters of the Pelagians* 1.2.5–3.6 (NPNF 5:378–79).
105. Ibid., 1.3.7 (NPNF 5:379).

P's view of the power of the will

304 In addition to this difficulty he mentions two further evils, the will's idleness and its being accustomed to sinning. These cause it to deliver itself into bondage and subsequently to hold on to or recover its authority only with § difficulty. Not that this happens because even then it has lost its innate freedom, but because the bondage to which it has submitted is pleasant to it. As long as that is the case, it cannot be released, because it does not wish to be. But when it begins to feel displeasure in earnest, then it shakes off that bondage and conquers it. Even so he does not deny that in this victory there is difficulty, because it is necessary to do battle with the flesh, which is an enemy within, and with a long-standing habit. Therefore he allows that in this battle it needs the help of divine grace in order at length to come off as the victor. He concludes finally that the loss of liberty which took place through sin consists only in this: whereas our first parents had the movements not only of the will but of all their members as well and their whole bodies under their control without any difficulty or opposition, our flesh is hostile to us and rebels against the authority of reason.

P's Pelagianism

But all this has not just a whiff of Pelagius's teaching, but is in large part an undiluted expression of Pelagian ungodliness. For in the first place [Pighius] leaves the will free in itself, so that it has its own motions in either direction under its own control, and he does not recognise that this power was either lost or diminished through original sin. Now let us hear what Augustine's view is on that. In writing to Vitalis of Carthage, after laying down twelve points, he concludes: "You realise that I did not want to say everything pertaining to the faith but only what pertains to that issue of ours about the grace of God—whether this grace precedes or follows the human will. That is, to express it more clearly, whether it is given to us because of the fact that we will or whether God through this very thing brings it about that we will" (*Letter* 217).[106] Again later: "These and other proofs show that God by his grace takes away the stony heart from unbelievers and preempts the merits of human good wills. [He does this] in such a way that the will is prepared by antecedent grace, rather than grace being bestowed because of the antecedent merit of the will."[107] Also in book 13 of the *City of God:* "The human will takes the initiative in doing evil, but in doing good it is the will of the Creator which takes the initiative, whether in making that which did not exist before[108] or in remaking that which

opposed by Augustine on prevenient grace

106. *Letter* 217.5.17 (FoC 32:88). The second half of this passage is quoted again in *BLW* 5.354 (at n. 39).

107. *Letter* 217.7.28 (FoC 32:94). This passage is quoted again in *BLW* 5.354 (at n. 38); see also 6.380 (at n. 52).

108. I.e., the initial creation of human will.

had fallen."[109] In the second book on *The Merits and Forgiveness of Sins*: "People toil to discover in our will what good of our own there is, and I do not know how any can be found" (ch. 18).[110] Also in the fourth book to Boniface: "And how can anyone have a good purpose unless the Lord first has mercy on him, since a good will is precisely one which is prepared by God?"[111] Likewise, when he had in another place stated that God does not show mercy until the [human] will has taken the lead, he withdraws that statement "because the mercy of God precedes the will itself, and if it were not there the will would not be prepared by the Lord" (*Retractations* 1).[112] Also, when he had elsewhere written that what we will is under our own control, he withdraws this too in the following way: "But this power to live well we also receive from above, when the will is prepared by the Lord."[113]

§ 305

What ropes will Pighius use to drag these words and make them agree with his godless lies? He wants to have the will deprived of nothing by original sin except its rule over the members of the body; that it is more inclined to evil than to good [he believes] results from laziness, slackness, and bad habits, not from the fact that it does not have the ability to resist. But Augustine shouts back that the will is evil and held prisoner by evil until it is set free.[114] And yet this dog is of such deplorable shamelessness that he dares to brand Augustine with the ignominy of the suggestion that he has him as a supporter of his own godlessness! Then he allows the initiative in conquering the desires of the flesh to be held by the will, as if it began the battle, and he associates the aid of divine grace with it as a kind of supporter. But everywhere Augustine shouts back that the will conceives nothing except evil until it is preceded by the Spirit.[115] And so it was also resolved by the Council of Orange: "If anyone argues that God waits for our desire that we should

Original sin

and prevenient grace

---

109. *City of God* 13.15 (NPNF 2:251).
110. *The Merits and Forgiveness of Sins* 2.18.28 (NPNF 5:56). This passage is quoted again in *BLW* 3.311 (at n. 173), 3.313 (at n. 207), and 5.358 (at n. 80). The quotation is also added in the 1543 *Institutes* 2.3.7 (LCC 20:299).
111. *Against Two Letters of the Pelagians* 4.6.13 (NPNF 5:422). This quotation is repeated in *BLW* 3.308 (at n. 145) and 5.354 (at n. 43).
112. *Retractations* 1.26 (FoC 60:114–15), where Augustine is discussing *Eighty-three Diverse Questions* 68.5 (FoC 70:163–64).
113. *Retractations* 2.1.2 (FoC 60:120–21), where Augustine is discussing *To Simplician* 2.1.4 (PL 40:131).
114. According to L. Smits, *Saint Augustin dans l'oeuvre de Jean Calvin* (Assen: van Gorcum, 1958), 2:71, this might be a loose quotation from *Against Two Letters of the Pelagians* 3.8.24 (NPNF 5:414). It is more likely, however, to be Calvin's summary of Augustine's position as he has presented it in many quotations.
115. According to Smits, *Saint Augustin*, 2:71, this might be a paraphrase of *The Spirit and the Letter* 3.5 (NPNF 5:84–85) (cited by Luther in *The Bondage of the Will* [LCC 17:174, 180]). But since this is what Augustine teaches "everywhere," it is again more likely to be Calvin's summary of Augustine's position.

be cleansed from sin, and does not acknowledge that it is by the work of the Holy Spirit in us that we are caused to want cleansing, he resists the Holy Spirit."[116] Since he claims[117] to give allegiance only to the church, what escape route will he find now, when he is declared an enemy of the Holy Spirit by an orthodox council?

Grace not just optional

Then he thinks that the will is hindered by the resistance of the flesh in such a way that it can nevertheless be victorious in the struggle if it makes use of its own strength. And even when it is held entangled by the allurements of the flesh, he imagines that the assistance of divine grace is sought just to help it in the recovery of its own authority, because it cannot easily win the victory in any other way. There is no reference at all to necessity.[118] But what did the ancients resolve about the matter? There survives a decree of the Council of Milevis in the following words, which is repeated in the African councils: "Whoever shall say that the grace of justification is given to us to enable us more easily through grace to fulfil by means of free choice what we are commanded, as if we could do it without grace, albeit with difficulty, let him be anathema."[119] Even though I do not wield those verbal thunderbolts with which Pighius rages against us, I hope nevertheless that it will be sufficiently clear from this discourse how alien and distant this new madness of his is from the view of Augustine, with whose name he, with remarkable confidence, dares to adorn it.

P unscriptural

306

It would be worthwhile to show how much he contradicts the whole of Scripture, if [this issue] did not recur in his fifth § book, which will be a more suitable place [to deal with it].[120] For the same reason I will also forbear to refute at the present time the nonsense which he talks about original sin, lest I should have to say the same thing twice over. But the order of the argument will not allow me to remain silent about the fact that there is nothing too absurd in what he says for him not to hold out Augustine's name-tag to give it approval. This, he says, is what Augustine says in the third book of the *Hypognosticon*:[121] We did not lose the

3. Hypognosticon

---

116. Council of Orange (529), canon 4 (Leith 38). On the further uses of this passage see *BLW* 2.289 n. 244.

117. The first edition has "he is supposed," which later editions correct to "he claims."

118. I.e., to the fact that grace is necessary, not just desirable.

119. Council of Milevis (416), canon 5 (CCL 149:363) = Council of Carthage (418), canon 6 (often numbered as 5) (CCL 149:71, 76), which is found in the later compilation *African Councils in the time of Boniface I and Celestine I*, canon 80 (J. D. Mansi, *Sacrorum Conciliorum Nova et Amplissima Collectio*, vol. 4 [Florence, 1760], 505). The condemned statement is taken from Pelagius's *Free Choice* (CCL 149:71). See *BLW* 2.289 n. 251 for Calvin's source and the confusion between Milevis and Carthage.

120. Calvin's response appears in *BLW* 5, esp. cols. 365–71.

121. Hypognosticων, with two Greek characters. This work is the *Hypomnesticon [Book of Reminders] against the Pelagians and Celestians*, also called *Hypognosticon [Book of Notes]* (PL 45:1609–10).

freedom to will, but to be able or to perform [the good].¹²² Firstly, I have already shown that Augustine so often teaches differently.¹²³ Secondly, it is the established scholarly opinion that that book is not by Augustine.¹²⁴ Thirdly, Pighius gives a wrong interpretation of the passage which he quotes. That writer (whoever he be) certainly says that "after the loss of the benefit of the power [to act well], we were left with only the choice so to will, and that was maimed."¹²⁵ But in what sense he meant it is quite clear if one connects it with what follows afterwards. He acknowledges that "there is free choice involving rational decision, yet not of such a kind that it would be fit either to begin or to fulfil without God's help any duty towards God, but only in actions of this present life."¹²⁶ What (I ask) is meant by free choice beginning if not the first movement of the will? Just as to fulfil is a firm resolve accompanied by effective exertion.

which is inauthentic

and teaches prevenient grace

But perhaps Pighius is not yet content. I will ensure, therefore, that he is compelled to become absolutely speechless. [The author] adds some time later: "When we are dealing with free choice, we are not dealing with a part of man, but with the whole, because when the first man sinned, he offended not with some part only, but entirely in the nature in which he was created."¹²⁷ You hear that it was not some portion in man that became corrupted, as Pighius with his unholy philosophical imagination conceives, but that the whole of human nature was subjected to depravity. What next? "Therefore, since his free choice has been corrupted, the whole man has been corrupted; hence without the assistance of the grace of God he cannot begin what is pleasing to God, nor is he sufficient to fulfil it."¹²⁸ Where is that idea which Pighius has thought up, that all the corruption was confined in the body as if in a sewer? Let us proceed. "But the medicine comes first, so that in [Christ] the corrupted will is healed and restored and prepared."¹²⁹ You hear that the corruption lies in the will itself; you hear that it can conceive nothing good until it has been healed, restored, and also prepared.

Whole of human nature corrupted

so prevenient grace necessary

On the subject of this preparation there follows: "Therefore man, whose will still limps through the corruption of his free choice, does not

God makes the first move

---

122. This is Pighius's summary (49b) of *Hypognosticon* 3.1.1 (PL 45:1621). Pighius goes on to quote from the same passage. Pighius's summary is in line with his own position as expounded by Calvin (cols. 303–4).
123. See cols. 304–5 (at nn. 106–15).
124. Its inauthenticity had already been shown in the ninth century (E. Portalié, *A Guide to the Thought of Saint Augustine* [London: Burns & Oates, 1960], 71).
125. *Hypognosticon* 3.1.1 (PL 45:1621).
126. Ibid., 3.4.5 (PL 45:1623); cf. n. 166.
127. Ibid., 3.5.7 (PL 45:1624).
128. Ibid., 3.5.7 (PL 45:1624–25).
129. Ibid., 3.5.7 (PL 45:1625), following on from the previous quotation.

anticipate God so that he knows and seeks that grace, as though he were going to receive it in accordance with his merits. But God in his mercy precedes, as I have already said, the will of man, who is not yet seeking him, so that [God] causes [man] to know him and seek him."[130] What else does a writer who removes all preparation from man leave to him except a crooked will? But later he makes his meaning still clearer: "It was said of the unbeliever, in whom there are no good works, that to know and to believe is not of him who wills or of him who runs. For since his senses are unreliable and the understanding that belongs to free choice is clouded in darkness, § he cannot see the true light, unless God who commanded light to shine out of darkness shall have first shed light in his heart. But when he has received the Spirit of the Lord, he will have within himself the freedom to embrace the commands of the Lord."[131] Now, I ask, what freedom to choose and to will is there in one who cannot of himself see anything? Of believers and those who already serve God he speaks as follows: "This also happens in their case, when through the compassion of grace they suddenly attain to those good works which they neither willed nor ran to."[132] Eventually he concludes: "Therefore whatever man wills, whatever he can do, is from the Lord."[133]

307

The good will is a gift of God

To will the good Pighius allows to man, teaching that it is only the ability to fulfil it (and that in part) which man receives from the Lord. On whose authority? He holds up "Augustine." But you hear how well [Pseudo-Augustine] defends himself against this false charge when he acknowledges that to will no less than to be able is a gift of God, and he does so without exception. But [it will be objected] later he says that he who has denied free choice is no catholic Christian.[134] Certainly, provided that the condition is added that without God one can neither begin nor complete any good work.[135] Then he quotes Pelagius's objection that it is because man wills in the first place that God wills, which he refutes as follows: "[Pelagius] is making it a merit, so that there is no longer grace but a wage."[136] Finally, quoting and expounding the famous saying of the apostle (Gal. 1),[137] he says: "'When it pleased God, who called me from the womb, not when I willed but when it pleased him who chose me, not through my merit but through his grace'—so that he might be a believer, not according to the merit of his

---

130. Ibid., 3.5.7 (PL 45:1625); cf. n. 167.
131. Ibid., 3.9.15 (PL 45:1630).
132. Ibid.
133. Ibid., 3.9.16 (PL 45:1630); see n. 168.
134. Ibid., 3.10.18 (PL 45:1631).
135. Ibid., following on from the previous quotation.
136. Ibid.
137. Gal. 1:15.

own will but through the gift of God."¹³⁸ I shall be surprised if Pighius dares to hold his head high after being proved wrong and confounded by such a dazzling beam of truth as this.

I pass by the fact that by an entirely irrelevant comment he wretchedly mutilates a most glorious statement of Paul about those who are free from righteousness and slaves of sin.¹³⁹ For by a nice play on words [Paul] describes as free from righteousness those who have been set free from the rule of righteousness. But he calls them slaves of sin because they do slave-service under the domination of unrighteousness up until that liberation which he mentions in the same breath. Pighius tries to evade this with some tasteless stupidity.

P twists Paul

And in an effort to wrest from my hands the passage of Augustine which I had quoted from his book *The Spirit and the Letter*,¹⁴⁰ he twists it with undue violence. For although Augustine ascribes the sum total of good works and each individual portion of them to the grace of God, [Pighius] (as though no such statement existed in [Augustine's] words) limits this to being one possibility. Where Augustine puts rebellion, he replaces it with weakness.¹⁴¹ And he thinks that he has escaped if he has said that these words are appropriate against the Pelagians, but not against him and those like him. But when Augustine cries that this name which rings of freedom is applicable only to those who are ruled by the Spirit of God, since all others are the slaves of sin, and that not in part but entirely,¹⁴² Pighius jumps over this, as if it had nothing to do with him. Perhaps he once heard that it is an oratorical trick to pass

4. *The Spirit and the Letter*

---

138. *Hypognosticon* 3.14.32 (PL 45:1638).
139. Rom. 6:16–22.
140. *The Spirit and the Letter* 30.52 (NPNF 5:106), from which Pighius summarises the first half and quotes the second (50a). Despite Pighius's assertion, which Calvin appears to accept, this passage is cited neither in the 1539 *Institutes* nor in any other work of Calvin prior to Pighius's work. (His editors have detected an allusion to it in the 1539 *Institutes* 2.3.14 [LCC 20:308], but the passage concerned derives clearly from another work of Augustine's, and Pighius would have had no grounds for accusing Calvin of misquoting *The Spirit and the Letter*, which he had not named.) In the 1543 *Institutes* 2.2.8 (LCC 20:265–66) Calvin introduces a long quotation from the end of the passage. The 1543 *Institutes* appeared *after* the present work, but was *completed* before it (OS 3:xix–xx), a consideration which could explain why Calvin accepted the charge of having quoted *The Spirit and the Letter* (having forgotten when the quotation was added), but not why Pighius should have thought that he had quoted it. It could be that they are both thinking of debates about the passage at Worms or Regensburg (see *BLW* 1.233 nn. 1, 3).
141. Having chided Calvin for wrongly citing the passage, Pighius himself (50a) proceeds to quote it loosely, stating that the healing of the will brings the possibility of doing the good. In his comment on the passage he states that grace heals the wound, the weakness of human free choice. Neither the word "possibility" nor the word "weakness" is found in the Augustine passage—but neither is the word "rebellion." Pighius and Calvin are offering rival interpretations of the passage.
142. Paraphrase of the end of *The Spirit and the Letter* 30.52 (NPNF 5:106), a passage which, rather than "jumping over," Pighius quotes at length (50a). For the uses of the passage in this work see n. 100.

308

Against Two Letters of the Pelagians

No merit before grace

Prevenient grace

over in silence what would make the defence of one's case too difficult. But there is no room for pretence in a matter as open as this. §

Afterwards [Pighius] gathers together other statements on which there is no need for us to delay long, because it will not take much trouble to refute the accusations which he tacks on, since [the texts] most clearly support us. When [Augustine] replies to that text quoted back by Pelagius, "If you are willing and hear," he writes that he has no objection if [Pelagius] acknowledges that that will is prepared by the Lord.[143] You see, [Pighius] says [Augustine] does not condemn in the case of the Pelagians the fact that they affirmed freedom of choice, but that they ascribed to it the meriting of grace without the help of grace. No, on the contrary what he condemns is that they should claim even one drop of good for man. "Let the new heretics answer me," he says, "what good there is in people who are hostile to the Christian cause. For they not only have no merit, but they have the most evil merit. We pray for them. What then do we ask but that instead of being unwilling they should be made willing, instead of rebelling be made acquiescent, instead of attackers be made loving? But by whom, except by him of whom it is written: 'By the Lord the will is prepared'?" (in the same place, i.e., book 4 of *Against Two Letters of the Pelagians*).[144]

You see now what Augustine means by the preparation of the will: without doubt that it is tamed from being evil and perverse to being good. "For how," he says, "can anyone have a good purpose unless the Lord first has mercy on him, since a good will is precisely one which is prepared by the Lord?"[145] Still better and more clearly is it said in the first book of the same work: "We pray for the wicked, that their evil will may be changed to a good one. And by the secret grace of God many are suddenly drawn to Christ. Those who reject this are in conflict not with me but with Christ who cries: No one can come to me, unless my Father draws him.[146] For he does not say 'leads,' which might encourage us to understand that there in some way the will comes first. Who is drawn if he is already willing? And yet no one comes unless he wills. Therefore, so that he does will, he is drawn in wonderful ways by him who knows how to work within the very hearts of people, not so that they should believe unwillingly, which is impossible, but so that they may become willing instead of unwilling."[147] Do you see that peo-

---

143. *Against Two Letters of the Pelagians* 4.6.12 (NPNF 5:421–22), referring to Isa. 1:19–20.
144. Ibid., 4.9.26 (NPNF 5:428–29), quoting Prov. 8:35; see *BLW* 2.287 n. 232. For further brief allusions to this passage see 4.342 (at n. 163) and 5.368 (at n. 140).
145. Ibid., 4.6.13 (NPNF 5:422). For the other uses of this passage see n. 111.
146. John 6:44.
147. *Against Two Letters of the Pelagians* 1.19.37 (NPNF 5:389). There is a similar quotation in *BLW* 5.354 (at n. 41); see also 6.396 (at n. 168).

ple can will only evil until by a wonderful transformation their will is changed from evil to good? What then does Pighius gain by diminishing [God's work], so as to make it a part instead of the whole?

But, [Pighius says, Augustine] explains more exactly at the end of the first book what the orthodox condemn both in the case of Mani and in the case of Pelagius. [They condemn] the former for saying that it was not by the good God that human beings were created, marriage was instituted, and the law was given by Moses. [They condemn] the latter for opposing the grace of God and saying that it was not given freely but according to our merits, that man merited grace by making good use of his free choice, and that little children are secure in such a way that they are not saved by Christ.[148] If this is an accurate description of their doctrines, then on what pretext did Pighius earlier[149] make us the disciples of Mani? For we do not § deny either that man was created by God or that marriage was instituted by him or that the law derived from him. But [he will say] the Manichees added other doctrines too. Then his whole argument collapses. You see, he says, the chief articles of Pelagius's blaspheming, among which is not included that he affirms free choice. If that argument is valid, why is not this one valid likewise? You see the chief articles of Mani's blasphemies, in which none is included of which Pighius accuses us. For there could not be. It follows then that it is a wicked and untrustworthy liar who charges us with being disciples of that heretic with whom we share no similarity at all.

I would not say this for any other purpose but to make it clear that Pighius, while he devotes himself more to deceptive subtlety than to true proofs, loses the argument by giving himself away, as they say, like a shrew-mouse.[150] Now I come to my substantive reply. Although we have here[151] a brief summary of Pelagius's errors, yet I say that they are not clearly displayed. There is no more reliable witness to this than Augustine himself. He elsewhere lists twelve principal points which he requires those wanting to purge themselves of Pelagianism to concede to him (*Letter* [217] *to Vitalis*).[152] These contain more than is stated here.[153] In addition, there is nothing here about the perfection of righteousness, to which [the Pelagians] imagined that a man could attain, so that he would be without sin[154] in this life. There is nothing about

P falsely accuses C of Manichaeism

309

The essence of Pelagianism

---

148. Ibid., 1.24.42 (NPNF 5:390).
149. See *BLW* 2.262–64.
150. Erasmus *Adages* 1.3.65 (CWE 31:289). (The translation here follows later editions, which correct the first edition [*iudicio* becomes *indicio*] to bring it into line with the proverb.)
151. I.e., in *Against Two Letters of the Pelagians* 1.24.42 (NPNF 5:390), cited above (at n. 148), the passage to which Pighius is appealing (51a).
152. *Letter* 217.4.15–5.17 (FoC 32:86–88).
153. See n. 151.
154. "Without sin" is in Greek.

subsequent grace, nothing about its extension to individual actions throughout life, and finally nothing about the gracious election of the faithful and the predestination of the wicked to death.[155] It is known that these were the most important points of controversy between them. Who then does not see that Pighius is fooling around too much like a child?

5. The Grace of Christ

But the other passage, from the first book on *The Grace of Christ and Original Sin*, puts more pressure on him. There [Augustine] affirms that there will be no dispute if Pelagius, just as he acknowledges that our ability comes from God, would add at the same time that to will and to act [well] are also [from God]. In other words, if he would recognise that "not only the power in man (even if he neither wills nor acts well) is the result of divine aid, but so are the will and action themselves (i.e., that we will and act well). These are not in man except when he wills and acts well. [Pelagius should recognise] that without that aid we neither will nor do anything well, and this aid is the grace of Christ through which, by his righteousness, not ours, he makes us righteous. That then is our true righteousness, which we have from him."[156] For these are Augustine's words, but not as they are reported by Pighius.[157]

We can do nothing without grace

Our will and action are given by grace

Here of course I must toil energetically to loosen this knot. But now I have found a very easy way. For I acknowledge that what Augustine says is true; provided that there is genuine agreement on those three things, not only am I ready to abandon the contest, but I will say that there is none [between us]. Pelagius would acknowledge that [human] power is aided by the grace of God, § but he said that the will and the effect were under man's control. Although Augustine shows that [Pelagius] seeks a hiding place for his deceit in the word "power,"[158] he is still not satisfied even if that obfuscation were to be removed. But he constantly safeguards the doctrine that the will is made good by the grace of God and we are effectually directed by it until we perform the good work. "It is not only our ability," he says, "which God has given and aided, but he also brings about in us to will and to act. Not that we do not will or do not act, but that both happen with his help" (ch. 25).[159] But what this means will be understood better from the fourteenth chapter: "If it is the case, as the truth teaches, that all come who have learned from the Father—then whoever does not come has assur-

---

155. Of the points that Calvin mentions, Augustine's support is clear on all except the last one, predestination to death, on which his testimony is ambiguous. Predestination to evil was anathematised with utter abhorrence at the Council of Orange (529) (Leith 44).
156. *The Grace of Christ and Original Sin* 1.47.52 (NPNF 5:235).
157. Pighius quotes the same passage (51a), but somewhat differently.
158. *The Grace of Christ and Original Sin* 1.47.52 (NPNF 5:235).
159. Ibid., 1.25.26 (NPNF 5:227).

edly not learned."[160] Later: "Therefore when God teaches, not by the letter of the law but by the grace of the Spirit, he teaches in such a way that what each has learned he not only perceives in an intellectual way but also strives towards by willing it and completes it by his action. And by that divine way of teaching the will and action are aided, not merely the power to will and act. For if merely our ability were aided by grace, the Lord would say this: Everyone who has heard and learned can come. But he says not only that [everyone can come], but that he does come.[161] Pelagius places the ability to come in nature, or even in grace, by which he says the power itself is aided. But [actually] to come involves the will and the action. Moreover, it does not follow that he who can come also does come, unless he has willed [to do so] and done so. But everyone who has learned from the Father not only can come but does come, where already there are both the power as the point of departure, and the desire of the will and the execution of the action."[162]

What more could Pighius want or require? I declare that I embrace this covenant with my whole heart, that there shall be no disagreement between us once this doctrine is established among us. What does he himself say? He holds that it is only human ability that is flawed. This too he imagines is aided by the grace of God in such a way that the will, if it wills, has the ability [to act]. But from the effectual operation of grace he shrinks back in fear as though from a most hazardous rock or rather from imminent shipwreck. Anyone who wants to have a shining example of his good faith and integrity should weigh carefully what alterations he has made in treating this passage.

P rejects effectual grace

There is no more difficulty for us in the passage which he subjoins from the third book of the *Hypognosticon*.[163] That free choice be denied is forbidden by that writer[164]—for all scholars are of the opinion that he is not Augustine.[165] But what does he hold on to except the name [of free choice]? For he bears witness that it is useless without the grace of God both to begin and to complete a good work;[166] he affirms that God is not anticipated by our will, so that we seek his grace, but that he in mercy freely conferred brings about a good will in us;[167] and finally he leaves nothing to man but to be strong, wise,

Hypognosticon affirms free choice

but not in P's sense

---

160. Ibid., 1.14.15 (NPNF 5:223), quoting John 6:45.
161. John 6:45.
162. *The Grace of Christ and Original Sin* 1.14.15 (NPNF 5:223).
163. *Hypognosticων*, with two Greek characters; cf. n. 121.
164. *Hypognosticon* 3.4.5 (PL 45:1623), cited by Pighius (51a).
165. See n. 124.
166. Paraphrase of *Hypognosticon* 3.4.5 (PL 45:1623), cited by Pighius (51a) and quoted above in col. 306 (at n. 126).
167. Paraphrase of *Hypognosticon* 3.5.7 (PL 45:1625), quoted above in col. 306 (at n. 130).

311

No need to fight over words

We affirm 1. inability before grace

2. grace is prevenient

and efficacious

and continuous

Augustine supports C

and righteous in God, having § none of these things in himself.[168] Where we have excellent agreement with this writer in substance, why does Pighius bring us into conflict over a mere term,[169] as though we were at odds throughout? As my *Institutes* bear witness, I have always said that I have no objection to human choice being called free, provided that a sound definition of the word is agreed between us.[170] Augustine does so on this condition and in so doing follows not the proper sense of the word but common usage.[171] Or is it after all fitting that [Augustine] should be a difficulty to us for this reason? [Pighius] cannot marvel enough at our stupidity and negligence in that we infer from diverse passages of Augustine that he ascribes no part, no power to [human] choice. But all that we say amounts to this. First, that what a person is or has or is capable of is entirely empty and useless for the spiritual righteousness which God requires,[172] unless one is directed to the good by the grace of God. Secondly, that the human will is of itself evil and therefore needs transformation and renewal so that it may begin to be good, but that grace itself is not merely a tool which can help someone if he is pleased to stretch out his hand to [take] it. That is, [God] does not merely offer it, leaving [to man] the choice between receiving it and rejecting it, but he steers the mind to choose what is right, he moves the will also effectively to obedience, he arouses and advances the endeavour until the actual completion of the work is attained. Then again, that [grace] is not sufficient if it is just once conferred upon someone, unless it accompanies him without interruption.

But what does Augustine [say]? Already indeed we have reported many sayings of his, and it will be worthwhile afterwards also to report more. But, so that Pighius may recover a little from that amazement, let him now hear briefly from one passage that nothing which causes him surprise is without Augustine's full support. "But people toil," [Augustine] says, "to discover in our will what good of our own there is which does not come from God, and I do not know how any can be found."[173] [Then he gives] the reason. "For if we have a kind of free will from God which can still be either good or evil, and a good will is from us, then

---

168. Not a quotation but a summary of the thrust of *Hypognosticon* 3; e.g., 3.5.7; 3.7.9; 3.8.11; 3.9.15–16; 3.11.19 (PL 45:1625–28, 1630–32), some of which Calvin quotes in cols. 306–7.
169. I.e., "free choice."
170. *Inst.* 2.2.7–8 (LCC 20:264–66); cf. col. 303 (at n. 103).
171. As Calvin both argues in *Inst.* 2.2.8 (LCC 20:265–66), a passage he defends at the beginning of this book (cols. 292–94), and has been arguing in the rest of this book to this point.
172. Literally, "the spiritual righteousness of God."
173. *The Merits and Forgiveness of Sins* 2.18.28 (NPNF 5:56). For the other uses of this passage see n. 110.

what we have of ourselves is better than what we have from him" (*The Merits and Forgiveness of Sins 2*).¹⁷⁴

But [Pighius says] Augustine denies that grace is sufficient without free choice, as well as that free choice is sufficient without grace.¹⁷⁵ I agree, but all that he means is that God is working in a human being, and not in a stone, since he has a will,¹⁷⁶ born and prepared for willing, as they say. By bending it to the good, [God] makes good the will which by the corruption of nature is wicked and perverted. So it is just as if he said that a human being cannot will well unless he already has a will, and it is self-determined. Since he has the latter from nature and the former from grace, Augustine rightly says that without free choice there is no room for grace.¹⁷⁷ For what the term "free choice" means § for him has already been seen. If you want this explained to you more clearly, think of it like this: the human will is like matter which has been subjected to the working of grace, so that it may receive its form from it.¹⁷⁸ So it follows that the will with its self-determined movement comes from nature, wickedness from the corruption of nature, [while] goodness results from the grace of the Holy Spirit and so is his own work.

The next statements in Pighius's book are the confused utterances of a madman. Augustine says that he does not condemn "those good works done by free choice after it has been prepared by prevenient grace apart from any merit of free choice. Grace itself does them, guides them, and completes them."¹⁷⁹ So [Pighius] like a victor taunts me and criticises both my foolishness and my obstinacy, saying that I have no discernment. Shall I not say that he is a madman who aims straight at his own throat when he thinks he is striking his foe? Let us leave on one side the expression "free choice" itself, about which dispute would be otiose. Those works which Augustine declares to be good and worthy of praise are precisely those which the Spirit of God prepares to be done, and this happens by the prevenience of grace without any merit

Hypognosticon again, on free choice

312

and good works

---

174. Ibid., 2.18.30 (NPNF 5:56). Calvin's marginal reference appears slightly lower than this, but belongs here. This passage is quoted again in *BLW* 5.355 (at n. 50).

175. Pighius is quoting (51b–52a) from *Hypognosticon* 3.11.20 (PL 45:1633), without any indication of source. In his response Calvin shows no awareness that Pighius is quoting Pseudo-Augustine. Indeed the misplaced marginal reference (see n. 174) might indicate that he thought that Pighius was quoting from *The Merits and Forgiveness of Sins*, though that fault is more likely to have been the typesetter's.

176. Calvin's response in the rest of this paragraph is a general summary of Augustine's teaching, but the opening part is found in *The Merits and Forgiveness of Sins* 2.5.6 (NPNF 5:46), repeated in *BLW* 3.313 (at n. 203) and 5.358 (at n. 77).

177. See at n. 175.

178. Note the Aristotelian distinction between matter and form; see Introduction §6.

179. *Hypognosticon* 3.13.29 (PL 45:1635–36), which Pighius again quotes with no indication of source (52a). In his response Calvin again shows no awareness that Pighius is quoting Pseudo-Augustine. The passage is quoted again in *BLW* 6.392 (at n. 142).

of the will.¹⁸⁰ If our will is preceded by the grace of God, without any merit of its own, where is that good motion and preparation¹⁸¹ which Pighius fabricates? If the same grace effects, guides, and finishes whatever good works there are in us, why are we still in dispute? Pighius thunders in a clamorous voice that I should hear this. I do indeed gladly both hear and acknowledge it. But [he says] Augustine affirms that good works [come from] free choice,¹⁸² which we deny. Have I ever denied that good works are voluntary? But [he says] I ascribe no part in good works to free choice. Certainly, except that it should act while it is acted upon, since by itself it can do nothing. If this does not agree with what Augustine says, then one egg is not like another.¹⁸³ But Augustine reckons [people to be] holy on the basis of good works,¹⁸⁴ while I deny works, whatever they may be, any power for attaining righteousness; [I deny this] to the extent that they are wicked if they have this intention. I answer that now is not the place for a discussion about how men attain righteousness before God.¹⁸⁵ As far as the present issue is concerned, that statement of the saint sides entirely with us. For whenever he wants to prove that human righteousness is of grace, he immediately has the argument on his lips that we serve the righteousness of God "not by free choice, which is innate in us, but through the Holy Spirit, which is given to us."¹⁸⁶

Third Group

P's boasts

Now Pighius invites us to [consider] the third group¹⁸⁷ of Augustine's works. But before he comes to that he sings a festive hymn to himself, as if the victory were already won, and he admits that he is continuing to do battle only so as to pay in full what he promised. Perhaps he had persuaded himself of this when without the benefit of another's com-

---

180. A comment on the passage quoted at n. 179.
181. I.e., the idea that people can prepare themselves to receive God's grace.
182. Calvin quotes Pighius (52b), who is referring to his earlier quotation (52a) from *Hypognosticon* 3.13.29 (PL 45:1635).
183. Cf. Erasmus *Adages* 1.5.10 (CWE 31:393); Calvin here appeals to the interpretation of Augustine presented throughout book 3.
184. Calvin quotes Pighius (52b), who is again referring to his earlier quotation (52a) from *Hypognosticon* 3.13.29 (PL 45:1635–36).
185. Calvin is making the distinction between the doctrine of justification (on what basis people are accepted by God) and the doctrine of grace and free will (how it is that people come to respond to God). He rightly observes that the position taken on one of these issues does not determine the position taken on the other. This suits him as Augustine supports him on the latter, but not the former.
186. *The Spirit and the Letter* 3.5 (NPNF 5:85) is the closest source. *Nature and Grace* 64.77 (NPNF 5:148) is similar, but not quite so close.
187. I.e., writings from the third period mentioned in col. 294.

ment and criticism he was reading on his own what he had written. Now that he has read our response, he will recognise, I hope, that he gave himself applause that was too inappropriate and hasty.

He brings forward from the second book of *The Merits and Forgiveness of Sins*, [addressed] to Marcellinus, § Augustine's complaint about the Pelagians, which is not that they affirm free choice, but that they exalt it too much.[188] But it has already been said too often to need repeating that he was in the habit of allowing his enemies [the use of] the expression "free choice" precisely so as not to incur ill will for pedantry on account of a word that was generally accepted.[189] So [Pighius] must bring forward something else if he wants to put pressure on us. He testifies that neither [Augustine] nor any of the orthodox has doubted the fact that no one sins without freely willing it.[190] We too assent to these words, if you understand "freely" as being put in place of "of his own accord," as it was the writer's intention to understand it.[191] After this follows [in Pighius]: And [neither Augustine nor any of the orthodox has doubted] that God has commanded nothing which does not lie within our power.[192] Of course, if the will were sound, so that it could apply all its strength to the observance of the law, as [Augustine] himself replies concerning the perfection of righteousness.[193] But now, when the faculties of the whole soul are entirely corrupted and useless for acting well, that power which will be sufficient for the righteousness of the law is no longer to be sought

1. The Merits and Forgiveness of Sins
313

Free choice

Sin is freely willed

Commands are possible?

---

188. Pighius (53a–b) quotes at length from *The Merits and Forgiveness of Sins* (2.2.2–2.3.3; 2.5.5–2.6.7 [NPNF 5:44–47]). Calvin loosely paraphrases the first sentence, and does so again in *BLW* 5.357 (at nn. 67, 69).

189. In *Retractations* 1.15.4 (FoC 60:67), quoted above in col. 298 (at n. 52), Augustine states something similar about the use of the term "free *will*"; but here Calvin is referring rather to his own earlier claims made for Augustine (see cols. 302–3, 311).

190. Calvin is quoting Pighius's comments (53b) following his quotations (53a–b) from *The Merits and Forgiveness of Sins* 2.2.2–2.6.7 (NPNF 5:44–47); in particular the reference is to 2.6.7 (NPNF 5:47), where Augustine states that with God's help it is possible to be without sin, if one so wishes. Calvin refers to this again in *BLW* 5.358 (at n. 70).

191. As with "free choice," Calvin insists that he accepts what Augustine meant by "freely," even if he is less than happy with the word itself. He argues this by appeal to the author's intention in using the word.

192. Calvin is quoting Pighius's comments (53b) following his quotations (53a–b) from *The Merits and Forgiveness of Sins* 2.2.2–2.6.7 (NPNF 5:44–47); in particular the reference is to 2.6.7 (NPNF 5:47), where Augustine is responding to the Pelagian view as expressed in 2.3.3 (NPNF 5:44). Calvin refers to this again in *BLW* 5.358 (at n. 71).

193. Augustine makes this point in *The Merits and Forgiveness of Sins* 2.3.3 (NPNF 5:44–45) in response to Pelagius's claim that God's commands are possible to natural man. The perfection of righteousness is the theme of 2.3.3–2.6.7. The French translation takes this as a reference to Augustine's *Perfection of Righteousness*, but Calvin is not here referring to that work. The flow of the argument is about the work *The Merits and Forgiveness of Sins*; in addition, the particular point made here is not really covered in *The Perfection of Righteousness*; see also n. 196.

in us, but from heaven.¹⁹⁴ These are not my words, but those of Augustine himself.

> "Help" implies a human role?

But [Pighius says] he is always using the word "help," by which he seems to indicate that [God] himself does not do everything but leaves us some role in our actions.¹⁹⁵ Firstly, this joker either does not notice or pretends not to notice that in those books¹⁹⁶ Augustine is not dealing systematically with the nature or power of free choice, but makes reference to it in passing. For there the first question is whether death is due to natural necessity or is the punishment for sin;¹⁹⁷ the second is whether anyone can be found who is ἀναμάρτητος, that is, without sin,¹⁹⁸ from which is derived a third question, about original sin.¹⁹⁹ So on free choice he speaks there not to the extent that would be sufficient to explain the whole issue, but as much as the occasion allowed in the course of his treatment of another subject.²⁰⁰ In addition, if you examine his conclusion, it embraces exactly what we teach: namely that it is God's work to fulfil through grace what he commands by the law.²⁰¹ But [Pighius says] later he qualifies this by saying that prayer alone is not enough.²⁰² Of course, so as to counter the crazy and ungodly illusion of those who imagine that God works in a human being as he does in a stone, that is, without (so to speak) an inward movement of his will.²⁰³ Finally, if readers remember the statements which I lately quoted from that same book,²⁰⁴ they will recognise that Augustine puts forward far more in the course of his argument than this man touches on. For he does not speak only of God's aid,²⁰⁵ as though God helped

---

194. This is the thrust of *The Merits and Forgiveness of Sins* 2.5.5–2.6.7 (NPNF 5:45-47). It is also a recurring theme in *The Perfection of Righteousness* (e.g., 2.2–3; 3.6; 4.10–6.12; 10.21–22), should Calvin after all be referring to that work.

195. Calvin is referring to Pighius's comments (53b–54a) following his quotation of *The Merits and Forgiveness of Sins* 2.5.6 (NPNF 5:46).

196. I.e., the two books on *The Merits and Forgiveness of Sins*, together with *The Baptism of Infants*, which although originally a separate letter has come to be counted as book 3 of *The Merits and Forgiveness of Sins*. The fact that Calvin refers to books in the plural confirms that he is not thinking of Augustine's single book on *The Perfection of Righteousness* (see n. 193).

197. The starting point of *The Merits and Forgiveness of Sins* book 1.

198. The starting point of *The Merits and Forgiveness of Sins* book 2.

199. This issue figures predominantly in *The Merits and Forgiveness of Sins* book 1 and, to a lesser extent, book 2. Alternatively, Calvin may have in mind book 3, *The Baptism of Infants*, which also contains a substantial discussion of original sin.

200. This is a general statement about *The Merits and Forgiveness of Sins*, which is confirmed by Augustine's comment that he is making a brief statement without prejudice to a more careful examination (2.17.26) (NPNF 5:55).

201. Ibid., 2.5.5 (NPNF 5:45–46), which is quoted by Pighius (53a–b).

202. Pighius (53b) is simply quoting *The Merits and Forgiveness of Sins* 2.5.6 (NPNF 5:46).

203. *The Merits and Forgiveness of Sins* 2.5.6 (NPNF 5:46), also part of Pighius's quotation (53b). For Calvin's other uses of this passage see n. 176.

204. I.e., the quotations from *The Merits and Forgiveness of Sins* 2 in cols. 304, 311 (at nn. 110, 173–76).

205. As in ibid., 2.5.5 (NPNF 5:45–46), quoted by Pighius (53a–b).

us in such a way that we convert ourselves when we are being converted by him, as Pighius falsely declares. But he affirms that uprightness both of mind and of will is entirely the work of God alone,[206] and he admits that he does not know what good can be found in the human will at all.[207] §

The texts which he quotes from *The Spirit and the Letter*[208] do not need long discussion, if they are given a straightforward interpretation—that is, not like Pighius's, who leaves no stone unturned so that he may distort by the worst of false allegations things that were well said. Augustine set faith within our free control, since it depends on our will, because by a free choice we can either incline to faith or turn to unbelief.[209] If the whole argument ended with this, Pighius would, I admit, have cause for elation. But since [Augustine] at the same time testifies that this power is conferred on us by an exceptional gift of God and does not arise from our free choice,[210] and that the will to believe too is not conceived by innate goodness but is made and formed by the Holy Spirit,[211] surely it is now easy to infer what he means in those earlier words! Namely that the power and the will are ours only when each of them has been given to us, as he teaches in the ninth chapter of that work, when speaking about righteousness and faith. "Each of them is ours, but it is said to be of God and of Christ for the reason that it is through his generosity that it is granted to us."[212] As for the fact that, having employed the distinction between being able and willing, [Augustine] says that in Scripture there is no occurrence of the formula "There is no will except from God" comparable to what is said of power, here he in every respect supports our position. For shortly afterwards he adds the explanation: it is of course to prevent anyone from attributing evil wills to God. But that a good will is properly and deservedly attributed to God just as it is produced by him, he allows.[213]

But [Pighius objects] he divides the responsibility between God and man in such a way that "the decision to consent to God's call or to reject

314

2. The Spirit and the Letter

Later passages qualify earlier

Our assent to grace also God's gift

---

206. E.g., *The Merits and Forgiveness of Sins* 2.17.26; 2.19.33 (NPNF 5:55, 57).
207. Ibid., 2.18.28. For the other uses of this passage see n. 110.
208. Pighius quotes (54a–55a) *The Spirit and the Letter* 31.53–54; 33.57–34.60 (NPNF 5:106–10).
209. This is a summary of the argument of *The Spirit and the Letter* 31.53–33.59 (NPNF 5:106–110), drawing especially on the beginning of 32.55 and of 33.58. In his discussion of the origin of faith, Augustine defers the mention of prevenient grace to 34.60.
210. At the beginning of *The Spirit and the Letter* 33.57 (NPNF 5:108) Augustine poses a question similar to the statement which Calvin here attributes to him.
211. In *The Spirit and the Letter* 34.60 (NPNF 5:110–11) Augustine answers the question (see n. 210) along the lines indicated by Calvin's summary here.
212. Ibid., 9.15 (NPNF 5:89).
213. Ibid., 31.54 (NPNF 5:107), referring to Rom. 13:1.

it lies within the free movement of the will."²¹⁴ Combine with this what immediately follows in Augustine (which Pighius craftily suppresses) and the problem will be resolved. "If anyone drives me into a corner with the deep mystery of why one is convinced when he hears [the gospel] and another is not, I have two possible replies: 'O the depth of the riches . . .,' and 'There is no unfairness with God.'"²¹⁵ Why does he add this, unless because he recognises that even that assent which he had placed within man's power is a work of God? For God would achieve little by awakening our will unless he directed and guided it right into a firm assent. However even Pighius cannot restrain himself in the end from giving us his own support too. Augustine acknowledges, he says, that he made a mistake, because he had thought that it was within our ability to assent to the gospel.²¹⁶ What reason then is there for him to bother us, as though this were an innate ability of free choice? It follows from this admission that God bends our heart so that we assent to the gospel. That assent is properly called ours, but not in such a way that it should be understood to derive from us. So [he says also] elsewhere: "It is that faith which God demands from us, and he does not find what he demands unless he has already § granted it so that he may find it" (*Sermon on John* 29).²¹⁷ Very well then! Let us embrace without pretence the statement with which Pighius concludes, that we affirm freedom of choice in such a way that we do not acknowledge that there is anything in us which is derived from ourselves,²¹⁸ and peace will be established between us. But because he is hurrying along at full tilt to manufacture pretences, he does not notice what this means!

But he interposes another sentence, from *Homily on John* 53, although he does not indicate the place: Let no one dare to defend free choice in such a way as to deny that the help of grace needs to be called in; nor let anyone so deny the choice [exercised] by the will that, as necessarily follows, he should dare to excuse sin.²¹⁹ But what right had Pighius to add on this supplement²²⁰ on his own account and insert it into the context in such a way that it should seem to be part of it? By what necessity does it more follow that sin is excused if free choice is denied

---

214. Ibid., 34.60 (NPNF 5:110), which is quoted by Pighius (54b). Calvin includes a phrase ("it" in English) which Pighius omits.
215. Ibid., 34.60 (NPNF 5:110–11), quoting Rom. 11:33; 9:14.
216. *The Predestination of the Saints* 3.7 (NPNF 5:500); cf. col. 320 (at n. 272).
217. *Sermons on John* 29.6 (on 7:17) (NPNF 7:185), quoted already in *Inst.* 2.5.7 (LCC 20:325, where Calvin's reference is suppressed); cf. *BLW* 5.368 (at n. 141).
218. This is Pighius's comment (55a) immediately after his quotation from *The Predestination of the Saints* 3.7 (NPNF 5:500), which is longer than Calvin's (at n. 216).
219. *Sermons on John* 53.8 (on 12:39–40) (NPNF 7:293), following the text of Pighius's quotation (55b) rather than Augustine's original. Calvin knew the source of the passage (not given by Pighius) because he had himself quoted it in *Inst.* 2.2.8 (LCC 20:265).
220. The phrase "as necessarily follows" is not part of Augustine's text.

than that the aid of grace is annulled if it be established? There is a danger that by the affirmation of free choice a wrong may be done to the grace of God, and again that by denying that same thing an opportunity may be given for the wicked to excuse themselves. Augustine warns [his readers] to beware of both [dangers], just as we carefully do. If it is inevitable, according to Pighius, that sins are excused where free choice is denied, why will it be less inevitable for the grace of God to be overthrown if it is affirmed? If he had said this on his own account, I would order him to be off to a far country with [all] his nonsense. But now that he has falsely attributed it to Augustine, why should I not name him a forger? Away then with this false addition—what then remains in the text which might be contrary to our position? Augustine wants care to be taken lest some opportunity be given to the wicked to excuse their sins. Do we not meticulously ensure that this care is taken? For we say both that all who sin do so of their own accord and that by this very fact they are held guilty, so that they may not free themselves from the charge. Those who have outraged God's righteousness, to which it is fitting that we should all be subject, are condemned by his righteous judgment, and truly it is in vain that they plead their natural weakness and impotence, the blame for which they ought to attribute to themselves. Therefore what Pighius was mistakenly glad to brandish against us helps us not a little. For since Augustine was satisfied with the qualification "that people not excuse their sins," who does not see that he agrees fully with us? For when we deny free choice, but add the same qualification, we faithfully perform what he demands.

But Pighius thinks that he has a formidable engine of war from the books which the same Augustine addressed to Valentinus.[221] For since many people then suspected that free choice could not be defended without doing injury to grace, he says, the first book to Valentinus was written by the saint to refute this error. In it he so qualifies his teaching about grace and free choice that they are in harmony with one another.[222] For in the very opening of the book he as it were takes it for granted that free § choice is adequately attested in the Scriptures,[223] and he also later proves it from the commandments as well as by other arguments.[224]

4. *Grace and Free Choice*

Augustine affirms free choice

316

---

221. I.e., *Grace and Free Choice*, which Pighius quotes together with Augustine's accompanying *Letter* 215 to Valentinus (55b–56b), and on which he comments (56b–57a). Calvin refers to "books" (plural), meaning this work ("the first book") and *Rebuke and Grace*, which is discussed in *BLW* 3.323–24 and 4.340–42.

222. This is Pighius's summary of *Grace and Free Choice* (55b). But while Augustine acknowledges the existence of those who so affirm free choice as to deny grace, in this work he is dealing with those who so affirm grace as to deny free choice (*Grace and Free Choice* 1.1 [NPNF 5:443–44]).

223. *Grace and Free Choice* 2.2 (NPNF 5:444).

224. Ibid., 2.2–3.5 (NPNF 5:444–46); see also *BLW* 4.329 (at nn. 22, 25) and 5.358–59 (at n. 83).

and himself shows what he means

I will do here what I have normally done up till now. For I consider that there is no one to whom the responsibility of explaining his own mind could more suitably be entrusted than Augustine himself. Now what he understands by the term, when he ascribes free choice to man, he later defines in these words: "The human will is always free, but it is not always good. For either it is free from righteousness, when it is serving sin, and then it is evil; or it is free from sin, when it is serving righteousness, and then it is good. Indeed it is always by the grace of God that [the will], which had previously been evil, is good. And through [grace] it also happens that the good will itself, which has now begun to exist, is increased."[225] We hold that the will can be called free only because it moves by a self-determined volition. But Pighius demands something far different, namely that it should have a free ability to choose either good or evil. Augustine says, it is free because it is evil of its own accord.[226] Pighius argues that it is free because it is capable of choosing freely in either direction. Do you then want to know briefly in what sense [Augustine] unites free choice with grace? At the end of the book he finally replies in a few words: "the human will is not abolished by grace but changed from evil to good and, when it has become good, is helped."[227] Now you hear that man does have a will to hand by nature, but one which is evil and cannot be good of itself or aspire to the good, and it is not annulled by the grace of God, so as not to exist, but it is corrected and turned from being evil, so as to be good.

All is of grace

I have no fear that anyone who has read the whole book carefully and with the application of judgment[228] will doubt whether he ought to give his vote in my favour. But since not all have the time to read it, I will relate a few of his words from it, to make clear how much power he allows to human choice, which he defends there. "We are fashioned, that is, formed, in good works which we ourselves have not prepared, but God prepared them for us to walk in them."[229] Moreover the manner of this formation follows next. "For he himself begins by working in us so that we will [the good], and also completes the work by co-operating with us when we will. Thus he works without us to cause us to will, but when we will and will so as to act, he cooperates with us; but without his help (whether by working so that we will or by co-

---

225. Ibid., 15.31 (NPNF 5:456), also quoted in *BLW* 3.322 (at n. 288) and more briefly in 4.329 (at n. 32); it is paraphrased in 5.359 (at n. 85).

226. A summary of the previous passage (see at n. 225).

227. *Grace and Free Choice* 20.41 (NPNF 5:461), quoted more fully in *BLW* 4.330 (at n. 36) and more loosely in 6.399 (at n. 209). It is also quoted in *Inst.* 2.3.14 (LCC 20:308).

228. At the end (24.46 [NPNF 5:465]) Augustine, using language which Calvin here echoes, urges the reader to read *Grace and Free Choice* carefully.

229. *Grace and Free Choice* 8.20 (NPNF 5:451).

operating when we do will) we are powerless to do the good works which are our duty."²³⁰ But perhaps the human will is prepared in some way to receive this grace. Not at all, says he: "for can we say that the merit of a good will was already present in man, so that his stony heart should be removed, when that stands for nothing but a most stubborn will and is altogether unyielding towards God? And when a good will is already present, there is certainly no longer a stony heart."²³¹ But perhaps the grace of God moves the will only far enough to make it inclined towards good, but does not arouse an effective volition in it. § On the contrary, he says, "we have to ask God that we may will as much as is sufficient for us to act willingly. It is indeed certain that it is we who will when we will, but it is he who causes us to will the good. It is indeed certain that it is we who act when we act, but it is he who, by providing the will with fully effective powers, causes us to act, as he says: I will cause you to walk in my commandments."²³²

Yet someone will say that [Augustine] implies that once grace has been received the first time, we cooperate with God. Of course, since the will which has now been made good through the power of the Holy Spirit is ours, and we act by means of it after previously being acted on by God, it is not at all surprising if a part of the action is ascribed to us. Accordingly, when he finishes, he says that "God will repay the faithful both with good for evil, that is, with grace in return for unrighteousness, and with good for good, that is, with grace in return for grace."²³³ Here we learn what it means for God to act without us: this is obviously when he makes children of Abraham out of stones²³⁴ and when he grafts slips from a wild unfruitful olive into a vigorous fertile olive.²³⁵ For there is nothing that is ours there. Then [we learn] what it means for him to act with us: this is obviously when, by the continuous supply of his aid, he assists, increases, and strengthens that power which he has granted us, both for the completion of each particular work and for final perseverance through life.²³⁶ Or if you like to maintain that fine image of Paul's, it is when he invigorates by his own heavenly warmth the olives which have already been made fertile and waters them with dew, so that they may bear fruit.²³⁷ And indeed in this image there is an

> No preparation for grace

> 317
> Grace is efficacious

> Cooperation with grace

---

230. Ibid., 17.33 (NPNF 5:458); see also at n. 236.
231. Ibid., 14.29 (NPNF 5:455–56). For another summary of this passage see *BLW* 4.329 (at n. 31). Calvin also refers to it in 6.380 (at n. 51).
232. *Grace and Free Choice* 16.32 (NPNF 5:457), quoting Ezek. 36:27. A very similar quotation is found in *BLW* 3.323 (at n. 303) and again in 4.330 (at n. 34).
233. *Grace and Free Choice* 23.45 (NPNF 5:464).
234. Matt. 3:9/Luke 3:8.
235. Rom. 11:17–24.
236. A summary of the passages from *Grace and Free Choice* that Calvin has cited, esp. 17.33 (see at n. 230).
237. See at n. 235.

easy and rapid answer to all Pighius's sophistries. We are by nature wild olives, of no value and barren. When God regenerates us into newness of life, he removes this barrenness from us and makes us into olives fit to bear fruit. For by the light of the truth he both enlightens our minds, which are blind and buried in darkness, and transforms our wills from their innate wickedness to obedience to his law. What is there in that which we can claim for ourselves? But after we have begun to be guided by the Spirit of holiness, we are now olives which are green and lively, drawing their vigour from their good root. Of our own accord, then, we are now disposed towards bearing fruit. But is that our own doing or may we boast of it even in smallest measure? [No,] it is entirely derived from the root. Moreover, the root itself is [ours] not by nature but by grace; and even it is still not sufficient, unless God supplies from heaven continual power for life.

<small>Augustine is on C's side</small>

Since Augustine so clearly speaks on our side throughout this work, how do those loud, fine-sounding declamations of Pighius, with which he celebrates his own victory, differ from the silly shrieking of children? Augustine lauds grace in such a way that he still leaves free choice its proper role.[238] But [in the *Institutes*] I had conceded the contest over the term to him.[239] Therefore now it was necessary to inquire § how much power Augustine bestows on free choice, not to insist on the use of the proper term. There is no sin, [Pighius] says, except one that is voluntary.[240] What is the point of saying this except to instil suspicion in the unlearned, who do not read our works, that we teach differently, although this very statement appears repeatedly in our writings?[241] Everyone, he says, ought to attribute to himself the fact that he sins.[242] And what [else] do those words mean which he earlier quoted from my *Institutes*?[243] Our merits, he says, win a crown—provided you understand that they are God's gifts.[244] It will be surprising if the more sober of the Romanists do not here suspect him of changing sides, when he pleads our case just as if he had been hired by us.

---

238. I.e., in *Grace and Free Choice* as a whole.

239. *Inst.* 2.2.8 (LCC 20:265–66).

240. Pighius's observation (56b) refers back to his quotation (55b–56a) from *Grace and Free Choice* 2.4–3.5 (NPNF 5:445–46).

241. For the statement that sin is voluntary see, e.g., *Inst.* 2.3.5; 2.5.1–2 (LCC 20:295–96, 317–18); *BLW* 2.287 (at n. 237).

242. *Grace and Free Choice* 2.4 (NPNF 5:445), quoted by Pighius (56a) and cited again in his concluding summary of *Grace and Free Choice* (56b).

243. Probably a reference to Pighius's quotations (book 1, ch. 3 [9a–15a]) from the second chapter of Calvin's 1539 *Institutes*.

244. *Grace and Free Choice* 6.15 (NPNF 5:450), quoted by Calvin in *Inst.* 2.5.2 (LCC 20:318–19) and by Pighius (56b), and cited again in *BLW* 4.337 (at n. 105) and 6.386 (at n. 99). This thought is also found in many other places in Augustine's writings (see *BLW* 4.337 nn. 107–8, 110).

But sensing that he has reached a point too slippery and dangerous for himself, he quickly retraces his steps and sets off on a different way. For he passes to another book, which survives under Augustine's name among his works, and has the title *The Dogmas of the Church*.[245] But he acts with his accustomed candour in that he misuses the name of the saint while quoting from a work of whose inauthenticity he is no less aware than are those who will now, after my reminder, recognise it. First, although Augustine claims that he composed a list of all his works in the *Retractations*, there is no mention [there] of this work. In addition, although he is everywhere in his writings most attentive to orderly exposition, that work contains a confused mixture, a hodgepodge of different matters piled up without any arrangement. When [its author] deals with the matter now under discussion, he does nothing but collect divergent quotations from hither and thither.[246] Innocent, the pope of Rome who was made bishop a long time after Augustine,[247] he calls his master.[248] He speaks of the African synods of Milevis and Carthage as though he had never taken part in them,[249] although it is certain that Augustine was supreme in them by his counsel and his authority. Indeed the opinions which he borrows from Augustine and his contemporaries he calls "the definitions of the fathers of old."[250] However it is foolish of me to write so many words on a matter that is by no means obscure, except that I at least gain the advantage that Pighius's shamelessness will be obvious to all!

Now let us hear what advantage he wants to secure with the help of that ghost of an Augustine! That the heretics may know, [Pighius] says, that he affirmed freedom of choice not on the basis of his own private opinion, but of a definition of the church, which none of the faithful should dare to contradict. Can it really be that so much weight is given

5. *The Dogmas of the Church*

which is inauthentic

Freedom of choice affirmed there,

---

245. *The Dogmas of the Church* was written in the latter part of the fifth century by Gennadius, a presbyter at Marseilles who has been accused of semi-Pelagianism. Passages from Innocent I and the councils of Carthage (418) and Orange (529) were later added. The Erasmian edition used by Calvin declares that it is not by Augustine.

246. *The Dogmas of the Church* 21–51 (PL 58:986–93). For the sources of the quotations see the notes in PL 58:1023–26. Some might feel that Calvin by implication credits Augustine with greater powers of orderly arrangement than is warranted.

247. Innocent was bishop of Rome from 402 to 417. Calvin's point (contrary to Smits, *Saint Augustin*, 1:188) seems to be not that the author was guilty of anachronism, but that Augustine was the senior bishop, having been consecrated in 395.

248. *The Dogmas of the Church* 25 (PL 58:986) quotes Innocent's letter to the bishops at Milevis (*Letter* 30.3 [PL 20:591]), identifying the author simply as "the master." In the Erasmian edition used by Calvin it is stated at the beginning of the work that ch. 25 contains a letter by Innocent.

249. For Milevis see n. 248. Carthage is not named, but *The Dogmas of the Church* 28–29, 33–37 (PL 58:987–90) constitutes canons 4–5, 1–2, 7–9 of the 418 Council of Carthage, for more details of which see *BLW* 2.289 n. 251.

250. *The Dogmas of the Church* 49 (PL 58:992).

to compositions thoughtlessly assembled from all over the place by an unknown author (I will say nothing worse for the moment)? But how far is freedom affirmed there? To the extent that there remains to us after the fall [the ability] to choose either alternative, but with the addition of these qualifications: that there is no such power except "when God admonishes us and invites us to receive salvation"; secondly, § that "it is within our power to assent to divine inspiration"; thirdly, that "our not falling away once we have obtained the gift of salvation is equally the result of our own carefulness and of heavenly assistance."[251] What if the writer is not consistent with himself a little later? For what he quotes from the synod at Milevis—"if anyone supposes that God waits for our desire that we should be cleansed from sin, and not rather that he causes us to want cleansing, he resists the Holy Spirit"[252]—is scarcely consistent with the aforementioned[253] freedom to choose. Further, when he says that God works in us so that we will and do what he wills,[254] that is absolutely contradictory to what he had said [before], that it is within our power to assent.[255] For in the one place the effective operation of the Holy Spirit is affirmed, while in the other it is said that through grace the power of at least choosing good or evil is conferred. As for those three statements, it has already been seen in part[256] how far removed they are from the mind of Augustine, and it will be seen still more fully.[257]

Finally, [Pighius] puts down the conclusion from some public oration which is attributed to Augustine.[258] Whether it is from him I leave to others to judge, although it seems to me to have very little of the flavour of Augustine's genius. Certainly one may, even from these words which Pighius cites, make an inference that is not entirely without substance,

---

251. Ibid., 21 (PL 58:985–86); cf. nn. 253, 255. An abbreviated form of this passage reappears in the twelfth-century Pseudo-Augustine *The Spirit and the Soul* 48 (PL 40:814; 58:1023).

252. *The Dogmas of the Church* 41 (PL 58:990). This canon does not come from Milevis but is canon 4 of the Council of Orange (529) (Leith 38). While Calvin seems to have accepted the ascription of the canons of Carthage (418) to Milevis (see *BLW* 2.289 n. 251), this particular canon has already twice been quoted as from Orange (see *BLW* 2.289 n. 244 for details); the error is probably due to the pressure of time.

253. As quoted above (at n. 251). If the canons of the Council of Orange are added to the work of a semi-Pelagian author (n. 245), it is not surprising that inconsistency ensues.

254. *The Dogmas of the Church* 32 (PL 58:988).

255. As quoted above (at n. 251).

256. I.e., the three qualifications listed at n. 251. For Calvin's response see cols. 304–5 (at nn. 106–15), col. 308 (at nn. 143–47), col. 310 (at nn. 159–62), cols. 314–15 (at nn. 210–13, 215–17), cols. 316–17 (at nn. 225–37). "In part" is an indication that the third statement (the human contribution to final perseverance) has not yet been covered.

257. I.e., in cols. 320–25. On the third issue see cols. 324–25 (at nn. 311–13).

258. Pighius quotes (58a) the end of Pseudo-Augustine *Sermon* 236 (PL 39:2183). This is in fact, with minor verbal changes, the *Confession of Faith to Pope Innocent* which Pelagius submitted to Rome (PL 39:2181; cf. 45:1716–18).

that it is either not from him or was delivered by him when he was still a young man. For when he was describing two opposite heresies which err by an excessive tendency in this direction or that, and had placed the Manichees on one side, he set opposite them not the Celestians or the Pelagians, but Jovinian.[259] Would he, I ask, have omitted the Pelagians, to whom he was always so bitterly hostile and whom it was the more necessary to name in public, if they had existed then? For at that time[260] Jovinian was no trouble to the African churches, but the notoriety of the Pelagians had spread through almost the whole world. However, even apart from this inference, the very style betrays that it carries Augustine's name falsely. But however that may be, let us hear what it contains: "So that we may acknowledge human free choice, we say that we are able both not to sin and to sin."[261] I reply that if this man's understanding (whoever he be) is that it is by the power of choice that man is able not to sin, then he is a heretic, not [only] in my judgment but in that of Augustine himself. But if it[262] is by the grace of God, then scholars who are well practised in the reading of Augustine know how his argument on this possibility tends to go. For since the Pelagians falsely accused him of detracting from God's power, he acknowledges that God can [bring this about] if he were to will it, but no such case has ever occurred or ought to be expected, since Scripture declares otherwise.[263]

After he has refuted me with such sure proofs, Pighius again performs a victor's dance—not surprisingly, since he sings inwardly to himself and his Muses,[264] or at least is content if he can obtain applause from a small number of people like himself. These people, having already despaired of the possibility of the truth of God being overthrown, look everywhere for any ways of delaying and obstructing its progress and, when they are § found, applaud them furiously but blindly. But I am sure that I have exposed the whole subject too clearly for him to gain even the slightest advantage from those arrogant[265] displays of his with those who bring to the reading of this controversy a sound judgment and a calm and composed mind. For I think that I have more than adequately washed away the colours with which he had painted Augustine to make him seem to be opposed to us.

and ambiguous

P boasts of Augustine's support

320

---

259. Pseudo-Augustine *Sermon* 236.6 (PL 39:2183). For the Celestians see n. 66. Jovinian was a monk who at the end of the fourth century combated excessive asceticism. He was accused of teaching that some Christians can no longer sin.
260. I.e., in the later period of Augustine's life, the period that Pighius is supposedly covering (see n. 187).
261. Pseudo-Augustine *Sermon* 236.6 (PL 39:2183).
262. I.e., "that man is able not to sin."
263. Augustine argues this repeatedly in his anti-Pelagian works, e.g., *The Merits and Forgiveness of Sins* 2.6.7–2.28.46; *The Perfection of Righteousness* passim.
264. Greek goddesses of poetry, literature, music, and dance.
265. The Latin (*flatuosis*) can also refer to the breaking of wind (cf. English "flatulent").

Augustine Supports Calvin

More proof that Augustine supports C

But now some may perhaps require also of me, as a bonus, that I next confirm more fully and with more evidence my boast that Augustine is certainly on our side. In carrying this out I am hindered not so much by the difficulty as by the extent of the task. For if I were to begin to collect all [the evidence] which, if it were quoted, would be of use for the confirmation of our position, I should have to put together a long volume, and sometimes even whole books would have to be included. For what else do the four books [addressed] to Boniface,[266] the two to Prosper and to Hilary,[267] and also the two to Valentinus[268] contain, what else does the book *Nature and Grace* [contain], and also the other one *The Perfection of Righteousness*, what do the three books [addressed] to Marcellinus,[269] what do the letters of about the same number as the books which I have named[270] [contain]—except a pure and so enduring exposition of our teaching? But lest I seem, like my opponent, to want to win my case by oratory alone, and also so that I may satisfy in part the wishes of those who, although they desire to see our agreement with Augustine, have neither the leisure nor the opportunity to read through all these [books], I will add a summary compiled from a few passages which will remove all doubt on the matter. And I will select those books above all to which Pighius allows the most authority, lest when he is refuted he may take refuge in his usual objection, that many words fell from Augustine's lips in the heat of an argument which not even the author himself wanted to be believed. Now he acknowledges that those books which were written after the violence of the argument had subsided are the most reliable witnesses to what Augustine thought and wanted to be accepted with certainty.[271] Therefore, if I prove from these that he is in agreement with us, then I shall have an undisputed victory, even on the admission of my opponent.

Summary from his last books

Corruption of human mind and will

First, we say that man's mind is smitten with blindness, so that of itself it can in no way reach the knowledge of the truth; we say that his will is corrupted by wickedness, so that he can neither love God nor obey his righteousness. Both of these doctrines Pighius rejects. Let Augustine now come forward between us, like an arbitrator. In the book *The Predestination of the Saints* he admits that at one time he held the erroneous view that it is within our power, having heard the gospel, to assent to it. But afterwards [he says] he was convinced by those words

---

266. *Against Two Letters of the Pelagians.*
267. *The Predestination of the Saints* and *The Gift of Perseverance.*
268. *Grace and Free Choice* and *Rebuke and Grace.*
269. *The Merits and Forgiveness of Sins* and *The Baptism of Infants* (see n. 196).
270. In this work Calvin cites *Letters* 36, 145, 194, 214–15, 217.
271. See col. 294.

of Paul, so as to change his mind: What do you have that you have not received?[272] Accordingly he concludes that both the beginning and the perfection of faith are the gift of God,[273] since it is not in our power even to think anything good, which however is much less than to believe.[274] But he wanted to leave no loophole § for the sophistry that faith is a gift of grace in that by a general inspiration God invites and stirs everyone to believe. So he confronts it by adding that "this gift is given to some and not given to others."[275] And "if the question is raised and discussed how each is deserving [of his lot], there are not lacking those who say that it is because of human will, but we say that it is by divine grace and predestination."[276] But God demands faith from mankind. I agree, he says, but it is nonetheless a gift from God. For at the same time he promises them that he will cause them to do what he orders to be done.[277]

But people commonly imagine that man is prepared to receive the grace of God by a movement of his own—a view which Pighius also strongly defends. So [Augustine] responds: "This opinion is refuted by the apostle when he says: What do you have that you have not received? From whom [do you have it] but from him who distinguishes you from another to whom he has not given what he has given to you?"[278] And he brings forward a proof of this in Paul himself: "Being alienated from the faith, which he ravaged, and violently opposed to it, he was suddenly converted to it, grace being more powerful, so that he not only became willing to believe after being unwilling, but also turned from being a persecutor to being ready to endure persecution."[279] Again: "When God promises that he will cause people to do what he commands, he remains silent not about their merits, but about their evil deeds. He thus shows them that he repays good for evil by the very fact that he causes them thereafter to have good works."[280] Later: "A most clear pointer to predestination and grace is the Mediator himself between God and mankind. By what merits of its own, I ask you, whether of faith or works, did the human nature which was in him win the right to be this? Because its goodness, whatever that was, came first? Since I am a human being, as he was too, why am I not the Son

Faith is a gift of God

321

No human preparation for grace

---

272. *The Predestination of the Saints* 3.7 (NPNF 5:500), citing 1 Cor. 4:7. Cf. col. 314 (at n. 216).
273. Ibid., 8.16 (NPNF 5:506), quoted again (more accurately) in col. 323 (at n. 300). For the same idea see 2.5 (NPNF 5:499–500).
274. Ibid., 2.5 (NPNF 5:499–500).
275. Ibid., 8.16 (NPNF 5:506).
276. Ibid., 10.19 (NPNF 5:507).
277. Ibid., 11.22 (NPNF 5:509), quoted more fully at n. 280.
278. Ibid., 5.10 (NPNF 5:503), citing 1 Cor. 4:7.
279. Ibid., 2.4 (NPNF 5:499).
280. Ibid., 11.22 (NPNF 5:509); cf. at n. 277.

of God as he was? But he had that nature and status by grace. Why is grace different where nature is the same?²⁸¹ Let it be clear to us that the source of grace itself is in [our] Head. For he who for us made Christ in whom we believe made us believe in Christ; he who made the man Jesus, the beginner and perfecter of faith, makes in men the beginning and perfection of faith in Jesus."²⁸² Again: "Therefore just as he chose us, so he calls us, according to the decision of his will, lest, where so great a benefit is concerned, we should boast in the decision of our own will."²⁸³ Again: "Let them consider how they are mistaken who think that it is of ourselves, and not something given to us, that we ask, seek, and knock; who say that the consequence of grace is brought about by our own merit which precedes it, when asking we receive and seeking we find; and who are not willing to understand that it is a divine bounty that we ask, and seek, and knock."²⁸⁴

Fallen man not free to do good

322

But the question is asked whether freedom to choose good or evil does not naturally reside in man. He replies *(Rebuke and Grace, to Valentinus)*: "It must be acknowledged that we have free choice to do § both evil and good. But in doing evil each one is free of righteousness and the slave of sin, while in doing good no one can be free, unless he has first been set free by the Son of God.²⁸⁵ So people are freed from evil by the grace of God alone. Without this they do no good at all, whether by thinking, or by willing and loving, or by acting. This means not only that when [grace] shows them they know what they should do, but that when it enables them they gladly do what they know [to be right]."²⁸⁶ And he then explains this more briefly. "The human will does not obtain grace through its freedom, but rather freedom through grace."²⁸⁷ And he had said in the first book to Valentinus: "There is always a free will in us, but it is not always good. For either it is free from righteousness, when it serves sin, and then it is evil; or it is free from sin, when it serves righteousness, and then it is good. But the grace of God is always good, and through this it comes about that a person has a good will."²⁸⁸

---

281. Ibid., 15.30 (NPNF 5:512).

282. Ibid., 15.31 (NPNF 5:512–13). In 1559 Calvin added to the *Institutes* a quotation which overlaps with this and the previous one (2.17.1 [LCC 20:528–29]).

283. *The Predestination of the Saints* 18.36 (NPNF 5:516), where Augustine is discussing Eph. 1:5.

284. *The Gift of Perseverance* 23.64 (NPNF 5:551), where Augustine is discussing Matt. 7:7.

285. *Rebuke and Grace* 1.2 (NPNF 5:472), summarised in *BLW* 6.399 (at n. 212).

286. Ibid., 2.3 (NPNF 5:472), the first half of which is quoted again in *BLW* 6.400 (at n. 217).

287. Ibid., 8.17 (NPNF 5:478), quoted already in *Inst.* 2.3.14 (LCC 20:308). It is quoted more fully in *BLW* 6.400 (at n. 218).

288. *Grace and Free Choice* 15.31 (NPNF 5:456). For the other uses of the passage see n. 225.

But perhaps [God] offers light to human minds, and it is in their power to choose to accept it or to refuse it, and he moves their wills in such a way that it is in their power to follow his movement or not to follow it. To this [Augustine] replies: "If God causes our faith, working miraculously in our hearts so that we believe, why should we fear that he is not able to complete the work? And why does man claim for himself the initial part in it, to be the basis for his receiving the second part from God?"[289] Again: "Not wanting to go against such clear evidence in which faith is declared to be the gift of God, and yet wanting to have the fact that he believes derived from himself, he as it were makes a bargain with God. He claims part of his faith for himself and leaves part for him, and, what is more arrogant, he takes the initial part himself and gives the subsequent part to God."[290] You see how [Augustine] in no way divides [the gift of faith] in half or shares it between God and man, but yields it in its entirety to God.

It is all of grace

But later he sets it out much more clearly. "What is 'to come to Christ'[291] except to believe in Christ? That this should happen is granted by the Father. For what does it mean when it says, Everyone who has heard the Father and learned from him comes to me,[292] except that there is none who hears and learns from the Father and does not come to me? For if everyone who has learned from the Father comes, then certainly he who does not come has not learned."[293] A little later [he says]: "This grace which is secretly bestowed on human hearts is not received by any hard heart. For it is given for the very purpose that hardness of heart should for the first time be removed."[294] Again: "Far be it that he who has learned from the Father should not come.[295] But why, they say, does he not teach everyone? If we shall say, Because they do not want to learn, the reply will be, And where then is the text: 'Lord, you make us alive by converting us'?[296] Or, if God does not make the unwilling become willing, why does the church pray for its persecutors? Now when the gospel is preached, some believe and some do not believe. But those who believe, while the preacher is speaking externally, are inwardly giving ear § to the Father and learning from him. But those who do not believe hear outwardly, but inwardly they do not hear or learn—that is, it

Conversion is a gift of efficacious grace

323

---

289. *The Predestination of the Saints* 2.6 (NPNF 5:500).
290. Ibid.
291. John 6:37 is being discussed.
292. John 6:45.
293. *The Predestination of the Saints* 8.13 (NPNF 5:504).
294. Ibid., 8.13 (NPNF 5:505). Augustine wrote that "this grace is not *rejected* by any hard heart," which Calvin has inadvertently changed to "not received," softening the emphasis on the sovereignty of grace.
295. Ibid., 8.14 (NPNF 5:505), referring to John 6:45.
296. Ps. 84:7 in the Vulgate (85:6).

is granted to the former to believe, but not to the latter. [Christ] declares this even more openly afterwards: No one can come to me unless my Father has drawn him."[297] Again: "[No one can come to me] except him to whom it has been granted by my Father.[298] Now to be drawn to Christ and to hear and learn from the Father is nothing other than to receive the gift of faith. For he distinguishes not hearers from nonhearers but believers from nonbelievers when he says: No one comes to me, unless it has been granted to him.[299] Faith, therefore, both at its beginning and in its perfection, is the gift of God."[300] Again: "God promised what he himself would do, not what men would do. For although men do good things pertaining to the worship of God, it is he who causes them to do what he has commanded, not they who cause him to do what he has promised. Otherwise the fulfilment of the promises of God lies not in God's power but in man's."[301] Again: "When God speaks like this, 'I will put fear of me in their heart,' what else does this mean but that the fear of me which I will put in their heart will be of such a kind and such a magnitude that they will persevere in clinging to me?"[302] Again: "It is certain that it is we who keep the commandments if we will to, but because the will is prepared by God, we must seek from him that we will it to a sufficient degree for us to do them. It is certain that it is we who will when we will, but it is he who causes us to will the good. It is certain that it is we who act when we act, but it is he who, by providing the will with fully effective powers, causes us to act."[303] Again: "Or will you dare to say that even when Christ asked that Peter's faith should not fail, it would have failed if Peter wanted it to fail? As though Peter would in any way want something different from what Christ had prayed for him to want! Therefore when he asked that his faith should not fail, what did he ask but that he should have in believing a will that was free, strong, unconquerable, and constant to the utmost degree?"[304]

Adam compared to fallen humanity

Indeed, when [Augustine] gets down to a comparison of the first man and his descendants, he finishes this whole section[305] in such a

---

297. *The Predestination of the Saints* 8.15 (NPNF 5:505–6). In Augustine the quotation of John 6:44 in the last sentence precedes the first half of the sentence ("[Christ] declares this even more openly afterwards").

298. John 6:65.

299. *The Predestination of the Saints* 8.15 (NPNF 5:506).

300. Ibid., 8.16 (NPNF 5:506); cf. at n. 273.

301. Ibid., 10.19 (NPNF 5:508), quoted more briefly in *BLW* 6.379 (at n. 45).

302. *The Gift of Perseverance* 2.2 (NPNF 5:527), quoting Jer. 32:40. The quotation is repeated in *BLW* 5.356 (at n. 53).

303. *Grace and Free Choice* 16.32 (NPNF 5:457). For the other quotations of this passage see n. 232.

304. *Rebuke and Grace* 8.17 (NPNF 5:478), discussing Luke 22:32.

305. The "section" comparing Adam and his descendants is found in *Rebuke and Grace* 10.26–12.38 (NPNF 5:482–87).

way that Pighius now ought to be silent, or that, if he continues to growl, he will at least have nothing to bite! For after explaining the original state of innocence, then the fall, and also the punishment for the fall (that is, this wretched condemnation of our race which followed from it),[306] [Augustine] then turns to [our] restoration and writes as follows: God the Father deemed the human nature in Christ, through no merits of its own [but] by his own gracious benevolence, worthy of such honour that a man conceived in the womb of a virgin should be called the Son of God. And that was on the terms that "the human nature which was taken up by God in this way should permit no movement in itself of an evil will. In the same way through this Mediator God showed that he makes those whom he redeemed by his blood, who were evil, to be eternally good.[307] The first man did not have that grace through which he would never wish to be evil. But he had grace which was such that if he were willing to § remain under its control he would never be evil, and without which, even possessing free choice, he could not be good. But he could by free choice abandon it."[308] Next: "For the assistance was of such a kind that he might abandon it when he wanted and remain under its control if he wanted, but it was not such as to cause him to want. This is the original grace which was given to the first Adam, but [the grace given] in the second Adam is more powerful. For the first [grace] causes someone to have righteousness if he wills; the second can do more and even causes him to will, and will so much and love with such ardour that through the will of the Spirit he overcomes the will of the flesh which lusts against it. The first [grace] was certainly not a small thing. But the second is so much the greater that for man merely to recover his lost freedom through it would be insufficient, and, finally, for it merely to make it possible for him either to perceive the good or to persist in it, if he willed it, would be insufficient. What it requires is that he also be caused to will [the good] by it."[309] Again: "And through this God did not want the saints to boast of their own powers even in regard to perseverance in [doing] the good, but to glory in him. He not only gives them help of the kind which he gave to the first man, without which they could not persevere if they wanted to, but also causes them to will. This means that, since they will not persevere without being both able and willing to do so, both the power and the will to persevere are

---

306. Ibid., 10.26–11.29 (NPNF 5:482–83).
307. Ibid., 11.30 (NPNF 5:484), moving from summary to quotation.
308. Ibid., 11.31 (NPNF 5:484).
309. Ibid. This and the previous quotation reappear, with minor variations, in *BLW* 5.355 (at n. 48). A summary of part of this quotation appears in *Inst.* 2.3.13 (LCC 20:307) and is repeated in *BLW* 6.401 (at n. 229). The final part is repeated in 6.402 (at n. 237).

granted to them by God's generosity. For their wills are so fired by the Holy Spirit that they are able for the very reason that they so will, and they will for the reason that God works so that they will. For if, when our weakness in this life is so great, people were left with their own wills, so that they would continue to have the help of grace, without which they could not persevere, only if they willed to do so, and God did not cause them to will, among so many and so great temptations the will itself would succumb through weakness, and they would not be able to persevere. This is because their weakness would let them down, and they either would not will to [persevere] or through weakness of will would not will in such a way as to be capable of it. Therefore help has been given to the weakness of the human will, so that it should be driven by divine grace without the possibility of turning aside or detaching itself,[310] and thus, although weak, should not fail or be overcome by any opposition."[311]

Perseverance also God's gift,

Will Pighius continue here to exclaim and pour out his poison against us on the ground that we affirm that God effectually drives human wills? But we are doing nothing but following Augustine! To write a lot about perseverance as well would be a waste of time, since he everywhere unites the two together, both effective desire and constancy in persevering. And he had previously said, as I have not yet mentioned, that "after the fall of the first man God wanted it to belong to his grace alone that man should come to him, and he wanted it to belong to his grace alone that man should not depart from him."[312] He names both things, the beginning and the end. In both he leaves not even the slightest loophole for man, while Pighius bestows on him the leading role.

not given according to our merits

325

One thing remains, that whatever grace is bestowed on us to the very end of our lives is freely bestowed on us, not § repaid for our gratitude, as though by using earlier favours well we merit this of ourselves. This is confirmed by Augustine in the following way: "I have shown quite clearly that the grace to begin and to persevere to the end is not given according to our merits, but is granted according to his own most secret and at the same time most just, most kind, and most wise will, since those whom he has predestined he also has called."[313]

---

310. "Without the possibility of . . . detaching itself" is the reading of the early-sixteenth-century editions, including the Erasmian edition used by Calvin. The correct reading is "invincibly." See NPNF 5:487 n. 6.

311. *Rebuke and Grace* 12.38 (NPNF 5:487), quoted more briefly in *BLW* 6.402 (at n. 242); cf. 6.403–4 (at nn. 246–47). This passage had already been quoted, more briefly than here, in *Inst.* 2.3.13 (LCC 20:307).

312. *The Gift of Perseverance* 7.13 (NPNF 5:530), quoted again in *BLW* 5.356 (at n. 55).

313. Ibid., 13.33 (NPNF 5:538), quoted again in *BLW* 5.356 (at n. 56) without the last clause.

What will Pighius now hold up to evade this (for to escape is quite beyond his powers)? Will he complain that I have pulled out mutilated, maimed statements which do not at all show how Augustine thought?[314] But everyone would refute his roguery if he did so. Or that I did not quote accurately? But I have written the passages out word for word.[315] Or that I deliberately omitted what would contradict me? But I took everything[316] from just four books, and these not so very lengthy ones, which it would not be a great trouble to read completely. I could have piled up far more statements from all over the place, but I refrain, partly out of a desire to save space and partly so that it would be easy for readers, without trouble or toil, to check how faithfully and candidly I have expounded the true authentic thought of Augustine. If anyone is not entirely satisfied by this, then let those four books come forward: the two addressed to Valentinus, of which one bears the title *Grace and Free Choice* and the other *Rebuke and Grace*; two also addressed to Prosper and Hilary, of which one is *The Predestination of the Saints* and the second *The Gift of Perseverance*. Then let judgment be given between us on the basis of these, for I will readily allow the whole controversy to be settled on that basis, and I am not afraid that it will do even the slightest damage to our case. Or will he say that here Augustine was driven beyond the limit by the heat of the controversy, so as in this way to diminish his reliability? But these are the books to which he acknowledges that authority should be granted without qualification, and from which alone he declares that it is possible to determine for sure what Augustine's view was.[317] And what does Augustine teach here?

These points proved by quotations

from just four works

[He teaches] that the human will is indeed free, but only to [will] evil. And this epithet[318] is not applied to it in the true sense, since it is the slave of iniquity. For it is evil by nature and for that reason is held bound and captive under the yoke of sin, until it be freed through Christ. This corruption extends to our being unable not only to will or resolve anything good, but even to conceive the thought of it. Therefore God is not induced by our preparation to bestow his grace on us, but in every way he goes before us, so that the beginning is in his pure

Summary of Augustine's teaching in these works

---

314. This is Pighius's charge (37b–38a) against Calvin's use of Augustine in the 1539 *Institutes*, to which Calvin has responded at the beginning of this book (cols. 292–94).

315. Calvin's claim to copy out word for word is not strictly true by today's standards in that he very rarely quotes without minor verbal alterations. These rarely affect the sense of the passage. See Introduction §5.

316. I.e., everything quoted in cols. 320–25 is taken from the four works about to be mentioned.

317. See col. 294 (at nn. 18–19). Pighius's choice of battleground was probably his worst mistake since the late works of Augustine are those which most support Calvin.

318. I.e., "free."

326

mercy. For all human faculties are corrupt, so that of themselves they can bear only evil fruit. In addition this grace is not given to all without distinction or generally, but only to those whom God wills; the rest, to whom it is not given, remain evil and have absolutely no ability to attain to the good because they belong to the mass that is lost and condemned § and they are left to their condemnation. In addition, this grace is not of such a kind as to bestow on [its recipients] the power to act well on condition that they will to, so that they thereafter have the option of willing or not willing. But it effectively moves them to will it; indeed it makes their evil will good, so that they of necessity will well. In addition, this does not happen once, so that people are subsequently left to themselves, but they are steered on a steady course, so that their perseverance in goodness is no less the gift of God than their beginning it. Moreover, in taking people up for direction by his Spirit, and in continuing to direct them, after he has taken them up, till the very end of their lives, and in confirming them in perseverance, God is led by only one consideration. This is his own free goodness without respect for any merit at all, since in fact they can have no merit, either in their works or in their wills or even in their thoughts.[319]

Augustine on C's side

If anything is detected in this summary which is not taken from those four books, I offer no reason why the whole world should not judge me a man of no credibility. But what that is different is contained in all our teaching? Therefore even though Pighius may make much ado, we cannot be deprived of the fact that Augustine is on our side. What remains to stop him from declaring that [Augustine] has sunk to the level of a brute beast, as he announced that he would do if [Augustine] could be shown to support our case?[320]

---

319. This paragraph is a summary of Augustine's teaching as expounded in cols. 320–25.
320. See col. 298 (at n. 58).

On Book Four [of Pighius]

Introduction

To remove any doubt about what he has thus far achieved by his long-winded arguments, Pighius intones afresh a victory hymn, splendid but fanciful and unreal. The opposition, he says, were laid low at the first assault. But I must be very insensitive not to be aware of this onslaught. For I think I am still standing up straight and firm. And to display his achievement as the greater if he has shown the views of the ancients to be opposed to ours, he again[1] belches out that sacrilegious saying of his. Namely that no one is permitted to believe anything on the basis of any Scripture, however clear (at least in our judgment) and perspicuous it may be, if it is contrary to the clear and united judgment of the orthodox fathers, or contrary to the universal definition of the church. For it is possible that each one of us may be mistaken in our understanding of Scripture, but that the church should err in those matters which pertain to the truth of the faith is impossible, because it is the pillar and support of the truth.[2]

P boasts

and proclaims infallibility of church

But it is nothing new, and is agreed to have occurred in all ages, for those who are on other occasions the most bitter enemies of the church to conceal themselves falsely in her shadow and to arrogate her name. So how shall we agree to distinguish between the true church and the false?[3] By numbers, says Pighius. But I thought that such judgment should be based on the word of God, so that what § adhered to Scripture would be deemed to be the church, while what departed from it would be discounted, irrespective of the name with which it put itself forward.[4] The word, he says, is unclear, and so all certainty about it depends on the mind of the church. But I thought, and so I had been taught, that the

Test of true church:

not numbers but Word of God

327

---

1. See *BLW* 2.266–78.
2. 1 Tim. 3:15.
3. See *Institutes* 4.1 (on the true church) and 4.2 (on the false church) (LCC 21:1011–53), parts of which are from 1539.
4. Here is the classic Reformation divide: for the Reformers, the true church is that which truly preaches the Word of God; for Rome the true meaning of the Word of God is that given to it by the church.

foundation comes before its building. And Paul bears witness that the church is founded on a teaching which is not one which it constructed itself, but that of the apostles and prophets.[5] [Pighius] will perhaps respond that this teaching is indeed prior to the church, but its interpretation is founded on the church. That reply is sufficiently refuted by its own absurdity. So when we want to determine with certainty what is the true church, let that rule of Christ prevail: that those are his sheep who hear his voice.[6] Accordingly, just as the church is a pillar and support of the truth[7] because of the fact that it faithfully guards that teaching on which it was founded, so we ought to recognise as the church only that body in which we find that teaching. This is the chain, this is the bond of holy wedlock, with which Christ united the church to himself, a bond which Pighius tries to break by a wicked, sacrilegious divorce when he puts the church in the more important place and relegates the teaching of God to a lower seat. And that [teaching he holds] not in the form in which it was delivered by God, so that its truth should remain clear and perspicuous for us, but as men have preferred to interpret it.

P claims all Scripture proves free choice,

But let my readers consider a second amazing example of the man's subtlety. For having initially declared that he would contend with us by using proofs from Scripture, when he comes to the point he finds an ingenious excuse for declining to do so, namely that the whole of Scripture, however vast its extent, proves freedom of choice. For since it everywhere bears witness that God will render to each according to his merits, contains laws and commands for living well, and everywhere urges us towards goodness, bans sins, threatens punishments, it is certain that everywhere it proves the power of free choice.

but he has forgotten the promises of grace

If Pighius understands "everywhere" in the sense that [Scripture] is entirely devoted to this and pursues this alone, then he has not yet learned the first rudiments of the faith. For he is leaving out the principal and more necessary part of its teaching which is contained in the promises of grace; when this is recognised, he achieves nothing by his claims. For after God has commanded us to walk in his commandments, he promises that he will cause us so to walk, that is, he will give us the mind and feet. But all the law, all the commands, as well as all the exhortations, rebukes, and threats, direct us and as it were lead us by the hand to the promises, where God reduces all our goodness to nothing by attributing every portion of our good works to himself and his grace. So, therefore, he who measures human powers by the law and the commands betrays the fact that he does not yet grasp the first principles of the faith. However, I shall for the moment not spend long on

---

5. Eph. 2:20.
6. John 10:27.
7. 1 Tim. 3:15.

On Book Four

resolving this problem, since it will have its due place § shortly.[8] For Pighius follows his usual custom here of repeating the same thing ten times! As for the fact that he mentions that God's judgment would not be just if he did not render to each according to his merits, I reply, as Augustine did: Woe to the whole human race, if in judgment God were to weigh our merits! As far as the reward which God promises to his servants is concerned, the righteous Judge will indeed grant them the crown of righteousness. But it must also be asked what is the origin of that righteousness of the saints which will be crowned then. And it is sure that it is nothing but a pure gift from God.[9] Why then does he infer human powers from this?

And because he has a bad conscience about his weak defences in Scripture, he at once shifts ground to that customary bolt-hole of his by claiming that this was the view of Origen, Tertullian, Hilary, and the rest.[10] But even if I should so allow myself to be tied and bound by their authority as to abandon the sure truth of Scripture and assent to what they determined—which I am not going to do, nor is it right to do so— yet I have already[11] shown what a dishonest interpretation he uses to twist their statements against us. For their assertion that the law is of no use unless there is the power to obey it, and similar statements, would deserve to be made if this bondage which keeps us penned in and deprives us of strength were in our nature and not due to our own fault. But as it is, since it is constantly evident that whatever weakness or failing there is in us is to be put down to our own fault, all these objections are answered and removed. And that is how Augustine answers them both in those books which I went through a little while ago[12] and in the book *The Perfection of Righteousness*.[13] So it is too shameless and brazen when he here misuses the testimony of Augustine as well. Yet [he says that Augustine] states clearly in his own words that what cannot be avoided is not a sin.[14] And where nature or necessity has the upper hand, there he teaches that no basis for blame can be found.[15] Against

328

P turns from Scripture to the Fathers

on our power to keep the law,

to which Augustine responds

---

8. See cols. 339–42, 346–48.
9. Calvin is not claiming to quote Augustine here, merely to be following his teaching. *Grace and Free Choice* 6.14 (NPNF 5:449), which is quoted in col. 337 (at n. 103), is similar.
10. Pighius appeals to "Peter" (in Pseudo-Clement), Tertullian, Irenaeus, Origen, Basil, Hilary, Jerome, and Augustine (58b-59b).
11. In *BLW* 2.280–86. Calvin echoes the language of Pighius, who accuses the "heretics" of twisting obscure passages of Scripture (58b).
12. I.e., in *Grace and Free Choice, Rebuke and Grace, The Predestination of the Saints,* and *The Gift of Perseverance* (see *BLW* 3.320–25).
13. *The Perfection of Righteousness* 6.13 (NPNF 5:163).
14. Pighius quotes (59b) *Free Choice* 3.18.50 (LCC 6:201), which he had quoted earlier (42a). See *BLW* 3.296 (at n. 43).
15. Pighius's summary (59b) of Augustine's position, looking back to *Free Choice* 3.1.1 (LCC 6:170), which he had quoted earlier (39b, 42a).

this, [Augustine] protests that it is no use raising objections against him based on such books which he had written long ago when he was a young man.[16] "For it was for just this reason that I undertook the revision of my works, so as to show that I had not remained fixed in my views on everything. But I consider that I have made progress in my writing, and was not perfect from the start" (*The Gift of Perseverance, to Prosper*, chs. 12 and 21).[17] This indeed is how in the *Retractations* he counters that false charge of Pighius: "It is one thing to inquire into the origin of evil, but another to ask how there can be a return to the original state or an advance to a greater good."[18] A little later he quotes this earlier statement of his: "Since man cannot rise up of his own accord in the way that he fell, let us take hold with sure faith of the right hand of God which is stretched out to us." And so on.[19] And yet he apologises that even in these words he did not include the whole of what needed to be said.[20] Again in *The Perfection of Righteousness*: "It was through freedom of choice that man came to be a sinner, but now the corruption which followed as a punishment has turned freedom into necessity."[21] §

329

Augustine affirms free choice

but in what sense?

But [says Pighius] even in [Augustine's] latest writings he teaches that freedom of choice is addressed whenever God commands or exhorts.[22] I acknowledge that he did indeed dwell at length on the association of free choice with grace, lest the preaching of grace should seem to abolish free choice. But we ought not to overlook what he meant by this term, if we desire to reach his true meaning and not lay traps and nets with words. He himself makes it sufficiently clear all through the book that his meaning is only that it is with a will that is self-determined that people act both well and badly, but by nature they can only sin, while it is by grace that they begin to do what is good and persevere in it.[23] And so, having begun by saying that he was writing that work because of those who denied or seemed to deny free choice by affirming grace,[24] he piles up a number of passages which indicate that free choice is present

---

16. *The Gift of Perseverance* 12.30 (NPNF 5:536–37), where Augustine explicitly refers to *Free Choice*.

17. *The Gift of Perseverance* 21.55 (NPNF 5:548). "Revision" is *retractanda*, a clear reference to his *Retractations*.

18. *Retractations* 1.9.2 (LCC 6:103; FoC 60:33), quoted more fully in *BLW* 3.295 (at n. 23).

19. *Retractations* 1.9.4 (LCC 6:104; FoC 60:37), quoting *Free Choice* 2.20.54 (LCC 6:169). The passage is cited, more accurately, in *BLW* 3.295 (at n. 30).

20. *Retractations* 1.9.2, 4 (LCC 6:102–3; FoC 60:32–33, 35).

21. *The Perfection of Righteousness* 4.9 (NPNF 5:161). For the other uses of this passage see *BLW* 3.293 n. 8.

22. Pighius quotes (60a) from *Grace and Free Choice* 2.2, 4 (NPNF 5:444–45).

23. A summary of *Grace and Free Choice*, as Calvin is about to expound it.

24. *Grace and Free Choice* 1.1 (NPNF 5:443–44).

in man. That is, a will by which he does what he does of his own accord. And it is this alone which [Augustine] is doing in the second chapter, which Pighius brings forward.²⁵ But immediately afterwards he warns that "one must fear the understanding of these evidences as a defence of free choice in such a way that no place is left for the grace of God."²⁶

Therefore everything now depends on our knowing what he then apportions to free choice and what to grace. For from that it will also be established what free choice means. He bears witness, both often and in clear statements, that whatever good we do is the gift of God, because he causes it in us.²⁷ Indeed the grace of God is not given as a reward for our merits, but it is granted to us at a time when we have no merits, except bad ones. It is from there that good merits begin, but such as are the pure gifts of God, and in no way from us.²⁸ At this point he enters on the argument about how eternal life is at the same time a reward and [a gift of] grace.²⁹ He resolves it by saying that God does indeed reward good works in the saints, but in doing so he is only continuing his freely given compassion towards them, since he bestowed freely upon them whatever good works there are. And there he deals with how God shapes and forms us when he regenerates us by his Spirit, how he prepares good works in us, and we ourselves do not prepare them.³⁰ At the same time he refutes the error of those who imagine that man prepares himself by some good movement to receive the grace of God. For the first action of grace is to pluck out from us our stony heart, which means nothing other than the will, which is very hard and incapable of responding to God.³¹ Then he begins to define what the word "freedom" means. "The will is always free in man, but it is not always good." He in fact bears witness that it is evil by a corruption of nature, but becomes good by grace.³² You see now that he makes the will free when nonetheless it can by itself do only evil things.

Augustine on role of grace and free choice

He replies later to those arguments which are commonly thrown back on the basis of the law and the commandments. "The Pelagians think they have a strong point when they say, God would not command what he knew was impossible for man to do. Who could be ignorant of this? But he § commands some things which we cannot do, with the

Augustine: what law commands, grace gives

330

---

25. Ibid., 2.2–3.5 (NPNF 5:444–46). See n. 22. For the other uses of this passage see *BLW* 3.316 n. 224.
26. Ibid., 4.6 (NPNF 5:446). This is the very first sentence of 4.6 ("immediately afterwards").
27. E.g., ibid., 4.8; 5.10; 16.32; 17.33 (NPNF 5:447–48, 457–58).
28. Ibid., 6.13 (NPNF 5:449).
29. Ibid., 8.19 (NPNF 5:451).
30. Ibid., 8.20; see also 9.21 (NPNF 5:451–52).
31. Ibid., 14.29 (NPNF 5:455–56). For the other uses of this passage see *BLW* 3.316 n. 231.
32. Ibid., 15.31 (NPNF 5:456). For the other uses of this passage see *BLW* 3.316 n. 225.

very intention that we should know what we ought to seek from him. For it is faith itself which obtains by prayer what the law commands."[33] Again: "It is certain that it is we who keep the commandments, if we will to. But because the will is prepared by the Lord, we should seek from him that we will it to a sufficient degree for us to act by our willing. It is certain that it is we who will when we will, but it is he who causes us to will the good. It is certain that it is we who act when we act, but it is he who, by giving the will fully effective powers, causes us to act."[34] He then goes on afterwards to show from a number of passages of Scripture that God does those selfsame things in us which he commands us to do.[35] At last when he reaches his conclusion, he speaks thus: "I think that I have argued enough against those who vigorously fight against the grace of God, by which the human will is not abolished but changed from evil to good and, when it has been changed, is helped, and that I have argued in such a way as not to say more than divine Scripture has said, with truth most clear. If Scripture is carefully examined, it shows that God has in his power not just the good wills of human beings, which he himself produced out of bad ones and now, having made them good, leads into good deeds and eternal life. But those also who follow the ways of this creaturely world are so in God's power that he causes them to incline where he wills when he wills."[36] "But he has the power, whether through angels, good or evil, or in whatever other way, to work in the hearts of the wicked, in accordance with their merits. He himself did not make their wickedness. It was either derived at the beginning from Adam himself or grew through their own will. So why should it be surprising if he who has brought it about that their hearts should become good instead of evil works good things through the Holy Spirit in the hearts of the elect?"[37] See the praises that he would heap on free choice there! And yet, with his usual modesty, Pighius charges us with deliberately closing our eyes so as to avoid seeing the brightest light. And he is so pleased with himself that he hopes to be able to enchant his readers simply and solely by having his mouth open!

Discussion of "Absurdities" in the *Institutes*

P attacks *Institutes,*

But since in my *Institutes,* after expounding our own teaching, I had refuted the arguments with which those who want to attack it are accustomed to arm themselves, he now takes up this role himself, to persuade

---

33. Ibid., 16.32 (NPNF 5:457).
34. Ibid. For the other uses of this passage see *BLW* 3.317 n. 232.
35. Ibid., 16.32–19.40 (NPNF 5:457–61).
36. Ibid., 20.41 (NPNF 5:461). For the other uses of this passage see *BLW* 3.316 n. 227.
37. Ibid., 21.43 (NPNF 5:463).

everyone that my answers are either without force or not full enough or inappropriate or useless. To do this he makes up a dialogue in which he introduces me as a speaker, though to his own advantage. For whenever it suits him, he breaks off the speech.[38]

I had said in my *Institutes* that those who opposed our teaching were piling up some [alleged] absurdities to make it disagreeable as being alien to common sense, and then attacking it with evidence drawn from Scripture. Because I declare that I will drive back both siege engines in turn,[39] he criticises my pride with theatrical denunciations to the effect that I, a wretched little mite, am assaulting at the same time so many elephants of such size and that noble assembly of eagles, that is, all the saints of old. And again § he recites that catalogue of his which I already earlier tore to shreds and wiped out with my pen.[40] But I declare that I am not at war with the ancient fathers—only with Pighius and those like him, whether dogs or pigs, who some of the time befoul the sacred saving truth of God with their vile, filthy snouts, and at other times trample it underfoot or tear it with poisonous teeth or pursue it with their barking. But if I wanted to persist in refuting his verbosity there would be no end to the matter. So I ask my readers not to let themselves be diverted from the real subject. If they will grant me this, I will see that they do not find anything lacking in my replies.

appealing to early fathers

331

First "Absurdity"

Now then, the first "absurdity"[41] which I quote is: "Once sin is of necessity, it ceases to be sin; if it is voluntary, then it can be avoided." But I add that Augustine was once troubled with this dilemma by Pelagius.[42] This madman cries that I am lying! But I have said nothing which Augustine himself did not enunciate. For he sets out this ninth argument of Pelagius in his book *The Perfection of Righteousness*.[43]

Necessity incompatible with sin?

Augustine responds

---

38. For the rest of book 4 (60a–72a) Pighius quotes short passages from the 1539 *Institutes* and then responds to them. Calvin might have shown more appreciation for the fact that Pighius allowed him to speak for himself!
39. A loose quotation in indirect speech of passages from *Inst.* 2.5.1 (LCC 20:316–17), quoted by Pighius (60a–b).
40. I.e., those church fathers listed in n. 10, with the addition of Ambrose. Calvin's reply is found in *BLW* 2.280–87.
41. In *Inst.* 2.5 (LCC 20:316–40) Calvin answers objections to his doctrine, in particular four "absurdities" which his opponents saw in it. The situation is confused by the fact that Calvin later (col. 338) switches from calling them "absurdities" to calling them "objections."
42. *Inst.* 2.5.1 (LCC 20:317), quoted by Pighius (60b–61a).
43. *The Perfection of Righteousness* 2.2 (NPNF 5:160), quoted in *BLW* 3.299 (at n. 70). In the first edition of *BLW* this is referred to as Pelagius's "new" argument, in all later editions as his "ninth." In fact it is his second. The similarity of the ninth (*The Perfection of Righteousness* 4.9 [NPNF 5:161]) could have caused the confusion, especially as Calvin appears to be alluding to that passage shortly afterwards (cf. at n. 55).

What madness then is this, to deny the existence of what is on view before our eyes? But [he says] Augustine used a similar argument against the Manichees.⁴⁴ He did, quite properly and for the best of reasons, since they imagined that sin was implanted in man by God as a substantial evil, and they did not allow that it occurred through the fault of his own will.⁴⁵ But our case is different. So then just as the Romanist theologians attack us today by throwing up this absurdity, so in former times Pelagius assailed Augustine in the same way. For a book survives which bears witness to this.⁴⁶ What will Pighius gain by denying it? And yet how much nobility there is in what I had added, but Pighius left out! "I do not want our enemies to be too encumbered with the name of Pelagius, until we have dealt adequately with the issue itself."⁴⁷ I did this as follows. "Sin is no less rightly imputed to us for its being necessary. The reason is that if someone would argue with God and escape judgment by the excuse that he could not do otherwise, [God] has his reply ready: Ruin is yours, O Israel; in me only is your hope.⁴⁸ For whence does that inability come but from the corruptness of our nature? Moreover, whence the corruption if not because man rebelled against his Maker? Since we are all guilty of this rebellion, I say that it is in this necessity which restricts us that there lies the clear cause of our condemnation," and therefore it is far from having any force as an excuse.⁴⁹

P appeals to early fathers

332

Here Pighius dissolves completely into laughter, that I should trust to have escaped by so worthless an argument! But what has he to put against it? He sings back that § song of his which he has so often repeated: that he has proved from the Fathers that the law was given in vain if it cannot be fulfilled; there will be no place for merit or demerit if the will is not free both to do good and to do evil. And, so as to overwhelm us with the multitude of his witnesses, he brings forward that whole crowd which we have reviewed before.⁵⁰ As far as that spectre

---

44. Pighius (61a–b) cites *Free Choice*, books 2 and 3, and *Two Souls*, referring back to his exposition of them in book 3.
45. *Retractations* 1.9.2 (LCC 6:102; FoC 60:32–33). The Latin contains the contrast between *substantiale* and *accidisse*. See Introduction §6.
46. See n. 43.
47. *Inst.* 2.5.1 (LCC 20:317). This is the sentence that Pighius has left out, between quoting what precedes (at n. 42) and what follows (at nn. 48–49) it. Ironically, Calvin seems to have misquoted himself. In 1539 he wrote that he did not yet wish to crush his enemies by the weight of his [Augustine's] name; here the "his" has become "Pelagius," necessitating a different translation.
48. Hos. 13:9 (very close to the Vulgate translation).
49. *Inst.* 2.5.1 (LCC 20:317), most of which was quoted by Pighius (61b–62a). Part of the passage (including the Hosea quotation) was dropped from later editions of the *Institutes,* and so does not appear in the English translation.
50. Here he mentions Peter, Tertullian, Irenaeus, Basil, Hilary, Jerome, and Augustine. For Calvin's response see *BLW* 2.281–86.

of a Peter and that counterfeit Clement are concerned, away with them! For I will not count them worthy of a single word.[51] Of the others I have already said as much as is required. However, there is no surer interpreter of all their own teaching than is Augustine when he explains his own thought in the common cause. For he warns that his statement that no basis for blame can be found where nature or necessity holds sway[52] is valid only when considering a nature that is healthy and whole. For now human beings are subject to necessity, but that necessity which the first man by a voluntary fault brought upon them. The punishment, he says, has become our nature.[53] And the penalty of the first man which was [for him] a punishment is our nature. Since therefore the necessity is a punishment for sin, the sins which derive from it are deservedly blamed (Ps. 37),[54] and the blame for them is deservedly imputed to us, since their origin is voluntary.[55]

but Augustine interprets them

Now, therefore, what reason is there for Pighius to despise and ridicule with so much disdain the answer that I have proposed? I say nothing of Augustine,[56] who was, I think, no less clever a logician than Pighius, who thinks that when he has provided this or a similar answer, he has done all that is required of him. But let us inquire of the common sense of the devout whether this is not sufficient to make man guilty, when he is proved to have perished through his own fault. For God humbles his own people with just this accusation when he says: Ruin is yours, O Israel; in me only is your hope.[57] But [Pighius says] there he is censuring a people who have refused to obey his word. I agree, but since the statement is universal, we must see what it comprehends. Doubtless it means that man is deprived of all excuse if he is perceived to have been the cause of his own ruin. But Pighius complains that this is not the case, unless he can both escape ruin and ruin himself. One who stammers, or rather grunts, like this betrays the fact that he does not hold to that first axiom of our faith, that we and all our power to act well perished in Adam. Nor does he here make any secret of his abhorrence of [that axiom] when he so often locates only

We all sin through our own fault

---

51. On the issue of the authenticity of "Clement" see *BLW* 2.261–62.

52. See at n. 15.

53. Cf. *Nature and Grace* 67.80–81 (NPNF 5:149–50); *Retractations* 1.9.5 (FoC 60:37–38). Both passages are responding to *Free Choice* 3.18.50, which, though not the statement mentioned by Calvin (see at nn. 15, 52), is similar.

54. Ps. 37 seems to be an error for Ps. 25:17 or 31:7 (in the Vulgate translation, where they are numbered 24:17 and 30:8), both of which are quoted by Augustine in the passage which appears to be in mind (see n. 55).

55. Cf. *The Perfection of Righteousness* 4.9 (NPNF 5:161–62). For the other uses of this passage see *BLW* 3.293 n. 8.

56. I.e., Calvin's own answer suffices against Pighius without the need of Augustine's support.

57. Hos. 13:9, as at n. 48.

in the members of the body the corruption which derives from our first ancestor.

I also said [in the *Institutes*] that there was a flaw in the other half [of the argument], where they conclude that if sin is voluntary it can be avoided. I denied the validity of the argument, because from "voluntary" it infers "free."[58] [Pighius] tries to refute me by responding with Augustine, who he says argues just so everywhere.[59] But I have already brought Augustine forward so often[60] to interpret his own meaning that to repeat the exercise again would be distasteful to me. For in the statements that Pighius continually echoes back with his usual verbosity, [Augustine] is writing about a nature that is healthy and whole. But where he is talking about a corrupt nature, he plainly declares it[61] to be a sin, "whether it can § be avoided or not. For if it can, the present will does it; if it cannot, the past will did it."[62] And he adds that it can be avoided, yet not by man's own power, "nor when his proud will is eulogised, but when in humility it is aided" (*The Perfection of Righteousness*, response 15).[63] Moreover, he had determined the meaning of these words at the outset [by saying] that "sin can indeed be avoided, but on condition that the corrupt nature is first healed. But as it is, it is not healthy, either because through blindness it does not see what it should do or [because] through weakness it does not fulfil it."[64] What clearer words could you want than these? But Pighius thinks he is well on the way to victory if he has by any means whatever put up Augustine's name against us.

Excursus: Coercion versus Necessity

But since I have already quite often[65] mentioned the distinction which we maintain between coercion and necessity, on which this argument primarily hangs, and have touched on it only in passing, we must now examine it a little more carefully.[66] For even though Pighius rejected it in a previous book,[67] we put off a defence of it to this point. Now those who protect free choice against the grace of God say that there is no sin

---

58. *Inst.* 2.5.1 (LCC 20:317).
59. Pighius (62b) cites *Two Souls* 11.15 (see *BLW* 3.298 at n. 56) and *Free Choice* 3.18.50 (see at n. 14), both of which he had quoted earlier (42a, 44b).
60. E.g., *BLW* 3.299.
61. "It" is the human deed where love is lacking.
62. *The Perfection of Righteousness* 6.15 (NPNF 5:163).
63. Ibid.
64. Ibid., 2.1 (NPNF 5:160).
65. *BLW* 2.280; 3.302.
66. Calvin introduces an excursus (cols. 333–36) in which he leaves his response to book 4 to take up unfinished business.
67. Book 3.

or virtue where there is necessity.⁶⁸ We reply that God is good of necessity, but he obtains no less praise for his goodness because of the fact that he can only be good. Again, [we reply that] the devil is evil of necessity, but his wickedness is no less culpable [for that]. Nor is this an argument that we fabricated. So spoke Augustine,⁶⁹ so spoke Bernard⁷⁰ before us. What does Pighius say? That God has a status distinct from his creatures. For what inheres in them as a necessary consequence of their creation redounds not to their praise but to God's, and in them only those qualities merit praise which they have acquired themselves by improving the talent which God lent to them. But his status is different, since his infinite goodness cannot be transferred elsewhere. Is this capable of undermining what we say? Our opponents want to force us to agree that being voluntary is inconsistent with being necessary. But we have shown that both are combined together in the goodness of God. They say that it is absurd that those things which people do in such a way that they are not able to do otherwise should be attributed to their fault or blame. We solve this contradiction by introducing the comparison. We do not argue that people are good or evil of necessity because God is good of necessity, but show by means of an example only that it is not contrary to reason for a quality which exists of necessity nevertheless to be deemed worthy of praise or censure. But Pighius's philosophising about the necessary consequence of creation is entirely beside the point. Natural endowments, as they call them, whether good or bad, are rightly not reckoned as vices or virtues, since they are such as people can use both badly and well. But a good will and the actions which derive from it are of a different order. So this § is irrelevant.

But what of God or the devil?

Example shows necessity compatible with praise/blame

334

He adds besides that God does not do or will of necessity anything at all which is outside himself. This philosophising is to be rejected, not only because of its trifling, petty inquisitiveness, but also because it introduces a blasphemous separation between the righteousness of God and his works. As for his adding again that he does not know what it means for God to will to be righteous of necessity—in saying that he comes close to revealing that he considers God to be like a tree trunk or stump. Will, he says, is inferior to nature. Now God is good by nature. Therefore it is inappropriate to say that God wills to be righteous, when he is so by nature. But [Pighius] would have acted in a more ap-

P objects to example of God

---

68. Augustine *Nature and Grace* 65.78 (NPNF 5:149) quotes Jerome's statement to this effect. This is quoted more fully in *BLW* 3.299 (at n. 71).
69. Augustine *Nature and Grace* 46.54 (NPNF 5:139); *Letter* 217.3.10 (FoC 32:82).
70. Bernard *Grace and Free Choice* 4.9; 10.35 (CFS 19:65–66, 90–91) makes the same point, though in different words. He maintains that God/the devil is unalterably good/evil while retaining free choice = freedom from necessity.

propriate, more fitting way if he had maintained up to this point that distinction which he made not long ago between God and his creatures. While creatures by nature have many attributes which are not within the scope of the will and are not subject to the choice of the will, yet to imagine anything comparable in God is a blasphemous fabrication. For he is what he is by nature in such a way that he wills to be so, and he also wills what he wills in such a way as to have it naturally. For since God's goodness, wisdom, power, righteousness, and will are united together by a kind of, so to speak, circular connection, it is the work of a wicked, devilish imagination to break this bond apart. Since, then, God wills to be whatever he is, and that of necessity, there is no doubt that just as he is good of necessity, he also wills to be so, a state which is so far from coercion that in it he is to the greatest degree willing.[71] I would say "free," if it were agreed between us that this should be understood as "self-determined."

Example of the devil

He answers our argument about the devil as follows: the very fact that he is evil of necessity is the punishment for the sin which he committed under no coercion from any necessity. As though this argument did not equally apply to human beings! For we do not locate the necessity in human nature, as has been said so many times,[72] but in the corruption to which we say that the human race is subject. We teach that there is only this difference: that the devil has been consigned to eternal bondage in which there is no hope of liberation, whereas we have been left with a remedy, so that by the grace of the Holy Spirit we may escape from it. Finally he concedes that necessity is not in conflict with will as such, but with the will of those who are still pilgrims in this world. By this ruse he certainly thinks that he can evade our reply, but it is as open to us to deny [his ruse] as it is for him to affirm it.

Necessity affirmed by Augustine,

Augustine [he says] is speaking about pilgrims when he lays down the lasting incompatibility between necessity and will.[73] On the contrary, he bears witness that he is speaking about the condition of the first man before he had fallen into this wretched condition beneath whose burden we who are his offspring all toil.[74] But that now, after his fall, the yoke of necessity, from which we should otherwise have been

---

71. "Willing" is *voluntarius*, usually translated "voluntary."
72. E.g., *BLW* 2.259, 263 (at nn. 25, 61–62).
73. Pighius (41a) is referring to his earlier quotation (39b) of Augustine *Free Choice* 3.3.8 (LCC 6:175–76); see *BLW* 3.295 (at n. 27).
74. In the passage referred to, Augustine is in fact referring to "pilgrims," as Calvin would not have known since he was not himself using the work (see *BLW* 3.295 n. 23). If Calvin had realised to which passage Pighius was referring he would, as before, have appealed to *Retractations* 1.9.5 (cf. *BLW* 3.295 [at n. 28]). *The Perfection of Righteousness* 4.9 (NPNF 5:161–62) responds to the alleged incompatibility of free choice and necessity precisely as does Calvin, by contrasting the state before and after the fall.

free and exempt, § has been laid upon us, is the unanimous teaching of [Augustine] himself[75] and Prosper[76] and Bernard.[77] However, so as to look generous, [Pighius] boasts that he freely grants me this, although my arguments do not prove anything of the sort. I will allow him to bestow this applause on himself in his own home, provided that his vanity is publicly exposed to all. To bring that about, let us define necessity. Now will Pighius not allow me that it is a fixed, steady state in which a thing cannot be otherwise than it is? In Aristotle at any rate the existence of alternative possibilities[78] is always the opposite of necessity.[79] And common sense lays down that we should regard as necessary whatever has to be as it is and cannot be otherwise. In this way unchangeability is included in necessity, from which it also immediately follows that God is good of necessity.[80] But if his goodness is necessary, why am I not permitted to deduce from this that he wills the good as necessarily as he does it? Indeed since he continues unchanging in this respect, he is in a certain sense a necessity to himself, he is not coerced by another, nor however does he even coerce himself, but of his own accord and voluntarily he tends to that which he does of necessity. The devil, on the other hand, both is evil and acts in an evil way necessarily, but no less wilfully. From this what I wanted [to prove] seems to have been proved with clarity: what is voluntary is not so different from what is necessary that they cannot sometimes coincide.

Now I come to man, lest anyone should think that I am incorrectly drawing a parallel between these cases and his [situation]. We say that he is evil because he comes from an evil descent, like a bad branch from a bad, corrupt root. Therefore, as long as he continues in his own nature, he cannot will and act except in an evil way. Indeed we deny that it is in his power to abandon his wickedness and turn to the good. Since, then, he can of himself be nothing but evil, we determine that there is necessity in his case. And that not indeed without qualification, but insofar as he originates from an evil root and maintains his original character, that is,

---

75. The "yoke of necessity" could be said to be the teaching of the mature Augustine rather than the early Augustine; see *BLW* 3.299–300, 301–2.
76. Calvin is probably thinking of Prosper's *Letter to Augustine* (= 225 in Augustine's *Letters*; see *BLW* 5.364 n. 113), which prompted the latter to write *The Predestination of the Saints* and *The Gift of Perseverance* (ACW 32:38–48). Cf. Prosper *Grace and Free Choice*, esp. 13–14 (ACW 32:104–14).
77. *Sermons on the Song of Songs* 81.6–9; 82.5 (CFS 40:162–66, 175, where the Latin *necessitas* is confusingly translated in a variety of ways). The other references to Bernard in this work are to his *Grace and Free Choice,* the thrust of which is that the will is *not* constrained by necessity. But Bernard does there twice refer to necessities to which people are subject (5.14; 8.24 [CFS 19:70, 82]) and, more importantly, teaches that fallen humanity has lost freedom from sin (3.6–7; 4.9–10; 8.24 [CFS 19:61–63, 65–66, 81]), the point that Calvin is here making.
78. "The existence of alternative possibilities" is in Greek.
79. See *Categories* 10 (12b–13a [Loeb 88–91]); *Topics* 2.6 (112b [Loeb 354–57]).
80. For the examples of God and the devil see cols. 333–34.

Sidenotes:
335
Prosper, and Bernard

Testimony of Aristotle

Fallen man is necessarily evil

Aristotle on culpable impotence

for as long as he is not led by the Spirit of God. When Aristotle distinguishes what is voluntary from its opposite, he defines the latter as τὸ βίᾳ ἢ δι' ἄγνοιαν γιγνόμενον, that is, what happens by force or through ignorance.[81] Then he defines as forced what has its beginning elsewhere, something to which he who acts or is acted upon makes no contribution (*Eth. Nic.* 3.1).[82] And he shows what he means by the word "beginning" in the fifth chapter, when he teaches that the unjust and weak[83] are such of their own accord, just because at the beginning it was possible for them not to be so, even though they now cannot be anything else. And to explain this he uses analogies. For a sick person will not get better when he wants to, and yet perhaps he is sick of his own accord, if by living in an unrestrained way he has brought the illness on himself. So then it was possible for him not to become ill, but when he has reached this point it is not so. Just as when someone has thrown a stone, he can no longer take it back, but it was in his power either to hold on to it § or to throw it.[84] We see here a pagan philosopher acknowledge that it is not always in man's power to be good, indeed that he can be nothing but evil, and yet he is what he is wilfully, and not by force, because at the beginning the free decision by which he gave himself over to obedience and bondage to his desires was within his own power. But surely it is the native philosophy of Christians that our first ancestor corrupted not only himself but all his offspring at the same time, and that it is from this that we derive the habit[85] which resides in our nature. Now then, if you join this teaching about our faulty beginning to Aristotle's philosophy, you will with no trouble understand how sin, which it is not in our power to avoid, is nonetheless voluntary.

Second "Absurdity"

Without free choice, no punishments/ rewards?

The second "absurdity" which I quote from our opponents is: "Unless both virtues and vices derive from a freely chosen decision,[86] it is not proper for man either to have a punishment imposed on him or to be paid a reward."[87] Before I reply to this, I interpose these words: "Al-

---

81. *Nicomachean Ethics* 3.1 (1109b–10a [Loeb 116–17]). For Calvin's use of Aristotelian philosophy see Introduction §6.
82. Ibid., 3.1 (1110a [Loeb 116–17]).
83. A technical term in Aristotle for someone who knows what is right but does not do it. On the later history of the idea see R. Saarinen, *Weakness of the Will in Medieval Thought* (Leiden: Brill, 1994).
84. *Nicomachean Ethics* 3.5 (1114a [Loeb 146–49]).
85. For habit see Introduction §6.
86. "Freely chosen decision" is *ex libera arbitrii electione*.
87. Calvin is quoting from *Inst.* 2.5.2 (LCC 20:318). This and the next passage (see at n. 92) are quoted in full by Pighius (62b–63a). For the opponents quoted, see, e.g., J. Eck, *Enchiridion of Commonplaces*, ch. 31 (Grand Rapids: Baker, 1979), 213.

though this argument is from Aristotle,[88] I do however acknowledge that it was taken over by Chrysostom[89] and Jerome.[90] Yet it was, as even Jerome bears witness,[91] popular with the Pelagians."[92] In an effort to demolish this last claim, Pighius struggles to show what a great difference there is between his own case and that of Pelagius. As if indeed the Pelagians had used this argument any the less for their having slightly different views, or at least using slightly different words, from Pighius. In the second place he lays against me the grave charge of malice, because I mentioned only two names when there were many.[93] As though I were actually obliged by some duty to go through in order all those in whose writings that view is found! Why then did Pighius not keep me supplied with books, of which I had none to hand at that time except one volume of Augustine which had been given to me on loan?[94] I myself consider that I deserve to be excused for naming the two proponents of a single view whom, at a time when I was so short of books, I could remember, and for leaving out the others who did not then come to mind.

"As for punishments, I reply that they are rightly poured out on us, from whom the fault derives, and that it makes no difference whether we sin with a free or a servile judgment, provided that our desire is voluntary."[95] [Pighius] does not disapprove, provided that along with Augustine and all the others I allow that "voluntary" means precisely what is in our power.[96] But, with Augustine, I object that this ability which he is looking for depended on our being of sound nature;[97] and just as our first father had received this, so he lost it by misusing it.[98]

Sin is voluntary

My reply on rewards, to the effect that there is nothing absurd in their depending on God's kindness rather than men's own merits,[99] he

Rewards depend on God's grace

---

88. *Nicomachean Ethics* 3.5 (1113b [Loeb 142–45]).
89. Esp. *Homily on Genesis* 22.1 (on Gen. 5:32) (FoC 82:71, where it is numbered 22.5). In *Inst.* 2.5.3 (LCC 20:319) these homilies are cited as the source of his opponents' objection.
90. *Letter* 21.6 (ACW 33:114) and *Against Jovinian* 2.3 (NPNF2 6:389), both quoted by Pighius (see *BLW* 2.286 n. 223). For further uses of the latter see *BLW* 3.299 n. 71.
91. *Letter* 133.5 (NPNF2 6:275–76) and *Dialogue against the Pelagians* 1.4–6 (NPNF2 6:451).
92. *Inst.* 2.5.2 (LCC 20:318).
93. Pighius (63a), in addition to Chrysostom and Jerome, names Peter (in "Clement"), Tertullian, Irenaeus, Origen, Basil, Hilary, Ambrose, and Augustine.
94. An important reminder that Calvin, not only when writing the 1539 *Institutes* but also when writing this work, did not have at his disposal a complete library of the Fathers.
95. *Inst.* 2.5.2 (LCC 20:318), quoted by Pighius (63b).
96. Pighius (63b) sets against Calvin "your Augustine" and all the forenamed (n. 93) fathers, summarising their teaching, as Calvin notes, in words of Augustine (*Free Choice* 3.3.8 [LCC 6:175–76]) which he had earlier quoted (39b). See *BLW* 3.295 (at n. 27).
97. Calvin is here summarising the response which he had given in *BLW* 3.295 (at nn. 28–31) to the passage quoted by Pighius (see n. 96). There, as here, it is followed by a citation of *Enchiridion* 30.9.
98. *Enchiridion* 30.9 (NPNF 3:247). For the other uses of this passage see *BLW* 3.293 n. 9.
99. *Inst.* 2.5.2 (LCC 20:318), cited by Pighius (63b).

declares to be not only without substance but blasphemous. But since this is the subject of another argument, he refutes it with only a passing comment. The apostle, he says, bears witness that God rewards those by whom he is sought.[100] What follows? Where there is reward [says Pighius], there is also acknowledgment of both service and merit. Over service I agree. Merit, if he understands by it § the worth of the act, I deny; but if it means simply obedience accepted by God, then I have no complaint.[101] After he has collected some texts in which reward is mentioned, he brings in as his finale that passage from Paul about the crown of righteousness which the righteous Judge is to award to his servants.[102] But what if I respond using Augustine's words? "To whom could the righteous Judge award the earned crown, unless the merciful Father first gave unearned grace?"[103] We agree that labour and striving are needed on both sides. Nor do we deny that the struggle is of such a kind as both to involve the utmost difficulty and to require the greatest efforts and the whole of a person's dedication. The question is only whether we fight for God with our own strength, or he supplies from heaven the skill, the courage, the hands, the strength, and the weapons. Pighius grants a tiny part to the grace of God, but claims for us the greater role. I say that in us is fulfilled what God once promised to the people of Israel, namely that while we are at rest he fights for us.[104] It is not that we ourselves do nothing or that we without any movement of our will are driven to act by pressure from him, but that we act while being acted upon by him. We will as he guides our heart, we endeavour as he rouses us, we succeed in our endeavour as he gives us strength, so that we are animate and living tools, while he is the leader and the finisher of the work.

Augustine: God crowns his own gifts in us

[Pighius] complains that I quote in an abbreviated and mutilated form, against the actual sense intended by its author, Augustine's statement that God crowns his own gifts in us.[105] But when it comes to proving it he flounders. First, although I mentioned there that [the statement] repeatedly recurs in Augustine (as is true), he treats it as though it was said only once.[106] How many times [Augustine] insists on it both

---

100. Heb. 11:6.
101. Cf. *Inst.* 3.15.2–3 (LCC 20:789–91).
102. 2 Tim. 4:8.
103. *Grace and Free Choice* 6.14 (NPNF 5:449), commenting on 2 Tim. 4:8. Cf. n. 9. This passage was already quoted in *Inst.* 3.18.5 (LCC 20:825–26).
104. Exod. 14:14; 2 Chron. 20:29–30.
105. *Grace and Free Choice* 6.15 (NPNF 5:450). Calvin quotes this saying fairly closely in *Inst.* 2.5.2 (LCC 20:318). Pighius (64b) accuses him of citing it in an abbreviated form (this accusation is true) and against Augustine's clear meaning, which is the point at issue. For Calvin's other uses of it see *BLW* 3.318 n. 244.
106. In *Inst.* 2.5.2 (LCC 20:318) Calvin comments "how often" the thought recurs in Augustine. Pighius (64a–b) quotes at length from *Grace and Free Choice* 6.15.

in [his homilies on] the Psalms[107] and in [those on] the Gospel of John[108] (not to mention his polemical works)! About his meaning—if it is unclear to anyone—he removes all doubt in his letter to Sixtus: "Just as we from the time when we began to believe have obtained mercy not because we were faithful but so that we might be, so at the end he will crown us, as it is written,[109] in mercy and compassion. Consequently even eternal life itself, which shall be enjoyed at the end and will certainly be granted on the basis of preceding merits—even that life is nevertheless called grace, because those merits for which it is granted were not acquired by us through our own ability, but were done in us through grace. [It is called grace] precisely because it is given freely—not that it is not given for merits, but that those very merits, for which it is given, were themselves a gift."[110]

What doubt do these words leave, if only they receive a sound interpretation? But suppose some [doubt] remains; the quoted passage[111] alone would suffice. What is contained in it? The Pelagians' interpretation was that only the grace by which God forgives sins is given apart from any merits, whereas that which shall be given at the end is granted for already existing merits. Augustine was ready to allow them this, if they recognised that [the merits] were gifts of God, and not men's own. For whatever is such, that is from men themselves, is evil, but good things are the gifts of God.[112] Pighius already has the whole passage.[113] What then? You see, [Pighius] says, § that the merits of the saints are [in this passage] not abolished but established. Certainly, just as elsewhere Augustine himself teaches that free choice is established through grace, because by [grace] it is set free, although it is by nature in captivity and so useless for everything good.[114] But I feel no pain from this wound. I add later [in the *Institutes*] that there is not the least reason for us to be afraid of coming to where the Holy Spirit distinctly calls [us] to come. For this sequence and these steps of God's mercy are described for us, so that he may glorify those whom he has justified, justify those whom he has called, and call those whom he has chosen. From this we learn that the faithful are crowned precisely "because it

Merits are the gifts of God's grace

338

---

107. *Expositions on the Psalms* 70(2).5; 102.7; 137.18 (NPNF 8:324, 505, 635, where they are numbered differently). The last of these is quoted in *BLW* 6.386 (at n. 100).

108. *Sermons on John* 3.10 (on 1:16) (NPNF 7:22).

109. Ps. 103:4.

110. *Letter* 194.5.19 (FoC 30:313). An overlapping, but briefer and looser, quotation is found in *Inst.* 3.15.7 (LCC 20:795).

111. I.e., the passage which Calvin had quoted in 1539 (see n. 105).

112. A close paraphrase of *Grace and Free Choice* 6.15 (NPNF 5:450); see at n. 105.

113. I.e., Pighius (64a–b) quotes fully from *Grace and Free Choice* 6.15 (NPNF 5:450), covering all of the material referred to by Calvin.

114. A summary of *The Spirit and the Letter* 30.52 (NPNF 5:106). For the other uses of this passage see *BLW* 3.303 n. 100.

is through God's mercy, not by their own diligence, that they have been chosen and called and justified."[115] Pighius recoils from this statement so much that he says that God would not be just if it were true. But since that is pure insult and open calumny against the Holy Spirit, why should I expend much trouble in refuting it? Besides, this relates to the question of election, which will have its own proper place.[116]

Third "Absurdity"

However, lest I pass by something which deserves to be noticed, [the reader should note that] Pighius confuses two of my opponents' objections which I had put in separate places by themselves.[117] For having finally answered their allegations about the merits and rewarding of works, I had in the third place reviewed the following objection: "If good actions were not in our power to choose similarly to evil actions, how does it happen that some fall away from faith and good works, while others persevere?"[118] To give a satisfactory answer to this question, I had referred the cause of the difference to the free election of God, just as in fact [election] is the foundation of our calling not only in that he initiates it, but even in that he establishes it to the end and completes it.[119] There is nothing of mine in that. For Augustine insists on it everywhere, though he at the same time maintains that he is not inventing it out of his own mind but takes it from the mouth of God himself.[120] But Pighius holds God guilty of the utmost savagery and cruelty if that is how the situation is.

There follows in my *Institutes:* When Paul questions one of us [and asks] who it is that sets him apart, and [when Paul] forbids us to boast because we have received everything, surely "he removes everything from the realm of free choice, precisely so as not to leave any place for merits."[121] Here Pighius quibbles that [Paul] does not detract at all from free choice when he warns that everything we are and have and can do, even free choice, ought to be attributed to God as something received. Then, as though he has obtained his victory, he taunts us.

Why do some fall away, others persevere?

Election

P equates grace and free choice

---

115. *Inst.* 2.5.2 (LCC 20:319), echoing Rom. 8:30. Calvin begins with loose summary and moves on to quotation. This passage is quoted by Pighius (63b).
116. I.e., in Calvin's *Concerning the Eternal Predestination of God.*
117. Pighius moves from the second to the fourth objection, without explicitly considering the third objection, which Calvin treats briefly here.
118. A loose summary of the third objection, found in *Inst.* 2.5.3 (LCC 20:319–20).
119. *Inst.* 2.5.3 (LCC 20:320).
120. Calvin is not thinking of specific passages, but of Augustine's teaching "everywhere" (no doubt especially in *The Gift of Perseverance*, e.g., 7.14; 13.33 [NPNF 5:530, 538]), and of his claims to be basing his teaching on Scripture.
121. Calvin, quoting 1 Cor. 4:7, moves here from loose summary to quotation of *Inst.* 2.5.2 (LCC 20:319). This passage of the *Institutes* is quoted by Pighius (63b, 65a).

How, he says, is this teaching opposed to either merits or free choice? For I am seriously wrong if I think that they are so crazy as to believe that free choice is in man of himself, and not as a gift of God. How worthily Pighius boasts like this of his victories, which he wins so easily, without blood and sweat! Where he can find somewhere to lie low, he quickly hides himself there, and when he sees the enemy no more, he thinks that [the latter] has been put to flight and overcome. But if he now pokes his head out a little, he will feel me, or rather the apostle, nearby, menacing § him and approaching him. It was with this same disguise that Pelagius of old used to cover his godlessness, as Augustine bears witness in more than fifteen places.[122] For when [Pelagius] had, as a member of the Council of Palestine, anathematised those who taught that the grace of God was paid as a reward for earlier merits, and was later charged with bad faith,[123] he justified himself by saying that men could merit nothing when they did not yet exist.[124] So free choice was both a portion of grace and granted without any merits, but freely given. But Augustine robs him of that stratagem. "For," he says, "the apostle is not at all lauding that grace by which we were created, to be men, but the grace by which we were justified, to be righteous men" (*Letter 186, to Sixtus*).[125] So why should we use a longer proof here? For we are comparing nature with grace when we say that the latter is the one and only cure for the healing and removal of the corruption of the former. So it has been necessary throughout this discussion for them to be kept apart as if they were things opposed to one another. If Pighius will say that we have done badly to separate things which are united together, we will defend ourselves with the authority of the apostle.[126] What then is he now hoping to gain, that he confuses the

339
as did Pelagius

Augustine insists on distinction between nature and grace

---

122. Pelagius sometimes by the word "grace" simply means the gift of creation, especially free choice. See Augustine *Nature and Grace* 51.59 (NPNF 5:141); *The Proceedings of Pelagius* 10.22; 14.31; 17.41; 23.47 (NPNF 5:192–93, 196–97, 202–3); *The Grace of Christ and Original Sin* 1.3.3 (NPNF 5:218); *Grace and Free Choice* 13.25 (NPNF 5:454); *Letters* 175.2; 177.2, 6, 9 (FoC 30:86–87, 95, 98–99, 100). For the remainder of the more than fifteen places see the two following notes.

123. For Pelagius's anathematising of this statement at the Council of Diospolis in Palestine (415) and the ensuing accusation of insincerity, see Augustine *The Proceedings of Pelagius* 14.30; 17.40; 35.65 (NPNF 5:196, 201, 211); *The Grace of Christ and Original Sin* 1.3.3; 1.22.23; 1.31.34 (NPNF 5:218, 225–26, 229); *Against Two Letters of the Pelagians* 1.19.37; 2.5.10 (NPNF 5:388, 395); *Grace and Free Choice* 5.10 (NPNF 5:448); *The Predestination of the Saints* 2.3 (NPNF 5:499); *Letter* 194.3.7 (FoC 30:305–6). Calvin refers again to this in BLW 5.365 (at n. 117).

124. *Letter* 194.3.8 (FoC 30:306); cf. *The Merits and Forgiveness of Sins* 2.18.29 (NPNF 5:56); *Letter* 177.7–8 (FoC 30:99); *Sermon* 26.7.8 (Works III/2.97). Since the only work common to nn. 123–24 is *Letter* 194 and since Calvin proceeds to quote from it, this is his probable source.

125. *Letter* 194.3.8 (FoC 30:306). (Calvin gives the wrong number of the letter—106 instead of 105 in his edition.)

126. As does Augustine in the passage just quoted (at n. 125), where he goes on to quote Rom. 7:24–25.

whole basis of the debate by diverting us from the particular benefit of regeneration to the universal grace of creation? But it is of course a case of what Augustine writes elsewhere, that the enemies of grace are always seeking out the technique of hiding behind the praise of nature.[127]

Fourth "Absurdity"

Exhortation, warning, and criticism imply power

The fourth objection which I bring up in my *Institutes* in the name of my opponents is this: "Exhortations are undertaken in vain, the use of warnings is without point, and criticisms are absurd, unless it is within our power to obey."[128] To add strength to this argument Pighius mentions that many of the ancients had commonly used it, of whom he places Pseudo-Peter, with that ghost of a Clement,[129] in the front line. Concerning Tertullian and Irenaeus it has already been stated that their argument is only that God would have given the law in vain to man if he had not also bestowed the ability to choose freely both good and evil.[130] But it is one thing to ask what abilities man received at the beginning and another [to ask] what remains now that he has been deprived of his abilities and reduced to utter poverty. The very different condition in which he now is ought not in the least to be confused with that earlier state. The same reply would perhaps also be adequate for the statement of Origen. But I will not delay so long on him, since I have already acknowledged that he somewhat disagrees with us.[131] The fact that [Pighius] also calls in Cicero[132] to support him does not much help his case. For we allow, as is true, that all this teaching about the inherited wickedness of our nature and its gracious renewal was totally hidden from carnal reason.[133] So there is nothing surprising if it escaped the notice of a whole crew of orators and philosophers.

But what about the fall?

340

Augustine supports C

But it was my intention [in the *Institutes*] to answer this § question with Augustine's words rather than with my own, and to borrow the answer from his book *Rebuke and Grace*. So I state in passing the reason for which that book was written, which was of course that similar

---

127. *Against Two Letters of the Pelagians* 2.1.1 (NPNF 5:391), where Augustine is attacking those who use the defense of the goodness of creation (against the Manichees) as an excuse for undermining the reality of grace (Pelagianism). This text is also cited in *BLW* 2.259 (at n. 24).

128. *Inst.* 2.5.4 (LCC 20:320), quoted by Pighius (65b).

129. I.e., the legend of Peter's confrontation with Simon Magus, described by Pseudo-Clement in *Recognitions*. See *BLW* 2.260–62.

130. *BLW* 2.281–82.

131. *BLW* 2.280–81; for why Calvin feels confident to acknowledge disagreement with Origen see 2.291.

132. Pighius (65b–66a) cites Cicero's *Nature of the Gods*, summarising his teaching in words which owe more to Pighius than to Cicero; cf. *Nature of the Gods* 1.15.39–40; 1.20.55; 3.6.14; 3.8.19; 3.35.85; 3.36.87–88; and *BLW* 2.266 (at n. 88).

133. As Calvin argues in *Inst.* 2.1.1–3; 2.2.2–3 (LCC 20:241–44, 256–58).

objections were being made against Augustine himself.[134] Here Pighius attacks me with his usual ferocity and accuses me of lying and impudence, because I dare to associate Augustine with us. But tell us, how does he prove it? To begin with he states the purpose for which [Augustine] wrote a different book, which is irrelevant to the present issue.[135] For his only way to win a victory is to distract the eyes of the readers for a while from the current issue by tossing in a red herring,[136] as it were interposing a little cloud. In that book,[137] he says, Augustine teaches that free choice is quite consistent with grace. The actual words, and the meaning of his teaching, I have faithfully explained above.[138] But now another question is being discussed: what drove Augustine to write *Rebuke and Grace*? Why then does [Pighius] here, as they say, jump from his horse to his donkey?[139] But I could somehow bear this, if only along the way in passing he affirmed something worth listening to! But he does nothing of the sort.

From the two letters to Valentinus he piles up many quotations from which he proves that those who deny free choice altogether are criticised just as much by Augustine as are others who affirm it without grace.[140] And so a moderate position is established between these two extremes: namely that choice is indeed free, but "it is helped by the grace of God, so that human beings may both know and do what is right, so that when the Lord comes, he may find our good works, which he prepared for us to walk in."[141] I acknowledge of course that the saint does there take trouble to prevent both the denial of free choice and its affirmation "in such a way that it is separated from the grace of God, as though without the latter we could in any way think or do anything in accordance with God's will, which we cannot do at all."[142] For this is what he says. Again: "Believe, he says, the oracles of God, that there are both free choice and the grace of God, without whose help it is impossible to turn to God and to make progress in God."[143] Again, in the second letter: "The catholic faith does not deny free choice, whether to

> P says Augustine holds grace and free choice together

> He does affirm free choice,

---

134. *Inst.* 2.5.4 (LCC 20:320), quoted by Pighius (66a).
135. Pighius (66a) states why Augustine wrote *Grace and Free Choice*, the companion volume also addressed to the monks of Hadrumetum. Pighius cites it to indicate the nature of the situation at Hadrumetum, to which Augustine later wrote *Rebuke and Grace*.
136. "Red herring" is in Greek.
137. I.e., in *Grace and Free Choice*.
138. *BLW* 3.315–18 (at nn. 221–44); see also 322–23 (at nn. 288, 303).
139. Erasmus *Adages* 1.7.29 (CWE 32:83).
140. Pighius (66b–67a) quotes at length from *Letters* 214.1–2, 4, 6–7; 215.4–7 (NPNF 5:437–40).
141. *Letter* 214.1 (NPNF 5:437).
142. *Letter* 214.2 (NPNF 5:437).
143. *Letter* 214.7 (NPNF 5:438). This passage had been paraphrased in *Inst.* 2.3.14 (LCC 20:309).

[live] a good life or a bad one. Nor does it ascribe to it such power that it could have any strength without the grace of God, whether so as to turn from evil to good or to make progress in the good by perseverance or to attain to the eternal good, where at last it need not fear the possibility of failure."[144] These are the very words with which Pighius is carried away, and rushes at me in a crazed attack and thunders at the top of his voice that both my cunning and my ill will have been exposed. But there is no doubt that [Augustine], here as elsewhere, by the term "free choice" is establishing that there is in man[145] a will which is capable of both good and evil, and which is thus the source and origin of good works as well as evil. However, he also holds that this will is evil by the corruption of our nature, and becomes good [only] by the correction of grace. But if you are still in any doubt about [Augustine's] views, do what he himself tells you to do there,[146] that is, derive a clearer interpretation from his other letter to Sixtus,[147] and you will have § little difficulty in seeing what, or how much, he allows to free choice.

<small>but what does he mean by it?</small>

341

<small>Augustine faced the same objection as does C</small>

But after he has spent a long time rambling, he at length returns to the point. He tells me to bring forward, if I can, where, when, or by whom Augustine was ever faced with the objection that the commandments are passed on in vain, and exhortations are undertaken in vain, if human ability is of no avail for acting well. As though indeed the whole book did not proclaim this![148] But to save me from having to put together a longer proof of it, let my witnesses be those very objections which [Augustine] relates, of which the first is: "For what purpose are we preached at and commanded to avoid evil and do good, if it is not we who do this, but God works in us both to will and to do?"[149] Second: "But come, let our superiors command what we ought to do; and pray for us, that we may do it; but let them not rebuke us, if we have not done it."[150] "For if the will is prepared by God, why do you rebuke me when you see me not being willing to do his commandments, and not rather ask God to work in me even to will [to do them]?"[151] Third: Since [grace] is not given to all, "why are we rebuked, criticised, blamed, accused? What [can] we do, who have not received [grace]?"[152] What else, I say, are these and the similar false charges which he there

---

144. *Letter* 215.4 (NPNF 5:439).
145. The first edition here repeats the word "choice," an error which is corrected by the later editions.
146. *Letters* 214.3–4; 215.3 (NPNF 5:437–39).
147. *Letter* 194 (FoC 30:301–32).
148. *Rebuke and Grace* in general.
149. Ibid., 2.4 (NPNF 5:473).
150. Ibid., 3.5 (NPNF 5:473).
151. Ibid., 4.6 (NPNF 5:473).
152. Ibid., 6.9 (NPNF 5:474).

deals with but sacrilegious mockeries by the wicked to expose the preaching of grace to laughter and ridicule? But according to Pighius, as much as these charges were wrongly addressed to Augustine, they would rightly be addressed to us. Suppose they would. Does that mean that I was lying when I said that he was troubled by such false charges? I grant that he did not deserve them. What difference does that make to me? I am only stating the facts. Pighius makes trouble for me about their legitimacy, and afterwards he begins shouting loudly, as though he has caught me in the act of lying. That is what all hired speakers are like: provided that they boast with the dishonourable impudence of a prostitute, they think that they have won a victory worthy of three triumphal processions! You would never find a spark of shame or character in a man who makes his money from the gift of the gab.

But now let us see what is the difference by which he separates us from Augustine. Against you, he says, it would rightly be said that "it is folly to teach, exhort, and rebuke." For you affirm that it is the consequence of a single divine decree that, when we are all afflicted with the same sickness, he extends his healing hand to [the elect], [but] passes by others and lets them waste away in their own rottenness. But not so against Augustine, who has an entirely different view. But what does Augustine say to that? After he has taught that wickedness is inborn in everyone by nature, he says that "the damnable origin [of our condition] should be rebuked. This is so that out of the pain of rebuke a will for regeneration may arise (if indeed the one rebuked is a child of the promise), in order that by the noise of the rebuke resounding externally and scourging him God may also, by hidden inspiration, work internally in him so that § he may will [the good]" (ibid., ch. 6).[153] You hear that a person is not changed by words or warnings, unless God inwardly forms the will through the Spirit. You hear that this is not given indiscriminately to all, but only to the children of the promise. Again: "We ought to understand that no one can be separated from the mass of perdition, which came about through the first Adam, unless he possesses this gift. And whoever has it, has it because he has received it by the grace of God."[154] "Further, those whom he chose, he also called. None of them perishes, because they are all chosen. But they are chosen because they are called according to a decision, and that is not their own decision but God's" (ch. 7).[155] Again a little later: "God knew who are his. Their faith, being effective through love, either never fails or (if there are any whose faith fails) it is renewed before this life is

P claims difference between C and Augustine,

but Augustine refutes this

342

---

153. Ibid., 6.9 (NPNF 5:475). This quotation is repeated, more loosely, in *BLW* 6.400 (at n. 222).
154. Ibid., 7.12 (NPNF 5:476).
155. Ibid., 7.14 (NPNF 5:477).

ended, and by the wiping out of the iniquity which had intervened it is counted as perseverance to the end. But those who are not going to persevere, and so are going to fall away from faith, are not separated, in the foreknowledge and predestination of God, from that mass of perdition. For that reason they are not called in accordance with a decision and therefore they are not chosen."[156] "But as far as we are concerned, we cannot distinguish those who are predestined from those who are not, and so we ought to want everyone to be saved. We ought therefore to administer a harsh rebuke to all as a medicine, lest they perish or lest they cause others to perish. But it is God's work to make it beneficial to those whom he has foreknown and predestined" (ch. 16).[157]

P fails to show difference between C and Augustine

Surely now everyone can see the truth of what I just said[158] in Pighius's case. Those with a tongue that is available for hire could not care less about the kind of things which they say, provided that they are not altogether silent. These objections, [Pighius] says, are deservedly levelled against those who say that people are separated by God's decree alone, and that while some are granted grace, others are passed by and left without it, as God has decided; but they are not at all relevant to Augustine. But it is quite obvious that throughout the book Augustine is speaking of just this.[159] It is justifiable, says [Pighius], for Augustine to speak as follows: "O man, learn by the commandment what you ought to do; learn by rebuke that it is by your own fault that you do not have it; learn by prayer from where you may receive it."[160] But how could Calvin say this, when he denies that it is in a man's power to seek grace or desire it before he receives it? On the contrary, why does [Pighius] allow Augustine more than me, when, no less than I, he constantly has this doctrine on his lips? For what does that saying [of his] mean: "Could you be converted unless you were called? Surely he who called you when you had turned away was himself responsible for your conversion. Do not therefore claim the credit for your conversion for yourself, because if he did not call you when you were on the run you could not be converted" *(On Psalm 84)*?[161] What, again, of this second saying? He calls us without us *(Grace and Free Choice)*.[162] What of this

---

156. Ibid., 7.16 (NPNF 5:478).
157. Ibid., 16.49 (NPNF 5:491). This quotation is repeated, in a shorter and looser form, in *BLW* 6.400 (at n. 225). It was already quoted, more briefly, in *Inst.* 3.23.14 (LCC 21:964).
158. I.e., at the end of the paragraph before the last.
159. I.e., throughout *Rebuke and Grace* Augustine is speaking of election.
160. Ibid., 3.5 (NPNF 5:473), quoted in *Inst.* 2.5.4 (LCC 20:320) and by Pighius (68a).
161. *Expositions on the Psalms* 84.8 (on Ps. 85:6; 84:7 in the Vulgate) (in NPNF 8:406, this passage is rendered by ". . .").
162. That God calls people to himself effectually, without waiting on their response, is taught repeatedly by Augustine, e.g., in *Grace and Free Choice* 5.12 (NPNF 5:449). The actual phrase "without us" is found in 17.33 (NPNF 5:458) ("He operates, therefore, without us, in order that we may will") and is cited again in *BLW* 5.368 (at n. 139).

third one: "Not only to make the unwilling willing, but also to make rebels submissive"?[163] And § countless others like them?[164] But this[165] is all right for Pighius, who has hired out his services in the Roman Antichrist's brothel!

Be that as it may, when I have to reply to this criticism [in my *Institutes*], I say that we are not alone in this dispute, but Christ and all the apostles are united with us. And I corroborate this by the fact that although they everywhere teach that human abilities are of no importance and are completely useless for the attainment of the good, this does not stop them from commanding and exhorting and rebuking.[166] Here Pighius tears into me with abuse for calling in Christ to support me in my dispute. For [Christ] bears witness that he knocks so that we may open the door of our heart to him, and reproaches the city of Jerusalem for being unwilling, through persistence in its own stubbornness, for its children to be gathered together when he wanted to do this.[167] This trivial argument leads him to scoff at us, as though he has made out Christ to be strongly opposed[168] to us. But this is exactly what we so strongly maintain, that the way is not in the least barred to exhortation and rebukes, however unable man may be to obey if his will is not formed towards obedience by the Spirit of God. He brings forward a similar instance in Paul, when he states that grace is praised by him in such a way that he does not deprive free choice too of a place. Where is his evidence? [Paul, he says,] does not deny that we will or run.[169] But if he understands this to refer to a good will, then what about the statement that God works in us both to will and to do?[170] If each of these is the peculiar work of grace, it follows straightaway that they do not depend on our natural strength.

But I see what is happening. Pighius has been taken in by that widespread delusion that because it is "not of him who wills or him who runs,"[171] it follows that willing and running are ours. [Pighius has been taken in] despite the fact that Paul argues in the opposite direction that

343

Christ and apostles support C

Rom. 9:16

---

163. *Against Two Letters of the Pelagians* 4.9.26 (NPNF 5:429). For the other uses of this passage see *BLW* 3.308 n. 144.
164. See, e.g., the passages quoted in *BLW* 3.321–23.
165. See n. 158, with particular reference here to the way in which Pighius seeks to separate Calvin from Augustine.
166. Summary of *Inst.* 2.5.4 (LCC 20:320–21).
167. Pighius (68b), having quoted from *Inst.* 2.5.4 (LCC 20:320–21), responds by quoting Rev. 3:20 and Matt. 23:37.
168. Where the first edition has "to want to be opposed," later editions rightly emend this to "to be strongly opposed."
169. Pighius (68b–69a) argues thus, echoing Rom. 9:16 and Phil. 3:14 and quoting 1 Cor. 9:24–27.
170. Phil. 2:13.
171. Rom. 9:16.

the reason why we do not obtain the grace of God by willing or running is that there is no good will in us, no good running, which could merit it in advance. And that is what Augustine says: "How is it 'not of him who wills or him who runs,' except that the will itself is prepared by the Lord? Otherwise, suppose it was said 'not of him who wills or him who runs, but of God who has mercy,' because of the fact that it is done with participation from both sides, that is, from the human will and from the mercy of God. In other words, suppose that we should understand the saying 'not of him who wills or him who runs, but of God who has mercy,' as if it said that the human will is not sufficient by itself if it is not accompanied by the mercy of God. Then it follows that the mercy of God is also not sufficient by itself if it is not accompanied by the human will. But if it was rightly said that 'it is not of man who wills, but of God who has mercy,' for the reason that the human will does not fulfil it alone, then why can the reverse not also rightly be said? Namely that 'it is not of God who has mercy, but of man who wills,' because the mercy of God does not fulfil it alone. But no Christian will dare to say that 'it is not of God who has mercy, but of man who wills,' lest he quite openly contradict the apostle. So it remains the case that the statement 'not of him who wills or him who runs, but of God who has mercy,' is rightly understood to have been said in order that the whole [action] should be attributed to God, who both prepares § a good will in man, so that it may be helped, and helps it when it has been prepared. For a good will comes before many of God's good gifts, but not all. And of those which it does not precede it is itself one."[172]

344

Warnings and rebukes not pointless

But Pighius says that our teaching is without foundation when we preach grace in such a way that we leave free choice no part in right living. For to urge those who are incapable of it to obedience is just the same as if someone commanded his slave to run this way and that when he had him shut up in prison and bound in fetters. This comparison would perhaps be somewhat appropriate if it did not totter on one side and fall in a heap on the other. For if we professed that we are held captive by the tyrannical power of God and not by our own wickedness of heart, then it would have some attraction. But as it is, since both the cause of the evil and the blame attach to us, and we have on us no chains to bind us but those of our own crookedness, and [so] are unable to run, there is a great amount of difference in the comparison. In addition, since the primary use of warnings and rebukes looks to the

---

172. *Enchiridion* 32.9 (NPNF 3:248), discussing Rom. 9:16. The first edition has the erroneous reference *[Letter] To Vitalis*, which later editions rightly drop. A quotation overlapping this one is found in *BLW* 6.392 (at n. 137). A shorter version is added in the 1550 *Institutes* 2.5.17 (LCC 20:337–38).

needs of the elect, it is a sign of the utmost blindness not to consider their purpose—or at any rate to consider it and pretend not to is a sign of a wickedness that is utterly lost. For God commands [the elect] what they are to do; and when they do not obey, they have both their wretchedness and their wickedness pointed out to them and in some measure rebuked, for the very purpose that a way may be cleared for the Holy Spirit to set them free.

I trust that I have treated this topic in such a way that from his barking Pighius will gain little in the hearing of those who have any intellect. But if anyone desires to be satisfied at greater length, that book of Augustine's is available which was put together with this matter in mind throughout.[173] Nor is it such a complicated issue that it cannot be resolved in a few words. If, they say, man does not have the ability to obey, God is wasting his effort in teaching and warning him. He would be wasting it, I agree, if he used outward teaching alone—I mean as far as true benefit is concerned. But as it is, since he renders the teaching effective by his Spirit, it is far from being the case that he speaks without benefit. Paul declares that all those who plant or water are nothing.[174] How so, except that the ministers of Christ achieve nothing more by their teaching and preaching than they would if they were striking the air with their breath? But why is it that their labour is so useless, except because they are speaking to stones until, by his miraculous and secret operation, God introduces into people's minds and breathes into their hearts what, by their own efforts, could not reach beyond their ears? So he concludes that God alone, who gives the increase, is everything.[175] This is not because in doing everything by the power of his own Spirit [God] excludes the ministry of his servants, but so as to secure the entire praise for the action for himself, just as the effectiveness derives from him alone, and whatever labour people do without him is empty and barren.

In this teaching Pighius says that there is contained so great an accumulation of absurdities that it would be an endless task to § examine them all. As a result he thinks that he has a clever way of getting ahead, so that he may leap on further in an uninterrupted run when he says that there are countless places where I contradict myself. But to avoid seeming to say this without any proof at all, he next brings one of them forward. I say: "God works in his elect on two levels, externally through the word, and internally through the Spirit. By enlightening our minds by his Spirit and forming our hearts to love and cultivate righteousness, he makes a new creation; and by the word he arouses us

> Cf. *Rebuke and Grace*

> God works through outward and *inward* means

> P claims that C contradicts himself
>
> **345**

---

173. *Rebuke and Grace.*
174. 1 Cor. 3:7.
175. Ibid.

to seek, search for, and pursue that renewal."[176] That I here clearly contradict myself he shows in the following way. For either, he says, the preaching of the word comes before the action of the Spirit, or it comes after it. But this second alternative is contrary to reason, because it would be pointless for the faithful to search for and desire the regeneration[177] which they had already obtained. But that it comes before [the Spirit's action] does not fit in with my teaching, which declares that man while under the control of his old nature cannot even desire the good. A crafty workman indeed, who can weave spiders' webs so well![178] But my reply is that the word is preached to the faithful when they are already regenerate, and that effectually and to their benefit, not so that new creatures should be born, but that they may grow and mature, even as we ought to grow and advance all through our life. If total perfection were reached at the first step, those who had heard once would indeed be taught to no purpose. But our experience is different. Already, then, one part of the web[179] has been broken off.

But [Pighius says] unless we are wrong,[180] no one will be able to be aroused by the word to seek the Spirit of God before he is regenerate. Augustine rightly warns [us] in another place that this teaching [that God is externally heard and internally teaches us to come] is far removed from the carnal mind.[181] But even though human beings, being drunk with their own foolish thoughts, may not be able to be persuaded, they can nevertheless be convicted, so that they no longer contradict God. To begin with I will put Paul in my place, since he will be stronger and better prepared to stave off Pighius's attacks. For he teaches that faith comes from hearing, and yet he immediately adds that it is possessed only through the secret revelation of the arm of God.[182] You hear that a person is changed from an unbeliever to a believer by the preaching of the word; you hear, on the other hand, that he remains an unbeliever until he has been enlightened by the Spirit of God. If these two things seem to involve any contradiction, Paul reconciles them by a single word, when he glories that the ministry of the Spirit has been entrusted to him and declares what he means by this. That is of course that God by his Spirit engraves on human hearts what

---

176. *Inst.* 2.5.5 (LCC 20:322).

177. The first edition has "this," which Calvin has taken from Pighius (69a) but made redundant by adding "the regeneration." Later editions rightly drop "this."

178. Cf. Erasmus *Adages* 1.4.47 (CWE 31:355).

179. In this paragraph Calvin is discussing preaching to the converted; in the next paragraph he discusses preaching to the unconverted.

180. The first edition has "he is wrong," which later editions rightly change to "we are wrong."

181. *The Predestination of the Saints* 8.13 (NPNF 5:504, 505).

182. Rom. 10:17; 1 Cor. 2:1–5, 6–16. For the same juxtaposition of texts, again with the assertion that one immediately follows the other, see *BLW* 1.247 (at nn. 63–64).

he speaks through his mouth to their ears, not before or after but at the same time.[183] So in preaching the seed is being sown, but that it puts out roots, germinates, and bears fruit is brought about by the Spirit of God inwardly.[184] Now, to come to my own words as well, people are aroused by the word to seek regeneration—when? When, it is clear, the Spirit of God § makes that instrument of his effective to inflame such desire. But it is not for us to lay down for God the moments and occasions for his working. Only let us keep hold of that connection which, as Paul describes, exists between the secret working of the Spirit and the outward preaching by human beings, and we shall be clear of all difficulty.

Both work together

346

Scriptures Quoted against Calvin

But since our opponents twist against us some texts from Scripture which seem superficially to have little in common with our teaching, in my *Institutes*[185] I show how falsely and incorrectly they are, as I have said, twisted to bear an unnatural meaning. For the sake of brevity I divide them into a number of types. Of these the first concerns the commandments. "Either," they say, "God is playing games with us when he gives commands, or he demands of us only those things which are within our power."[186] Here I reply that those who measure human strength by the commandments are without understanding.[187] Pighius comes back to that well-worn principle of his, that the observance of the law is not impossible, an idea which he utters with the more confidence because he has never given serious thought to the observance of the law. For this is what nearly [all] those high-minded giants are like today who philosophise about the possibility of fulfilling the law, the merits of works, and perfection. For with deep gasps they froth about the law being possible to observe, when they have never attained to any part of it at all, even with the tip of a finger. But if they once perceived with the slightest understanding what it means to "Love the Lord your God with all your heart, with all your mind, [and] with all your strength,"[188] they would surely recognise how far removed man must be from fulfilling it as long as he is enclosed within this mortal body.

Three types

1. Commandments
"Ought" implies "can"?

But we are still dealing with a different question [from this]. For we are saying that man is unequal not only to the fulfilling of the law, but

We cannot even begin *to keep the law*

---

183. 2 Cor. 3:1–8.
184. 1 Cor. 3:6–7.
185. *Inst.* 2.5.6–11 (LCC 20:323–31).
186. *Inst.* 2.5.6 (LCC 20:323).
187. Ibid.
188. Mark 12:30/Luke 10:27.

even to making a beginning on it. And we are saying that not only the completed and finished totality of righteousness but also its lowest and easiest part is beyond those abilities which Pighius so exalts to the sky. But I do not want anyone to learn from me whether that is true or not, but let each one of the faithful consider his own living experience of the faith.[189] Then he will agree to the facts with greater certainty than to [my] words [alone]. As for the very clear passages of Paul which [in the *Institutes*] I cite to confirm this view,[190] [Pighius] supposes that he has suitably disposed of them as soon as he has declared that they are not relevant to the present issue. Does the fact, he says, that the knowledge of sin comes through the law[191] thereby mean that the observance of the law is impossible? In fact I deduce from there that not only that but even the earnest desire to observe it is impossible, as the context of the passage inevitably demands. For, after raising the question of whether it is possible for righteousness to be obtained through the law, [Paul] uses only one argument to prove that it is impossible: through the law comes the knowledge of sin. § It is an argument from opposites, which would in no way stand up if there were any other effect of the law at all. So it is exactly as if he said that the law of itself brings people nothing except for making their sin plain to them. Now imagine that man does have some ability by his own strength; surely that whole argument will immediately collapse. It is still clearer in another passage, where he teaches that the law came in afterwards so that sin might abound,[192] which would not be true if any power to obey existed in man. Hence anyone who knows the purpose of the law will know that human power is not at all to be calculated from its commands. Therefore Augustine well said somewhere: "We say that by the law the hearing of what God wants to be done is brought about, but obedience to the law is brought about by grace. So the law produces hearers of righteousness, but grace produces doers" (*To Boniface* 3).[193] Elsewhere he says it even more distinctly: "God's righteousness depends not on the commandment of the law, by which fear is instilled, but on the aid of Christ's grace, to which alone the fear of the law like a tutor usefully guides us. He who understands this understands why he is a Christian" (*Nature and Grace* 1).[194]

---

189. Note that Calvin appeals not only to Scripture but also (as a secondary confirmation) to experience. See W. Balke, "The Word of God and Experientia according to Calvin," in *Calvinus Ecclesiae Doctor*, ed. W. H. Neuser (Kampen: Kok, 1979), 19–31.
190. In *Inst.* 2.5.6 (LCC 20:323–24) Calvin cites Gal. 3:19; Rom. 3:20; 5:20; 7:7–8.
191. Rom. 3:20.
192. Rom. 5:20; see n. 190.
193. *Against Two Letters of the Pelagians* 3.2.2 (NPNF 5:402).
194. *Nature and Grace* 1.1 (NPNF 5:121–22).

When [in the *Institutes*] I say that the law lays down what we should do, so that we should ask the Lord urgently for the power to obey,[195] [Pighius] says this is right, since we are acknowledging that both the fact that we exist and the fact that we are alive derive from the Lord. But [I reply] we exist and move in one sense as human beings and in another as the sons of God. The former grace is the common possession of everyone, but the latter is granted specially to the elect. The former is in a certain way implanted in our nature, but the latter is given to man as a supernatural gift, so that he may cease to be what he was and begin to be what he had not yet become. Secondly, [Pighius] tries to find in my words the appearance of a contradiction. Who, he says, will pray to be given grace, which no one desires before he has it? I for my part acknowledge that the Spirit of prayer is given by God, and if I kept silent, Paul would sufficiently prove it, when he bears witness that faith is the mother of prayer.[196] But in the meantime this does not in the least prevent God from also applying the outward instrument of instruction like a goad, so as to accomplish his work in man in his usual way. If Pighius grasped this, he would at last make an end of disputing.

Law points us to grace:

special grace, not grace of creation

In addition he criticises this deduction of mine: it is vain to seek in human nature the ability to fulfil the law, since it is the special gift of God.[197] For, he says, seeing is not denied to be within our competence just because we need the brightness of the sun to see. Pighius maintains that usual custom of his: he is deceived by foolish comparisons which have as great a difference from the matter in hand as heaven is distant from the earth. For grace does not occupy the same role for us as does the sun, to which we can direct our eyes if we so wish. [Grace] even gives us and opens for us eyes of the mind, so that we may gaze on the light of the § truth shining in [God's] word. This is the reason for that prayer of Paul's that God may be willing to give the Ephesians enlightened eyes of the mind to perceive what is the hope of their calling and to understand with all the saints what is the length, breadth, and depth (ch. 1).[198] No wonder, since elsewhere he says that the heights of spiritual wisdom do not rise into the heart of man (1 Cor. 2).[199]

P's analogy of the sun

348

[In the *Institutes*] I put in a second category those promises which have the condition attached: if we do what God requires of us. For [our opponents] use them as weapons against us in the following way. To what purpose would it be said that the fulfilment of those promises which God makes depends on us, if it were not in our power to bring

2. Conditional promises

---

195. *Inst.* 2.5.7 (LCC 20:324).
196. Rom. 10:14.
197. Summary by Pighius (70a) of the argument of *Inst.* 2.5.7 (LCC 20:324–25).
198. Eph. 1:18; 3:18.
199. 1 Cor. 2:14.

about their fulfilment? This is how I replied there. "Since the promises are held out to the faithful alongside the wicked, they have a use that is appropriate to each." For this is how the wicked are brought to see that it is their own unworthiness that deprives them of those benefits which God is wont to bestow on those who worship him. By the blessing they offer, [the promises] also have the task of making the devout the more keenly disposed towards fear and obedience towards God and true purity and innocence of heart—but relying on the Spirit of uprightness, not their own strength. Accordingly I teach that by such promises people are sent off to seek the grace of God, by which alone they can reach the place to which they are called.[200] Pighius thinks that [by them] people are kept dependent on free choice. To confirm this opinion he alleges that a different end was appointed by Moses.[201] For, after promulgating the law, this is what he says: Consider that today I have placed before your eyes life and death....[202] As though the apostle did not shout in opposition that the law, which had been appointed to result in life of itself, has been turned through the corruption of our nature to our ruin (Rom. 7).[203] The law is indeed what demands our bounden duty, but we are not at all able to pay it. The law shows that that priceless reward of eternal life is reserved for those who practise it. But there is no one who even by an earnest attempt can by his own power aspire to it. This is why Paul, having quoted the saying, "He who does [the works of the law] shall live by them," immediately, as though in desperation, teaches us to flee to a different refuge, so that we may obtain freely and without works what God promises there as a wage in return for works (Rom. 10; Gal. 3).[204] But Pighius insists on the fact that Moses shortly afterwards adds: so that you may do [the works of the law] and fulfil it with your might.[205] Certainly, so that after hearing this we may know the inevitability of our duty and, having made trial of our own strength and having been convinced of our weakness or rather of our impotence, be compelled to say to God: "Give what you command, and command what you will."[206]

They also point to grace

The third category consists of those statements where the Lord charges the people of Israel to the effect that it is their fault alone that

3. Accusations

---

200. Up to this point the paragraph is a summary of *Inst.* 2.5.10 (LCC 20:327–28), with a short quotation. *Inst.* 2.5.8–9 is not discussed because Pighius passes over that material.
201. I.e., that Moses saw the promises as having a purpose different from that proposed by Calvin.
202. Deut. 30:15 (cf. 30:19), quoted by Pighius (70b).
203. Rom. 7:7–13.
204. Rom. 10:5–9; Gal. 3:12–14.
205. A loose summary of Pighius's quotation (70b) of Deut. 30:16.
206. Augustine's famous prayer of *Confessions* 10.29.40; 10.31.45 (NPNF 1:153, 155). Cf. *BLW* 2.260 (at n. 30).

On Book Four 169

they do not enjoy all kinds of good things. For such charges seem not to fit those who have this response available to them: "Prosperity was dear to us, and we feared its opposite, and the fact that to secure the one and escape the other § we did not obey the Lord was due to its not being open to those who are subject to the domination of sin. Therefore it is unreasonable to have laid to our charge evils which it was not in our power to avoid."[207] I reply, as is true and straightforward, that the source of evil must be traced, so that from this it may be determined where the blame remains, or on whom it should be laid. Now no one can claim that anything else is responsible for his sinning except an evil will. Moreover, the evil character of the will has no other source but its inherited corruption. What then is to be gained by diverting to another the reproach for that which is rightly imputed to us? We find the root of the blame in ourselves; why then do we attempt to pass it on to someone else to secure a discharge for ourselves?

Pighius thinks that he has a strong enough counterargument to refute this reply by simply rejecting it with his usual contempt—except that he dwells with somewhat greater care on the testimony of Moses, which was also examined there.[208] For Moses, after the promulgation of the law, calls the people to witness as follows: This commandment which I command you today is not hidden or placed far away, but it is beside you, in your mouth and your heart.[209] Since this adjuration seems to lay great responsibility on mankind, it could also seem to be opposed to our earlier answer. And so [in the *Institutes*] I quoted it and expounded it. But at the same time I did not hide the fact that, if I had had it in mind to quibble, it would have been open to me to evade the conclusion by saying that the point [of the passage] was ability only to know [the law], rather than to observe it. But I showed from Paul what is, without doubt, the real and natural meaning: namely that it refers to the gospel and not to the law.[210]

Pighius spends a lot of labour on refuting the first answer, which I acknowledged to be of a quibbling kind. But when he comes to the second one, he thinks that nothing more absurd or more inconsistent with the words of Moses can be imagined than if it be true that the passage should be understood to refer to the gospel. Now I am not surprised that he presents himself as such a wild and ferocious opponent of us, when he is no more gentle towards the Holy Spirit. Surely the Spirit of Christ who had spoken through Moses pronounces through Paul's

349

Source of evil lies in us

Deut. 30:11–14

refers to the gospel

P denies this,

---

207. *Inst.* 2.5.11 (LCC 20:329), quoted by Pighius (71a). The response that follows is similar, but not identical, to the reply given in the 1539 *Institutes*.
208. Pighius (71a–72a) responds to Calvin's exposition in *Inst.* 2.5.12 (LCC 20:331–32).
209. Deut. 30:11, 14.
210. *Inst.* 2.5.12 (LCC 20:331).

_{contrary to Paul}

mouth what he meant (Rom. 10).[211] And its interpretation is not intricate or concealed. For a comparison is being made between the gospel and the law, namely that the law promises life only to those who have fulfilled its commands, while the gospel offers a righteousness that is freely given, by which men are reconciled to God and become heirs of eternal salvation. It is in relation to this that that passage is cited: The word is not far off, nor placed beyond your reach. And it is added: This is the word of faith, which we preach. If clarity is wanted, what could you desire which is easier to understand? If authority [is wanted], it is an oracle from heaven. Should then Pighius's blasphemies even be heard against it? But since this giant does not shrink from declaring war on heaven, let us observe for a moment what an effect he makes. The whole context, he says, unavoidably demands that it[212] be understood of the law. I acknowledge that it certainly first has reference to the law, so far as it is a pathway to the gospel and has the function of § leading people to Christ. But these words would be said to no purpose of the commandments alone, or at any rate they would be of little profit to man, being such as would lead only to his ruin on account of the corruption of his nature. For that reason Paul transfers them to the gospel, not by an improper use[213] but according to their proper and, so to speak, literal meaning.[214] But [Pighius objects] these words, "I command you to do . . . I set before you this day life and death," are a mockery if they are spoken to despisers [of the law] who must inevitably continue in their hardness of heart and obstinacy until God remakes their heart of stone. Not so according to Paul, who calls the law a ministry of death and condemnation precisely because it could only kill its disciples and send them to destruction, unless it was engraved on their hearts by a new covenant (2 Cor. 3).[215] After saying these things, as though like a judge he held me bound on trial before his judgment seat, [Pighius] declares that it has been sufficiently proved how opposed is all of Scripture to our opinion. But I advise him, if he wants to judge anything in future, that he should first pay a visit to Anticyra;[216] from there he may come back with a sounder and cleaner brain!

---

211. Rom. 10:5–9, which Calvin proceeds to expound.
212. I.e., Deut. 30.
213. "Improper use" is in Greek.
214. According to Pighius (71b), Paul in his use of the text was not annulling Moses' literal reference to the law.
215. 2 Cor. 3:3, 6–7, 9.
216. A town in Phocis (modern-day Aspraspitia, in Greece) famous for the medicinal plant hellebore, which was supposed to cure madness. Cf. Erasmus *Adages* 1.8.52 (CWE 32:153–54). Luther also offers Erasmus the same advice in his *Bondage of the Will* (LCC 17:106).

On Book Five [of Pighius]

Pighius Attacks Reformed Doctrine

In the fifth book [Pighius] lists again the heretics of old who were in error on the topic under discussion. He is endeavouring to show that his teaching and that of those like him is so restrained among the different and competing opinions of the sects that it avoids the extremes of both sides and holds a middle position.[1] We on the other hand [he claims] have drawn something from every one of those who diminished freedom of choice—and thus in part have a teaching which is a mixture of many different errors and in part have also added new falsehoods which surpass all the wickedness of previous heretics. For [he says that] with Marcion, Valentinus, Mani, and the like we misrepresent human nature as evil; with Wyclif and Lorenzo Valla we make man only an instrument of the will of God, so that he is acted upon rather than acting. Everything depends on the choice of God alone, so that nothing happens to us contingently, but everything by sheer necessity. But we hold one opinion which is worse than all the rest: we find the whole of [human] nature in its entirety guilty of such great perversity, even in the saints, that it can act only in an evil way, whereas they (that is, Valentinus, Marcion, and the Manichees) taught that it is good in part and evil in part. I have already said before,[2] as it were pointing with my finger, how filthy a slander it is that he so repeatedly associates us with Marcion and the Manichees, from whom we differ no less than Pighius himself does from us. The fact that we teach that § [human] nature is evil we could perhaps seem in a way to share with them. But then with the very next word we make it obvious that there is such a great difference between us that not even the least suspicion can attach itself to us. For they set a propensity to evil in the essence of our nature and imagine

P claims Reformers follow heretics,

especially over perversity of nature

351

Evil from the beginning versus evil from the fall

---

1. Pighius (72b–73a, 74a–b) represents his own position as a middle way between, on the one hand, that of Simon Magus and his followers (Cerdo, Marcion, Valentinus, Mani, Bardesanes, Priscillian, Abelard, Wyclif, Valla, Luther, and Melanchthon) and, on the other, that of Pelagius and Celestius.
2. In *BLW* 2.262–65.

that it has been like this from the beginning of creation. But our people laid down the principle that the defect is due to the corruption of that nature, and constantly affirm that it has been corrupted not by some influence from heaven, but by man's voluntary fall. So when the cause of evil is being sought, we ought not to go outside ourselves but ascribe to ourselves the whole of the blame. This is the extent of our agreement with Valentinus, Marcion, and the Manichees—as much as there is between fire and water. If anyone asks for confirmation of this, first of all our books are available, excellent and most trustworthy witnesses; and secondly you will read nothing here which is not quoted by Pighius himself from my *Institutes*.[3]

1. Whole of nature corrupted

But not content with having equated us with such irrational men, he shouts that we deserve [even] greater anathemas, because we condemn the whole of [human] nature. Of course, since man has sinned not with some part of himself but with his whole being, why should it be surprising if he be said to have ruined himself totally? But it makes a very big difference whether he is said to be in trouble through bringing the defect upon himself by his own fault, as we teach, or through its being imposed on him from elsewhere, as their crazed minds suppose. But if human support is needed, we have Augustine to vouch for all of this.[4] As for the necessary or chance occurrence of events, I prefer not to touch on this at the present time, lest by entwining different topics I confuse the order of my discourse.[5] We do indeed teach that man is so acted upon by the grace of God that he nevertheless [also] acts at the same time, but he acts in such a way that the effectiveness of the action is and remains entirely in the control of the Spirit of God.[6]

Human wickedness comes from the fall

And to make clear how much license and boldness he has gained from his constant practice of lying, [Pighius] not only takes no care to cover his lies with at least some disguise but, lest anyone should fail to recognise them, relates passages from my *Institutes* which expose them to public view.[7] For we do not locate the origin of our wickedness in creation or in the work of God, but in the fault of our first ancestor. For by a voluntary rebellion he brought upon himself his wretched condition of bondage, since he had been created free. But this is the single criterion by which Augustine was content to distinguish the orthodox from the Manichees and those like them.[8] You see then how this madman, immediately after he has spoken his word of condemnation, ef-

---

3. In *Inst.* 2.5.1 (LCC 20:317), quoted by Pighius (62a); see also *BLW* 4.331 (at n. 49).
4. See *BLW* 3.320–21, 325–26; 4.331–32.
5. Cf. *BLW* 1.250–51 (esp. at n. 78); 2.255–58 (esp. at n. 10).
6. Cf. *BLW* 3.316–17 (at nn. 230, 232).
7. Pighius (73a–74a) quotes extensively from ch. 2 of the 1539 *Institutes*.
8. See, e.g., *Retractations* 1.9.2 (FoC 60:32–33).

fectively acquits us.⁹ As for our saying that the whole person is corrupted in such a way that he cannot with any part of himself come near to God by himself, we affirm nothing other than that to which God himself bears witness. And no better judge than he can be found concerning man, since no one knows better what is in man.¹⁰ For it is not difficult to prove that the whole person is denoted by the word "flesh," however much those who are fond of an argument may contradict this. For whenever it is contrasted with the Spirit as its opposite, the word "Spirit" is without doubt understood as regenerating grace. § It follows then that "flesh" is what we have in our natural state before we are regenerated. It is precisely by the argument that what is born of the flesh is flesh that Christ proves that we need to be born again (John 3).¹¹ If only a part of man were "flesh," surely this argument would be the means of its own undoing. For the reply would be ready to hand that the superior part of man is by far a different thing from the "flesh." But what words of praise does Paul use to recommend this flesh? I know, he says, that no good thing dwells in me, that is, in my flesh.¹² Again: The mind, or thought, of the flesh is enmity towards God (Rom. 7–8).¹³ He who bears witness that the flesh is devoid of any good and who at the same time indicates the reason to be that it is entirely resistant to the righteousness of God and can think and consider only what is opposed to God, says nothing more or less than we do. And in case anyone should yet seize on the ambiguity of the word "flesh" itself, [Paul] had previously left no part of man whatever outside the range of his condemnation. Let his description of human nature which is contained in the third chapter of Romans be read.¹⁴ What does he leave man there that is untouched by condemnation? So then what I have declared about the corruptness of our nature is not my own judgment but that of the Holy Spirit.

Scripture supports C

352

But who cannot see that what I then add¹⁵ is the [logical] consequence of this? Namely that it is not in man's power to prepare himself to receive the grace of God, but his whole conversion is the gift of God. However, this point too has its own sure and clear evidence [in Scripture]. For when the Lord promises that he will give us a heart of flesh

2. No human preparation for grace

---

9. I.e., by immediately following the charge of Manichaeism with a quotation (73a) of Calvin's statement from *Inst.* 2.1.8 (LCC 20:251) that human corruption is the result not of God's creation but of original sin.

10. Cf. John 2:25.

11. John 3:5–7. At this point Calvin is reiterating the argument of *Inst.* 2.3.1–4 (LCC 20:289–94).

12. Rom. 7:18.

13. Rom. 8:7. In the first edition there is a second, inaccurate and redundant, reference to Rom. 7, which is rightly dropped in later editions.

14. Rom. 3:9–20.

15. I.e., in *Inst.* 2.3.6–9 (LCC 20:296–303).

in place of our heart of stone,[16] what room is left for preparation?[17] How shall he who is made willing[18] instead of unwilling, ready to obey instead of rebellious and obstinate, claim for himself the praise for his preparation? This is no less declared in the following words: I was found by those who did not seek me.[19] For even though the prophet is speaking about the calling of the Gentiles, yet in it he exhibits the universal pattern of the calling of all of us. So it is God's work to go before us, to convert us to himself. No wonder, for although it is a much lesser thing to think than to will, Paul does not even leave us the capacity to think anything good.[20] Accordingly let us acknowledge with the prophet that we had all like sheep gone astray, each one of us had turned to his own way, when the Lord led us back to his way.[21] Nor does the Lord allow even any part of this glory to be transferred elsewhere. For he cries that it is his work that we who were blind are enlightened,[22] that we are brought over from darkness into his light,[23] that we are renewed in mind,[24] that finally we are roused from death to life.[25] What kind of preparation will one who is dead use to call forth the grace of God?

3. Grace is efficacious

353

There follows the third point, on the effective operation of grace. [In the *Institutes*] I say, then, that grace is not offered to us in such a way that afterwards we have the option either to submit or to § resist. I say that it is not given merely to aid our weakness by its support as though anything depended on us apart from it. But I demonstrate that it is entirely the work of grace and a benefit conferred by it that our heart is changed from a stony one to one of flesh, that our will is made new, and that we, created anew in heart and mind, at length will what we ought to will. For Paul bears witness that God does not bring about in us [merely] that we are able to will what is good, but also that we should will it right up to the completion of the act. How big a difference there is between performance and will! Likewise I determine that our will is effectively formed so that it necessarily follows the leading of the Holy Spirit, and not that it is sufficiently encouraged to be able to do so if it wills.[26]

---

16. Ezek. 11:19; 36:26.
17. I.e., for the idea that people can pr epare themselves to r eceive God' s grace.
18. Latin *voluntarius*, usually translated "voluntary."
19. Isa. 65:1.
20. 1 Cor. 2:14.
21. Isa. 53:6.
22. E.g., Ps. 146:8.
23. E.g., Acts 26:18; 1 Pet. 2:9.
24. E.g., Rom. 12:2; Eph. 4:23.
25. E.g., John 5:24; 1 John 3:14.
26. This paragraph summarises points made in *Inst.* 2.3.6–11 (LCC 20:297–306), citing Ezek. 36:26; Phil. 2:13.

Moreover, what we say about one action should be extended to cover our whole life. For it would not be enough if God guided man's heart once, and did not always maintain it in a similar way and strengthen it to persevere. Now in treating perseverance, I remind you,[27] we must beware of two things. We must not imagine that man, by some power of his own, cooperates with God when he obeys the direction of the Spirit. And we must not suppose that subsequent grace is paid to him as a reward, as though by using the earlier well he has merited it. For I do not allow that human beings have any ability but that which has been given to them. And [I say] that God unceasingly so accomplishes his work in them that whatever he bestows on them right to the end is freely given—unless perhaps with Augustine we prefer to call it a reward because it is grace in exchange for grace, because God constantly adds to his kindness to the elect by giving them new gifts.[28] All of this, if I have any understanding, is comprehended by Paul in a single statement when he teaches that there is one God who effects in us both to will and to do according to his good pleasure.[29] He speaks not of a single day, but of a continuing course of action, whose sole cause he defines as God's good pleasure, that is, his gracious kindness which pays no attention to any merit.

4. Perseverance also a gift of God

My claim that Augustine supports all these teachings is received by Pighius with a delightfully dismissive wave of the hand.[30] But I am saying nothing which I have not previously placed before the eyes of readers. And there is not one point which does not appear almost word for word quite often in Augustine's works, nor is there any which may not be confirmed by a clear testimony of his.[31] I teach[32] that the whole of human nature is corrupt. What of Augustine? "Do not suppose that you achieve anything, except insofar as you are evil" *(On Ps. 142).*[33] Again: "Just as the Spirit of life in Christ regenerates believers, so the body of death in Adam had generated sinners. The latter is the generation of the flesh, the former that of the Spirit. The latter makes children of the flesh, the former children of the Spirit. The latter makes

Augustine supports C:

1. Whole of nature corrupt

---

27. Cf. *Inst.* 2.3.7, 9, 11–12 (LCC 20:298–99, 301–6).
28. *Grace and Free Choice* 8.19–9.21 (NPNF 5:451–52) on John 1:16.
29. Phil. 2:13.
30. With reference to *Inst.* 2.3.11, 13–14 (LCC 20:305–9) Pighius (73b) notes in one line that Calvin wishes his teaching to be both certain and the most clear opinion of Augustine.
31. I.e., Calvin here is simply reiterating the teaching of the 1539 *Institutes,* which is supported by Augustine, as he has shown by his appeals to Augustine there (2.3.13–14) and earlier in this work. This paragraph and the next three reinforce the claim, taking in turn the four points which have been outlined in the four previous paragraphs.
32. I.e., in *Inst.* 2.3.1–4 (LCC 20:289–94); cf. n. 11.
33. *Expositions on the Psalms* 142.10 (on Ps. 143:5; 142:5 in the Vulgate) (NPNF 8:653, where it is numbered 143.6). In the first and subsequent editions, this and the next reference are wrongly reversed.

children of death, the former children of the resurrection. The latter makes children of this world, the former children of God. The former makes children of mercy, the latter children of wrath. The latter binds people in original sin, the former frees them from every chain" (*The Merits and Forgiveness of Sins* 3.2).[34] Again: "We say that human beings are the work of God insofar as they are human, but they are under the control of the devil insofar as they are sinners" (*To Boniface* 1.18).[35] And he bears witness that the whole of man is so corrupted that whatever good qualities he seems to have of himself become sinful (*To Boniface* 3.5; *Against Julian* 4).[36]

[In the *Institutes*] I say that man is preempted by the freely given grace of God, that he attains to it by no merit of his own, indeed he cannot even aspire to it until this desire has been aroused in his heart.[37] Let Augustine speak: "It is obvious then that God by his grace takes away the stony heart from unbelievers and preempts the merits of human good wills. [He does this] in such a way that the will is prepared by antecedent grace, rather than grace being bestowed because of the antecedent merit of the will" (*Letter* [217] *to Vitalis*).[38] Again: This is the chief point on which the issue turns, "whether this grace precedes or follows the human will, or (to speak more plainly) whether it is given to us because of the fact that we will or whether through it God also brings it about that we will."[39] Again: "Because by the greatness of the first sin we lost the freedom of choice to love God, it is not of him who wills or him who runs that we believe in God and live devoutly—not because we have no obligation to will and to run, but because he brings about both in us."[40] Again: "To what end did the Lord command us to pray for unbelievers? Was it so that grace should be paid to them in return for their good will, and not rather so that their evil will should be changed into a good one? For he says: No one can come to me unless my Father draws him. He does not there say 'leads,' which might perhaps have encouraged us to understand that there the will comes first. Who is drawn, if he was already willing? And yet no one comes unless he wills. Therefore, so that he does will, he is drawn in wonderful ways

---

34. *The Merits and Forgiveness of Sins* 3.2.2 (NPNF 5:70). Book 3 of this work is also called *The Baptism of Infants* (see *BLW* 3.313 n. 196).

35. *Against Two Letters of the Pelagians* 1.18.36 (NPNF 5:388), which is quoted more fully in *BLW* 2.259 (at n. 27).

36. Ibid., 3.5.14 (NPNF 5:408–9), which is added twice in the 1543 *Institutes* (3.14.4; 3.18.5 [LCC 20:771, 826]); *Against Julian* 4.3.14–33 (FoC 35:176–98), cited in *Inst.* 2.3.4 (LCC 20:293).

37. *Inst.* 2.3.6–9 (LCC 20:296–303); cf. n. 15.

38. *Letter* 217.7.28 (FoC 32:94). For the other uses of this passage see *BLW* 3.304 n. 107.

39. *Letter* 217.5.17 (FoC 32:88), quoted more fully in *BLW* 3.304 (at n. 106).

40. *Letter* 217.4.12 (FoC 32:84), discussing Rom. 9:16. A shorter form of this quotation is added in the 1550 *Institutes* 2.5.17 (LCC 20:338).

by him who knows how to work within the very hearts of people, not so that they believe unwillingly, but so that they become willing instead of unwilling" (*To Boniface* 1.19).[41] Again: "Free choice is capable only of sinning, as long as it is a prisoner" (*To Boniface* 3.8).[42] Again: "How can anyone have a good purpose unless the Lord first has mercy on him, since a good will is precisely one which is prepared by the Lord?" (book 4, ch. 6).[43] Again: "By doing this for his own sake and not for theirs, God shows that he is not roused by any human merits to make them good, but rather repays them with good things in return for evil" (ibid.).[44] Again: "According to the pleasure of his will, lest we boast in the pleasure of our will" (*The Predestination of the Saints* 19).[45]

I consider that God does not merely give man the option, so that he has the ability both to will and to act well if it pleases him. But [God] effectively arouses [man's] heart, so that he wills, and [God] so guides it in its entirety that it does and completes by the action what has been granted to it § to will.[46] Now let Augustine speak. In correcting a certain view which had been uttered without due consideration, he said: "[It is] more appropriate [to put it] like this. [It was] the determinate will of God that you should come from unbelief to faith by receiving the will to obey and that by receiving perseverance you should continue in faith" (*The Gift of Perseverance, to Hilary and Prosper*, 22).[47] Again: "The first man did not have that grace through which he would never wish to be evil. But he had grace which was such that if he were willing to remain under its control he would never be evil, and without which, even possessing free choice, he could not be good. But he could by free choice abandon it. This is the original grace which was given to the first Adam, but [the grace given] in the second Adam is more powerful, and by it one is even caused to will, and to will so much, and to love with such ardour that through the will of the Spirit he overcomes the will of the flesh which lusts against it. That [first grace], which shows the power of free choice, was certainly not a small thing. For [free choice] was helped in such a way that without this help it would not remain in a good state, but it could, if it so willed, abandon this help. But the second is so much the greater that for man merely to recover his lost freedom through it would be insufficient, and, finally, for it merely to make it possible for him either to perceive the good or

3. Grace efficacious

355

---

41. *Against Two Letters of the Pelagians* 1.19.37 (NPNF 5:389), discussing John 6:44. The same passage, with a different beginning, is quoted in *BLW* 3.308 (at n. 147).
42. Ibid., 3.8.24 (NPNF 5:414). For the other uses of this passage see *BLW* 3.293 n. 12.
43. Ibid., 4.6.13 (NPNF 5:422). For the other uses of this passage see *BLW* 3.304 n. 111.
44. Ibid., 4.6.14 (NPNF 5:422). Augustine is here commenting on Ezek. 36:22–27.
45. *The Predestination of the Saints* 18.37 (NPNF 5:516).
46. As Calvin argues in the 1539 *Institutes*; see n. 26.
47. *The Gift of Perseverance* 22.58 (NPNF 5:549).

to persist in it, if he willed it, would be insufficient. What it requires is that he also be caused to will [the good] by it."⁴⁸ "Now those to whom such help is not given are being punished, but those who are given it are given it in accordance with grace and not in payment of a debt. And it is given, to those to whom God pleases to give it, so much more abundantly that not only the means to continue are provided (which are still needed even if we will to do so), but the aid is such and of such measure that we do will [to continue]. Indeed in our receiving good and holding perseveringly to it by means of this grace, there is in us not just the ability to do what we will to do, but also the will to do what we are able to do" (*Rebuke and Grace* 11).⁴⁹ And much else to the same effect. Again: "If we have a kind of free will from God which could be either good or evil, and a good will is from us, then what we have of ourselves is better than what we have from God" (*The Merits and Forgiveness of Sins* 2.18).⁵⁰

4. Perseverance also a gift

That same thought I also apply [in the *Institutes*] to perseverance: as the beginning, so also the completion of good works depends on God alone. And [I say], lest man fail, he is strengthened in such a way by the power of God that the course of pure, undeserved grace continues right up to the end of his life. Nor does man of himself cooperate with God so that some contribution of his own is added in, but [man cooperates] only in accordance with the measure which he has received, so that he acts only to the extent that he is acted upon.⁵¹ On this too let Augustine reply: "How can not only the will to believe at the beginning but also perseverance to the end be other than the work of the grace of God? For the end of life itself is not in man's control but God's, and God can certainly bestow on someone who is not going to persevere at least this, to prevent badness from changing his heart" (*Letter* [217] *to Vitalis*).⁵²

356 Again: We affirm that perseverance § to the end is the gift of God. "For when he says, I will put fear of me in their hearts, what else does this mean but that the fear which I will put will be of such a magnitude and of such a kind that they will persevere in clinging to me?" (*The Gift of Perseverance, to Prosper and Hilary*, at the beginning).⁵³ In addition, [Augustine] teaches everywhere that free choice in the first man, when

---

48. *Rebuke and Grace* 11.31 (NPNF 5:484). For the other uses of this passage see *BLW* 3.323–24 n. 309.
49. Ibid., 11.32 (NPNF 5:485), the second half of which is also quoted in *BLW* 6.402 (at n. 234).
50. *The Merits and Forgiveness of Sins* 2.18.30 (NPNF 5:56), also quoted in *BLW* 3.311 (at n. 174).
51. *Inst.* 2.3.7, 9, 11–12 (LCC 20:298–99, 301–6); cf. n. 27.
52. *Letter* 217.6.21 (FoC 32:90).
53. *The Gift of Perseverance* 2.2 (NPNF 5:526–27), quoting Jer. 32:40. The passage is first cited in *BLW* 3.323 (at n. 302).

it existed whole and unimpaired, yet had no power without grace.[54] But he says, "After the fall God wanted it to belong to his grace alone that man should come to him, and he wanted it to belong to his grace alone that man should not depart from him" (ch. 7).[55] Again: "By this I have shown that the grace both to begin and to persevere to the end is not given according to our merits. It is granted according to his own most secret and at the same time most just, most kind, and most wise will" (ch. 13).[56] Again: "These are the gifts of God which are given to the elect, who are called according to God's purpose—and among these gifts are both to begin believing and to persevere right to the end" (ch. 17).[57] So he concludes that "the grace of God is the whole merit of the saints" (*Rebuke and Grace* 7).[58] Why then is Pighius angry with me, if I make use of Augustine's support which he so generously offers me?

The last thing which vexes him is my statement that after regeneration the faithful soul is divided into two parts. Every time he mentions this he says that I am imagining or dreaming it. For today the theology of the Romanists is to consider as incredible what ought to be the most familiar knowledge to a Christian. But seeing that such people have no more spiritual experience than do brute beasts, at least the authority of Paul should suffice to put a gag on Pighius. Since it ought not to be in doubt that in the seventh chapter of Romans he portrays a person who is regenerated,[59] let us see whether he does not in that passage represent in living form that very thing of which I speak. So then he bemoans the common bondage of the faithful in [speaking of] his own person. For while he wills and desires the good, he does not find the ability to accomplish it. With his mind he agrees with the law of God, but in his flesh with the law of sin, and so he does not do the good which he loves, but rather the evil which he hates.[60] You see his will agreeing with righteousness. Where then does the obstacle come from, which prevents the action from following? Surely only from a contrary desire. Where, next, does that desire come from, if not from the fact that remnants of the old man which struggle against the Spirit live on in him? For he had said in the sixth chapter that the old man had died through the cross of

5. Souls of Christians divided

Testimony of Paul

---

54. This might be a paraphrase of *Rebuke and Grace* 11.31 (NPNF 5:484) (see L. Smits, *Saint Augustin dans l'oeuvre de Jean Calvin* [Assen: van Gorcum, 1958], 2:79), which is quoted at n. 48, but is more likely to be Calvin's summary of Augustine's position as he has presented it in many quotations. This is what Augustine teaches "everywhere."
55. *The Gift of Perseverance* 7.13 (NPNF 5:530), also quoted in BLW 3.324 (at n. 312).
56. Ibid., 13.33 (NPNF 5:538), also quoted in BLW 3.325 (at n. 313).
57. Ibid., 17.47 (NPNF 5:544).
58. *Rebuke and Grace* 7.13 (NPNF 5:477), very loosely quoted.
59. In fact, historically this point has been the subject of perennial controversy; see D. C. Steinmetz, "Calvin and the Divided Self of Romans 7," in *Augustine, the Harvest, and Theology (1300–1650)*, ed. K. Hagen (Leiden: Brill, 1990), 300–13.
60. Rom. 7:15–23.

Christ,⁶¹ but afterwards⁶² he adds that it is not dead in such a way as to cease causing a troublesome struggle. Now what he means by the old man can be inferred from other passages where he commands us to be renewed in heart and mind according to the image of God.⁶³ Hence whatever lies outside the scope of this renewal is a part of the old man and is referred to § under this name.

And—so as not to prolong the battle unduly—Paul complains that he is pulled this way and that by opposing desires, and that he feels a resistance when he desires the righteousness of God, and this imposes a delay on him, so that he does not run as quickly as would be appropriate. He says that the cause of this resistance is sin which dwells within him, and at the same time names the part of him in which it dwells—namely the flesh.⁶⁴ But Pighius understands him to mean the body when he mentions the flesh. The body, however, has of itself no feeling of its own, and Paul does not mean just any feeling, but a deliberate⁶⁵ desire which is opposed to the Spirit. Now the question is, what is the origin of the resistance if it is not from the imperfection which consists in the fact that both the human mind and the human will are not yet wholly reformed by the Spirit of God into newness of life, but in some part still smack of the flesh and the earth? Where such a desire is evident, so that will is opposed to will, desire conflicts with desire, wish is contrary to wish, who will not allow me to say that the soul is divided into two parts? Indeed who does not both experience this and speak of it?

Pighius Claims Middle Way

But after expounding the whole of our teaching, he contrasts us with the Pelagians (who, he says, fell into the opposite extreme by denying the grace of God altogether) so as to arrive at his own middle position, which is based on the combination of free choice and grace. And indeed first of all, to make what he is going to say credible, he secures favour for it by labelling it a definition of the church. But what argument then does he use to prove that it is a definition of the church? That Augustine said so. What? Does he dare again to misuse the testimony of the man whom we have so clearly claimed as our supporter? But he is not short of camouflage, for he scrapes together bits of sentences from inauthentic books⁶⁶ which seem to give equal roles to free choice and the grace

---

61. Rom. 6:6.
62. Rom. 7:14–25.
63. Col. 3:10; see also Rom. 12:2; 2 Cor. 3:18; Eph. 4:23.
64. Rom. 7:15–18.
65. Latin *voluntarium*, normally translated "voluntary."
66. Pighius (74b) repeats short quotations from Pseudo-Augustine *Sermon* 236.6 (PL 39:2183) (see *BLW* 3.319 n. 258) and *Hypognosticon* 3.11.19–20 (PL 45:1631, 1633).

of God. But it is good that he brings forward nothing into the discussion now which I have not already refuted. However, by his dishonesty he forces me to say something again on the same subject.

In the second book, [Pighius] says, of *The Merits and Forgiveness of Sins* [Augustine] does not criticise the Pelagians on the ground that they affirm free choice, but because they overstep the limits in their elevation of it. Here I would like readers to notice that this is the first work in which he began to argue with the Pelagians, and so there he is skirmishing rather than engaging in a regular battle. Then again it was not part of his present purpose to deal with the question of free choice there, as the context indicates[67] and as the author himself also bears witness in the second book of his *Retractations*.[68] So it is not surprising if he does not discuss in depth what he intended only to touch on lightly in passing. But, to take no account of this, what difficulty, may I ask, does it cause us that [Augustine] condemned the Pelagians not because they affirmed free choice, but because they exalted it excessively?[69] For since he allowed the term to popular usage, he conducted the dispute on the basis of the facts alone.

Merits and Forgiveness of Sins

So now we must see how big a role [Augustine] allows to free choice, and judge from that where he disagrees with us. He acknowledges, Pighius says, that no one sins unless he wills it.[70] What do we say? Do we place sin outside the will? He acknowledges also that God has commanded nothing which does not lie within our power.[71] Of course, if you understand by "power" not that which is implanted in our nature, but that which God specially bestows from heaven on his own, as [Augustine] himself so often explains it.[72] However, he immediately adds the true observation that there has never been such a case nor is one to be expected in the future.[73] He compares, [Pighius] says, grace to the brightness of the sun;[74] by this he implies that there is some strength in the soul, just as there is in the pupil of the eye an ability to see. But why does [Pighius] keep quiet about the correction which he added next? For there is a similarity in the fact that just as the eye is

§ 358
Augustine on role of free choice

---

67. The issue in *The Merits and Forgiveness of Sins* 2 is the possibility of living without sin (2.1.1), but the context is, as Pighius says (74b), that some were presuming too much on free choice (2.2.2 [NPNF 5:44]), cited by Calvin in *BLW* 3.312–13 (at n. 188).
68. I.e., in *Retractations* 2.33 (NPNF 5:12; FoC 60:187–89) there is no mention of free choice.
69. See n. 67.
70. Pighius's comment (74b), repeating his earlier summary (mentioned by Calvin in *BLW* 3.313 [at n. 190]).
71. Pighius's comment (74b), repeating his earlier summary (mentioned by Calvin in *BLW* 3.313 [at n. 192]).
72. E.g., *The Merits and Forgiveness of Sins* 2.17.27 (NPNF 5:55–56).
73. Ibid., 2.20.34 (NPNF 5:57–58).
74. Ibid., 2.5.5 (NPNF 5:45), cited by Calvin in *Inst.* 2.2.25 (LCC 20:285).

enlightened by the brightness of the sun when it directs its gaze, so the human will which turns to God is aided by his grace. But when Augustine noticed that the comparison was defective in that conversion is not within the power of the soul, he said, "God even helps us to turn, which the external light does not accomplish for the eyes in our body."[75] As [he says] elsewhere too: "What soundness is to the eyes so that they may see the sun, grace is to our minds so that we may fulfil the law" (*Against Faustus the Manichee* 15).[76] But [Pighius says] he recognises that only those who try of their own accord are helped. Certainly, for God does not work in people merely by outside pressure but through a voluntary movement. For he is indicating the form of the action only so that he should not seem to be making people like brute beasts or stones.[77] Moreover, he makes no secret later on of the origin of that self-determined arousal, that voluntary effort. For when he has borne witness that it is the work of grace to make both what was hidden known and what was unpleasant sweet,[78] after he has taught that it is not by human ability but by God's gift that we either know the good or delight in it,[79] he says: "People toil to discover what good of our own there is in our will, and I do not know what can be found" (idem, 17–18).[80] If we believe Pighius, Augustine demands of man that he endeavour of his own accord by himself. What does Augustine himself say? I pass by his other books, but in the one which Pighius quotes he defends himself strongly against this allegation. Man could, he says, if he had not fallen away from his original condition into his present wretchedness, have pursued and striven for righteousness without difficulty.[81] But as things are, a fault has resulted from the punishment for his rebellion, so that now it is difficult for him to obey righteousness. [God] does indeed command us to endeavour anxiously and to pray earnestly, but also to understand that our ability so to endeavour and so to pray is ours by his gift (ch. 19).[82]

Grace and Free Choice

However, [Pighius] thinks that he has in the first book [addressed] to Valentinus an excellent text to establish this combination of free choice and grace which he advocates. There commands from Scripture are quoted which, while they limit free § choice, do indicate that it is

---

75. *The Merits and Forgiveness of Sins* 2.5.5 (NPNF 5:46), also cited by Calvin in *Inst.* 2.2.25 (LCC 20:285).
76. *Against Faustus the Manichee* 15.8 (NPNF 4:218).
77. *The Merits and Forgiveness of Sins* 2.5.6 (NPNF 5:46). For the other uses of this passage see *BLW* 3.311 n. 176.
78. Ibid., 2.17.26 (NPNF 5:55).
79. Ibid., 2.17.27 (NPNF 5:55).
80. Ibid., 2.18.28 (NPNF 5:56). For the other uses of this passage see *BLW* 3.304 n. 110.
81. Ibid., 2.22.36 (NPNF 5:59).
82. Ibid., 2.19.33 (NPNF 5:57).

present in man; and then others are contrasted with them, which show that whatever things are required of us are gifts from God.[83] I have already[84] described, as honestly as I could, what that whole contrast signifies, that is, its purpose and its components. It consists of two parts: that people sin of their own accord when they sin, and by their own movement of the will, and therefore it is fruitless to divert the blame elsewhere. And that, when they are guided by the Spirit of God to the good, their will is not thereby excluded, since grace consists precisely in the turning of their will to love and seek the good. Then, having shown that man acts voluntarily both in good works and in bad, [Augustine] begins to debate the nature of the will itself, what power it has of itself, and also the effectiveness of grace. [He says] that the will is certainly by nature always evil, so that it can do nothing but obstinately resist the righteousness of God. Only by grace does it become good, and that in such a way that it then necessarily loves and follows the righteousness to which it was previously averse (ch. 15).[85] What of us? Do we exclude the will by preaching of grace? Pighius must therefore put on some other disguise if he wants to deceive even those of ordinary intelligence. For it cannot escape anyone's attention how closely Augustine's thoughts and words are in agreement with ours when he writes like this.

But it is now high time to yield a place to Pighius's hallowed definition,[86] so that it may appear the more clearly with what justification he engages the universal church in conflict with us, so as also to claim its support for himself. Before he reveals his own views on the subject itself, seeing that in this discussion the treatment of the grace of God is of the utmost importance, he does list the different meanings of the expression. But he introduces nothing which had not been carefully noticed and taught by our people long ago, although he subsequently shows his gratitude in the worst possible way. And yet, so that you may see what an expert theologian he is, whenever he inserts some idea of his own, he corrupts and spoils by his own padding things which elsewhere had been finely spoken.

P appeals to the church's definition

P on grace

Then he turns to an explanation of the corruption of our nature which flowed from the fall of the first man, as beyond any doubt the whole dispute hinges on knowledge of this. However, I wonder why it has now occurred to him to use such an introduction, since elsewhere he has written that nothing is more contrary to reason. The church's

P on corruption of nature

---

83. *Grace and Free Choice* 2.2–3.5 and 4.7–5.10 (NPNF 5:444–48). For the other uses of this passage see *BLW* 3.316 n. 224.
84. Calvin expounds *Grace and Free Choice* carefully in *BLW* 3.315–18 and 4.329–30.
85. Ibid., 15.31 (NPNF 5:456). For the other uses of this passage see *BLW* 3.316 n. 225.
86. I.e., Pighius's appeal to the definition given by the church. See Calvin's reference to "the church's definition on free choice" in the following paragraph and the text just before n. 66.

definition on free choice, he said, is clear and known to all; the question of original sin has always been difficult, obscure, and confused. How absurd it is then to complicate a matter that is, of itself, straightforward with unnecessary difficulty! He was saying this, it is true, to get away from ground that was unfavourable to him, but now, conquered by the power of argument, he does what he had [previously] rejected. Of course it was a mark of excessive idleness and folly to want to eliminate original sin from the present discussion, when its principal part depends on it. § Of course Pighius will argue in his weighty tome[87] that God bestowed free choice on man. Why does he wear himself out with such senseless toil? For he will at last achieve only one thing, when he has sweated long and hard, which is that we shall acknowledge the truth of what we have always admitted and what he perhaps could not have uttered so eloquently if he had not had the benefit of our instruction. Now we affirm that the human race, on losing that freedom which it had received in creation, fell into wretched bondage. This Pighius allows. We say that man in this state of bondage is not endowed with a free ability to choose both good and evil, so that he could conform to whichever he pleased. For he is held bound under the yoke of sin, so that he cannot in any way desire the grace of God until he is freed by the grace of Christ. Here is the sticking point where Pighius opposes us, and yet he forbids there to be any mention of it in the investigation of the dispute. But now, as I have said, forced by the power of truth, he has moved into the place which he used so much to avoid.

P says nature undiminished by the fall

From now on, lest I be too long-winded in relating his dreamings, I will briefly note only the main points of the matter. He considers that it is an ungodly, crazy fabrication that we teach that our nature is so corrupted by original sin that man cannot do anything other than sin. For our nature was not taken away from us, but only the supernatural gift[88] which rendered our nature better and more complete than it would have been in itself. Is this the reason why he has so often snatched Augustine from us, to make him a witness and a supporter of his own viewpoint? Augustine cries that in this debate we should look not at our nature as it was created by God, but at the distortion of a corrupted nature, and he does not do this in a single place, but is wholly and everywhere insistent upon it.[89] Against this Pighius thinks that there was no diminution in our nature, and yet at the same time he defends himself with Augustine's testimony.

---

87. Pighius (78b) refers to his discussion of these issues in the *Controversies*. See Introduction §2.

88. In the 1559 *Institutes* Calvin approves the Scholastic doctrine that through the fall humanity's natural gifts were corrupted and supernatural gifts taken away (2.2.12 [LCC 20:270]).

89. As Calvin argues in much of *BLW* 3, e.g., in cols. 293, 295–300.

But, he will say, he does not hide the fact elsewhere that [Augustine] is opposed to him on this matter. But since this matter on which they are diametrically opposed is the chief point and one of the greatest importance in the whole dispute, why does he later boast as if there were full agreement between them? Add the fact that there is no error which Augustine refutes more often and more fiercely in the Pelagians than their boasting of the intactness of our nature, while he maintained that it was wounded, corrupted, and ruined.[90] So why does [Pighius] go so far as to anathematise the Pelagians, when he openly subscribes to their first axiom? Mortality and corruption, [Pighius] says, [derive] from the creation of our nature, not from a fault in it. How does he prove this? The body [he says] is in this state as a result of the elements of which it is composed and the mode of its composition. But by the same argument it could be proved that after the resurrection too it will be subject to death, and that the soul is mortal now. For from what element did it arise if not from nothing? Indeed if he said that that perfection which God conferred on man at the beginning did not so subsist in his nature that he had it by himself and of himself, I would gladly yield to his opinion. § For in that way we do not allow either that the soul is immortal of itself. Indeed Paul also teaches the same when he ascribes immortality to God alone.[91] But we do not on that account acknowledge that the soul is by nature mortal, since we judge nature not from the initial character of its essence but from the permanent condition which God has imparted to his creatures.[92] So although man had been created with the intention that he should never experience death or corruption, he brought death upon himself by his own fault. So when the apostle argues about the origin of death he does not ascribe it to nature but to sin.[93] Accordingly, to have been free from the necessity to die was the wholeness of [man's] nature, but his present subjection to the judgment of death is a disease. This is the wholesome and simple philosophy which is violently overturned by those wandering, fleeting speculations of Pighius. That the flesh, he says, is in conflict with reason and hinders it and disturbs it in its obedience to righteousness belongs to nature, not to its corruption.

Does he not in fact confess publicly that he is a Manichee? Everyone knows the intoxication of Eck[94] and the foolishness of Cochlaeus.[95]

P on intactness of nature

361

P is a Manichee

---

90. Possibly an echo of *Nature and Grace* 53.62 (NPNF 5:142).
91. 1 Tim. 6:15–16.
92. Calvin's first theological treatise, the *Psychopannychia*, was written against the Anabaptist view of the mortality of the soul.
93. Rom. 5:12–21.
94. See *BLW* 2.260 n. 32.
95. Johannes Cochlaeus (1479–1552) was a German Roman Catholic theologian who engaged Luther in bitter controversy. Calvin would have met him at the colloquies of Hagenau, Worms, and Regensburg (see *BLW* 1.233 nn. 1, 3).

But of such disgraceful shamelessness no similar example exists that I know. More than a hundred times he has cast at us the name of Manichee, on the ground that we condemn [human] nature because we say that whatever is wrong in man should be ascribed to the corruption of that nature. But what now? That rebellion of the flesh, he says, which causes trouble to the reason, and which struggles against righteousness, is no different from what it was at our first beginnings, before sin began. You see how his foul mouth declares, to the dishonour of the Creator, that evil is part of man's essence? Unless perhaps he should wish to absolve obstinacy from being a fault—although he himself teaches that it is opposed to righteousness. But he would more quickly get himself out of the labyrinth[96] than explain away such a manifest blasphemy by any smoke screen. When earlier he falsely said that we make God the author of evil, that was the gravest charge with which he thought that we could be burdened. What does he now declare as his own opinion? That the rebellion which is experienced from the flesh against obedience to reason and righteousness is from our nature and from God, not from the corruption resulting from the revolt [against him]. Let him who wishes now read the ravings of Mani, as they are reported by the ancients,[97] and he will find that they are no different.

Effects of the fall

[Pighius] concludes then that man lost no part of his natural endowment, but only that he had been deprived of[98] the supernatural gifts which God had granted to him.[99] But he loses touch with reality in not being able to distinguish wholeness, which is the true, authentic state of our nature, from a contingent corruption.[100] Without this distinction it is not surprising if he gets everything confused. I will explain the nature of it in a few words. We too recognise as deriving from the original creation of our nature all the feelings which naturally occur in man, such as, for example, § married love, also the love of parents for children, friendship, joy at a happy outcome, sorrow at bereavement, widowhood, and all adversities; fear of hunger, cold, want, danger, disgrace, scandal, and on the other hand the desire and seeking after the necessary resources for life. We do not teach that these feelings developed through sin, but that they were implanted in our nature from its very creation. We do teach that the ἀταξία with which we are all too familiar, that is, the unregulated overflowing of the feelings which causes us

Human feelings

362

and their corruption

---

96. See *BLW* 1.240 n. 34.
97. E.g., Augustine *Heresies* 46 (Müller 84–97).
98. Latin editions all have "adorned with"; the French translation more plausibly has "deprived of," involving the change of a single letter in the Latin.
99. See n. 88.
100. Literally, "accidental corruption"; see Introduction §6.

to have evil desires and by these desires to become rebels against God, was born of our corruption, and was not inborn in our nature from the beginning. For this reason Augustine, in words we have already quoted, does not count the faculty of desire, in its present corrupted state, worthy of the name of will, but thinks that it should rather be called lust, because it recognises no limit to its longing.[101] Father loves son, husband [loves] wife. It is a pure love and one which even merits praise. But in the present corrupt state of [human] nature this love will not be found in man without some smack of defilement. Therefore from that root of corruption it results that the will generates nothing that is pure or unsullied; but, as it is itself spoiled, so it also bears fruit which is defiled and unclean.

And this is what we [too] say: precisely because that sickness of which we speak is always firmly fixed in the human will, it cannot generate anything but evil. For if desire for a thing which is otherwise an honourable example of its own kind and praiseworthy is never without some blemish because of some such excess, what [shall we say] when we lust after evil things? Such a corruption in our nature is also proved everywhere by the Scriptures. There you have in a few words an account of the distinction between a pure and a corrupted nature. Because Pighius does not recognise it, he gets everything wrong. He supposes this teaching does God an injustice, because it would not be at all compatible with his goodness to create a soul so bereft of all uprightness that it could do nothing but sin. What sort of commendation is it of [God's] grace, he says, when he is said to have produced such a nature? Yet it is not to our Creator that we owe whatever in us is evil, but to our first ancestor, who passed on this wretched inheritance to us. However, if Pighius is afraid that God may rightly be accused of cruelty if on account of the fault of one man he punished the whole race with such a severe form of punishment, he should not take action against us but do away with the whole of Scripture, where this judgment is proclaimed in many places.

Evil lusts

There follows in his book another passage on the renewal of [human] nature in which he shows well enough that he warms up only when he is being abusive. For since he had to be complimentary here or keep quiet, he is colder than any ice.[102] But this is what he eventually indicates to be his principal difference of view from us. He thinks that God does stretch out his hand to fallen humanity to raise § them up, but only to those who long to be raised up and do not neglect the grace which is available to help them, but rather lay hold of it, try

Preparation for grace

363

---

101. *Retractations* 1.15.4 (FoC 60:67), quoted in *BLW* 3.298 (at n. 52).
102. Luther similarly, in his *Bondage of the Will*, accuses Erasmus of being colder than ice (LCC 17:114).

with its help to return to God, desire to be saved by him, and hope for this—those who deliver themselves to him to be healed, enlightened, and saved. With these words, in regard to regeneration he attributes to free choice the role of willing, laying hold, trying, and obeying. To this he adds, as is inevitable, that all are equally able to receive grace because it is offered indiscriminately to all. Afterwards he goes much further: no wrong is done to grace if people are said to be able by their own nature and through the power of free choice to hate sin, renounce evil, turn to God, ask for pardon with a humble and lowly heart, seek mercy, and hope for grace. No, these are the preparations which must come first if God is to consider us worthy of his kindly look. And with teaching like that [Pighius] really thinks that the whole of Pelagius's blasphemy is adequately refuted. And he mocks at our foolishness when, fearing that such ideas will diminish the praise due to grace, we unnecessarily contend over nothing with so much violence.

<small>P condemned by Council of Orange,</small>

Two reasons prevent me from now refuting these delusions with Scripture: namely that a vast forest [of texts] would spring up around me here, and that this will be the subject which will occupy the whole of the next book. Add the fact that whenever his mind finds Scripture not to his taste he ignores it. But where is that respect which he pretends that he shows to the definitions of the ancient fathers? "If anyone teaches that both the increase and the beginning of faith and the very desire to believe [come] not as a gift of grace (i.e., through the working of the Holy Spirit reforming our will from unbelief to belief, from irreligion to religion), but are innate in us by nature," he is declared to be a heretic by a decree of a church council (Council of Orange, ch. 5).[103] Also, "if anyone argues that God waits for our desire that we should be cleansed from sin, and does not acknowledge that it is by the work of the Holy Spirit in us that we are even caused to want cleansing," he is condemned as an adversary of the Holy Spirit (ch. 4).[104] Again, "if anyone teaches that God's mercy is bestowed on us because apart from the grace of God we will, toil, knock, ask, and desire it, and does not acknowledge that it is from God through the Spirit that we are caused to believe, will, and be able to do all these things as we should," he is judged worthy of an anathema (ch. 6).[105] The following decrees were passed by the council in addition: "If anyone says that by the disobedience of Adam man was not entirely, that is, in both soul and body, changed for the worse, but believes that only the body was sub-

---

103. Council of Orange (529), canon 5 (Leith 39), also quoted in *BLW* 2.289 (at n. 250).
104. Council of Orange (529), canon 4 (Leith 38). On the other uses of this passage see *BLW* 2.289 n. 244.
105. Council of Orange (529), canon 6 (Leith 39), also quoted in *BLW* 2.289 (at n. 248).

On Book Five   189

jected to corruption, the freedom of the soul remaining unharmed, then he is deceived by the error of Pelagius" (ch. 1).¹⁰⁶ Again: "If anyone says that § grace is bestowed in response to human request, and not that it is grace itself which causes us to request it, he contradicts the prophet Isaiah" (ch. 3).¹⁰⁷ Again: "If anyone affirms that it is possible to think or choose by natural strength any good thing which has to do with eternal life, that is, to assent to the preaching [of the gospel] without the enlightenment of the Holy Spirit who gives to all their delight in assenting and believing, then he is deceived by a heretical spirit" (ch. 7).¹⁰⁸ Again: "God loves us as we shall be through his own gift, not as we are by our own merit" (ch. 12).¹⁰⁹ Again: "No one has anything of his own but falsehood or sin" (ch. 22).¹¹⁰

364

Now let Pighius show me one detail in the whole of his teaching which is not cut to pieces and condemned by those decrees! But if he despised the authority of the council, then at least he should be disturbed by the fact that the bishops who took part in it and signed its decrees do not make themselves out to be the originators of those clauses, but only to be approving them, since they had been sent to them from the apostolic see.¹¹¹ This is the same see whose every utterance Pighius maintains is to be received no differently from an oracle of the tripod,¹¹² nay no differently from a divine revelation from heaven to which both angels and prophets ought to defer. What will he say now that the anathema of that holy see has been pronounced against his own person?

which has papal backing

As for the fact that he so often boasts that he has nothing in common with the Pelagians, I know not what Pelagians he is inventing here. For not only does he resemble in many matters those whom Augustine describes, but he is much worse than some of them. Augustine had been informed by Prosper that there were some in Gaul who disagreed with him, but who had come so near [to Augustine], even on [Augustine's] own admission, as to believe that human beings are from birth subject to the sin of the first man, and that no one can be set free from that except through the righteousness of Christ. They also acknowledged that people's wills are preceded by the grace of God and that no one is self-

P worse than semi-Pelagians of Gaul

---

106. Council of Orange (529), canon 1 (Leith 38).
107. Council of Orange (529), canon 3 (Leith 38), which goes on to quote Isa. 65:1.
108. Council of Orange (529), canon 7 (Leith 39–40).
109. Council of Orange (529), canon 12 (Leith 41).
110. Council of Orange (529), canon 22 (Leith 42).
111. Council of Orange (529), preface (CCL 148a:55). This was a shrewdly aimed blow as Pighius held that the decisions of councils took their validity from the pope's approval (*Defence of the Ecclesiastical Hierarchy* 6).
112. The seat of the Pythian priestess of Apollo at Delphi. Cf. Erasmus *Adages* 1.7.90 (CWE 32:121–22).

sufficient for either the beginning or the completing of any good work.¹¹³ When [Augustine] began to dispute with them, he distinguished them from Pelagius,¹¹⁴ but nevertheless he was not at all satisfied with their declaration¹¹⁵—from which it is easy to recognise how far Pighius is still removed. They acknowledged that people's wills are preceded by God (*Predestination of the Saints* 1.1),¹¹⁶ not by a natural gift—for that would have been absurd—but by the special grace of the Holy Spirit. But [Pighius] shouts that no one who has not by willing and by hoping and by seeking first prepared himself is aided by the mercy of God. Where now is that immense disagreement between him and the Pelagians in which he glories?

> P wrongly claims to differ from Pelagius

365

He does indeed oppose Pelagius for making God a debtor to man. But with what argument? Even if, he says, man were guilty of no fault, what can he yet bestow on God or hold out to him, a slave to his master, a creature to his Creator, to bind him to himself § [and ensure] that he is adopted into inheritance of eternal life? But now, having fallen into guilt which brings eternal death, has he anything with which to rescue himself from damnation? Or with which to make satisfaction for his offence [and] besides deserve to be inscribed as both heir and son? What can he by his own strength present to God, to whom he owes all that he is and all that he can do? He is so sure that Pelagius is overwhelmed by such a powerful assault that he fiercely mocks as ridiculous our anxiety to safeguard the grace of God. But if one statement is removed, where he declares man to be subject to punishment of death for his fault, I say that Pelagius is in no way affected. Pighius praises with splendid panegyrics the benefits which God bestowed on human nature. Augustine bears witness that the same was done by Pelagius, much more excellently and much more splendidly. Indeed he also used to paint over his wickedness with a not dissimilar kind of oratory when in the Council of Palestine and often afterward he was asked his views on grace.¹¹⁷ What is man, or what does he have, that he has not received from God?¹¹⁸ What pride, and also what madness, it would be, therefore, if he claimed anything as his own, as though it had not been bestowed by the grace of God? Look what engines Pig-

---

113. Prosper *Letter to Augustine* (= 225 in Augustine's *Letters*) 3–6 (FoC 32:121–26) sets out their views, as does Hilary in his *Letter to Augustine* (= 226 in Augustine's *Letters*) 2–8 (FoC 32:130–37). Calvin here quotes loosely the summary given by Augustine himself in *The Predestination of the Saints* 1.2 (NPNF 5:498). Prosper's and Hilary's accounts portray the semi-Pelagians as being considerably more Pelagian than Augustine admits.
114. *The Predestination of the Saints* 1.2 (NPNF 5:498).
115. As is shown by *The Predestination of the Saints* as a whole.
116. See at n. 113.
117. See *BLW* 4.339 (at nn. 122–24).
118. 1 Cor. 4:7.

hius would use to ruin and overthrow Pelagius! All he does is subscribe to his confession.[119]

But [Pighius claims to] remove from man the possibility of imposing an obligation on God, which Pelagius affirmed. Again this is a ghost which he has invented for himself under the name of Pelagius.[120] Since, as he reckoned human merits only on the basis of the promises, he indicated well enough that he conceived God's obligation to pay a reward for human works as deriving only from the fact that he had of himself made himself a debtor by a voluntary undertaking. Finally he did not ascribe any virtue or righteousness to man which he did not explicitly and unambiguously attribute to God's grace. He taught that people had merit only because God considered their works worthy of that price, not by any necessity nor through any legal obligation, but in accordance with his own measureless kindness. While chanting this almost in so many words, Pighius congratulates himself on having overthrown the whole Pelagian heresy.

P follows Pelagius

Pighius on Grace

But he finds support in an irrefutable reason why he should believe that the grace of God is available to none but those who have prepared themselves to receive it: God ought to have a definite reason for imparting it to one rather than to another. For this befits one who is wise. I will reply in unison with Augustine: "Far be it that this decision should rest with the clay rather than with the potter."[121] God does indeed have a definite, real reason for what he does, but it is too secret, sublime, and concealed for it to be grasped by the measure of our mind, which is so narrow and mean. What is at issue, then, is simply this. We with fear and trembling reverence the wisdom of God, which Paul teaches is beyond the ability of our faculties to understand as regards this decision.[122] Pighius [on the other hand] § does not allow God to be wiser than he with his foolish brain can comprehend. From this follows that accursed blasphemy which says that if God punishes one of two people who are evil and liable to equal condemnation, and still disobediently persist in wrongdoing, and counts the other as worthy not only of pardon but of his love as well, his mercy will not be praiseworthy but foolish, irrational, and the softness of a mad lord who certainly deserves to

P opposes election

366

---

119. I.e., Pighius subscribes to Pelagius's confession of faith.
120. I.e., Pelagius's actual position, as set out in this paragraph, is different from that attributed to him by Pighius and is indeed close to Pighius's own position.
121. *Rebuke and Grace* 5.8 (NPNF 5:474), added in the 1559 *Institutes* 3.23.14 (LCC 21:963).
122. Rom. 11:33; cf. n. 126.

have all his servants be evil and disobedient. I will leave to God the defence both of his righteousness and of his wisdom. I will only ensure that he does himself take up his cause and declare with his own lips that he is on trial here. He promises through Isaiah that he will be found by those who have not sought him, and that he will appear and show himself to those who were not concerned to know him.[123] Did he bestow this benefit on all? By common consent [he bestowed it] only on some.

Grace is prevenient

But if you would like to know still better how [God] does not wait until people come to him, but draws to himself those who are hostile and estranged, look at those in whom this prophecy was fulfilled. Consider carefully what they were like before they were converted, and then you will be in doubt no longer on this matter. Then let us bring forward what Paul reports about the Ephesians: God displayed his mercy towards them, not when they stretched out their arms to welcome him, but when, dead in sins and trespasses, they served in Satan's army; when, sunk in evil desires, they paid allegiance only to the flesh and to the world; when they were by nature children of wrath, just like the rest; when they lived apart from Christ and apart from God.[124] I will not insist for the moment, as I am entitled to do, on how far such a condition is from preparedness. I would only like to learn from Pighius why [God] cherished the Ephesians rather than anyone else. If he cites to me their grief, their good thoughts, their devout desires, Paul's words leave no room for any such thing. Indeed, to prevent such a foolish idea from entering anyone's mind, he also explicitly shows that they had been entirely like others, from whom nevertheless they had been distinguished and separated by the undeserved favour of God. By nature you were children of wrath, he says, just like the rest.[125] As if he were saying that since all shared a common condition and an equal status, God did not find any reason in you to distinguish you from others, but he derived it from his own mercy. Now, if it is asked why he does so, he has already anticipated this question by that celebrated reply: I will have mercy on whom I will have mercy.[126] By this of course he set this discriminating character of his mercy in choosing people, which we are discussing, on an exalted plane, just as it is far higher than our understanding.

But Scripture teaches otherwise?

But [Pighius] brings forward passages of Scripture in which the Lord seems to indicate that his grace will be available to no others but those who have prepared themselves in advance. To whom, he says, will I have regard except him who is poor and broken in spirit, and trembles at my

---

123. Isa. 65:1.
124. Eph. 2:1–3.
125. Eph. 2:3.
126. Exod. 33:19; Rom. 9:15.

On Book Five 193

words?¹²⁷ Certainly God has regard to the humble, as David sings that the § sacrifice of a broken and contrite heart is acceptable to him.¹²⁸ But it is worthwhile also to know whence come that humility and reverence for God's words which the prophet so praises. Now it is certain that the human heart always swells with pride and blind self-assurance until it is tamed and subdued by the Spirit of God and settles into humble submission. Nor indeed do we deny that man is prepared in this way to receive the gift of righteousness, but it is by the direction of the Holy Spirit, not by his own strength.¹²⁹ It is only those who labour and are burdened that Christ calls to himself.¹³⁰ But it is he himself who also makes us feel our burden and groan under it. We agree that the popular proverb is very true: the one and only start for a cure is recognition of the sickness.¹³¹ Therefore¹³² for Christ to reveal himself to you as a doctor you must recognise your disease. Moreover, recognition of the disease will bring you to humility and fear of God, to a fear and horror of judgment and to dissatisfaction with your self. Now let us consider whether human beings can generate such an attitude naturally. But even experience itself cries that they cannot be brought to this state before they have entirely laid aside the natural mind, and Scripture everywhere testifies the same. So it is necessary for God to chastise us so that we may be rendered wise, since we are of ourselves like untamed calves, as Jeremiah says (Jer. 31).¹³³ And to prevent anyone understanding that of external correction, he himself at once interprets it differently: Convert me, O Lord, and I shall be converted. After you converted me, I repented; after you showed me [the way], I smote my thigh, I was perplexed, and I was ashamed.¹³⁴ You see how the prophet gives to God the credit for all these things, hatred of sin, fear of death, sorrow at his offence, desire for grace, which Pighius ascribes to the power of human choice.

367

However, [Pighius] thinks that he cleverly anticipates this objection when he acknowledges that we are continually aroused and moved by God—but only if we ourselves try, take trouble, and do not fail to assist his grace which is present to help us. But in that way he divides [the responsibility] between God and man, and indeed leaves in human control those matters¹³⁵ in which the whole power to repent is con-

We must assist grace?

---

127. Isa. 66:2.
128. Ps. 51:17.
129. This simple argument is Calvin's response to all passages of Scripture that set conditions on God's gifts: it is only by God's grace that people are able to meet these conditions.
130. Matt. 11:28.
131. Walther 38324g.
132. Where the first edition has "I," later editions rightly have "Therefore."
133. Jer. 31:18.
134. Jer. 31:18–19.
135. I.e., those listed in the last sentence of the previous paragraph.

tained. So how will this be reconcilable with the prophet's words,[136] which show that repentance in its entirety, and so in its first beginnings, proceeds from God alone? Grace, [Pighius] says, fails no one but him who fails himself. I agree, certainly; only let him grant to me in turn that all are lacking in a good will and bereft of strength, but those to whom God supplies each; and moreover that he who both wills well and makes effective endeavour does not fail himself. [God], he says, does not coerce anyone by violence. Certainly, but so that he may have willing[137] servants who follow of their own accord and obey, he creates a new heart in them and renews a right spirit in their inner nature.[138]

P's concept of threefold action of grace
368

After this he trims his sails somewhat. For he reports that he finds a threefold action of grace by which the Lord distinctively and specially helps and advances his elect, in addition to their § natural endowment and the common gift of free choice. The first is that in which he comes to us before our justification and incites us to desire the same, stretches out a helping hand to those endeavouring to attain it, [and] helps those who are labouring. What do I hear? If we are incited to desire grace, what has become of that declaration of twenty lines above, that God counts no one worthy of his kindly regard but him who, having forsaken sin and turned to him with a broken and humbled heart, begs for his mercy, seeks pardon, and hopes for mercy? Who would not call someone unduly forgetful who lets such contradictory, opposed statements fall from his lips in almost a single moment? Surely God has already counted as worthy of his kindly regard one whom he arouses to devout and holy desires. And what is this very thing, but to come before all good movements of the heart? But let us proceed. This, he says, is what holy doctors call "prevenient grace." They do indeed often speak of prevenient grace, but in a very different sense. For they do not imagine that a good will is established in us by it in such a way that we already [at this stage] cooperate, as Pighius wants to argue, but they affirm that this is entirely its own work. Nothing [happens] without us, says Pighius. But according to Augustine, [it happens] absolutely without us (*Grace and Free Will* 17).[139] For here are the words of them both. "Not only are the unwilling made willing, but rebels are made submissive," is the teaching of Augustine.[140] But this man maintains that to assent lies within our power. Augustine denies that this grace

contradicted by Augustine

---

136. As in the last sentence of the previous paragraph.
137. Latin *voluntarios,* normally translated "voluntary."
138. Ps. 51:10.
139. *Grace and Free Choice* 17.33 (NPNF 5:458), cited in *BLW* 4.342 (at n. 162).
140. *Against Two Letters of the Pelagians* 4.9.26 (NPNF 5:429). For the other uses of this passage see *BLW* 3.308 n. 144. The first two editions have a reference to "ch. 2." That this is an error is confirmed by the fact that the French translation drops it.

finds human wills [already] good; it makes them good.¹⁴¹ Again elsewhere: "But who flees to grace, except when 'a person's steps are guided by the Lord'? And this means that even to desire the help of grace is already the beginning of grace" *(Rebuke and Grace).*¹⁴² Pighius recognises no action of grace except where someone of himself wills well. Why then, on account of nothing but the bare similarity of the term, does he cover up his own wicked lie with the name of the ancient [fathers], to whom he is diametrically opposed in his definition of the actual facts? For it is just as if someone were to define God as a mortal animal with a body, and then add that this is what holy doctors call God. There follow a second action of justifying grace and a third of crowning grace, in the explanation of which he hardly dares to stammer out three words, in case something similar happens to him. Is this a definition, and not rather a disordering and confusing of everything which had been well enough analysed by itself elsewhere?

But he claims that his conception is no different from what is contained in those words of Ezekiel: I will give you a new heart, and I will put a new spirit within you, and I will take away the heart of stone from your flesh, and I will give you a heart of flesh, and I will cause you to walk in my commandments.¹⁴³ For he interprets as prevenient grace the melting of the hard § heart in the sinner and the making for him of a heart that is soft, responsive, and ready for divine influences. The second part, that he begins to walk in God's commandments, he takes as justifying grace. This of course is his usual trick of making anything mean whatever he likes when he is handling Scripture. The prophet is explaining in plain speech the metaphorical expression which he had used—for to make a heart of flesh out of a heart of stone is a metaphor. To cause people to obey the law is plain speech, free from any figure of speech. This clever commentator makes two things out of one. Now he seeks, by sly cunning, to appropriate the words of the prophet for his own purpose. When God promises that he will cause us to walk in his righteous ways, [Pighius] shows that he will give this grace only to those who cooperate [with it]. In this sense too David sings that we will practise virtue in God.¹⁴⁴ In the end it all comes down to this, that God does good works in men in such a way that at the same time men do them, and grace is effective only when we do not fail the help that is offered to us.

P cites Scripture:
1. Ezek. 36:26–27

369

---

141. Not a quotation but a summary of Augustine's teaching (e.g., of the thrust of *Grace and Free Choice*). Cf. *BLW* 3.314–15 (at n. 217); *Letter* 186.5.15 (FoC 30:202), cited in *Inst.* 3.22.8 (LCC 21:943).
142. *Rebuke and Grace* 1.2 (NPNF 5:472), quoting Ps. 37:23 and cited again in *BLW* 6.399 (at nn. 212, 214).
143. Ezek. 36:26–27; cf. 11:19–20.
144. Ps. 60:12, cited by Pighius (81a).

2. Paul

Meanwhile he does not notice that, according to the words of Paul which he quotes,[145] there is also included this aspect of grace, that it should not be held out to no purpose but should reach fruitfulness, that is, effectiveness. The work of God's good pleasure is said to be both the good will in man and the endeavour to which it gives birth up to the completion of the act. So the mere offering of grace, which will be useful only if someone is happy to receive it, is certainly less than the half of it. But [Pighius says] the same Paul teaches elsewhere that grace leads to condemnation if it is repudiated: Or are you ignorant of the fact that the goodness of God is drawing you to repentance? But you by the hardness of your heart are storing up wrath for yourself.[146] But Paul is speaking to hypocrites who, puffed up by the happy outcome of their affairs, even despise the judgment of God because they imagine that God is well disposed towards them and are not anxious about repentance. Therefore since they so misuse the kindliness of God, he threatens that God's vengeance will be the heavier the longer he puts it off. Now Pighius, who is by his own assessment such a skilled master craftsman in making distinctions, ought not to overlook what kind of goodness is the subject of Paul's argument there. For to confuse the exterior blessing of God, which he bestows on the good and the bad alike, with the spiritual grace of regeneration, of which he counts his elect exclusively worthy, is a mark of someone who does not think carefully enough. But his sin is not so much due to ignorance as to malice. For what mere boy would not notice and laugh at the fallacy in the following argument? Paul is attacking those who were made more obstinate in their indifference and their fleshly self-confidence by the very good gifts of God by which they had been meant to be summoned to repentance. Therefore, when the spirit of sanctification is offered it can be repudiated.

3. Rev. 3:20

Another argument follows. Christ says that he knocks at the door of our heart, so that we may open it.[147] Since then the door of our heart is closed § to him through our sins, he himself knocks, stirs, and by various ways and means invites us to open our hearts to him. So prevenient grace is not lacking to anyone, provided that he does not harden his heart against the sound of the one who knocks, which stirs and invites us. It is he who knocks, but it is we who must open to him before he will come in to us. As though indeed his way of knocking were not clearly indicated in that text, namely that he stirs us by his words of exhortation.[148] But he who opens the eyes of the mind to make himself

---

145. Phil. 2:13.
146. Rom. 2:4–5.
147. Rev. 3:20, cited by Pighius (81a–b).
148. "If anyone hears my voice" (Rev. 3:20).

understood is the very one who also opens hearts so that he is obeyed. Each of these is surely the work of Christ. What advantage, then, does Pighius gain by such childish nonsense? Christ declares that he knocks. I admit it, of course, in the sense that he explains it, that is, by warnings and exhortations. What then is it to open [our hearts]? To receive the warning in our hearts, and to obey the exhortations. Pighius imagines that this is placed in our control, but God claims it as his. I will circumcise your heart, he says, so that you will hear my voice (Deut. 30).[149] On the other hand, however, in the case of the Israelite people, Moses identifies the cause of their blindness, dullness, and obstinacy as being the fact that the Lord had not given them eyes to see, or ears to hear, or a heart to understand (ch. 29).[150] But Pighius rejoins that even though we are assisted by God, that still does not prevent it being partly also our responsibility to see and to hear and to understand. But I want proof, instead of which he brings in digressions which are absolutely irrelevant.

What he adds from the prophet is similar: Let the wicked forsake his way, and the Lord will have mercy on him.[151] To open the door to God, he says, is to renounce iniquity, [an act] which you see is put in your hands. Really? Does this mean that conversion to God, which is the true resurrection of the soul, is put back in man's power so that in this way he can rouse himself from death to life? But Pighius says we have to do it for God to have mercy on us, by which he understands that the grace of justification is indicated. If I should willingly allow him all [this], he will at once become the victor. But his whole position has stability of such a kind that it will immediately collapse at a blow from one little sentence. God demands repentance when he invites the people to [receive] the forgiveness of sins, and it was in these two elements that Christ also summed up the whole proclamation of his gospel.[152] Here Pighius constructs a fresh subtlety: that to turn back from iniquity is man's preparation, with which he steps forward to meet God, while the mercy of God is the grace of regeneration, by which he helps man. But as far as perseverance and the daily progress towards the goal are concerned, to show that man cooperates with God he uses this famous utterance of the apostle: The grace of God was in me not without effect.[153] But he ought to have noted the reason why [Paul] says this. The reason is that he has laboured more than all the rest. But lest, by boasting of his labours, he should seem to be claiming anything for himself,

4. Isa. 55:7

5. 1 Cor. 15:10

---

149. Deut. 30:6.
150. Deut. 29:4.
151. Isa. 55:7.
152. Luke 24:47.
153. 1 Cor. 15:10.

371

he immediately inserts a correction: Not I but the grace of God which was with me or which was beside me.[154] He had already given the pre-eminent role § to the grace of God and attributed to it nearly all the praise. But there was a danger that, after mentioning his own labours, he might give the impression, even by that single statement, that he was declaring that some portion of [his labours] at least was due to him. So he removes that suspicion by inserting the correction, saying that it had not been he who had laboured, but rather that this happened entirely as a result of the grace of God.

<small>P blends natural ability</small>

No plague is more hostile to the truth or a more deadly way of blinding someone completely than a false presupposition, especially when it is fixed obstinately in the mind. Pighius wants to combine the following two presuppositions. [He holds] that man is naturally endowed with the ability both to anticipate the grace of God by a good movement and to follow it, and that God's grace is offered to us only if we first stretch out our hand [for it], and is effective in us only if we support it with our own strength. Yet [he also maintains] that whatever grace God confers on us is his pure unmerited gift, that it is he alone who both begins and completes good works in us, that we are anticipated by him and made firm by him right up to the end. Pighius, I say, yokes these statements together just as if they fitted one another well. But you would more easily mix earth and heaven. What then is the reason why he rushes headlong, as if with his eyes shut, into such great absurdity? It is of course just this, that once he has conceived the idea in his mind that the grace of God is offered equally to all, provided that they show themselves to be worthy of it, he is held prisoner by this idea, so that he is incapable of further perception or judgment. And so after he has minimised the grace of God as much as possible by adorning human nature with his eulogies, he is at once moved by shame and exalts [grace] to the sky—but in manifest inconsistency. And he no more matches Augustine than an ape does a human being.

<small>and the gratuity of grace</small>

<small>P claims grace equal for all</small>

But what necessity constrains him to make the dispensation of grace equal [for all]? It is on the pretext that God declares that he does not will the death of one who dies, but that he should return and live.[155] But if we interpret this according to [Pighius's] view, why then does he die whom God wills not to die? For it is written: But God is in heaven, he has done whatever he willed.[156] Here certainly is the Gordian knot,[157] if you take that saying of Ezekiel, that God does not will the death of him who dies, to refer to his secret plan. For that reason it must

---

154. Ibid.
155. Ezek. 33:11.
156. Ps. 115:3.
157. Cf. Erasmus *Adages* 1.9.48 (CWE 32:207).

be understood in the way that Augustine also explained it in many places: God leaves nothing undone which would lead to people being led back into the way of salvation if only they were in a healthy condition. As for the fact that they do not return when they are called, it is only the disease of their own wickedness which stands in their way.[158] So God wills that the dying should live (so far as it is right for us to judge his will) in that he helps man by all [kinds of] support, lest he should be able to complain that anything other than his own guilt stood in his way. But meanwhile God's secret plan, by which he passes over one and chooses another, remains his own, and one should not inquire too curiously into it if one does not want to be overwhelmed by [God's] glory. If Pighius grasped this, he would not hold so tenaciously § to that false axiom about the equal distribution of grace. For after he has finished his speech, he finally descends to this conclusion, namely to assert with the Pelagians that "God's grace is given to us according to our merit, so that he may be with us; indeed our merit lies in this: that we are with God" (Augustine *Grace and Free Choice* 5).[159] Our whole position, on the other hand, comes back to this statement of Augustine: "Those to whom it is not given either do not will, or they do not fulfil what they will; but those to whom it is given will in such a way that they do fulfil it" (ibid., ch. 4).[160]

372

Conclusion

So, to bring this book finally to its close: It is in vain that Pighius tries either to detach himself from Pelagius, with whom we have so plainly proved his association and entanglement, or to attach us to Mani and other heretics, from whom we differ no less than he does from the orthodox thinking of the church. For even though he constantly holds up a pale shadow of it to cover his ungodliness, he nevertheless gains no more advantage from this with devout, intelligent readers than he would if he openly acknowledged that he has nothing in common with Christ or with the members of his body. It is in vain that he also seeks a middle position from the fact that he reconciles together [two] things which are more opposed than fire and water. Namely that whatever good things there are in men are the pure, unmixed work of God, and yet that men are strong in their ability of themselves to cause God to bestow grace upon them and, when he has bestowed it, to render it ef-

P vainly denies Pelagianism, accuses Reformers of Manichaeism,

and claims to hold a middle position

---

158. A summary of Augustine's teaching rather than a reference to any specific passages. There is a loose parallel with *Letter* 102.2.15 (NPNF 1:418); see Smits, *Saint Augustin*, 2:81.
159. The Pelagian view as summarised by Augustine in *Grace and Free Choice* 5.11 (NPNF 5:448).
160. Augustine's own view in *Grace and Free Choice* 4.7 (NPNF 5:447).

fective by a power which is distinctively their own. This, I say, is not to take the middle way, but rather to cast oneself and others into a labyrinth[161] from which no way of escape will afterwards open up. It is in vain that he strives to scrape together from every corner passages of Scripture which might share between God and man [the responsibility for] faith and the good works which are born of it, since the whole of Scripture assigns the goodness of both root and fruit entirely to God alone. It does indeed commend those who are devout in respect both of faith and of good works as being for that reason worthy of praise. Yet whenever it draws a distinction between man and God, it bestows the glory for all that is good on the latter as being the source, origin, and perfection of all righteousness, wisdom, and uprightness, and that not in part but so that he alone possesses it in entirety. On the other hand it strips man of all his glory, as being bereft of all righteousness and uprightness, lacking in any wisdom, not clothed or endowed with any strength, in such a way that it leaves him with nothing except the utmost wretchedness. When it urges us to devotion, to the fear of God, and to holiness of life, it teaches us that we can attain all those things only if it has been granted to us by God.

P caricatures Reformers' teaching

It is again in vain that Pighius struggles to arouse hatred against us from the allegation that human beings are made like stones if no role is left to them in acting well. For that is a false inference which he makes from our teaching. We acknowledge that the human mind sees, but [only] when it has been enlightened. [We acknowledge that] human judgment decides § and chooses, but under the control of the Spirit's guidance. [We acknowledge that] the human heart is willing,[162] but after it has been remade by the hand of God. [We acknowledge that] man himself endeavours and acts and applies his powers to obedience to God, but [he does this] in accordance with the measure of the grace which he has received. It is in vain, finally, that [Pighius] struggles, in extolling the goodness of God, to tie it to the necessity of its being equally accessible to all. For God himself speaks otherwise, judging that the praise of his goodness and mercy shines better if he exhibits the proof of it only in some, while in others he displays an example of his wrath and judgment.

P opposes election

He has no more reason to try to arouse hatred against us for malice because we say that the saving grace of God is conferred only on the elect. This, he says, is to limit it. But God does not want it to be extolled as generous in such a way that it ceases to be free. Moreover, its freedom resides in the fact that he bestows it on those on whom he will.

---

161. See *BLW* 1.240 n. 34.
162. Latin *voluntarium*, normally translated "voluntary."

However, if I wanted to examine how ignorantly and wickedly [Pighius] distorts whatever passages of Scripture he quotes on this topic, it will be an endless sea. It is written, he says, that we all have one Father, God.¹⁶³ Therefore he is not father to some and stepfather to others. But before whom are the words spoken? Before the faithful, I believe. What then is the relevance of this to the totality of mankind? In Malachi it is said: Is there not one father of us all? If we grant that here not Abraham but God is to be understood, is the prophet not speaking about Israel, that is, the special, elect flock of God? He is kind to all, sings David; surely his mercies also are upon all his works.¹⁶⁴ Will he then present the beasts of the fields and the fish of the sea and the birds of the sky with the Spirit of regeneration? But all enjoy this kindness who do not reject it by their bitterness. I agree. But the root of bitterness is plucked out of our hearts only by that Spirit through whom the elect are sanctified to be pure and holy temples of God.

<small>and twists Scripture</small>

---

163. Mal. 2:10.
164. Ps. 145:9.

On Book Six [of Pighius]

Pighius Opposes Calvin's Counterarguments

[Pighius] realised that his efforts thus far to condemn our teaching would be inadequate if he left untouched the many very strong counter-arguments by which we defend it.[1] So he begins in his sixth book to review and refute them. At least this is what he declares his intention to be.[2] But because he is aware of his feebleness in this part of the task, he soon applies the majority of his strength to completely diverting his readers not only from assessing our arguments but even from looking at them. Whatever passages of Scripture, he says, are brought forward, you should keep yourself shut up inside that fence which I built around you. For there is the consensus of the Catholic church, and to depart from it, even in the slightest matter, is fatal. But what if something different is proved beyond doubt from Scripture? You must, he says, be completely unmoved by it. Indeed even if § you see it [for yourself], you must suppose that your sight is bad. But later he fully recovers his usual confidence and undertakes to make everyone see that there is no strength in my arguments. Moreover, I had said [in the *Institutes*] that for many centuries past the view has been commonly accepted that man is endowed with a power that is free to do all things, both good and evil—in the sense that no one is subject to a necessity to sin, and no one is of necessity directed to the good by the Spirit of God.[3] So he once again leads out that band of ancient writers[4] into battle formation to prove that the view which I reject has been the common and agreed doctrine of the church. But his labour is in vain, for he quotes those with whom I have already, in my second book, negotiated and made my peace.[5]

Scripture versus consensus of church

374

---

1. I.e., in the 1539 *Institutes*.
2. In his subtitle to book 6 (84a).
3. *Inst.* 2.3.10 (LCC 20:303), cited by Pighius (84b).
4. Pighius (84b–86b) appeals to "Peter" (in Pseudo-Clement), Tertullian, Irenaeus, Origen, Basil, Hilary, Ambrose, Jerome, Chrysostom, and Augustine, referring to works which were discussed in *BLW* 2.
5. *BLW* 2.280–92.

Coercion?

However, Pighius distorts what I say, so that I seem to disapprove of all who do not agree that man is under forcible coercion—although I so often teach that a work must be voluntary before it can be good or evil, and I devoted myself with such care to excluding coercion and force.[6] So let us ensure that readers understand what his dispute with me is about: When we teach that God should be given the credit for whatever good there is in us, he testifies that he gladly accepts this. But when we begin to describe the way in which God is the source of all good things in us, he immediately objects, because he maintains that the whole [responsibility] can be attributed to God only on condition that a part is left for man. First, then, when I had brought forward the saying of the apostle, "He who began a good work in you will complete it,"[7] I had added that God begins a good work in us by arousing in us the love and wish and desire for righteousness, or more properly by forming, bending, and directing our hearts to righteousness.[8] The first part of my explanation Pighius welcomes without argument; with regard to the second he puts me under suspicion of departing from the ordinary language of the devout when I say that human hearts are formed, bent, and directed. Is it really the case that terms which both occur frequently in the Scripture and are constantly on the lips of the church's writers are deemed new and foreign to the common mind of the faithful? I could easily cite over two hundred passages from Augustine where he uses those words.[9]

Human role?

Scripture supports C

But what does the Holy Spirit say in the Scriptures, from which we should seek the rule for correct speech? Does he not prescribe the following form of prayer for the faithful: Incline my heart to your testimonies, O Lord (Ps. 119)?[10] Again: May the Lord incline our hearts to him, so that we may walk in all his precepts! (1 Kings 8).[11] Again: But may the Lord guide your hearts into the love of God and the hope of Christ! (2 Thess. 3).[12] Why [say] more? There is no prayer more often used by the saints than that they may be guided by the Spirit of God into the right way. Indeed since he says that he bends this way and that (as has seemed fit [to him]) the hearts of the wicked, who are not under the special direction of his Spirit, what [else] should we say of the faithful? For they live no more for themselves, but Christ lives in them. Like

---

6. In *Inst.* 2.3.5; 2.4.1; 2.5.1 (LCC 20:294–96, 309–10, 317–18).
7. Phil. 1:6.
8. In *Inst.* 2.3.6 (LCC 20:297).
9. A computer search of the passages where Augustine uses these words has revealed that he uses them frequently to describe the work of grace in human beings, but only a few times with specific reference to the human *heart*.
10. Ps. 119:36.
11. 1 Kings 8:58.
12. 2 Thess. 3:5.

On Book Six

streams of water, said Solomon, § so is the heart of the king in the hand of God; wherever he wills he will incline it.¹³

Why then is Pighius offended at the novelty and unfamiliarity of the word when I say that the heart of a believer, which the Lord has undertaken to rule in a singular way, is bent and formed by his Spirit?¹⁴ For he complains¹⁵ that I am introducing a new idiom to which the faithful are not accustomed. The saying in popular circulation is very true that fools have no doubt about anything, and it is derived from an ancient, more stylish proverb.¹⁶ For see how Pighius, armed only with his own ignorance, dares to declare war at the same time on both God and man! An expression is produced which first the Holy Spirit, and then also the holy doctors who follow his instruction, habitually employ. He boldly objects that it is alien to the usage of the Catholic church. Paul is brought in as a witness; before replying to him, [Pighius] unhesitatingly threatens him with an anathema if he has said anything different from what he himself is confident is the church's view. But with what kind of assurance? The saying is well known: "Ignorance begets confidence."¹⁷ A little later, however, having now become more restrained, he concedes that these words (not mine but the Holy Spirit's), however inappropriate they might be, would not trouble him very much if he had not noticed that I want secretly to introduce the poison of my wicked teaching into them. Namely that God uses our hearts and wills in good works as evil spirits use the bodily members of those who are possessed when they reply and say through them words which they themselves do not understand. But, seeing that I previously took away from him every reason for suspecting me of this, why does he speculate where there should be no anxiety whatever? I had explained [in the *Institutes*] that it is of their nature that human beings have it in them to will. But as a result of the corruption of that nature it came about that we can will only in an evil way. Therefore it is God's own gift that we will well.¹⁸ What syllable will he find here to provide material for such an allegation?

But [he says] later on I reveal without pretence that this was my view, because I am not satisfied if someone should say that the will, which is at other times not thoroughly evil but is weak and feeble, is aided by the help of grace. And I use the evidence of the prophet to make that point: I will give you a new heart and put a new spirit within

375

P objects to C's terminology,

which is scriptural and patristic

Ezek. 36:26

---

13. Prov. 21:1.
14. See at n. 8.
15. Reading "queritur" for "quaeritur," following OC and the French translation.
16. For the ancient proverb see at note 17; cf. Prov. 14:15.
17. Erasmus *Adages* 4.5.54 (LB 2:1066D–E); cf. Prov. 14:16.
18. *Inst.* 2.3.5 (LCC 20:294–95), quoting Bernard *Grace and Free Choice* 6.16 (CFS 19:72).

you; I will remove from you your heart of stone and give you a heart of flesh (Ezek. 34).[19] Then I add: "By this comparison God does not mean to indicate that there exists in our hearts a softness which at other times can be turned to obedience to what is right, but which, being weak of itself, has need of the support of his grace. [He means] that absolutely nothing good will be extracted from our hearts unless they are changed. For if stone is transformed into flesh when God converts us to a desire for what is right, then whatever belongs to our will is abolished and what takes its place is entirely from God."[20] At this point he rants at me with that shameless insolence of which he is so very capable. He cries that a false prophet in sheep's clothing[21] has been detected, who misleads simple souls, that is, he leads them away from the sheepfolds. For he is so self-satisfied in his senseless § deluded mind that he is not content with having betrayed his lack of taste once [only]. His aim, lest you should suppose him to criticise without cause, is that, whatever the words of the prophets may declare, his own opinion should prevail since he relies on the church's authority.

But eventually he comes to the point. Earlier, he says, [Ezekiel] had placed the sum total of our perfection within our power, without any reference to [God's] aid, when he said: Cast away your iniquities from you, turn to me, make yourselves a new heart and a new spirit.[22] Here, likewise,[23] he ascribes the same thing to God alone, passing by our ability. [Pighius] demands, therefore, that the two passages should be taken together to produce that combination of free choice and grace which he has described. As though indeed I would allow him to deduce from commandments the extent or nature of human ability to obey![24] From Paul we learn that the effect of the law in giving commands is to kill.[25] Why, unless because it is capable only of placing man in subjection to disobedience? We know that it is also its function to teach man to take refuge in grace, after he has been cast down by the recognition of his own wretchedness.[26] Therefore we should turn away from the exterior preaching of the law so as to come to the spiritual writing of it of which Jeremiah speaks. For there the Lord promises that he will make a covenant—not like the one which he had made before, because it had been invalidated by the rebellion of his people, but a new covenant in which

---

19. Ezek. 36:26, cited in *Inst.* 2.3.6 (LCC 20:297).
20. An inaccurate quotation from *Inst.* 2.3.6 (LCC 20:297).
21. Matt. 7:15.
22. Ezek. 18:31.
23. See at n. 19. "Likewise" refers to the fact that both passages speak as if only one agent is involved.
24. See *BLW* 4.339–44, 346–48.
25. Rom. 7:9; 2 Cor. 3:6.
26. Cf. *Inst.* 2.7.3–9 (LCC 20:351–58).

he would write the law on the hearts of his people and inscribe it on their inward parts (Jer. 31).[27] You see the reason why that covenant which was based on exterior preaching was annulled. It was because, of course, it had been broken by men. You see too the need for the making of a new one. It was of course because [a covenant] would not be permanent until it had been inscribed on [human] hearts by the Spirit of God. If Pighius had even the merest taste of this effect, or if he were at least touched by some awareness of his own helplessness, he would not go on objecting that what people are commanded [to do] is placed within their power.

Indeed, just how empty and worthless his reasoning is can be seen from the following [example]: If we should infer from the promises that conversion is the work of God alone (because in them he mentions only himself as its originator), Pelagius [Pighius claims] will with equally good reason show from the commandments that we can do everything without any help from the grace of God (because in them it is from us that complete righteousness is required, without any mention of grace). As though indeed the commandments are given so that what grace lacks should be supplied by the assistance of our strength, and not rather so that they may lead us by the hand to grace after convincing us of our own impotence! The reason for the promises is different. The Lord says, *I will give you a mind so that you may see and choose what is right; I will give you a heart of flesh so that you may obey; I will cause you to walk in my law.*[28] He does not make the fulfilment of what is promised depend on us, but plainly puts it solely in his own hands. But in commanding [us] he neither bestows any new ability on us nor commends that which we have, but shows us that we have no ability at all, so that we may learn to seek from elsewhere what we utterly lack. So let us say good-bye to that feigned moderation § of Pighius until he has proved to us that from the promises we are sent back to the law to find our righteousness there, just as [we know that] the law leads us by the hand to the promises.

Relation of law to promise

377

That we are corrected from wrongdoing to righteousness not as the result of the power of our nature, but through the gift of his grace, is plainly stated by God. Now let Pighius reverse that, if he can, and make it reciprocal: "not as a result of a pure gift of grace, but by the strength of our nature"! On the contrary, when the Lord speaks about us, he does not leave us even a drop of goodness. And he does not merely find us guilty of weakness, but he eliminates all respect for our own capacity. So let Pighius stop concocting for us this dangerous, poisonous

Grace alone, not human capacity

---

27. Jer. 31:33.
28. Ezek. 36:26–27.

mixture of his whose only aim is, by raising man to partnership with God, to cast him down more heavily from a greater height. For what else do his words mean but that in the most excellent work of all, that is, in the soul's resurrection, man has an equal part with God? Man, he says, is converted by God; but nonetheless he converts himself, he crucifies the old man, he mortifies his flesh, he renews himself, and he puts on the new man, even though he is at the same time renewed by God. He is circumcised by God, nonetheless he circumcises himself. And what is the basis on which [Pighius] constructs this equality? The fact that, just as God promises that he will do all these things in man, he also demands that man should do them. But the promises surely declare and define not only what God can do but what he will do. The law, however, was given not to bear witness to man's power but rather to prove his weakness, so that, having been reminded by the commandment that he can do nothing, he may rest on God's strength, not his own.

Meaning of "stony heart"

Moreover, because I think that the description of the heart as "stony" shows that no good will ever be extracted from our hearts unless they are made utterly different,[29] he shouts out like one thunderstruck that he does not comprehend what sort of monstrosities these are. If, however, I did not know that, blinded by madness, the man cannot see, and so strikes aimlessly at trees, animals, the ground, the very air, or whatever comes his way, as if it were an enemy, I would wonder how he could be so stupid as to imagine such a strange interpretation for a simple straightforward statement. For he sets out on a long argument to prove that the substance of the heart is not removed, but its quality is changed and a fault is corrected. If rational proofs were not enough, he confirms by a quotation from Ambrose that no new product, no new creature is made, but there is merely the removal of a fault which was not naturally present.[30] What reward do you think someone deserves who has brought to light so recondite an issue in this way? But, [Pighius argues], I say that a new heart is made, while Ambrose says that nothing in the substance is changed.[31] As if indeed it were possible to believe that I conceive that before regeneration the substance of the human heart is stone! When the prophet says that the heart is made fleshy instead of stony,[32] it is beyond doubt for Pighius that this is to be understood of its quality. When I say that it is changed or made different, he interprets me to be speaking of its substance. § Then, when David prays to have a pure heart created in him, and a right spirit re-

---

29. Pighius (88b–89a) quotes from *Inst.* 2.3.6 (LCC 20:297).
30. Pighius (89a) quotes (Pseudo-)Ambrose (i.e., Prosper) *The Call of All Nations* 1.7–8 (ACW 14:34–36).
31. I.e., in the passage referred to at n. 30.
32. Ezek. 36:26.

newed within him,³³ what will be the meaning of these words? Does not the creation of a new heart mean the same as to be made different? What a feeble slanderer to grasp at such slight and worthless trifles for his charges!

But he devises a clever little mousetrap which he is convinced I can in no way escape. For since, as I myself also acknowledge, the heart signifies the will, what I say cannot be understood of an act of the will. For I would pour out words to no purpose if I said that only evil desires ought to be destroyed. It remains therefore that I am thinking of that power whereby we will, refuse, hate, and love. Just now he was talking about the substance, now he has jumped across to power. But [what] if he complains that he denotes one thing by these two words? Then he is wrong to cite Ambrose, who included under the terms "product" and "creature" something more than power.³⁴ But never mind that; I say that the logic by which he claims that I am caught without any hope of escape is invalid. Or is Pighius still so uneducated as not to recognise anything in between the substance of the will, or the faculty of willing, and its actions or its actual effects? He has certainly disappointed me enormously. For I thought that he was trained in at least the first principles of logic. Now I see that he is completely bereft of education and of common sense. Since no one is so unlearned as not to set habit in between.³⁵ For what is the point of these forms of speech, "someone of a good or evil mind," if not to indicate his quality? Nor indeed did I fail to mention this. For in relation to the present issue, following Bernard I proposed three things for consideration: to will per se, that is, simply to will; then to will badly; and [to will] well.³⁶ The first is the faculty of willing or, if preferred, the substance. To will well and badly are qualities or opposed habits which belong to the power itself. I had omitted its acts, because they contribute nothing relevant. Having defined these three things, I had taught that the will is perpetually resident in our nature, that the evil condition of the will results from the corruption of that nature, and that by the regeneration of the Spirit the evil condition is corrected and in that way the will is made good instead of evil. Pighius boasted that if I could break this knot he would accept any treatment whatever from me. What if I were now to accept this promise?³⁷

Between substance and acts of will

there is its habit/quality

---

33. Ps. 51:10.
34. I.e., in the passage referred to at n. 30.
35. "Habit" is a philosophical term adopted by medieval Scholastic theology; Calvin here voluntarily introduces it into the debate. See Introduction §6.
36. In *Inst.* 2.3.5 (LCC 20:294–95) Calvin cites this distinction of Bernard, which is found in his *Grace and Free Choice*, esp. 6.16, 18–20; 8.24–26 (CFS 19:72–77, 81–83); see also col. 391 (at n. 130).
37. The Latin word *(sponsio)* is a legal term signifying an agreement that the losing party should pay a sum to the winner, a sort of wager at law.

But I will refrain, because I acknowledge that I have not untied any knot, since there was none. For what child even would be at a loss here? On the contrary, since Pighius had quite often mentioned the quality of the will and distinguished it from the substance, how is it that when the time came for this analysis, he passed over the former element in silence? So should one believe that the man is in his right mind who, having opened all the doors for me to get out, thinks that no escape is open to me?

Will evil by corruption of nature

379

To be brief: I say that the will is evil not by nature (that is, by God's creation) but by the corruption of nature, and that it cannot be otherwise until it is changed § to be good by the grace of the Holy Spirit. Nor do I imagine that a new product or a new creature is made in such a way that with the destruction of the former substance a new one takes its place. For I explicitly mention[38] that the will remains in man just as it was originally implanted in him, and so the change takes place in the habit, not in the substance. By a renewal of such a kind I say that the heart is made different—David says that a new heart is created.[39] But Pighius, after first saying that he is dumbstruck at such terrible monstrosities, attacks me with plentiful abuse on the ground that I say that the substance is changed. You can see now just how much intelligence he has got! And how does he himself interpret [the passage]? [He says that] the heart, which has become inflexible through a prolonged habit of sinning, must abandon its stony hardness and be softened, so as to become sensitive, responsive to impulses from God, yielding, and pliable. It is of course with good reason that he confers on the Scripture which he despises the reward of having its sacred dignity befouled by such tasteless and impious interpretations. But we remember that those pearls which pigs trample upon[40] must be adored by us with special devotion and be guarded with the utmost dedication.

Grace changes habit, not substance

Liberation in the Old Testament

Having recounted the benefits which he had conferred on his people, the Lord reproached them for the lack of gratitude which they had shown.[41] He then urged them to penitence, which is the proper preparation for the grace of the gospel, and finally promised deliverance from the Babylonian captivity. After this he at once passed from the external type to the [inward] reality.[42] For the release of the people from the tyranny of Babylon and their restoration to the Promised Land are a slight benefit compared with that priceless grace through

---

38. Calvin is probably thinking of the passage cited in n. 36, where the change is that the evil will becomes good, but without any mention of substance or habit.

39. Ps. 51:10.

40. Matt. 7:6.

41. Calvin is not thinking of a specific passage of Scripture but is responding to Pighius's survey (91a–93a) of how the prophets called Israel to conversion.

42. Here Calvin is probably thinking especially of Jer. 31:31–34; Ezek. 36:26–27.

which[43] they are set free from bondage to sin, Satan, and death by the Spirit of God [and are brought] into a free condition of righteousness. He began to bestow this grace on the people of Israel when he released them from the Babylonian exile by his own hand and brought them back to their city and temple. But he poured it out more fully and richly on all the nations under the kingly rule of Christ. Nevertheless, he there[44] shows that until he softens the hardness of [men's] hearts, that is, their obstinacy, exhortations and teaching are no more effective with men than if he were speaking to stones. For that which he promises to do he takes over into his power alone. "Otherwise the fulfilment of his promises will lie not in his power, but in man's," says Augustine (*The Predestination of the Saints* 10).[45] Certainly, therefore, a comparison is made here between grace and nature. For the hardness of the stony heart means nothing but the hostility of the flesh towards God, by which not a tiny number of human beings but the whole race is said to be troubled. God testifies that this can be subdued only by himself. And to what end? Not [just] so that they may be able to walk in the right way, as Pighius falsely says to minimise the praise due to grace, but that they may actually walk in it. When the Lord says that he will cause us to walk in his precepts,[46] he is not promising that he will merely render the heart § capable of turning in either direction, so that it will be as ready and inclined to resist him as to obey. It is rather that, being entirely formed and prepared for obedience, it already has the righteousness of God impressed and engraved upon it. For no one is so dull-witted as not to see both Pighius's remarkable malice and his shameless and almost despairing rashness in restricting the grace of God here. The Lord says that he will cause us to serve him.[47] [Pighius] renders it that he will make us able either to walk or not to walk [in his ways]. The Lord speaks in a similar way in another passage, saying that he will write his laws on our hearts (Jer. 13).[48] Pighius renders it that he will make our hearts capable of receiving this impress, but not actually [make them] have it. [God] makes a general statement. Pighius limits it to those who have been corrupted by evil habit. God calls the obstinacy and rebellion which are implanted in human beings through the corruption of their nature a stony heart.[49] Pighius declares that the hardness was incurred through bad habit. Just as if one of the philos-

Inward grace necessary

Ezek. 36:26–27

380

---

43. Correcting a minor error in the first two editions (reading *qua* for *quam*).
44. Esp. Ezek. 36:26–27.
45. *The Predestination of the Saints* 10.19 (NPNF 5:508), quoted more fully in *BLW* 3.323 (at n. 301).
46. Ezek. 36:27.
47. Ibid.
48. Jer. 31:33. The faulty reference to Jer. 13 is dropped in the second edition.
49. Ezek. 36:26.

ophers' crew should say that by evil living a person had become hardened or callous towards evil.

Efficacy of grace

I trust therefore that what I said will now be clear to all: In this passage[50] the prophet makes it plain enough that the weakness of the human will is not merely strengthened by the aid of grace to the end that it might aspire effectively to a desire for the good. And Pighius is ready to endure any abuse from me if I can bring forward one of the orthodox writers who did not share his opinion. But, since I am anxious to be economical, I bring forward Augustine, who both at the beginning of *Grace and Free Choice, to Valentinus*[51] and in his *Letter* (217) *to Vitalis*[52] teaches just so. For in both places, in his interpretations of this passage from the prophet,[53] he strongly maintains that it is not the case that some good notion in the will comes first, which God assists subsequently, but that the will is corrupt and rebellious against God until it is put right. Even so I will abstain from abuse. Pighius has branded himself with signs of his shamelessness which are obvious enough.

taught by Augustine

Grace eradicates not nature but corruption,

Then, since I add that everything which is ours should be obliterated when we are regenerated by the Lord,[54] he first asks what I mean by those words. He then quickly anticipates me by answering that they can be understood to refer only to all parts of our nature, among which are both soul and body. Therefore, according to my words, it follows that people are resurrected bodily as soon as they turn to God. If he were alive, Chrysippus[55] would not pursue his foe in debate with more confidence, but he would hold him better and with more lively arguments. To silence the barking of this dog in a few words, I reply first that this way of speaking is neither new nor my invention. For this is how Augustine spoke before me: "Let no one flatter himself. For of himself he is nothing but Satan. For what do you have of your own but sin? Take away the sin, which is yours. For you have no righteousness except by

§ 381

God's gift" (*Homily on John* 49).[56] Nor is a reply difficult on the issue itself. By "whatever is ours" I understand that which belongs to us. Moreover, I define this as what we have in ourselves apart from God's creation.[57] It is the corruption which abides not in some part of us but

---

50. Ibid.
51. *Grace and Free Choice* 14.29 (NPNF 5:455–56), which is in the middle rather than the beginning of the treatise. For the other uses of this passage see *BLW* 3.316 n. 231.
52. *Letter* 217.7.28 (FoC 32:94). For the other uses of this passage see *BLW* 3.304 n. 107.
53. In the former passage Augustine refers to the parallel passage in Ezek. 11:19–20.
54. *Inst.* 2.3.6 (LCC 20:297), quoted by Pighius (89a).
55. A leading Stoic philosopher (c. 280–207 B.C.) and an effective debater. Cf. Erasmus *Adages*, introduction (CWE 31:27): "acute as Chrysippus."
56. A loose quotation, with some paraphrase, of *Sermons on John* 49.8 (on 11:8–10) (NPNF 7:273). For the other uses of this passage see *BLW* 2.265 n. 82.
57. In the 1559 *Institutes* 2.3.6 (LCC 20:297) Calvin adds a similar qualification immediately after the passage here being discussed.

throughout our nature. For "the first man ruined it entirely in himself," as Augustine writes to Vitalis (*Letter* 217).⁵⁸ So one who can distinguish between the original creation of our nature and the corruption of it which later supervened as a result of sin will, without much trouble, extricate himself from all difficulty.

But Pighius enters upon a deep argument which he thinks holds me too tightly for me ever to be able to escape from it. For by reason and will, which I maintain need to be totally renewed, must be understood [Pighius says] either the essence of the rational soul or at any rate activities and powers which derive from it. And these have a reciprocal connection between them, so that they can no more be separated than heat-giving power can from fire, or light-giving power from the sun. He concludes that it would be impossible for our will and reason to be removed from us unless the substance of the rational soul itself were also removed, and a new, different soul entered in its place. But I would like to know from him whether he does not allow that those powers of the soul can have accidental⁵⁹ qualities. For if this is allowed, those chains with which he exulted that I was bound are broken. His reply is of no concern to me. I say, as the facts themselves declare, that our power of reasoning, which has its seat in the mind, and our ability to will, which resides in the heart, are both defective and corrupted by sin. I say that man thinks, chooses, wills, attempts, and does nothing except evil because of that corruption which has taken the whole of the human soul under its control. And it is in this sense that I say⁶⁰ that whatever is from us needs to be destroyed and renewed.

which is accidental to soul

I then add that the will, which is by its natural disposition thus estranged from God, is converted by the power of God alone in such a way that it has no active part except insofar as the Lord takes the initiative. And so I conclude, as Augustine teaches elsewhere, that it is not the leader but the led.⁶¹ By saying this I indicate that I recognise no good movement in it which does not derive from a renewal by the Spirit. Pighius considers that in the first part [of this statement] there is contained an intolerable blasphemy against God, because I mean to imply that the will is estranged from God of necessity through a corruption of its nature. But I have adequately proved before⁶² that the evil which man has brought upon himself by his own fault should not be blamed on God. So he has no reason to complain that what the truth

No good in heart apart from grace

---

58. *Letter* 217.3.11 (FoC 32:83).
59. Note the contrast with substance in the previous sentence. See Introduction §6.
60. See at n. 54.
61. *Inst.* 2.3.7 (LCC 20:298) (quoted by Pighius [90a]), where Calvin quotes Augustine *Letter* 186.3.10 (FoC 30:198); see also col. 391 n. 125.
62. See *BLW* 2.259, 263, where Calvin quotes from *Inst.* 2.1.10 (LCC 20:254).

everywhere proclaims about the wickedness of the human heart (even if I say nothing) amounts to an insult against God.

Why does God urge conversion if impossible?

382

But he takes it upon himself to criticise more vigorously the second part [of my statement],[63] where I deny that the will makes any contribution to its own conversion except insofar § as it has been remade. For, he says, if no power remains with us to effect our conversion, but it is in the control of God's good pleasure alone as to where, when, and how he wills, why does he waste his effort and indeed expose himself to mockery by so often demanding of us that we be converted? It would surely be gross and senseless to demand from a debtor who is poor a payment which is in other cases justified and right. However, as I have already said,[64] it is with a quite different purpose that the Lord urges his people to conversion. For he requires of them what at the same time he promises to give them. So by his command he prepares them to receive his promise. But [asks Pighius] why does he vainly summon us with words? Why does he not rather speak to himself so as to convert those whom he wants converted? But at the same time that he speaks them in our ears, he is writing the same words on our hearts with his finger, that is, through the Holy Spirit (2 Cor. 3),[65] so that in this way the human ministry which he uses may be spiritual. So is it for us to lay down the law for him and say that he should not do so?

Why preach to the reprobate?

But [asks Pighius] what about the reprobate, to whom nothing is offered except the mere dead letter? My reply is that it is indeed characteristic of God's instruction that it should bring salvation to those who hear it, but when it has fulfilled this function in believers a punishment is ready for those who are rebellious and obstinate. Yet Pighius supposes that God wants all to be corrected and therefore offers his help equally to all—so it is within our power to assent or refuse. Unless we have first assented, he for his part does not turn towards us. For this is what the prophets in the clearest of words declare when in the person of God they say: Return, and I will heal you.[66] Again: Return, and I will not turn my face away from you.[67] I, however, observe that all that is contained in those words is that God promises that, provided [men] come to a better mind, he will remit both their sins and the punishments with which they suffer because of their sins. Now, since repentance is a spiritual resurrection from the dead, I say that it is no more within man's power than it would be to create himself—indeed less, insofar as it is a more excellent thing to make oneself righteous than it would be to make oneself a man.

---

63. Found in the first sentence of the previous paragraph.
64. See *BLW* 4.348.
65. 2 Cor. 3:3.
66. Jer. 3:22, quoted by Pighius (91b).
67. Jer. 3:12, quoted by Pighius (91a–b).

On Book Six

But why [asks Pighius] do the prophets make speeches about repentance? Because this is the order of regeneration, that people should take refuge in the mercy of God through being affected by a real dissatisfaction with themselves and both a true hatred of sin and a true desire and love for righteousness. But why does God demand from them what he knows is nothing but the work and gift of his Spirit? Because although he is able to accomplish the secret work of his Holy Spirit without any means or assistance, he has nevertheless ordained outward preaching, to use it as it were as a means. But to make such a means effective and fruitful he inscribes in our hearts with his own finger those very words which he speaks in our ears by the mouth of a human being.[68] So he makes his work spiritual and living, when it would otherwise be of the letter and dead.[69]

But [Pighius argues] God everywhere requires two things of us before he promises to show favour to us, namely repentance and humility. So he says through Isaiah: To whom will I have regard, but to the humble and § broken of spirit?[70] That quotation will not be a problem for anyone who remembers what I drew attention to somewhere in my *Institutes*: God has regard to men and as a result counts them worthy of his mercy in two ways.[71] Peter says that he perceived in the case of Cornelius that there is no respect of persons with God, because whoever, from any nation, does what is good is approved by him.[72] But Paul says that the Romans were reconciled to God when they were God's enemies and opposed to his righteousness;[73] that the Corinthians were justified when they were fornicators, and drunken, and adulterers, or defiled by other shameful acts;[74] that the Ephesians were received into favour when they were dead in sins, without God and without hope, when, in bondage to the desires of the flesh, they served Satan;[75] and the Colossians, too, were reconciled at the time when they were estranged and showed hostility of mind in evil works; and they were awakened to righteousness and life at the time when they were dead through their sins.[76] But why mention any more instances, since his letters abound throughout with such statements? Even if he had said

Why preach repentance if it is God's work?

God requires repentance and humility,

383

but grace precedes them

---

68. See at n. 65.
69. Cf. 2 Cor. 3:6.
70. Isa. 66:2.
71. In *Inst.* 3.17.4–5 (LCC 20:806–7) Calvin speaks of God's "double acceptance" of people, citing Acts 10:34–35. God accepts people and has mercy on them when they turn to him, but they turn to him only because he has previously had mercy on them and drawn them to him.
72. Acts 10:34–35.
73. Rom. 5:10.
74. 1 Cor. 6:9–11.
75. Eph. 2:1–2, 12.
76. Col. 1:21–22; 2:13.

nothing of this, his own conversion is, without further comment, a signal proof of that point. For with what trace whether of humility or of dissatisfaction with himself did he prepare himself and so merit that kindly regard of God as a result of which he was called a chosen vessel? Pighius will object that it was in the very fact that he was obedient to the call of God. But here the argument is only about whether [this obedience] preceded the grace of God. In any case it is mistaken to suppose that the voice which said, "Saul, Saul, why do you persecute me?"[77] sounded only in his ears and that the law of obedience was not inscribed on his heart by the instruction of the Holy Spirit in such a way that he immediately did what he was commanded. Through that inscribing, I say, he was made not only willing instead of unwilling, but also a follower instead of a persecutor.

Grace is prevenient

Moreover, what is the meaning of that saying which comes from a prophet and is so very famous: "I was found by those who did not seek me"?[78] The apostle explains that the Gentiles, who were not seeking righteousness, have obtained righteousness.[79] It was with no different kind of preparation[80] that Abraham and his descendants had drawn near to God at the beginning, as Moses[81] and Joshua[82] tell us. He who is not convinced by these and similar proofs to acknowledge a twofold acceptance of men before God[83] is unduly obstinate. So God has regard to his elect, and cherishes, loves, and welcomes them even before their call, but in Christ. By calling them he shows himself as favourable and well disposed to them. That is, he makes known to them the love which he was previously bestowing, so that they may perceive it in their minds and enjoy it. Now the call is manifest in repentance and faith. But the first part of repentance (or rather its beginning) is, with a mind that is humble and meek, to be dissatisfied with oneself. Only after this § humility is God said to have regard to men with reference to their knowledge and perception, since he then declares himself to them as their father and gives them the proof of his kindness.

For P, grace is only exhortation

Moreover, although he has already exalted human powers beyond limit or measure, now that he wants to show that [man] turns himself towards God by a movement all his own [Pighius] betrays his godlessness still more freely and openly than before. God wants the godless to turn, but he does not make him turn by his own all-powerful will; he invites him and encourages him to turn himself. Consequently it is for

---

77. Acts 9:4; 22:7; 26:14.
78. Isa. 65:1.
79. Rom. 9:30.
80. I.e., with no human preparation for grace.
81. E.g., Gen. 12:1; 28:10–15.
82. Josh. 24:2–3.
83. See n. 71.

us to return and be converted, and it is for him to take us up and revive us when we return. What, I ask, does he seem to leave to God but exhortation? And for what was Pelagius condemned if not for this?[84] But he at once covers this blasphemy with some disguise when he acknowledges that God does assist us in our turning to him, provided only that we ourselves first make an attempt at it. It is certainly something when after giving man the first place, he at least yields God the second. This was Pelagius's second fabrication, after he had been compelled to withdraw his view that man can attain to eternal life by his own strength.[85]

However, a little later he shows that he is not even satisfied with being half a Pelagian. For when he wants to define how God converts us, he says: By his goodness and patience in not punishing us at once, but giving us time and space for repentance; by calling, provoking, and stirring us to it and also by many means and opportunities, by exhortations, by kindnesses, and by scourgings. Here Pelagius[86] is certainly vomiting his profanities to the skies at full strength. For citing only the external means by which God summons men, he encloses in them the whole work of grace in conversion, while maintaining a deep silence about the inner movement of the heart, its renewal by the Spirit.[87] Nor indeed is there any justification for him to parry this by saying that he is far from denying the latter, however silent he keeps. For he undertakes to define the way in which God turns us [to himself]. Accordingly, by proposing such a definition [as he has], he excludes any renewal of the heart produced by the secret power of the Holy Spirit.

P is a Pelagian

Scripture Cited by Pighius

And yet, please God, he gathers some support from the Scriptures to confirm such evident, gross godlessness! That man begins his conversion, he says, is attested in Jeremiah: If you turn, I will cause you to turn (ch. 15).[88] There God addresses the prophet, who, being tested by extreme despair, had protested to him with many complaints. He therefore by new promises stirs him to pull himself together. And that is what these words mean if they are properly understood: If you will return, and I cause you to return, you shall stand before my face. If you separate the precious from the valueless, you shall be, as it were, my

1. Jer. 15:19

---

84. By "grace" Pelagius understood the gifts of creation (especially free will), the law in all its forms, and the forgiveness of sins; see *BLW* 4.339 n. 122. What he did not include was the inner work of the Holy Spirit. Calvin is accusing Pighius of the same failure.
85. Cf. *BLW* 4.339 (at nn. 123–24).
86. I.e., in Pighius's work it is Pelagius who is speaking again.
87. For Pelagius's silence concerning the inner work of the Holy Spirit, see *Nature and Grace* 23.25 (NPNF 5:129–30); *The Grace of Christ and Original Sin* 1.30.31 (NPNF 5:228).
88. Jer. 15:19.

mouth.⁸⁹ He had lost heart through seeing that he was robbed of success and had begun to waver just as if his faith no longer rested on God's promises. So the Lord rebukes this irresolution and lack of faith, and then orders him to § return both to boldness and steadfastness of faith and also to obedience, that is, to the way of his calling, by setting before him the better hope of a good and happy outcome. So he says: If you will return, you shall remain in my presence, even though the world slay you. If you will stand firm in right judgment and not abandon your duty, even though the world may give your teaching no honour, yet will I give it my approval, as having proceeded from my mouth. The addition of "and I will cause you to turn" you can see is inserted as a parenthesis, by way of correction, by which the Lord declares that it will be an act of his own kindness if the prophet returns to the [right] way. Behold how skilfully Pighius quotes from the Scriptures! But then he gathers a vast pile of quotations. From the fact that God blames the stubborn because they abuse his own kindness and refuse to turn, [Pighius] of course deduces that it is our own achievement if we do turn. But Scripture, just as it bears witness that man through his own wickedness of heart is prevented from turning to God, also forbids him to claim for himself any glory for his conversion, when it teaches that this is the work of the Holy Spirit.⁹⁰

2. Ezek. 33:10–11

But there are passages which he supposes to be clearer and which he therefore goes on to review in a separate list and to expound one by one. These I will briefly run through. He alleges that unfortunate people are driven by our teaching to think and utter those despairing words on account of which God is so gravely angry with Israel in Ezekiel: Our iniquities are upon us, and in them we are consumed.⁹¹ If these two things are alike, that man is turned from sin to righteousness by the direction of the Holy Spirit, not by his own strength, and that man has been abandoned by God without hope of pardon and is now consigned to destruction, then I will agree that a basis for despair is engendered by our teaching. But if it is obvious for all to see how great a difference there is [between them], then the unworthiness of this allegation of Pighius will escape nobody. If, he says, the conversion of man lies within God's good pleasure, what else will a sinner think but that he is destined to rot until he is raised up by the hand of God? As though indeed when people are taught about their own weakness they were not by that means raised to hope of assistance, if they are in fact God's elect—or if they are reprobate, compelled at once by God's judgment to acknowledge that it is their own fault that they perish. And, to make it

---

89. Ibid.
90. See *BLW* 5.352; 6.374.
91. Ezek. 33:10.

even clearer just how apt is the turning of that prophecy against us, it should be noted that the people then did not complain about their misfortunes so much out of despair as out of obstinacy, not unmixed with hatred of God that he should be so implacably harsh. So this cry could already be heard everywhere: What could we do once God determined to destroy us and utterly annihilate us? Accordingly, since there would be no point in our thinking about appeasing him, let his judgment come when he wills. By such stubbornness they got themselves into a state of insensibility so that, with their minds hardened, they kicked against the pricks. The Lord objects that he does not desire the death of the ungodly,[92] for the teaching which he imparts through his prophets is a ministry of reconciliation.[93] From this § Pighius concludes, without hesitation, that it is within our power to make such reconciliation sure. But I say that we must ask how that ministry becomes effective. The prophets reply, and Paul after them, that this happens when the teaching which otherwise our ears would receive in vain and without benefit is written on our hearts by the Spirit of God.[94]

The second passage which he cites is from Jonah.[95] Why did the king of Nineveh, in response to Jonah's proclamation, decree by an edict that everyone should turn from his evil way, unless common sense declared that man's conversion was in his own hands? I reply that it was the duty of a king who had already been converted himself to summon others to follow his example. At any rate the civil edict of the king will have no more weight for proving what Pighius has in mind than will the many prophetic speeches which clearly agree with it both in sense and in wording. For just as a prophet's duty when he wants to instruct people in the worship and fear of God is to plant and water, so also is a king's. But God reserves for himself the prerogative that he alone gives the increase,[96] and that by his sovereign freedom, where and as much as he pleases. It is, however, suggested that God was merciful because he saw their works, to the extent of course that they proceeded from their free choice.[97] This is the interpretation of Pighius, who imagines that man has of himself and by nature all the good that he has. But we who have learned from so many passages of Scripture[98] that coming to one's senses and conversion are the peculiar gift of God [expound the verse] otherwise: just as God had granted [the Ninevites] to be converted, he

386

3. Jon. 3:8–10

---

92. Ezek. 33:11, quoted by Pighius (92b).
93. Cf. 2 Cor. 5:18.
94. Esp. Jer. 31:33; Ezek. 11:19–20; 36:26–27; 2 Cor. 3:3.
95. Pighius (92b–93a) quotes Jon. 3:8–9.
96. 1 Cor. 3:6.
97. The first half of this sentence ("God . . . works") is Pighius's quotation of Jon. 3:10; the second half ("to the extent . . . choice") is his gloss on the verse (93a).
98. See n. 90.

also welcomed them after their conversion and withdrew his hand, so as not to punish them in accordance with his earlier proclamation. For he is first merciful on man who is naked, needy, and bereft of all good, endowed only with wretchedness; but then, when he has clothed and adorned him with his gifts, he pursues him with his mercy. But conversion, says Pighius again, could not be ascribed to them as a means of meriting or obtaining grace if God had taken the initiative so that they might be converted. See how great a gap there is between this man and Augustine. For this is how Augustine speaks: "If you have your merits from yourself, they are evil, and therefore they are not crowned. Therefore for them to be good they must be gifts from God" (*Grace and Free Choice* 6).[99] Again: "If you see my works, you condemn them; if you see yours, you give a crown. For even any good works that I possess I have from you, and therefore they are yours rather than mine. Therefore you will not despise the works of your hands" *(On Psalm 137)*.[100] But Pighius thinks it is absurd if God has regard to the works of his hands, so as to augment his previous gifts with others.

4. Luke 10:13

387

He also argues from the following statement of Christ: Woe to you, Capernaum. For if the miracles that you have seen had been done § in Tyre or Sidon or Sodom, they would have repented in sackcloth and ashes.[101] For, he says, if God did not will by his absolute, effective will to grant repentance to Sodom, Tyre, and Sidon, was he going to give it if he had displayed his miracles there? And why would he have given to them the grace to come to their senses on account of miracles rather than to his own city, where he was exhibiting the same miracles? I reply that in these words Christ is not at all concerned with the source of repentance or why, in God's secret plan, it is given to some rather than to others. But he simply draws a comparison on the basis of what had happened, namely that those other cities which he was naming, which had not enjoyed teaching and miracles, would have more excuse before God than would Capernaum. The latter, being hardened through deliberate wrongdoing and ungodly, heinous rebellion, could not be diverted by so many and such extraordinary warnings both by teaching and by signs. As if he said: There has never yet been a people so stiff-necked and untamed, with heart so unyielding and obstinate, that it would not be moved by those signs which were held up to such contempt and mockery by the people of Capernaum. But if Pighius presses

---

99. *Grace and Free Choice* 6.15 (NPNF 5:450). For the other uses of this passage see *BLW* 3.318 n. 244.

100. *Expositions on the Psalms* 137.18 (NPNF 8:635, where it is numbered 138.13). Cf. *BLW* 4.337 (at n. 107).

101. Pighius (93a–b) quotes Luke 10:13, with a change in word order derived from Matt. 11:21. Calvin adds the reference to Sodom (Matt. 11:23).

more obstinately the statement that "long ago they would have repented,"[102] let him now answer me, why then did God not think those cities which he knew would not fail to respond to his exhortation were worth exhorting to repentance in suitable ways? If he has any sense, he must, I think, be aware that he is now tangled up in his own traps. But let us have done with those foolish quibbles, since it is clearly agreed that by such manner of speaking Christ intended nothing other than if someone today were to say: There is no Turk so stubborn and rebellious against God, or so disinclined to true religion, that he would not already, long ago, have been brought to his knees if he had read, heard, and seen those things by which Pighius on the other hand could not be put right!

After this, to prove that it is within our ability to prepare our hearts for God as well as to assent to him when he calls us to goodness, [Pighius] unrolls a long list of commandments. There is certainly no doubt that we have been defeated a hundred times if it is acceptable to measure human powers by the commandments of God. It is madness, he says, to exhort people to do things whose accomplishment is beyond their ability. However, God, in declaring that he has the best possible reason for giving orders, can defend himself against this insult, even if there is not in man the ability to fulfil them. Nevertheless, it is worth the trouble to repeat and examine individually some of the texts which [Pighius] quotes. In Jeremiah, he says, we are taught how men can effectively prepare themselves for the grace of God: *Let us examine our ways, and return to the Lord; let us lift up our hearts with our hands to heaven, saying, We have done wickedly.* . . .[103] To hate, says Pighius, and loathe one's former life, and to flee to the Lord with contrite heart, to repent from the heart and in true faith to seek mercy—this § is preparation.[104] And the lifting up of hearts is conversion. Even readers of a modest intellect will recognise here Pighius's usual system of logic, the first rule of which is: Always split one thing into many, and mix up things which are different into one! What lifting up hearts and hands to heaven[105] means is well enough known: namely, to call upon God with one's hands spread out to the heavens, and with an earnest desire of the heart. Pighius, however, concocts the childish fiction that "to lift up hearts" means "to free our desires from earthly, perishable things," and "with our hands" means "by our works." And these are the interpretations, of course, which he wants to command trust just like the re-

5. Commandments

6. Lam. 3:40–42

388

---

102. See at n. 101.
103. Pighius (94a) quotes Lam. 3:40–42.
104. I.e., preparation of one's heart to receive grace.
105. Lam. 3:41.

plies of the Delphic oracle,[106] when nothing either more trifling or more of a joke could be imagined.

7. Acknowledgment of guilt

Immediately afterwards he assigns acknowledgment of guilt and prayer for pardon (both of which he had previously subsumed under preparation) to conversion, that is, the second part of repentance. But to pardon him such gross mistakes—I will ask what in fact he thinks he has proved. That repentance is entirely within man's power. But the very thing which Pighius himself also makes the beginning and, as it were, first step [of repentance] (namely that the sinner, in shame at the recognition of his wrongdoing, is ill at ease with himself), is put among God's other benefits by Ezekiel, in whose book God addresses his people as follows: Although you have despised your oath, so as to break covenant, yet will I remember my covenant which I have made with you, and I will make an everlasting covenant. And then you shall remember your ways so as to be ashamed. I will make, I say, my covenant with you, that you may remember and be ashamed (Ezek. 16).[107] Pighius imagines that this is the preparation with which men anticipate God and go to meet his grace in advance. But the Lord affirms that he takes the initiative with men, to cause them to acknowledge their sins. On the other point it has already been said elsewhere[108] that it is no more in man's power to renew his life than it is to rise by his own power from the dead.

8. Prayer

On prayer, how easy it is to refute his madness! By calling on God, he says, men preempt his grace. For when they plead for it in their prayers they do this of themselves. But Paul [says] against this: How shall they call on him in whom they have not believed?[109] Certainly by these words he shows that calling on God proceeds and is born from faith, like a daughter from her mother. But where does faith come from? Or will he put forward the ludicrous idea that this too is part of our preparation? And why should he not do so, since he has dared to speak in the same terms of hope, which is however both in second place to faith, and like it also as it were the source of calling upon God. Men, he says, have of themselves the power to knock, but it is God's part to open the door.[110] But Augustine [says]: "It is soundness of faith which causes us to pray so that we are heard, to seek so that we find, to knock so that the door is opened to us. He who argues § against this closes the door of God's mercy against himself" *(The Perfection of Righteousness)*.[111]

---

106. See *BLW* 5.364 n. 112.
107. Ezek. 16:59–63.
108. Col. 382.
109. Rom. 10:14.
110. Matt. 7:7–8/Luke 11:9–10.
111. *The Perfection of Righteousness* 19.40 (NPNF 5:174), quoted again in col. 397 (at n. 183).

But surely Solomon says in a statement, not a command, that the ability to prepare his heart belongs to man.¹¹² Here too you have an explanation of a text that is worthy of Pighius. Solomon there derides the audacious confidence of human beings when there is no plan that they will not consider, no effort that they will not dare to undertake apart from God, though they cannot even utter a word (which is a much lesser thing) except through him. It is man's work to prepare the heart—and it is God's to guide the tongue! Who cannot see that [this statement] is an ironical description of human pride which claims for itself all the greatest things when it does not even have the smallest thing in its power? But Pighius deduces from [this statement] that the grace of God is preempted by man.

9. Prov. 16:1

Now he proves from David those preparations which he imagines are pleasing to God. For God heard the petition of the poor: your ear heard the preparation of their heart.¹¹³ But if only, seeing that he is not capable of translating, he had preferred to follow a good translator¹¹⁴ rather than adding to his ignorance the vice of obstinately sticking to his mistake as well! Literally, [the text of] David is as follows: God heard the petition of the poor; you will prepare their heart, your ear will hear. Pighius, following in the footsteps of a poor, unreliable translator, twists it to mean a preparation by means of which human beings can compete with the grace of God. You see how appropriate the proof is to the question! And yet he tosses those candlewicks with no less ferocity than if he were brandishing thunderbolts from heaven.

10. Ps. 10:17

He adds that the reason brought forward to explain why Rehoboam was deprived of his kingdom is that he did not direct his heart so as to obey the Lord.¹¹⁵ If man can, he says, no more prepare his heart to seek God than touch the heavens with his finger, why does Scripture particularly mention this as a cause of Rehoboam's faulty disposition when it is equally characteristic of all the godly and ungodly alike? And he has no doubt that, whatever I may invent, this problem cannot be solved. I will reply that the cause of his rejection is not said to be that he did not have of himself a tractable heart which he might, without the direction of the Spirit, turn to the service of God by an impulse derived from his own nature—we teach that this is common equally to everyone. But [the cause] is that in actual fact he did not direct his heart to God, which is characteristic and distinctive of the ungodly. It is a habitual failing of Pighius, when he makes no distinction between very

11. 2 Chron. 12:14

---

112. Pighius (94a) quotes Prov. 16:1.
113. Ps. 10:17.
114. Pighius (94a) is quoting from the Vulgate translation not of the Hebrew, but of the Greek Septuagint, where this verse is 9:38.
115. Pighius (94a) quotes 2 Chron. 12:14.

different things, later on to produce complete and utter confusion. Hardness and wickedness of the heart, which makes us inclined towards evil and incapable of attaining the good, is a universal disease of the human race until the Lord applies the cure by his Spirit. But when he has produced a heart of flesh[116] in one, and left a stony one (according to its natural character) in another, there is now a great deal of difference between them. The former has a heart that is tractable to obedience to God, indeed he has the law of God written in his heart[117] so that he conforms to his righteousness with the full commitment § of his will. The latter, with a heart that is untamed, stubborn, and rebellious, rejects both God and his yoke. Though the obedience of the former is the work of God, the latter has no one else to blame for his obstinacy but himself. Therefore, those who in their original condition did not differ at all are now distinguished by the grace and judgment of God. Readers will see that I am inventing nothing, and yet no trouble remains any more.

12. Commandments again

Afterwards, as is his constant custom, he reverts to the commandments. But, foreseeing that we were not lacking in a reply, he goes on to say that the faithful have always fulfilled what God commands there. For just as David urged the people to offer their hearts to the Lord,[118] and Hezekiah too urged them not to be stiff-necked after the manner of their fathers, but to yield themselves,[119] so the holy record reports that some came from all over Israel and surrendered their hearts to serve the Lord.[120] Who denies [that]? Provided that he accepts that what is plainly stated elsewhere ought to be understood [here], namely "those whose hearts the Lord had touched."[121] For we do not deny that these and similar things are done by men. The only issue which is debated between us is whether they do this through an impulse deriving from their nature or by the leading and direction of the Holy Spirit.

13. Wisdom given to humble

Finally, to cover up at least to some extent the ungodliness which he had too openly revealed, he returns to the joining of free choice with grace. He is anxious to show an example of this in one case, so that a similar view may then also be taken about the rest. For [he says] wisdom is certainly the gift of God alone, but it is given selectively, not forced on a person. Moreover, it is given only to those who ask for it, who turn their hearts towards it. For it is for the humble, not for the proud.[122] What? Is not humility also a gift from God? And though Pig-

---

116. Ezek. 36:26.
117. Jer. 31:33.
118. 1 Chron. 22:19, quoted by Pighius (94b).
119. 2 Chron. 30:8, quoted by Pighius (94b).
120. Pighius (94b) quotes 2 Chron. 30:11, 22.
121. 1 Sam. 10:26.
122. Pighius's argument here (94b–95a) appeals especially to Prov. 2:2–6; Matt. 11:25–26.

hius may deny it, by what devices will he pluck this conviction from the minds of the godly, where it is deeply rooted? So then, is God deprived of part of the praise due to him because he bestows his favours in stages, so that the one is a preparation for the other, as though he only followed human [action] with his good gifts and did not also take the initiative? But [he will say] if God should reckon someone worthy of his favours without taking any account of his preparation, he will be cruelly unjust to others whom he at the same time neglects. Certainly if God were brought before Pighius's judgment seat, his case would quickly fail with so implacable a judge. For [God] declares that it is only by him that we are distinguished, since otherwise we are in all respects similar.[123] What else is Pighius doing by such criticism but throwing stones up to heaven, only for them to fall straight back on his own head? So he may cry a thousand times that those who allow man no ability to merit the grace of God and who teach that [man's] will is so disinclined to righteousness that of himself he cannot bring forth anything but evil are opposing the Holy § Spirit and the whole of Scripture. He may a hundred times threaten an anathema on those who so think. But he will gain no more by such shouting than he would by barking, until he produces other proofs from Scripture. For the truth of God, which we teach, is supported by too firm a buttress for it to collapse so easily under the windy blast of his arguments.

Pighius Opposes Calvin's Arguments and Appeal to Scripture

With this part of the debate so effectively dealt with and concluded, [Pighius] moves on to the next. I wrote [in the *Institutes*] that the human will should not even be considered a follower of grace's leadership, as though it cooperated by itself and by a separate impulse all its own. On the contrary this response of the will too (which they call cooperation), whether for receiving or for maintaining the impulse of the Holy Spirit, derives from the fact that, having now been reformed, the will presents itself as ready and compliant to the Spirit.[124] He first of all declares this to be so unclear that not even I understand what I mean. Then [he says] that it is a pile of ungodliness which it would be impossible to enlarge, and that it is to no purpose that I pretend that I have the support of Augustine,[125] who himself has shown that he is utterly

Cooperation with grace

---

123. 1 Cor. 4:7.
124. A loose summary of *Inst.* 2.3.7, 11 (LCC 20:298–99, 305–6). Cf. *Inst.* 2.2.6 (LCC 20:263).
125. Pighius (95b) quotes from *Inst.* 2.3.7 (LCC 20:299), where Calvin refers back to his earlier quotation of Augustine *Letter* 186.3.10 (FoC 30:198); see also col. 381 (at n. 61).

opposed to me. The reason why I went astray in using his words is that I have looked at him only hastily in passing and never read him carefully and attentively. If only [Pighius] had studied the Scriptures with the same attention and care and become so well acquainted with their meaning as I may claim that I have carefully read Augustine and become well acquainted with his thought! But I prefer to leave the facts to judge on that matter.

*Chrysostom*As far as the present issue is concerned—I had criticised Chrysostom's statement that neither the will without grace nor grace without the will could accomplish any good thing.[126] [Pighius] charges me with malice because I ascribe to Chrysostom alone something which was taken from a general definition of the church and is also affirmed, in nearly the same words, by Augustine. He quotes the passage from the third book of the *Hypognosticon*.[127] Its conclusion, I admit, is not very unlike, in its wording, what Chrysostom says, but I maintain that the meaning is utterly different. Whoever is the author of that book[128] teaches that good works are done by means of grace and free choice, just as a journey is completed both by a horse and by its rider, as the horse indeed does the running, but does it while being guided by the hand of the rider to keep to the correct way. Moreover, he declares that the way is Christ. He teaches that free choice wanders in worldly vanities, like a beast that has strayed off its way, until the Spirit of God comes to dwell in it and lead it from wandering after its lusts back to the way of righteousness. Once it has been brought back, he steers it with continuous guidance until it reaches its destined goal. Therefore he concludes that free choice does "run," but it is God who makes it run on the right course.[129]

And how is this different from what I have always taught, namely that the will has from nature the ability to will, but that to will well is a favour of grace, not a natural ability?[130] In this sense I have no objection at all to the idea that the will goes alongside grace, just as of § necessity the matter underlies the form.[131] The will is as it were the matter, suited and able to receive form; before it is renewed, it is badly formed through natural depravity. But when it is renewed so as to acquire goodness by the Spirit of God, it as it were puts on another form. To

---

126. Chrysostom *Homilies on Matthew* 82.4 (NPNF 10:494–95), cited in *Inst.* 2.3.7 (LCC 20:299).

127. Pighius (95b–96a) quotes at length from *Hypognosticon* 3.11.20 (PL 45:1632–33). For an earlier, partly overlapping citation see *BLW* 3.311 (at n. 175).

128. See *BLW* 3.306 n. 124.

129. *Hypognosticon* 3.11.20 (PL 45:1632–33).

130. See *Inst.* 2.3.5 (LCC 20:294–95), a passage which cites Bernard and to which Calvin refers in col. 378 (at n. 36).

131. On this Aristotelian distinction see Introduction §6.

will, therefore, is in man's possession; but for him to will good, he is preceded by God. For these latter words are present there.¹³² It does not say "so that he may be able to will," but it ascribes the actual effect [of the will] to grace,¹³³ just as somewhat earlier where it said that the will is both repaired and prepared to make what was evil good.¹³⁴ But what of Chrysostom? He makes the will the companion of grace in such a way that the effectiveness of the latter depends on the former.¹³⁵ That is exactly how Pighius understands him too. Why then does he use the similarity of [Chrysostom's and "Augustine's"] words in an effort to deceive, when their [actual] views are so different? If he still does not accept this, let our readers remember what we have reported elsewhere,¹³⁶ that Augustine regards it as a gross absurdity if anyone says that God's mercy is not sufficient unless the human will helps as well. "It is not of him who wills or runs. [This means] that the whole [action] should be attributed to God, who both prepares the human will so that it may be helped and helps it when it has been prepared; who goes before the unwilling agent to cause him to will and, when he does will, follows after him so that he may not will to no effect" *(Enchiridion, to Laurentius)*.¹³⁷

but not with Chrysostom

But [Pighius objects] in that earlier passage it is implied that free choice is not, as I claim, annulled by grace but, being wounded, is caught so that it may be tamed and reformed to obey God.¹³⁸ As though I have ever either taught or even dreamt that the substance of the will needs to be annihilated!¹³⁹ For I have always spoken about its quality; so when this writer¹⁴⁰ demands its reformation, how does he disagree with me at all? But these are ploys of our would-be Hercules,¹⁴¹ who is always manufacturing monsters, so that when they are defeated he can lead them in a secret triumph! To make everything correspond, he recites to himself as a triumph song that we are rebuked by the following words of Augustine: "Hear, O heretic, O fool, O enemy of the faith. We do not condemn good works done by free choice after it has been pre-

Substance of will not annihilated

---

132. I.e., the previous sentence is a loose paraphrase of a sentence in *Hypognosticon* 3.11.20 (PL 45:1633) which comes after the passage quoted by Pighius (see n. 127).
133. The actual words are that God precedes and teaches "so that they may wish and be able [to do] the good."
134. *Hypognosticon* 3.11.19 (PL 45:1631).
135. See at n. 126.
136. *BLW* 4.343–44 (at n. 172).
137. *Enchiridion* 32.9 (NPNF 3:248), discussing Rom. 9:16. For the other uses of this passage see *BLW* 4.344 n. 172.
138. Calvin is quoting Pighius's summary (96a) of part of the passage that he has quoted (see n. 127).
139. See cols. 377–79.
140. I.e., the author of *Hypognosticon*.
141. The Roman form of the name of Heracles, the most popular of the Greek heroes, known especially for his labours, which involved fighting various monsters.

pared by prevenient grace apart from any merit of free choice. Grace itself does them, guides them, and completes them, so that they multiply with free choice."[142] He is both so blind and so evil that he does not see that all this is written just as if one of us had dictated it, and is sure that by his own impudence he will be able so to deprive others of sense and judgment that they will not see it either.

Passages Calvin had cited:

1. Jer. 32:39–40

He then proceeds to the refutation of my remaining arguments [in the *Institutes*] with the same good fortune as hitherto. But he begins, to avoid wasting labour on something superfluous, by saying that an ample reply has already been given to my quotations from Jeremiah: I will put the fear of my name into their hearts, so that they will not turn away from me.[143] Again: I will give them a new heart, so that they will fear me all their days.[144] However, the only reply I have heard is his bold contradiction of these statements. For it is the Lord himself who § bears witness[145] that he causes us not to turn away from him. If we ask the way [this is done], he replies again [that it is] by giving [us] a new heart. If that is still too unclear, he adds as a clarification that he implants the fear of his name in our hearts. What reply does Pighius make to this? [He says] that the ability, if we so please, not to turn away is bestowed on us by the grace of God, and nothing else besides. However, he does not allow this without qualification. For we anticipate God, and he gives his grace only to those who seek it. These are Pythagorean[146] responses which he wants to be accepted without any argument.

2. Prayers of saints

When I cite the prayers of the saints in which they ask the Lord to direct their hearts,[147] to [create] a new heart, and to renew a right spirit within them,[148] he objects that on the other hand many commandments occur in which God demands like things of us. But it ought to be common ground that by their prayers the saints bear witness to what belongs to God, while God in giving commands is not at all demonstrating how much strength and ability the saints have to fulfil them.[149] He adds that there also occurs the statement that the saints directed their hearts to God when they obtained grace. As though answering an objection were achieved by joining in with different words but the same meaning! Finally he adds that such prayers are signs of the devout desire with which they long for grace, and that is diametrically opposed

---

142. *Hypognosticon* 3.13.29 (PL 45:1635–36), quoted in *BLW* 3.312 (at n. 179).
143. Jer. 32:40, quoted in *Inst.* 2.3.8 (LCC 20:300).
144. Jer. 32:39, quoted in *Inst.* 2.3.8 (LCC 20:300).
145. I.e., in the two passages just quoted.
146. A reference not to Pythagoras's mathematics but to his mysterious religious teachings.
147. 1 Kings 8:58, quoted in *Inst.* 2.3.9 (LCC 20:301).
148. Ps. 51:10, quoted in *Inst.* 2.3.9 (LCC 20:301).
149. An important hermeneutical principle for Calvin.

to our position, which denies that man prepares himself [for it]. As though it were less God's business to continue [his work] than to begin it! David and Solomon cry: Direct our hearts, O God.[150] Now this prayer is certainly an indication of a directing [of the heart]. What then do they mean? It is just as if they said: Complete, O Lord, what you have begun, and confirm what you have partly effected in us.

So Pighius has not yet wrenched away from me [the teaching] that to direct men's hearts to righteousness is the work of God alone. I had said that God demands nothing of us more solemnly than that we should observe his Sabbath, and moreover that it is a spiritual observance of it when we take rest from our works.[151] Pighius replies that what is demanded of us is rest from all servile work, but not from the fear of God and observance of his law. A fine escape! But for what purpose did I quote this if not to show that the fear of God is not our own work? For when the Lord, who does not want us to grow weary in well-doing, commands us to rest from our works, surely by that very word he declares that all our works are evil. And so Isaiah bears witness that the Sabbath is violated when our will intrudes.[152] So there is no doubt that the reality of the Sabbath is what Paul is talking about in the sixth chapter of Romans, the crucifixion of our old man[153]—something of which Pighius takes no account.

3. Sabbath

Next is that comparison in which I had said that a clear enough testimony to the grace of God appears, unless we were unduly prejudiced: I am the true vine, you are the branches. Just as a branch cannot bear fruit of itself, unless it abides in the vine, so neither § can you, unless you abide in me, because without me you can do nothing (John 15).[154] In these words Pighius finds the clearest proof of his own view. For since it is the task of the farmer to tend, while it is [in] the nature of the vine to supply moisture and sap and of the branch to put forth the fruit, he considers that in this distinction there appears a most beautiful combination of free choice and grace. But this comparison which Christ uses should be applied to its corresponding reality in accordance with his words and not Pighius's cleverness. The application according to the intention of Christ is simple and ready to hand. Just as the branch can neither bear leaves nor flower nor bring forth fruit when separated from the vine, but quickly becomes completely dry [and] even on the vine requires constant care and pruning—so we apart from him have

4. John 15:1-5

394

---

150. Ps. 119:36 (added after the quotation of 1 Kings 8:58 in the 1559 *Institutes* [LCC 20:301]); 1 Kings 8:58 (cf. n. 147).
151. In *Inst.* 2.3.9 (LCC 20:301).
152. Isa. 58:13, quoted in *Inst.* 2.8.31 (LCC 20:397).
153. Rom. 6:6. In *Inst.* 2.8.31 (LCC 20:397) Rom. 6:4 is quoted with reference to the Sabbath.
154. *Inst.* 2.3.9 (LCC 20:301-2), where John 15:1, 4-5, is quoted.

absolutely no strength or power to attain to true (that is, spiritual) life and the actions proper to it, but are altogether useless.[155] But once we have been grafted and implanted into him, we are tended by the constant activity of God,[156] so that we continue to be fruitful. One who is content with this agreement between the things which are compared with one another here will be in no danger at all of being disappointed by [the words of] Christ, the bogey with which Pighius seeks to discourage the immature.

<small>P's objection</small>

But what does [Pighius] himself say against this? Comparing the nature of the vine with our own, he deduces that the fruits of good works are technically produced by us and by the life-giving force which is in us, even though we have received it from the vine and our heavenly farmer. If [by this] he understands the will with which we will (which is implanted in us by nature), the judgment with which we choose, the power to endeavour with which we endeavour, I have no objection—provided that he allows at the same time that we acquire righteousness of will, judgment, and endeavour by grace alone. For these three are naturally corrupted by wickedness in us. But if he means to assign any part of the praise for our good works to us, rather than letting it be entirely God's, then he must seek support for his error from somewhere other than the words of Christ. For since works of both kinds—that is, both good and evil—are called fruits,[157] we are indeed made by nature for bearing fruit, but of ourselves we bear fruit with sin, leading to death.[158] For us to be fit to bring forth the good fruits that belong to life, we need to be made such by grace. Therefore by nature we are useless and unfruitful for the bearing of good fruits, but only too fruitful for evil. And even now I should like to learn from Pighius whether he thinks that everyone is naturally grafted into Christ, or acknowledges that this is a special gift surpassing the state of nature. For if I can extract this second alternative from him, as I am bound to do, what will become of those preparations in which he usually locates the particular power of free choice? And Paul brings to an end all argument about this matter when he compares those who are not yet grafted into Christ to wild olives.[159]

<small>Cooperation with grace?</small>

<small>395</small>

But as regards the cooperation wherein our will follows on the grace of God, he thinks that he has won the argument. For if the branch cannot bear fruit unless it abide in the vine,[160] then it will bear [fruit] § of

---

155. John 15:4–5.
156. John 15:1–2.
157. Not in John 15 but elsewhere, as in Matt. 7:16–18; Rom. 7:4–5.
158. Rom. 7:5.
159. Rom. 11:17, 24.
160. John 15:4.

itself if it does abide. Accordingly, he who like a branch abides in Christ will of himself, that is, by his own nature, bear fruit. It is amazing how much he celebrates through confidence in this craftiness. But everyone understands how childishly stupid he is being in spreading out such verbal traps. For although it is generally agreed to understand Christ as meaning that the branch is not fruitful of itself but only on condition that it abides in the vine, this trifler looks for a knot in a bulrush.[161] But if he is still fighting, let him answer me what he understands by the phrase "of itself." Will he deny that these two phrases, "of itself" and "in the vine," are opposites? But I will not wait for him. The matter is abundantly clear—those two phrases, "of itself" and "in the vine," are opposites, and from this it is straightforward to infer that "of itself" has just the same meaning as if he had said "pulled off or separated from the vine."

In response to Paul's statement that it is God who works in us both to will and to do according to his good pleasure,[162] he says that he too affirms this, but in such a way that the [human] will acts as well. With this twist he thinks that he has escaped, when I still have him held tight around the waist. For the question is not whether the will acts—which is beyond doubt—but whether it acts of itself or according to the measure of God's action. Or (to use, if I may, a cruder expression) whether the action of the will is distinct and separate from the working of God or, as people say, subject to it. For who is not aware that it is by means of the will that man wills? But Paul is affirming in that passage that the will is directed by the Spirit of God to turn to the good and seek after it, and so any good which we conceive in our minds is [God's] own doing. Therefore Pighius's answer is a puff of smoke.

5. Phil. 2:13

But [Paul's] other statement—that God does all in all[163]—he evades in the following way: There is indeed none besides him who can do all in all, but his creatures perform the actions, each in its turn, which he has ordained. According to this fabrication someone who attributes the action to the creature as its own, apart from God, will be saying nothing different from Paul's meaning. But it is surer than sure that Paul ascribed everything to God precisely so that we might learn that nothing happens except through him. So we may infer from this that no one does anything of himself, since God alone accomplishes all in all. The apostle is not, however, talking about the universal working of divine providence by which the whole world is governed, but the special direction by which, through the Spirit of sanctification, [God] guides the faithful to obedience to his righteousness. As Pighius knows

6. 1 Cor. 12:6

---

161. Cf. Erasmus *Adages* 2.4.76 (CWE 33:229).
162. Phil. 2:13, quoted in *Inst.* 2.3.9 (LCC 20:302).
163. 1 Cor. 12:6, quoted in *Inst.* 2.3.9 (LCC 20:302).

nothing of this, he irrelevantly philosophises about the natural order in general.

Chrysostom, But when he wants to establish Chrysostom's view that "whomever he draws he draws with their consent,"[164] he erroneously opposes to us the agreement of everyone down the centuries.[165] He then repeats those arguments which I have already refuted so often—that God stands at the door of our heart so that we may open it to him,[166] and such like. But, in his usual way, he attacks what he does not understand, or at any rate he is using unsuitable weapons. With Ambrose we consider that both § Christ and Satan choose for themselves and purchase volunteer soldiers.[167] But we say that all those whom Christ wants to have as volunteers for the good must be made such by his Spirit. God draws us, Augustine says, without force and not unwillingly, and therefore as those who follow of their own accord—but with a will which he has made.[168] Hence I disagree with Chrysostom[169] not when he says that those who are drawn are ready of themselves[170] to follow, but [only] because he assumes that they must follow in a movement that is all their own. Whatever efforts Pighius makes, therefore, he will not be able to deprive us of this: our will is effectively influenced by God, and not merely so lightly affected that we then have the option either to resist or to obey.

Ambrose,
396

and Augustine

7. John 6:45 Nor will he, by his tasteless criticism, succeed in diminishing the power of that witness of Christ which I quoted to confirm it: Everyone who has heard and learned from my Father comes to me.[171] Learning, he says, is here understood of assenting. So not everyone whom the Father teaches comes to Christ, but only he who allows himself to be persuaded. I will leave to my readers to reckon how much weight this in-

---

164. *Homily on Reproaches to Be Borne* 6 (PG 51:143), quoted in *Inst.* 2.3.10 (LCC 20:303). A number of other possible sources have been suggested, but while these convey the same idea the wording is different. It is possible that Calvin may have known the quotation via the 1535 edition of Melanchthon's *Loci communes* (*Melanchthon on Christian Doctrine*, ed. C. L. Manschreck [Grand Rapids: Baker, 1982], 60, has the same passage in the 1555 edition). "With their consent" is *volentem*, normally translated "willing."
165. See the debates of *BLW* 2.
166. Rev. 3:20; see *BLW* 5.369–70 (at nn. 147–48).
167. Calvin echoes Pighius's quotation (98a–b) from Ambrose *Jacob and the Happy Life* 1.3.10 (FoC 65:125); Pighius had earlier quoted this passage at greater length (see *BLW* 2.286 [at n. 226]). "Volunteer," here and in the next sentence, is *voluntarios*, normally translated "voluntary."
168. This appears to be a summary of Augustine's teaching rather than of a specific passage. L. Smits, *Saint Augustin dans l'oeuvre de Jean Calvin* (Assen: van Gorcum, 1958), 2:82, mentions *Sermons on John* 26.2–5 (on 6:43–44) (NPNF 7:168–70); *Sermon* 131.2.2 (Works III/4.317); *Against Two Letters of the Pelagians* 1.19.37 (NPNF 5:389). For the other uses of this last passage see *BLW* 3.308 n. 147.
169. See at n. 164. Calvin is clarifying the stance that he had taken in the 1539 *Institutes*.
170. Latin *spontaneos*, usually translated "self-determined."
171. John 6:45, quoted in *Inst.* 2.3.10 (LCC 20:303).

terpretation ought to have, once I have, in a couple of words, reminded them of what Christ is driving at in that passage. It is simply of course to show how big a difference there is between the outward preaching of a human being, which strikes only the ears, and that secret, more inward instruction of the Holy Spirit by which the mind is enlightened and the heart touched. Nor indeed should we overlook what the situation was that brought [Christ] to deal with that distinction. He saw that he was achieving nothing by his teaching in the presence of the blind, deaf, and rebellious. And so he showed that teaching is fruitful only when both the light of understanding and the disposition to obey are given by God.[172] And this is the relevance of the passage which he quotes from Isaiah to the effect that all will be taught by God.[173] For in that passage the prophet indicates a special kind of teaching of which the Lord deems his elect to be worthy. For the ungodly are also taught,[174] but in a different way, with the result of course that they hear only a man, not that they learn from God.

But in an effort to prove that Christ's words can be understood in a way different from what I think, he brings forward the interpretation of Cyril, which is different from mine.[175] As though it would really immediately follow that [Christ's words] can be differently understood because Cyril understands them differently! But if that argument is accepted, then I have Augustine on my side, one who comes before Cyril in time as in everything else,[176] and who altogether denies that the words can be understood in any other way.[177] But let the facts themselves and the truth suffice to ensure that we are believed. Christ bears witness that all, without exception, who have heard and learned from the Father come to him.[178] From that I infer that the teaching by which the Lord through his Spirit instructs us inwardly is effective. Pighius parries by saying that this learning depends on our choosing. I say that this is in flagrant contradiction with the intention of Christ, and I am saying only what it is possible for everyone to see clearly. For he is declaring that his teaching is received only by those to whom it has been given [to receive it]. And what, despite this, does Cyril [say]?[179] That he who is drawn is not forcibly coerced. Who objects to this? [Pighius]

Cyril's interpretation

versus Augustine's

---

172. See John 6:41–45.
173. Isa. 54:13, quoted in John 6:45.
174. The first edition has "teach," which in later editions rightly becomes "are taught."
175. Pighius (98b) quotes Cyril *Commentary on the Gospel according to S. John* 4.1 (on 6:45) (Oxford: James Parker & London: Rivingtons, 1874), 400–401.
176. For the relative authority of Augustine and Cyril see A. N. S. Lane, "Calvin's Use of the Fathers and the Medievals," *Calvin Theological Journal* 16 (1981): 167–73.
177. *The Predestination of the Saints* 8.13–15 (NPNF 5:504–6), cited in *Inst.* 2.3.10 (LCC 20:303) and quoted at length in *BLW* 3.322–23 (at nn. 291–99).
178. John 6:45.
179. See n. 175.

397

then adds another clause about § free choice, which he stitches on in accordance with a carnal fabrication.[180]

"William of Ockham"

Having accomplished this so well, he concludes by affirming the utter truth of William of Ockham's well-known statement (which throughout smacks of Pelagianism): God does not deny his grace to one who does what he can.[181] For [he says] my teaching that no one can seek the grace of God except one who is moved by the Spirit of God makes human beings straight into tree stumps. How so? Because from [my teaching] it follows that grace is available to no one and that no one has to seek it, since it is something which cannot be sought before it is possessed, and it is pointless to seek what is already possessed. But he is arguing just as if I had already conceded to him that there are not two different graces, a godly desire and its attainment.[182] In fact I have already proved elsewhere from Augustine that "it is soundness of faith [which causes you] to ask so that you receive, to seek so that you find, to knock so that the door is opened to you."[183] Moreover I think it is not the sick person but the physician who must be considered to be the author of this health.

versus Augustine

Perseverance not merited

With respect to the gift of perseverance, Pighius's philosophy is that it is indeed bestowed upon us gratuitously, and yet it is also paid as a reward for merits. How did it happen that an idea of such subtlety did not occur to the Holy Spirit when he was dictating[184] to Paul arguments that were totally opposed to it? For since the inference "if it is of grace then it is not of works"[185] was familiar to him, he argues elsewhere that what is paid as a reward for works is a debt. To one who works, [Paul] says, a wage is paid not according to grace but in accordance with a debt (Rom. 4).[186] How will this agree with the principle put forward by Pighius, who wants us to merit God's grace by our own goodness, and yet to obtain it gratuitously?

8. Parable of talents

However, on the basis of that well-known parable of Christ about the talents repaid with interest [Pighius] claims that God rewards the right use of earlier graces by [the gift of] later ones.[187] But I have never

---

180. Pighius (98b) adds: "Nor can we in any way deny the free power of man (which we call free choice) according to the dogmas of the church and of truth."

181. Quoted by Calvin in *Inst.* 2.3.10 (LCC 20:303–4) and quoted from there and defended by Pighius (98b–99a). Calvin's ascription to Ockham is hesitant ("unless I am mistaken"); the most likely source is in fact Gabriel Biel *Collectorium circa quattuor libros Sententiarum*, book 2, distinctio 27, articulus 3, dubium 4 (Tübingen: J. C. B. Mohr [Paul Siebeck], 1973–84), 2:523–24.

182. See cols. 383–84.

183. *The Perfection of Righteousness* 19.40 (NPNF 5:174), quoted earlier in cols. 388–89 (at n. 111).

184. See *BLW* 2.270 n. 114.

185. Rom. 11:6.

186. Rom. 4:4.

187. Calvin in *Inst.* 2.3.11 (LCC 20:305) cites the parable from Matt. 25:14–30; Luke 19:12–27. Pighius (99b) cites the Lucan version.

denied this absolutely; I have only added this qualification, that a two-fold danger must be avoided: "God should not be believed to reward the right use of his grace as if man, by his own efforts, rendered the grace which is offered to him effective; and the rewarding should not be thought of in such a way that grace is no more gratuitous." On the contrary I had taught that the parable should be interpreted [as saying] that God constantly follows up his earlier gifts in us with new and greater ones.[188] Hence Pighius achieves nothing worth the trouble when he pours out such a torrent of words to extract from me what I have already of my own accord acknowledged:[189] [in the parable] God's graces are represented by the word "talents," ourselves by the part of the servants, and God himself by the head of the household. Since this is agreed between us without any doubt, let him derive from that anything he can to oppose me. God, he says, praises our faithfulness and bears witness that it is in payment for this that he heaps further gifts upon us. Of course, just as he crowns his gifts in us whenever he gives some reward.[190] That is also what it says in my *Institutes:* "The faithful are to expect the blessing that, the better they have used God's earlier graces, the § more they will receive in addition afterwards." But [I say] that their good use of them is also a gift of grace. Indeed, lest anyone should suppose that I had made this up myself, I added a quotation from Paul, who attributes to the pure good will of God the fact that he works in us both to will and to complete [the work].[191] What there is in the parable that is opposed to this I cannot see.

Then, [to show] that our will cooperates with the grace of God, he cites as a witness Paul, who testifies that he has laboured more abundantly than all others.[192] Later, adding a correction, [Paul] takes that back and transfers to God's grace what he had seemed to take for himself. Not I, he says, but the grace of God which was with me.[193] By this correction Pighius thinks that nothing else is meant but that [Paul] laboured with the help and cooperation of God's grace. But if that is what Paul meant, he would have moderated his words only as follows: he had not laboured alone, but the grace of God[194] was together with him. As it is, he uses not a partial qualification, but a complete correc-

398

9. 1 Cor. 15:10

---

188. *Inst.* 2.3.11 (LCC 20:305). The last sentence is a paraphrase of the sentence in quotation marks at n. 191.
189. I.e., in his interpretation of the parable in *Inst.* 2.3.11 (LCC 20:305).
190. The famous Augustinian principle; see *BLW* 4.337 (at nn. 105–12).
191. *Inst.* 2.3.11 (LCC 20:305), where Phil. 2:13 is quoted.
192. 1 Cor. 15:10. Calvin quotes this in *Inst.* 2.3.12 (LCC 20:306), where he opposes the interpretation of his opponents, possibly including Erasmus *Diatribe concerning Free Choice* (LCC 17:82, 85).
193. 1 Cor. 15:10.
194. I.e., omitting the word "which" ("the grace of God which was with me"), as does the Vulgate translation; in *Inst.* 2.3.12 (LCC 20:306) Calvin criticises the Vulgate for this omission.

tion. But [Pighius says] the race and the struggle and the punishment of the body involve labour, which [Paul] elsewhere recalls that he had accomplished.[195] That is so, and we do not shrink from the customary manner of speaking whereby people are said to run and to strive and to labour—provided that it is not denied to us that, for the struggle and for the race (or labour), both the desire and the strength are also bestowed on them by the grace of God. Or, if it is more pleasing for our meaning to be expressed in the words of a prophet,[196] we willingly allow that people act, but it is because God causes them so to do. So let Pighius either change Paul's words,[197] or let him be off and his interpretation with him! But Paul [claims Pighius] has the natural meaning of the word[198] to protect him, because it is not at all fitting for God to labour. Therefore the labour is entirely ours, but power for labouring is supplied by grace. And he says that I was misled by my mistake in not noticing this. I am indeed happy to bear the criticism of being a faithful rather than an eloquent interpreter.[199] However, he should really attack the apostle rather than me with that criticism, for these are Paul's words: It is not I who laboured, but the grace that was with me.[200] If I did not dare to make any change to this, why should Pighius quarrel with me on that account? But he presses upon me the weight of Augustine's authority, who took Paul's words as though he said that he had laboured, but with grace as his helper.[201] As though indeed it were not well known that Augustine here goes astray because he made do with the Latin translation, which is ambiguous and incomplete,[202] and did not look at what Paul's words convey. Observe Pighius's carefulness in gathering only the dross from gold.[203]

Parable of labourers in vineyard

Finally, he brings into the fray the parable of the labourers hired [to work] in the vineyard. Who then, he asks, is that workman whom Christ declares to be worthy of his hire?[204] For he thinks that we have

---

195. Pighius (100a) quotes 1 Cor. 9:26–27; 2 Tim. 4:7–8.
196. Ezek. 36:26–27.
197. As does the Vulgate of 1 Cor. 15:10 (see n. 194), and as Calvin is about to accuse Pighius of doing.
198. I.e., Pighius claims (100a) that the natural meaning *(sermonis proprietatem)* of the word "labour" cannot apply to God or to his grace; thus Calvin's interpretation is wrong.
199. I.e., of remaining faithful to Paul's statement that it was not he but the grace of God that laboured.
200. 1 Cor. 15:10.
201. Pighius (100a) quotes from *Grace and Free Choice* 5.12 (NPNF 5:448–49), and Calvin alludes to the end of this passage. In *Inst.* 2.3.12 (LCC 20:306) Calvin says that "otherwise good men" have made this mistake, possibly thinking of this passage.
202. See n. 194.
203. Cf. *Prefatory Address* to the *Institutes* (LCC 20:18)—when they read the Fathers, the papists "gather dung amid gold."
204. Pighius (100a) uses the phraseology of Matt. 20:1–2, 8, but without making reference to the actual point of the parable.

nothing else to reply but that it is the grace of God, which is utterly ridiculous. But why is he prophesying like this? For we do not at all deny that there are faithful workmen, but we say that it is from the grace of God that they have the heart with which they will, the strength with which they are able, and the hands with § which they labour. In this teaching it is clear that there is nothing absurd.

399

Augustine's *Rebuke and Grace*

There remains Augustine: to prevent anyone from being in doubt that he supports our opinion throughout, I had quoted passages of his both from other places and especially from the second book [addressed] to Valentinus.[205] Before replying to these, Pighius goes off himself (and takes the reader with him) on long and irrelevant verbal detours. So it is easy for everyone to see that the man has a bad conscience about his case, is confused through his lack of confidence, and wants by this device to distract his readers from the matter in hand—so that while they are being taken on a circuit of his digressions, the truth, which otherwise stands in front of them and is clear, may vanish from their sight. Therefore reporting in a long passage what Augustine deals with in the other book [addressed] to Valentinus, [Pighius] is confident that because [Augustine] there associates free choice with grace this is enough to ensure victory for him.[206] But we have proved elsewhere[207] what this association means and in what sense we should understand it. For since he denotes by the expression "free choice" simply the will, which he nevertheless acknowledges to be the slave of sin,[208] how does his meaning differ from what we preach? Indeed also, if we accept him as the interpreter of his own words, he elsewhere makes clear how his view is not at all different from ours, when he writes that "the will is not abolished by grace but changed from evil to good and, when it has become good, is helped."[209]

C's citation of *Rebuke and Grace*

P first cites *Grace and Free Choice*

Then Pighius comes to the book from which I had quoted[210] and again seizes an opportunity for wrestling over the expression "free

Augustine on free choice

---

205. Pighius proceeds (100a) to quote from the beginning of *Inst.* 2.3.13 (LCC 20:307). In 2.3.13–14 (LCC 20:307–9) Calvin gives a dossier of Augustine citations, which are drawn, as Calvin states, especially from *Rebuke and Grace* and also from *Letters* 194, 214, 217.
206. Pighius (101a–b) summarises and quotes the beginning of *Grace and Free Choice*, the first book addressed to Valentinus (esp. 2.4 [NPNF 5:444–45]).
207. See *BLW* 3.315–17 (at nn. 222–37); 4.329 (at nn. 22–32); 5.358–59 (at nn. 83–85).
208. Calvin is not (contrary to Smits, *St. Augustin*, 2:82) thinking of a specific passage, but of Augustine's teaching as he has expounded it in this work.
209. *Grace and Free Choice* 20.41 (NPNF 5:461). Calvin has an erroneous marginal reference to *Letter* 194. For the other uses of this passage see *BLW* 3.316 n. 227. The quotation in *Inst.* 2.3.14 (LCC 20:308) is identical except for the position of one word.
210. *Rebuke and Grace*.

choice"—as though I had not always from the beginning[211] declared that we did not care at all about the words, as long as there was agreement about the facts. What does Augustine say? He affirms that it is the prophetic and apostolic faith to recognise human free choice both for good actions and for bad, but that it is absolutely useless for good actions without the help of grace—indeed that it is free from righteousness and the slave of sin, and in relation to the good it is never free until it is set free by the grace of Christ. So much so that it can by no means aspire to the good unless it is guided by the Spirit of God. From this [Augustine] deduces that "to desire grace is already the beginning of grace."[212] From this Pighius infers that our teaching is full of ungodliness and dishonesty, since it is diametrically opposed to this faith. But I say that not even a shadow of this contradiction which he is dreaming up appears to those of a sound mind. Yet he himself is unduly forgetful. For he now embraces among the principles of orthodox faith what he had recently attacked,[213] with cries worthy of a drama, as being an accursed doctrine, namely that to desire grace is the beginning of grace.[214] Let him see what he is doing. For by this single word the whole foundation of his philosophy is overturned. But he gives no thought to what to say once he has placed his confidence in battle in the flow of his words.

Grace makes rebuke superfluous?

400

In addition he likewise brandishes against us the fact that Augustine reproves those who imagined that § grace should be affirmed in such a way, lest[215] rebukes should be superfluous.[216] Why? Has such imagining ever, even in a dream, crept up on us? But it follows [he claims] from our teaching. Why from ours more than from Augustine's? Because, he says, if no one can guard against evil and do good without the help of grace; if, in addition, [grace] alone, without us, works and accomplishes this in us, and it is not in our power to make it come or even to desire it before it comes, then it would be more ridiculous to urge someone to do the good than to urge a blind man to see. And what of all that does Augustine not affirm almost word for word? "People are freed from evil by the grace of Christ alone. Without this they do no good at all, whether by thinking, or by willing and loving, or by acting" (ch. 2 of

---

211. In *Inst.* 2.2.7–8 (LCC 20:264–66).
212. A loose summary with quotation of *Rebuke and Grace* 1.2 (NPNF 5:472), a text which is quoted by Pighius (101b). Parts are also quoted in *BLW* 3.321–22 (at n. 285); 5.368 (at n. 142).
213. See cols. 382–83.
214. *Rebuke and Grace* 1.2 (NPNF 5:472), quoted above at n. 212.
215. "Grace should be affirmed in such a way, lest rebukes should be superfluous" is what the Latin editions have. The French translation, Pighius, and Augustine (see n. 216) all indicate that it should be "grace is affirmed in such a way that rebukes are superfluous."
216. Calvin is quoting Pighius's introduction (101b) to his quotations (101b–102a) from *Rebuke and Grace* 2.4–4.6 (NPNF 5:473).

that book).[217] Again: "The human will does not obtain grace through its freedom, but obtains freedom through grace and, that it may persevere, delightful endurance and unconquerable bravery" (ch. 8).[218] Again: "God is within, who holds back hearts, moves hearts, and draws men by their wills, which he has worked in them" (ch. 14).[219]

On the other hand he claims that Augustine is showing that it is in the power of the hearer to receive admonition. Is it really the case that he, almost openly, carries his lies to unrestrained licence and yet tries to persuade people that he is telling the truth? Augustine more than ten times there[220] denies what this cheat alleges that he affirms. "Man benefits from rebuke when [God], who causes those [to benefit] whom he has willed to benefit (even apart from rebuke), has mercy on him and helps him" (ch. 5).[221] Again: "The multitude that deserves condemnation should be rebuked. This is so that out of the pain of rebuke a will for regeneration may arise (if indeed the one rebuked is a child of the promise) in order that, by the noise [of rebuke] resounding externally and scourging him, God may work inwardly in him so that he may will [the good]."[222] Again: "In whatever way rebuke is administered through man, nevertheless it is only through God that it is made to be beneficial" (ch. 6).[223] Again: "When people through rebuke either come or return to the way of righteousness, who produces salvation in their hearts? No one but God who, as anyone plants and waters, gives the increase—God whom no human choice resists when he wants to make it whole" (ch. 14).[224] Again: "Accordingly, as far as concerns us who cannot distinguish those who are predestined from those who are not, we ought to administer the medicine of rebuke to all lest they perish, or lest they cause others to perish. But it is God's work to make it beneficial to those whom he has predestined to be made conformable to the image of his Son" (ch. 16).[225]

And what about the fact, which Pighius himself later acknowledges when he has been snatched away by his own dizziness to another place,

Power to receive admonition?

Perseverance is unmerited grace?

---

217. *Rebuke and Grace* 2.3 (NPNF 5:472), quoted more fully in *BLW* 3.322 (at n. 286).
218. *Rebuke and Grace* 8.17 (NPNF 5:478), the first half of which is quoted in *BLW* 3.322 (at n. 287). It was also quoted in *Inst.* 2.3.14 (LCC 20:308).
219. *Rebuke and Grace* 14.45 (NPNF 5:490), which is added in the 1559 *Institutes* 3.23.14 (LCC 21:964).
220. I.e., in *Rebuke and Grace*.
221. *Rebuke and Grace* 5.8 (NPNF 5:474), which is added in the 1559 *Institutes* 3.23.14 (LCC 21:963).
222. *Rebuke and Grace* 6.9 (NPNF 5:475), quoted more accurately in *BLW* 4.341–42 (at n. 153).
223. *Rebuke and Grace* 6.9 (NPNF 5:475).
224. Ibid., 14.43 (NPNF 5:489), which is added in the 1559 *Institutes* 3.23.14 (LCC 21:963–64).
225. *Rebuke and Grace* 16.49 (NPNF 5:491), quoted more accurately in *BLW* 4.342 (at n. 157). This passage was already quoted, more briefly, in *Inst.* 3.23.14 (LCC 21:964).

that Augustine teaches the following? Not only that the conversion of the ungodly, his progress in the good, and his perseverance right to the end depend upon the gift and grace of God, but that this grace has not been § offered to all. Also that we cannot attain it either by our own desire or by our own endeavour, but it is bestowed by the good pleasure of God alone on those whom he himself wills.²²⁶ Having let slip these admissions, he is first compelled to make an open break with Augustine, and he then shows how, without denying the grace of God, the arguments which kept Augustine in perplexity should be answered. Namely by saying that conversion is the gift of God, but only those are converted who merit it by their free choice. Perseverance [he says] is likewise the gift of God, but depends no less on man; and each is in fact paid as a reward for earlier merits.²²⁷ In this way, with a couple of words, he extricates himself from all difficulty. But if he hopes that his readers' eyes can be blinded by such obvious, stupid nonsense, then he is fooling himself overmuch. I at any rate have decided to refute it by doing no more than bring it out into public view, since no one will be so obtuse and stupid as not immediately, at first glance, to recoil from such great absurdity.

Disputed passage

Finally, of the passages that I quoted [in the *Institutes*],²²⁸ he takes up one in which he thought he had a plausible reason for abuse and ample scope for boasting. I had reported the following words of Augustine (which I will now append), but I had declared that out of a desire for brevity I had made extracts from different places which would cover the whole of the subject: "Grace to persevere in the good would have been given to Adam if he had willed; it is given to us, so that we may will, and by our will overcome lust. So he had the ability, if he willed, but not the willing to make him able; to us are given both to will and to be able."²²⁹ Thus far Pighius recognises that I reported faithfully, however much he still tries to obscure so clear a truth by his evasions.

Not able to sin: when?

But I add immediately after the second sentence that "the original freedom was to be able not to sin, while ours is a much greater one, not to be able to sin."²³⁰ So he lashes me vehemently for being a dishonest

---

226. A close quotation of Pighius's summary (102b) of what is perplexing in Augustine's teaching, looking especially to *Rebuke and Grace* 8.17–19 (NPNF 5:478–79). The margin contains a reference to Pighius: "Folio 102, page 2."

227. The margin contains a reference to Pighius: "Folio 103, page 2."

228. *Inst.* 2.3.13–14 (LCC 20:307–9).

229. An exact quotation from *Inst.* 2.3.13 (LCC 20:307), where Calvin summarised and quoted loosely from *Rebuke and Grace* 11.31–32 (NPNF 5:484–85). For the other uses of the first half of this passage see *BLW* 3.324 n. 309.

230. An exact quotation from *Inst.* 2.3.13 (LCC 20:307), where Calvin quoted loosely from *Rebuke and Grace* 12.33 (NPNF 5:485). Calvin makes one alteration which is crucial to the disputed interpretation: where Augustine wrote of the first and *last* freedom, Calvin writes of the first and *our* freedom. Cf. at n. 238.

forger, since I transfer to the present situation of the saints what was said about their future condition after the resurrection. I myself do not deny that the fulness of that perfection which [Augustine] there describes does not yet exist, nor is it to be hoped for before the resurrection.[231] But from this it does not follow that it has no relevance to the present situation. For now there begins in the saints what will then be fully completed. Moreover the context shows sufficiently that this was Augustine's intention. For he explains that the strength to stand firm, which is now in the holy angels, is the reward for their perseverance, since they did not fall with the wicked [angels].[232] Then he adds that man too would have shared in the same reward if as a result of their example he had continued in obedience. As it is, by his transgression he is utterly fallen, and yet "in those who are set free that which was to have been the reward for merit has become a gift of grace" (ch. 11).[233] Is he here discussing the glory § of immortality, and not rather the present benefit of regeneration? Again: "Indeed in our receiving good and holding perseveringly to it by means of this grace of God, there is in us not just the ability to do what we will to do, but also the will to do what we are able to do."[234] Immediately afterwards he infers that "a careful distinction should be made between these two pairs, and a watchful eye should be kept on the difference between them: namely to be able not to sin and not to be able to sin, and to be able not to die and not to be able to die."[235] What are those pairs but the things which he had already[236] mentioned when he distinguished the condition of the first man from ours? And he had said that "a so much greater grace has been given to us, because for us [merely] to recover our lost freedom [through it] would be insufficient, and, finally, for it merely to make it possible for us either to perceive the good or to persist in it, if we willed it, would be insufficient. What it requires is that we also be caused to will [the good]" (ch. 11).[237]

Why then [asks Pighius] does he use the future tense when he continues with that distinction? Why does he say that the last freedom

After the resurrection

402
and now

---

231. In *Inst.* 2.3.13 (LCC 20:307) Calvin immediately proceeds to reject the view that Augustine was thinking of the future. In the 1541 French translation that view is described as a mockery put out by the Sorbonnists (Roman Catholic theologians at the Sorbonne). In the 1559 *Institutes* Calvin adds the statement that Peter Lombard falsely interpreted the passage as referring to the future. The concession made here does not, therefore, appear to be reflected in the *Institutes*. Cf. at n. 240.
232. *Rebuke and Grace* 11.32 (NPNF 5:484).
233. Ibid., 11.32 (NPNF 5:485).
234. Ibid., which is also quoted in *BLW* 5.355 (at n. 49).
235. *Rebuke and Grace* 12.33 (NPNF 5:485).
236. *Rebuke and Grace* 10.26–11.32 (NPNF 5:482–85).
237. *Rebuke and Grace* 11.31 (NPNF 5:484). For the other uses of this passage see *BLW* 3.324 n. 309.

> "will be" and not rather that it "is"?[238] The answer is simple: only a part of that freedom, according to the measure of our regeneration, is seen in this life, while the full completion is deferred until the day of resurrection, as he later indicates. "To the first man there was given the free will with which he was created, without any sin, and he made it into the slave of sin. But our will, when it was the slave of sin, was set free by him who said, If the Son has set you free, you will be free indeed. And by this grace we receive so much freedom that, although during our life here we fight against sinful lusts, yet we are not the slaves of sin which leads to death" (ch. 12).[239] Therefore when he declares that the last freedom will be not to be able to sin, he is merely honouring the lasting grace of the kingdom of Christ, which, while now manifested only in part, will finally exist whole and entire after the resurrection. But [Pighius says] I also do not allow anyone to understand [that freedom] as referring to the future perfection which follows immortality.[240] Of course, if anyone wanted so to drag it in that direction that it would not be right to apply it to this life. Moreover, this is [to say] only that the whole grace of regeneration is included here.

Part now; part then

On this matter I had said[241] that all doubt had been taken away from us by Augustine's own words. For a little later he adds: "The wills of the saints are so fired by the Holy Spirit that they are able for the reason that they so will, and they will for the reason that God works in them to will. And help has been given to the weakness of the human will, so that it is driven by divine grace without the possibility of turning aside or detaching itself, so that, however weak it is, it should not fail."[242] Pighius objects that this statement is of no help to me, because it has nothing at all to do with that earlier one. And lest his criticism should lack wit, he makes fun of me with a proverb from the marketplace. This tail, he says, belongs to a different calf.[243] He is indeed a remarkable slaughterer, § who knows how to make two calves out of one like this! For a second distinction follows in the same context in Augustine, which is exactly suited to clarify that matter. "There is one kind of aid without which something does not happen, and another by which something happens. Thus the first man, who in

Augustine confirms this interpretation

---

238. Pighius's comment (104b) on Calvin's quotation of *Rebuke and Grace* 12.33 (NPNF 5:485); see n. 230.
239. *Rebuke and Grace* 12.35 (NPNF 5:486), quoting John 8:36.
240. Pighius (104b, 105b) quotes *Inst.* 2.3.13 (LCC 20:307); see n. 231.
241. I.e., in *Inst.* 2.3.13 (LCC 20:307).
242. *Rebuke and Grace* 12.38 (NPNF 5:487), quoted more fully and more accurately in *Inst.* 2.3.13 (LCC 20:307), which is in turn quoted by Pighius (105b); see also nn. 246–47. The passage is also quoted more fully in *BLW* 3.324 (at n. 311).
243. For a similar proverb see Walther 15878.

that good [gift] by which he had been made righteous had received the ability not to sin, the ability not to die, and the ability not to forsake the good, was given the aid of perseverance. This was not such as to cause him to persevere, but such that without it he could not, by means of free choice [alone], persevere. But now the saints who have been predestined for the kingdom of Christ are given not only this kind of aid of perseverance, but such aid that perseverance itself is bestowed on them—not only a gift without which they could not persevere, but also a gift by means of which they could not but persevere. For he did not only say: Without me you can do nothing. He also said: You did not choose me, but I chose you, and appointed you, that you should go and bring forth fruit, and that your fruit should remain. By these words he showed that he had given them not only righteousness but also perseverance in it."[244]

Who now, I ask, will not grant me that Augustine is expounding essentially the same teaching in different words? How will Pighius then benefit by separating parts that are so thoroughly intertwined?[245] But so desperate is his impudence that he always regards having sounded off with the confused bawlings of his mouth as equivalent to victory! For Augustine declares that not only to be able is given to us but also to will; that God's grace is effective in us not only to the extent that, aided by it, we can obtain faith if we please and, having obtained it, remain steadfast in it, but absolutely. The result is that we are believers and do persevere in faith, that with an utterly unconquerable will we grasp what is good and with utterly unconquerable constancy we refuse to abandon it.[246] All this and similar statements [from Augustine] which you have already heard mean to Pighius only that we are aided in such a way that we are certain of victory if we ourselves are not § inadequate for our need. The gates of hell [he says] will not be too strong for us if we do not yield to them. Satan will have no power over us or over the grace that has been given to us—if we do not give him room through our corruption and negligence. But suppose one of the elect should either by his own slackness shut out or reject the grace of God that is offered or, having received it, throw it away by his lack of constancy or through the fault of weakness allow it to be snatched away from him. Where then is that action of grace from which (as Augustine puts it) there is no possibility of turning aside or detaching one-

Augustine clear, but P blusters

404

---

244. *Rebuke and Grace* 12.34 (NPNF 5:485), quoting John 15:5, 16.

245. I.e., why does he maintain, as in the previous paragraph (see at n. 243), that the different Augustinian passages refer to different things?

246. A paraphrase of *Rebuke and Grace* 12.38 (NPNF 5:487). There is no need (contrary to Smits, *St. Augustin*, 2:83) to seek an alternative source for the first sentence ("For Augustine declares...."). Much of the material for this summary can be found in the quotation in *Inst.* 2.3.13 (LCC 20:307); see n. 242.

self,[247] which does not leave people's wills to themselves so that they may remain in grace if they will, but even works [in them] so that they do will? [Where is that action] which not only bestows the ability to obtain faith, but actually makes people believers; which not only provides the means for persevering, but equips them with enough steadfastness for them to do nothing but persevere? Indeed where are both that unconquerable will to grasp the good and the unconquerable constancy to hold on to it? And yet he is not content to have escaped by that dog's bark of his unless, with a stupidity greater than Thrason's,[248] he can boast that it is more than sufficiently clear how Augustine contradicts me at every point.

Conclusion

Pighius's work consists of ten books, in the first six of which he discusses free choice, while in the remaining four he deals with the predestination and providence of God. Therefore, since they are distinct issues, I have so far discussed that former one as my ability and the shortness of the time allowed. But I have resolved that the treatment of the other should be deferred until the next market,[249] because there is no danger in delay, and then it will be more useful, if the Lord wills, when it comes out. But I feared that if I remained silent for too long, Pighius would blind some people's eyes with that well-known display of his. So it seemed best to publish this as a sample in the meantime and so both restrain his insolence a little and arouse the attention of good and godly people, so that as they see the truth of God stand unconquered in the face of the attack of this Cyclops[250] they may be more and more strengthened in it.

---

247. Two adjectives found in *Rebuke and Grace* 12.38 (NPNF 5:487); see also at n. 242; *BLW* 3.324 (at n. 310).
248. See *BLW* 1.237 n. 24.
249. I.e., until the 1544 Frankfurt book fair. For details of Calvin's delayed response to the final four books see Introduction §1.
250. The Cyclopes were one-eyed giants of Greek mythology, known especially from Homer's *Odyssey*.

Subject Index

Absolute necessity, xviii, xxviii, 26, 28, 35–36; relative and, xxviii
Absurdities in the *Institutes*, 142–46, 150–65
Abuses in the church alleged as the cause of schism, 16–17, 18
Accidental qualities of the soul, 213
Accidents and substance, Aristotelian distinction between, xxv–xxvi, 46, 47, 75, 144, 213
Accusations, 168–69
Acknowledgment of guilt, God's initiative in human, 222
Adam, 46–47, 172, 177, 187, 240, 241, 242–43; compared to fallen humanity, 132–33
Adrian VI, xvi
Aeons, 45
Against Heresies (Irenaeus), xxiii
All in all, God's doing, 231
Ambrose, xxii; on free choice, 78–79, 84
Antichrist, pope as, 5, 16, 18, 19
Apostles compared with Reformers, 12–13, 14–15
Arbitrium, xxxii
Aristotle: Calvin's use of, xxiv–xxvi; on necessity, xxv, 149; on the compatibility of necessary and voluntary, 150
"Article 36" (Luther's *Defence*), 24, 26, 36, 37, 48, 49
Assent to grace as God's gift, 119–20
Augsburg Confession, xvii, 23, 29
Augustine, xviii, xxi, xxii; as the only Father to speak clearly and consistently on free choice, xviii, xxi, 67, 87, 100; the accuracy of Calvin's interpretation of, xxiv; and Pelagianism, 42, 47, 88, 90, 98, 100, 101, 108, 110, 111–12, 117, 127, 141, 143–44, 156, 181, 185; and Manichaeism, 42, 48, 90, 94, 99, 102, 127, 144; on the corruption of human nature, 49–50; on the clarity of Scripture, 57–58; on Scripture and tradition, 64; three groups of the writings of, 90; development in the views of, 94, 140; polemical works of, 101–2

Basil, xxii; on free choice, 75–77, 84
Behaviour of Reformers and of Romanists, 14
Bending of the heart, 38, 204–5
Bernard, 85
"Body" (Matt. 24:28), 59–60
Bolsec, Jerome, xv
Bondage of the will, xviii, xix–xx, xxi, xxv, 47, 68–69, 87, 89, 92, 97, 104, 135, 184, 238
Bondage of the Will (Luther), xiii, xxvii, xxviii, 3, 14, 49
Bound, the will as, 69. *See also* Bondage of the will
Brevity, Calvin's commitment to, 10, 11
Bucer, Martin, 8

"Can" v. "ought," xxi, 41, 165
Capernaum, 220
Carthage, Council of (411), 82; (416), xxiii, 82, 99; (418), xxiii, 82, 99, 106, 125, 126

245

Catharinus, Ambrosius, 22
"Catholic," Calvin's use of the term, 26
Celestius, 82, 95, 97, 171
Cerdo, 42, 47, 71, 171
Cerdonians, 45–46
Cervini, Marcello, xiv
Chrysostom: on free choice, 79–80, 85; on will and grace, 226–27
Church: Christ's preservation of the, 16; abuses in the, as the alleged cause of schism, 16–17, 18; as guardian of the Word of God, 66; infallibility of the, 137; test of the true, 137–38; Scripture contrary to the consensus of the, 203
Cicero, 156
Cincius, Bernardus, xiv
Clement, the writings of, 44–45
Clement, Pseudo-, 145; the *Recognitions* of, xxiii, xxv, 43–45; on free choice, 70, 84
Cochlaeus, Johannes, 185
Coerced, the will as, 69
Coercion: freedom defined as the opposite of, 68; confusion of necessity with, 69, 101, 146–50; Calvin's exclusion of, 204
Commandments (*see also* Law), 161; the (im)possibility of obeying, 117, 141, 165–67, 206, 207, 221, 228; keeping, as God's gift, 118, 132, 138, 142, 167, 224; useless without the power to obey, 158; purpose of, 160, 207
Concilia omnia (Crabbe), xxiii, xxvii
Conditional promises, purpose of, 167–68
Consequent necessity, xxviii
Constantine, 63–64
Controversies (Pighius), xvii, 7–8, 23
Conversion, xxvi; as a gift of God's grace, xxi, 131–32, 160, 173, 182, 207, 214, 218, 219, 240
Cooperation with grace (God), 81–82, 105, 119, 123, 175, 178, 193, 194, 195, 197, 198, 199–200, 204, 208, 216–17, 225, 230, 235

Corruption of human nature (*see also* Evil; Sin), xvii, 26, 36, 40, 49, 107, 128, 135, 136, 171–73, 175–76, 187, 188–89, 209–10, 212–13; as part of the substance of humans since creation, xxv, 45, 46, 47, 71, 144, 171–72, 186, 213; Pighius on the, 183–84; rather than nature eradicated by grace, 212
Counterfeit names as witnesses, Pighius's use of, 84
Covenant, new, 206–7
Crabbe, Peter, xxiii, xxvii, 82
Created v. nature as fallen, nature as, xx, xxv, 40–41, 46–47, 70, 71, 72, 75, 84, 85–86, 91, 92, 98, 146, 148, 156, 182, 213
Crimes committed of necessity, punishment of, 37, 150–51
Crowning grace, 195
Crowning of God's gifts in humans, God's, xxi, 124, 139, 152–53, 220, 235
Cyprian on free choice, 72–73
Cyril, 233

Danish Church Order, xvii
Death, origin of, 185
Deceit of Reformers, alleged, 14, 28
Defence of All the Articles of Martin Luther..., xxvii, xxviii, 24, 26, 36, 37, 48, 49
Defence of the Ecclesiastical Hierarchy (Pighius), xvi–xvii
Devil, 39; as evil of necessity, 147, 148, 149
Diatribe concerning Free Choice (Erasmus), xxvii, 14, 37
Dictation of Scripture, 56, 80
Diligent and Lucid Exposition of the Controversies... (Pighius), xvii, 7–8, 23
Diospolis, Council of, 155
Directing of the heart, 38, 204–5; prayers for, 228–29
Divided self, 31, 179–80
Doctrine as cause of schism, 18

Dogmas of the Church (Augustine), inauthenticity of, 125
Double acceptance, 215, 216, 220, 234
Double justification, xvii, 26

"Eagles" (Matt. 24:28), 59–60
Eck, Johann, 42, 185
Effective teaching, 233
Effectual call, 160
Effectual grace, xx, 112–13, 114, 123, 131–32, 134, 136, 174, 177–78, 196, 211, 212, 232, 243
Election (*see also* Predestination), xxi, 136, 154, 159–60, 179, 199, 216, 218; Pighius's opposition to, 191–92, 200
Erasmus, 14, 37; and Luther, xxvii–xxix
Eternal Predestination of God (Calvin), xv, xxviii
Evil (*see also* Corruption; Sin): lusts, xx, 187; God as the source of (Manichaeism), xx, 39–40, 48, 71, 92, 144, 186; the will as, 37, 69, 77, 79, 103, 105, 107–8, 114, 122, 135, 141, 158, 169, 183, 187, 205, 209–10, 213; principles (gods), good and, 45–46
Exhortation (*see also* Preaching; Rebuke; Warning), 161, 196–97; role of, 138, 159; useless without the power to obey, 156, 158
Exsurge Domine, 26

Faith: as a gift of God, 31–32, 79, 82, 119–20, 129, 130, 131–32, 188, 244; attributed to preaching and grace, 164
Fallen v. nature as created, nature as, xx, xxv, 40–41, 46–47, 70, 71, 72, 75, 84, 85–86, 91, 92, 98, 146, 148, 156, 182, 213
False interpretation of Scripture, Pighius's warning against, 53, 58
Fathers: debate over the, xxi–xxiv; on Scripture and tradition, 61–67; and free choice, xxi, 67–80; ambiguous on free choice, 67, 75, 80, 85
Feelings, corruption of human, xx, 186–87
First Principles (Pighius), xvii
"Flesh": definition of, 49, 173, 180; weakness of the, 78, 103; heart of, 173, 195, 206, 224
Florents, Adrian, xvi
Form and matter, xxvi, 115, 226
Forming of heart to righteousness, 204–5
Frankfurt book fair, xiv, 11, 244
Free, the will as, 69
Free choice: definition of, xix, 67–69, 102–3, 113–14, 117, 122, 140–41, 158, 237–38; and grace, xix, 115, 120–22, 124, 140–41, 154–55, 157–58, 180, 182, 188, 206, 224, 226, 229, 237; the Fathers and, xxi, 67–80; Luther on, xxvii, xxviii, 26; sin excused on the basis of the denial of, 120–21; Augustine on the role of, 181
Free Choice (Pighius), xiv, xv, xvii, 4; synopsis of, xviii–xix; on Calvin, attack of, 8, 9
Freedom defined as opposed to coercion, 68
Fruits, good, 230

Gennadius, 125
God: as the author of sin (Manichaeism), xx, 39–40, 48, 71, 92, 144, 186; as good of necessity, 147–48, 149
Good and evil principles (gods), 45–46
Goodness of creation, xxv, 40, 47
Good will as a gift of God, 105, 108, 110, 112, 119, 122, 130, 161, 162, 177, 183, 194, 195, 205, 213, 226–27, 231
Good works, xxi, 26–28, 122–23, 141, 200, 226, 227, 230; as effected by grace, 115–16
Gospel and law, 170

Grace: free choice and, xix, 115, 120–22, 124, 140–41, 154–55, 157–58, 180, 182, 188, 206, 224, 226, 229, 237; no human preparation for, xx, 123, 129–30, 135, 141, 173–74, 176–77, 188–89, 192; human preparation for (Pighius), 187–88, 190, 191, 192–93, 221, 223, 228; and nature, 26, 99, 155–56, 198, 211; and the human will, 81–82, 104–5, 226–27; cooperation with, 81–82, 105, 119, 123, 175, 178, 193, 194, 195, 197, 198, 199–200, 204, 208, 216–17, 225, 230, 235; Augustine's emphasis on, 95, 100; necessity of, 106; doctrine of free will and, 116; first grace (Adam) and second, 133, 177, 240–43; promises of, 138; as the gift of creation (Pelagius), 155; the law as pointing to, 167; Pighius on, 183, 191–99, 216; equal for all (Pighius), 188, 198–99, 200; threefold action of, 194; Pelagius on, 217

Guidance of the heart, 204–5

Guilt, God's initiative in human acknowledgment of, 222

Habit, xxvi, 150, 209–10; changed by grace, 210

Hagenau, Colloquy of, 7

Heart: substance of the, xxvi, 208; bending of the, 38, 204–5; of stone, 123, 141, 174, 195, 206, 208, 211, 224; of flesh, 173, 195, 206, 224; new, 194, 195, 205, 208–9, 210, 228; prayers for directing of the, 228–29

"Help," God's (meaning in Augustine), 118

Heretics: Reformers compared to ancient, 12, 42–50, 171; twisting of Scripture by, Pighius's warning against, 53, 57; the Fathers' method of dealing with, 62–63

Hilary, 81–82, 85; on free choice, 73–75

Holy Spirit, inward work of the, 33, 65, 131, 163–65, 214, 215, 216, 217, 219, 233, 239

Human feelings, corruption of, xx, 186–87

Human nature. *See* Nature

Human powers, the Fathers' exaltation of, 74

Human responsibility, xxi, 169

Human will and the grace of God, 81–82, 104–5, 226–27. *See also* Grace

Humility, 216; as a gift of God, 193, 224; preceded by grace, 215

Hyperaspistes (Erasmus), xxvii

Hypognosticon, inauthenticity of, 107

Image of God, 72

Inability to sin, 240–43

Index of Prohibited Books, xv, xvii

Infallibility: of the pope, xvii, xxiii, 189; of the church, 137

Innocent I, 125

Institutes, xiii–xvi; "absurdities" in the, 142–46, 150–65

Instruments, God's use of, xxi, 32–33. *See also* Secondary causes

Intactness of nature (Pighius), 184–85, 186

"Interpretation," private (2 Pet. 1:19–20), 55–56

Interpretations of Scripture, Pighius's warning against false, 53, 58

Inward work of the Holy Spirit, 33, 65, 163–65, 214, 215, 216, 217, 219, 239; distinguished from outward preaching, 131, 233; necessity of, 210–11

Irenaeus, xxii–xxiii, 66, 81, 156; on the Clementine *Recognitions,* silence of, 44; on Scripture and tradition, 61–62; on free choice, 71–72, 84

Jacob, 22

Jeremiah to turn, God's urging of, 217

Subject Index

Jerome, 84, 85; on free choice, 77–78
Jovinian, 127
Justification, 116; Pighius's doctrine of, xvii; double, xvii, 26
Justifying grace, 195

Labour as God's grace, Paul's, 33, 197–98, 235–36
Labourers in the vineyard, parable of the, 236–37
Labyrinth, 15, 200
Law (*see also* Commandments): (im)possibility of keeping the, xx, 26, 27, 41, 51–52, 117, 139, 144, 156, 165–67, 168; role of the, xxi, 41, 138, 166–67, 206, 208; and gospel, 170; and promise, 207
Law and order by necessity, alleged undermining of, 38
Letter to the Senate and People of Geneva (Sadoleto), 12, 16
Liberation in the Old Testament, 210
Lusts, evil, xx, 187
Luther, Martin, xxiv, 14, 17, 171; toward Aristotle, attitude of, xxiv; and Erasmus, xxvii–xxix; on free choice, xxvii, xxviii, 26; character of, 21–22; on reason, 24; teaching of, according to Pighius, 26; Calvin on, 28; language of, softened by Melanchthon, 29; Pighius's accusations against, 42, 48; on the corruption of human nature, 49
Lutheran, Calvin's willingness to be called, 30

Manichaeism (*see also* Augustine and Manichaeism), 40, 42, 45–46, 47, 48, 92, 95, 171, 172; Calvin accused of, xx, xxv, 111, 173; Pighius and, 185–86; Reformers accused of, 199
Marcion, 42, 44, 71, 171, 172
Marcionites, 45
Matter and form, xxvi, 115, 226
Melanchthon, Philipp, xxviii, 11, 171; on free will, 3; dedication to, 3–4; softening Luther's language, 29
Merits: no, before grace, 110, 176; grace not according to, 134, 136, 141; rewards not according to, 152; as God's gifts, 153, 220
Method of *Bondage and Liberation of the Will*, xix, 10–11
Middle path of Pighius, xviii, 157, 171, 180–91, 199–200
Milevis, Council of, xxiii, 82, 99, 106, 125, 126
Mind and the will, 77; corruption of the, 128, 135, 213; accidental qualities of the, 213
Miracles, no need for new, 13–14
Montanus, 46
Mortality, origin of, 185
Mystery of Our Salvation and Redemption (Pighius), xvii, 7

Nature: corruption of human, xvii, 26, 36, 40, 49, 107, 128, 135, 136, 171–73, 175–76, 187, 188–89, 209–10, 212–13; as created v. nature as fallen, xx, xxv, 40–41, 46–47, 70, 71, 72, 75, 84, 85–86, 91, 92, 98, 146, 148, 156, 182, 213; and grace, 26, 99, 155–56, 198, 211; Pighius on the corruption of human, 183–84; undiminished by the fall (Pighius), 184–85, 186; not eradicated by grace, 212
Necessary compatible with voluntary, 101, 147, 149
Necessity: absolute, xviii, xxviii, 26, 28, 35–36; and sin, xx, 69, 88, 139, 143–50, 203; Aristotle on, xxv, 149; relative, xxviii; of consequence, xxviii; confusion of coercion with, 69, 101, 146–50; combined with self-determination, 70; and will, 93, 97–98, 101, 148–49; definition of, 149
Nehemiah, precedent of, 5
New covenant, 206–7
New heart, 194, 195, 205, 208–9, 210, 228

New Testament, clarity of the, 55
Nicaea, Council of, 63–64

Old man, 179–80
Old Testament: clarity of the, 54–55; liberation in the, 210
Olives (Pauline analogy), 123–24, 230
Orange, Council of, xxiii, xxvii, 81–82, 105–6, 126, 188–89
Origen, 61, 156; unreliability of, 66, 67, 84–85; on free choice, 70
Original sin, xvii, xx, 26, 40, 104, 105, 173, 184; Augustine's failure to expound, 94
"Ought" v. "can," xxi, 41, 165

Palestine, Council of, 155, 190
Papacy (*see also* Pope): and reform, 17, 20–21; evils of the, 19
Pardon as born of faith (God's gift), prayer for, 222
Passion, will as, 95
Paul: on reason, 25; labour of, as God's grace, 33, 197–98, 235–36; on the corruption of human nature, 49; on the impossibility of keeping the law, 52; conversion of, 129, 216; divided self of, 179–80
Pelagianism (*see also* Augustine and Pelagianism), 40, 42, 52, 72, 151, 153, 180, 234; of Pighius, xx, 104, 185, 189–91, 199, 217; benefit of the controversy with, 100
Pelagius, 95, 155, 171, 190, 217
Perfection, time of the beginning of, 241–42
Persecution against Reformers, 15
Perseverance, 160, 197, 243; as God's gift, xx, 134, 136, 175, 178–79, 234, 239–40, 244
"Peter" (in Pseudo-Clement), xxv, 43, 45, 84, 145, 156
Pighius, Albertus: life and works of, xvi–xviii; wordiness of, 10, 11
Plagiarism of Pighius, xviii, 22–24
Pope (*see also* Papacy): infallibility of the, xvii, xxiii, 189; as Antichrist, 5, 16, 18, 19; power of the, 14–15; and the Council of Orange, 189
Prayer for pardon as born of faith (God's gift), 222
Prayers of saints to direct their hearts, 228–29
Preaching (*see also* Exhortation; Rebuke; Warning): role of, xxi, 31–34, 214–15; simultaneous operation of grace and, 33, 131, 163–65, 167; useless without the power to obey, 158; distinguished from the inward work of the Spirit, 233
Predestination (*see also* Election), 129, 134; controversy over, xv; to death, 112
Preparation for grace, 187–88, 190, 191, 192–93, 221, 223, 228; no human, xx, 123, 129–30, 135, 141, 173–74, 176–77, 188–89, 192
Pressure on Reformers, 4–5
Prevenient grace, xx, 82, 104–5, 107–8, 110, 114, 115–16, 135, 176, 192, 194, 195, 196, 216, 228
Priscillian, 42, 171
Priscillianists, 46, 47
Private "interpretation" (2 Pet. 1:19–20), 55–56
Promise, relation of law to, 207
Promises of grace, 138
Protestant unity, 13, 28, 30
Providence: and human responsibility, xxi; reconciliation of human work and divine, 36–37; the Fathers' acknowledgment of, 51
Pseudo-Augustine, xxii
Pseudo-Clement. *See* Clement, Pseudo-
Punishment of crimes committed of necessity, 37, 150–51

Quality of the will, xxvi, 209–10, 227

Ratio componendorum dissidiorum et sarciendae in religione concordiae (Pighius), 7
Reason, 77; Luther's attitude toward, 24; Paul's attitude toward, 25

Rebuke (*see also* Exhortation; Preaching; Warning), 161; purpose of, 138, 159–60, 162–63, 238–39; useless without power to obey, 158
Recognitions (Pseudo-Clement), xxiii, xxv, 43–45
Reform, papacy and, 17, 20–21
Reformers: pressure on, 4–5; comparison of apostles and, 12–13, 14–15; compared to ancient heretics, 12, 42–50, 171; unanimity among, 13, 28, 30; task of, 14–15; alleged deceit of, 14, 28; alleged obscurity and disharmony of, 29–30; on the impossibility of keeping the law, 51–52
Regensburg, Colloquy of, xvi, 7
Rehoboam, 223
Relative and absolute necessity, xxviii
Religion by necessity, alleged undermining of, 38–39
Repentance, 197, 216; as a gift of God, 193–94, 222; not in human power, 214; preceded by grace, 215
Reply to Sadoleto (Calvin), 12, 16
Retractations (Augustine), xxii, 51, 98; Calvin's exclusive use of the, 91, 93, 95, 97
Rewards: without free choice, propriety of, 150; dependent on God's grace, 151–52
Roman Catholic Church, Calvin's assessment of the, 19. *See also* Papacy; Pope
Romanists, behaviour of the, 14
Rottmanner, Odilo, xxiv
Rule of faith, 52, 56

Sabbath as rest from all our works (which are evil), 229
Sadoleto, Cardinal Jacopo, 12, 16
Saints: corruption of the, 26, 27, 48, 49, 52, 171; in bondage, 68
Satan, 39, 147, 148, 149
Saws in God's hands, the wicked as, 48

Schism: abuses in the church alleged as the cause of, 16–17, 18; doctrine as the cause of, 18
Scripture: as the final authority, xxiii, 57; passages not to Pighius's taste, 50, 137, 203; and tradition, 50–67, 80, 203; Christ's reliance solely on, 53; false interpretations of, Pighius's warnings against, 53, 58; as unclear (Pighius), 54, 56, 58; process of the recording of, 60–61; subordination of, to tradition (Pighius), 65, 137; as the test of the true church, 137–38
Secondary causes, God's working through, 38. *See also* Instruments, God's use of
Self-determined, the will as, xix–xx, 69–70, 122, 140
Semi-Pelagianism, xxvii, 125, 126, 189–90
Silence, impossibility of, 4, 17–18, 19
Simon Magus, 42–45, 171
Sin (*see also* Corruption; Evil): and necessity, xx, 69, 88, 139, 143–50, 203; God as the author of, xx, 39–40, 48, 71, 92, 144, 186; God's use of, 40; Augustine's definition of, 96; God's initiative in human acknowledgment of, 222; inability to sin and ability not to, 240–43
Sinlessness, possibility of, 52, 117
Soul, two parts of the, 31, 179–80
Special grace, 167
Stony heart, 123, 141, 174, 195, 206, 208, 211, 224
Substance: and accidents, Aristotelian distinction between, xxv–xxvi, 46, 47, 75, 144, 213; corruption as part of the human, xxv, 45, 46, 47, 71, 144, 171–72, 186, 213; of the heart, xxvi, 208; of the will, 209–10, 227; habit rather than, changed by grace, 210
Sun, Pighius's analogy of grace and the, 167, 181–82
Supernatural gifts taken away at the fall, 184, 186

Sword: comparison of the wicked to a, 37, 38; Scripture as a, 57

Talents, parable of the, 234–35
Ten Books on Human Free Choice and Divine Grace (Pighius), xiv, xv, xvii, 4; synopsis of, xviii–xix; on Calvin, attack of, 8, 9
Tertullian, 66, 81, 156; on the Clementine *Recognitions,* silence of, 44; on Scripture and tradition, 61, 62–63; unreliability of, 66; on free choice, 71, 84
Tradition and Scripture, 50–67, 80, 203
Trent, Council of, xvii

Unanimity among Reformers, 13, 28, 30

Valentinus, 44, 45, 47, 71, 171, 172
Valla, Lorenzo, 171
Vincentian canon, 83
Vine and the branches, analogy of the, 229–31
Vineyard, parable of the labourers in the, 236–37
Voluntary: slaves, 78; compatible with necessary, 101, 147, 149; sin, 146
Voluntas, xxxii
Volunteer soldiers, 232

Warning (*see also* Exhortation; Preaching; Rebuke), 197; useless without power to obey, 156, 163; purpose of, 162–63
Waxen nose, Scripture likened to a, 54, 56
Weakness: of the flesh, 78, 103; in Aristotle, 150
Will (*see also* Bondage of the will; Evil, the will as; Good will as a gift of God; Human will and the grace of God): as matter, xxvi, 115, 226; quality of the, xxvi, 209–10, 227; and mind, 77; and necessity, 93, 97–98, 101, 148–49; as passion, 95; Augustine's definition of the, 95; Pighius's view of the power of the, 104; preparation of the, 110; corruption of the mind and, 128, 135, 213; substance of the, 209–10, 227; accidental qualities of the, 213
William of Ockham, 234
Wisdom: danger of worldly, 25; as a gift of God, 224
Wordiness of Pighius, 10, 11
Works, good, xxi, 26–28, 115–16, 122–23, 141, 200, 226, 227, 230
Worms, Colloquy of, xvi, 7
Wyclif, John, 171

Scripture Index

The Scripture index is intended to be comprehensive; that is, it is not restricted to the usages in Calvin's text.

Genesis
4:8   79
5:32   151
6:5   49
12:1   216
28:10–15   216
32:24–32   22

Exodus
14:14   152
33:19   192

Leviticus
26:26   32

Numbers
19:22   27

Deuteronomy
8:3   32
8:17   32
28:38   32
29:4   197
30:6   197
30:11–14   169
30:12–14   54
30:15   168
30:16   54, 168
30:19   168
30:19–20   54

Joshua
24:2–3   216

1 Samuel
10:26   224

1 Kings
8:58   204, 228, 229
18:17–18   20

1 Chronicles
22:19   224

2 Chronicles
12:14   223
20:29–30   152
30:8   224
30:11   224
30:22   224

Nehemiah
4:17   5

Psalms
2:5   73
7:1–2   76
10:17   223
14:3   49
19:7   56

25:17 (Vulgate)   88, 98, 145
31:7 (Vulgate)   145
37:23   195
49:12   72
51:10   194, 208–9, 210, 228
51:17   193
52:8–9   74
53:3   49
60:12   195
84:7 (Vulgate)   131
85:6   160
103:4   153
115:3   198
119:36   74, 82, 204, 229
119:105   56
119:111   74–75, 81, 82
119:111–12   74
143:5   175
145:9   201
146:8   174

Proverbs
2:2–6   224
8:35   79, 81, 110
14:15   205
14:16   205
16:1   36, 223

16:9 36
21:1 205

Isaiah

1:19–20 110
8:20 55
10:5 38
10:5–6 49
10:15 38, 48, 49
30:21 54
40:31 59
45:19 55
48:4 38
53:6 174
54:13 233
55:3 55
55:7 197
58:13 229
65:1 174, 189, 192, 216
66:2 193, 215

Jeremiah

3:12 214
3:22 214
15:19 217–18
17:9 49
31:18 193
31:18–19 193
31:31–34 210
31:33 206–7, 211, 219, 224
32:39–40 228
32:40 132, 178

Lamentations

3:40–42 221

Ezekiel

11:19 174
11:19–20 195, 212, 219
16:59–63 222
18:31 206
33:10–11 218
33:11 198, 219
36:22–27 177
36:26 xxvi, 174, 205–6, 208, 224
36:26–27 195, 207, 210, 211–12, 219, 236
36:27 123

Hosea

2:21–22 32
13:9 144, 145

Jonah

3:8–9 219
3:10 219

Micah

6:14 32
6:15 32

Haggai

2:13 27

Malachi

2:10 201
3:6 61
4:2 54
4:4 55

Matthew

3:9 123
4:4 53
4:7 53
4:10 53
6:13 73
7:6 210
7:7 130
7:7–8 222
7:15 206
7:16–18 230
11:21 220
11:23 220
11:25–26 224
11:28 193
20:1–2 236
20:8 236
22:37–39 27
23:37 161
24:5 58
24:26 58
24:27–31 59
24:28 59–60, 80
25:14–30 234
26:41 73
28:20 16

Mark

12:29–31 27
12:30 165
14:38 73

Luke

3:8 123
4:4 53
4:8 53
4:12 53
10:13 220
10:27 27, 165
11:9–10 222
17:20–21 58–59
17:37 59
19:12–27 234
22:32 132
24:47 197

John

1:16 153, 175
2:25 173
3:5–7 173
5:24 174
6:37 131
6:41–45 233
6:43–44 232
6:44 110, 132, 177
6:45 113, 131, 232, 233
6:65 132
7:17 120
8:36 88, 242
10:27 138
11:8–10 49, 212
12:39–40 120
15:1–2 230
15:1–5 229
15:4–5 230

Scripture Index

15:5   243
15:16 243
20:31 61

Acts

9:4   216
10:34–35 215
17:2–3   57
17:11   57
22:7   216
26:14   216
26:18   174

Romans

1:16   33
1:28   9
2:4–5 196
2:16   61
3:5   40
3:9–20 173
3:12   49
3:20   40, 166
4:4   234
5:5   98
5:10   215
5:12–21 185
5:20   166
6:4   229
6:6   179–80, 229
6:16   88
6:16–22 109
6:17   68
7:4–5 230
7:7–8 166
7:7–13 168
7:9   206
7:14   68
7:14–25 180
7:15–18 180
7:15–23 179
7:18   49, 173
7:23   68
7:24–25 155
8:7   49, 173
8:20   40
8:30   154
9:14   120
9:15   192
9:16   161–62, 176, 227
9:30   216
10:5–9 168, 170
10:14 167, 222
10:17 25, 56, 164
11:6   234
11:17 230
11:17–24 123
11:24 230
11:33 120, 191
11:33–34 40
12:2   174, 180
13:1   119
16:25 61

1 Corinthians

1:18   33
1:19   25
1:20–21 25
1:27–29 25
2:1–5 25, 164
2:3–5 12
2:4   33
2:6–16 25, 164
2:14   25, 167, 174
3:6   219
3:6–7 33, 165
3:7   163
3:18–19 25
4:7   82, 129, 154, 190, 225
6:9–11 215
8:11   19
9:24–27 161
9:26–27 236
12:6   231
15:1   61
15:3   61
15:10 197–98, 235, 236
15:52 59

2 Corinthians

1:12   9
2:16   14
3:1–8 165
3:3   33, 170, 214, 219
3:6   33, 206, 215
3:6–7 170
3:9   170
3:18   72, 180
4:3   61
5:18   219
10:4–5 15

Galatians

1:8   50, 60
1:15   34, 108
3:10–12 52
3:12–14 168
3:19   166

Ephesians

1:5   130
1:18   167
2:1–2 215
2:1–3 192
2:3   192
2:12   215
2:20   138
3:2–6 61
3:18   167
4:3–6 18
4:23   174, 180
6:17   57

Philippians

1:6   82, 204
2:13   161, 174, 175, 196, 231, 235
3:14   161

Colossians

1:21–22 215
2:13   215
3:10   180

1 Thessalonians

1:5   61

2 Thessalonians

2:3–12 16
2:8   20
2:14   61

3:5   204

1 Timothy
3:15   65–66, 137, 138
6:15–16   185

2 Timothy
2:8   61
3:16–17   57
4:7–8   236
4:8   152

Titus
3:10   63

Hebrews
1:1–2   61
4:12   57
11:6   152

1 Peter
2:9   174

2 Peter
1:19   55, 56
1:20   55
2:19   88

1 John
3:14   174

Revelation
3:20   161, 196, 232

Patristic and Classical Index

The patristic and classical index is intended to be comprehensive; that is, it is not restricted to the usages in Calvin's text.

Patristic References

Ambrose

Commentary on Luke
 1.10 79
 7.27 79

Flight from the World
 1.1 79

Jacob and the Happy Life
 1.3.9–11 78
 1.3.10 232
 1.6.20–21 78

Pseudo-Ambrose

The Call of All Nations
 1.7–8 208

Augustine

Against Faustus the Manichee
 15.8 182
 22.28 99

Against Felix the Manichee
 2.3–4 99
 2.8 99
 2.12 99

Against Julian
 1.3.5 42
 2.8.23 89
 4.3.14–33 176

Against Two Letters of the Pelagians, 102–6, 110–11, 128
 1.2.5 102, 103
 1.2.5–3.6 103
 1.3.6 89
 1.3.7 103
 1.18.36 40–41, 176
 1.19.37 110, 155, 176–77, 232
 1.24.42 111
 2.1.1 40, 42, 156
 2.5.10 155
 2.9.21 52
 2.10.23 52
 3.2.2 166
 3.5.14 176
 3.7.20 88–89
 3.8.24 88, 89, 105, 177
 3.9.25 48
 4.6.12 110
 4.6.13 105, 110, 177
 4.6.14 177
 4.6.15 89
 4.9.25 73
 4.9.25–26 72
 4.9.26 110, 161, 194

Baptism of Infants, 128
 2.2 175–76

City of God
 13.15 104–5

Confessions
 10.29.40 42, 168
 10.31.45 42, 168

Eighty-three Diverse Questions
 68.5 105

Enchiridion
    30.9   88, 92, 151
    32.9   162, 227

Expositions on the Psalms
    70(2).5   153
    84.8   160
    102.7   153
    137.18   153, 220
    142.10   175

Free Choice, 90–95
    book 2   144
    2.1.3   90–91
    2.20.54   92, 93, 140
    book 3   144
    3.1.1   139
    3.1.2–3   91
    3.3   91
    3.3.7   93
    3.3.8   91, 148, 151
    3.18.50   94, 139, 145, 146
    3.18.51   93, 94
    3.18.52   91, 92

The Gift of Perseverance, 128, 135
    2.2   132, 178
    6.12   73
    7.13   134, 179
    7.14   154
    9.21   64
    12.30   140
    13.33   134, 154, 179
    14.37   34
    17.47   179
    19.48–49   79
    19.48–50   79
    20.53   42
    21.55   140
    22.58   177
    23.64   130

Grace and Free Choice, 121–24, 128, 135, 157, 182–83, 194–95, 237
    1.1   121, 140
    2.2   121, 140
    2.2–3.5   121, 141, 182–83
    2.4   124, 140, 237
    2.4–3.5   124
    4.6   141
    4.7   199
    4.7–5.10   182–83
    4.8   141
    5.10   141, 155
    5.11   199
    5.12   160, 236
    6.13   141
    6.14   139, 152
    6.15   124, 152, 153, 220
    8.19   141
    8.19–9.21   175
    8.20   122, 141
    9.21   141
    13.25   155
    14.29   123, 141, 212
    15.31   122, 130, 141, 183
    16.32   123, 132, 141–42
    16.32–19.40   142
    17.33   123, 141, 160, 194
    20.41   122, 142, 237
    21.43   142
    23.45   123
    24.46   122

The Grace of Christ and Original Sin, 112–13
    1.3.3   155
    1.14.15   113
    1.22.23   155
    1.25.26   112
    1.30.31   217
    1.31.34   155
    1.47.52   112
    2.2.2–2.4.4   82
    2.33.38   97

The Greatness of the Soul
    36.80   98

Heresies, 42
    1   43
    11   45
    21–22   45–46
    26   46
    46   45–46, 48, 186
    70   46

Letters
    36.9.21   45
    102.2.15   199
    145.2   88

175   82
175.2   155
176   82
177   82
177.2   155
177.6   155
177.7–8   155
177.9   155
186.3.10   213, 225
186.5.15   194–95
194   158, 237
194.3.7   155
194.3.8   155
194.5.19   153
194.10.47   100
214   237
214.1–2   157
214.3–4   158
214.4   157
214.6–7   157
215   121
215.3   158
215.4   157–58
215.4–7   157
217   237
217.3.8   97
217.3.10   147
217.3.11   213
217.4.12   176
217.4.15–5.17   111
217.5.17   104, 176
217.6.21   178
217.7.28   104, 176, 212
225 (Prosper)   149
225.3–6 (Prosper)   189–90
226.2–8 (Hilary)   189–90

The Merits and Forgiveness of Sins, 90, 117–19, 128, 181
  book 1   118
  book 2   118
  2.1.1   181
  2.2.2   181
  2.2.2–2.6.7   117
  2.3.3   117
  2.5.5   118, 181, 182
  2.5.5–2.6.7   117–18
  2.5.6   115, 118, 182
  2.6.7   117

  2.6.7–2.28.46   127
  2.17.26   118, 119, 182
  2.17.27   181, 182
  2.18.28   105, 114, 119, 182
  2.18.29   155
  2.18.30   115, 178
  2.19.33   119, 182
  2.20.34   181
  2.22.36   182
  2.36.59   57–58
  3.2.2   175–76

Nature and Grace, 101–2, 128
  1.1   166
  23.25   217
  46.54   101, 147
  49.57   101
  51.59   155
  53.62   91, 185
  64.77   116
  65.78   77, 146–47
  65.78–66.79   98
  67.80–81   145

The Perfection of Righteousness, 128
  2.1   146
  2.2   143
  2.2–3   118
  3.6   118
  4.9   88, 98, 140, 143, 145, 148
  4.10–6.12   118
  6.13   139
  6.15   146
  8.17   52
  10.21–22   118
  19.40   222, 234

The Predestination of the Saints, 128, 135
  1.2   189–90
  2.3   155
  2.4   129
  2.5   129
  2.6   131
  3.7   120, 128–29
  4.8   94
  5.10   129
  8.13   131, 164
  8.13–15   233
  8.14   131

8.15   131–32
8.16   129, 132
10.19   129, 132, 211
11.22   129
14.27   83
15.30   129–30
15.31   130
18.36   130
18.37   177

The Proceedings of Pelagius
10.22   155
14.30   155
14.31   155
17.40   155
17.41   155
23.47   155
35.65   155

Rebuke and Grace, 121, 128, 135, 156–57, 160, 163, 237–44
1.1   64
1.2   130, 195, 238
2.3   130, 238–39
2.4   158
2.4–4.6   238
3.5   158, 160
4.6   158
5.8   191, 239
6.9   158, 159, 239
7.12   159
7.13   179
7.14   159
7.16   159–60
8.17   130, 132, 239
8.17–19   240
10.26–11.29   133
10.26–11.32   241
10.26–12.38   132
11.30   133
11.31   133, 177–78, 178–79, 241
11.31–32   240
11.32   178, 241
12.33   240, 241, 242
12.34   243
12.35   242
12.38   133–34, 242, 243, 244
13.42   89
14.43   239
14.45   239
16.49   160, 239

Retractations, xxii, 90
1.1.2   51
1.8   98
1.9.2   91, 92, 94, 140, 144, 172
1.9.3   93, 94
1.9.4   92, 93, 140
1.9.5   91, 92, 93, 94, 145, 148
1.9.6   93, 94
1.13.5   97
1.15.2   96
1.15.3   95
1.15.4   95, 96, 117, 187
1.15.8   99
1.26   105
2.1.2   105
2.8   99
2.33   181

Sermons
26.7.8   155
131.2.2   232

Sermons on John, 120–21
3.10   153
26.2–5   232
29.6   120
49.8   212
53.8   120

The Spirit and the Letter, 90, 109, 119–20
3.5   105, 116
9.15   119
30.52   102, 109, 153
31.53–54   119
31.53–33.59   119
31.54   119
32.55   119
33.57   119
33.57–34.60   119
33.58   119
34.60   119–20

To Simplician
2.1.4   105

True Religion, 96–98
8.15   100

Patristic and Classical Index

    14.27 97

Two Souls, 95–96, 144
    10.14 95
    11.15 96, 146
    13.20 99

Pseudo-Augustine

The Dogmas of the Church, 125–26
    21 126
    21–51 125
    25 125
    28–29 125
    32 126
    33–37 125
    41 126
    49 125

Hypognosticon, 106–9, 226
    3.1.1 106–7
    3.4.5 107, 113
    3.5.7 107–8, 113–14
    3.7.9 114
    3.8.11 114
    3.9.15 108
    3.9.15–16 114
    3.9.16 108
    3.10.18 108
    3.11.19 114, 227
    3.11.19–20 180
    3.11.20 115, 226, 227
    3.13.29 115, 116, 227–28
    3.14.32 108–9

Sermon 236, 126–27
    236.6 127, 180

The Spirit and the Soul
    48 126

Basil

Ascetic Constitutions
    4 76

Homilies
    9.5 75
    9.6–7 75
    9.7 75
    9.8 75–76

Homilies on Psalms
    2.2 76

Pseudo-Basil

Sermon on Free Choice (Pseudo-Macarius)
    25.1 76
    25.2 76

Bernard

Grace and Free Choice
    3.6–7 149
    4.9 147
    4.9–10 149
    5.14 149
    6.16 205, 209
    6.18–20 209
    8.24 149
    8.24–26 209
    10.35 147

Sermons on the Song of Songs
    81.6–9 149
    82.5 149

Cassiodore

Tripartite History
    2.5 63

Chrysostom

Homilies on Genesis
    19.1 79
    22.1 151

Homilies on Matthew
    82.4 226

Homily on Reproaches to Be Borne
    6 232

Pseudo-Chrysostom

Homily for the First Sunday in Advent, 31

Pseudo-Clement

Recognitions, xxiii, xxv, 156
    2.19–3.50 43

Cyprian

The Lord's Prayer
26   73

Testimonies
3.4   72

Cyril

Commentary on John
4.1   233

Eusebius

The History of the Church
3.16   44
3.38   44, 45
5.20   66

Hilary

Letter to Augustine
2–8   189–90

Treatise on Psalms
2.13–17   73
51.23   74
118.5.11–12   74
118.5.12   82
118.14.20   74–75, 81, 82

Irenaeus

Against Heresies, xxiii
1.23.1–4   42
3.1.1   62
3.2.2   62
3.3.1–3   44
3.3.3   66
3.3.4   66
3.5.1   62
4.4.3   71, 72
4.37.1–7   71
4.37.4   72

Letter to Florinus, 66

Jerome

Against Jovinian
2.3   77, 98, 151

Dialogue against the Pelagians
1.4–6   151

Letters
21.5–6   77
21.6   151
124.2   85
124.4–5   85
124.10–11   85
133.5   151
133.8   52

Questions on the Hebrew of Genesis
4.6–7   77

Origen

Commentary on Matthew
10.11   70

Commentary on Romans
preface   70

First Principles
preface   66
preface 2   70
preface 5   70
3.1.5–6   70

Pamphilus

Apology for Origen, 43
1   70

Peter Lombard

Sentences
2.25.8   31

Prosper

The Call of All Nations
1.7–8   208

Grace and Free Choice
13–14   149

Letter to Augustine, 149
3–6   189–90

Rufinus

The Adulteration of the Works of Origen, 43

Tertullian

Against Marcion
2.5–10   71

Patristic and Classical Index

The Prescription against Heretics
  7   63
  15–19   62, 63
  16   63
  17–18   63
  19   63
  20–21   63, 66
  29–35   62
  32   44, 66
  33   42
  37   63

Pseudo-Tertullian

Against All Heresies
  1   42

Theodoret

The History of the Church
  1.6   63, 64

Vincent of Lérins

Commonitory
  2.6   83

Councils

Council of Carthage (418)

  canons 1–2   125
  canons 4–5   125
  canon 6   106
  canons 7–9   125

Council of Milevis (416)

  canon 5   106

Council of Orange (529)

  preface   189
  canon 1   188–89
  canon 3   189
  canons 3–8   82
  canon 4   81, 106, 126, 188
  canon 5   82, 188
  canon 6   82, 188
  canon 7   189
  canon 12   189
  canon 14   82
  canons 18–20   82

  canon 22   189
  canon 23   82

Classical References

Aristotle

Categories
  10   149

Metaphysics, xxv, 43

Nicomachean Ethics
  3.1   150
  3.5   150, 151

Topics
  2.6   149

Cicero

Nature of the Gods
  1.15.39–40   156
  1.15.40   51
  1.20.55   38, 51, 156
  2.64.160   31
  3.6.14   156
  3.8.19   156
  3.35.85   156
  3.36.87–88   156

Tusculan Disputations
  4.31.67   9

Erasmus

Adages
  introduction   212
  1.1.40   31
  1.1.83   21
  1.3.65   111
  1.4.47   164
  1.5.10   116
  1.5.19   30, 93
  1.5.87   57
  1.6.9   45
  1.6.19   33
  1.6.70   21
  1.7.29   157
  1.7.33   21
  1.7.90   189
  1.8.52   170
  1.8.60   28

1.9.48 198
1.10.86 21
2.2.49 93
2.4.76 231
2.5.87 54
2.10.51 15
4.5.54 205

Aulus Gellius

Attic Nights
11.8 11

Horace

Art of Poetry
19–21 30, 93

72 102
143 10

Gnaeus Naevius

Hector's Departure, 9

Terence

Eunuchus, 11

Virgil

Aeneid
4.359 13
4.469–70 9

A. N. S. Lane is director of research and senior lecturer in Christian doctrine at the London Bible College, an associate college of Brunel University, and the author of a number of Calvin studies. G. I. Davies is reader in Old Testament studies at Cambridge University and former classics scholar of Merton College, Oxford.

www.ingramcontent.com/pod-product-compliance
Lightning Source LLC
Chambersburg PA
CBHW061432300426
44114CB00014B/1644